God's Generation of Hope

About Monday Blues to Sunday Pews

Monday Blues to Sunday Pews Ministry is a grassroots series of Christian books that will lead us on a journey through each book of the Bible, one step at a time. They will cover critical verses and topics within each chapter that were life-changing then—and are still life-changing today. They will inspire and encourage the "intentional" believer to move from that rut of complacency to a life that brings value to the Lord by how they live. Through this journey, we will broaden and deepen our knowledge of God's expectations for us. We will learn the importance of obtaining the message from God's word and sustaining it daily—real-life application!

Most importantly, Monday Blues to Sunday Pews will donate half of its profit proceeds to support the mission field, help the needy, and assist organizations in distributing God's word globally. Remember this passage in Matthew 16:24: *We're called to be intentional followers of Jesus Christ—daily!*

Monday—*M*editate on one scripture in an area where you need help to refresh your mindset.
Tuesday—*T*ell someone about your daily journey as you begin. Someone needs to hear it, too!
Wednesday—*W*alk with a close friend and share your experience as you're walking with God!
Thursday—*T*hankful for one thing that happened this week. Showing gratitude is a huge step.
Friday—*F*ocus on another area in your life that needs improvement; we all have them.
Saturday—*S*hare one significant impact from the week with someone who also needs uplifting.
Sunday—*S*erve in some capacity in your church or community—connect, serve, and grow.

God's Generation of Hope

A Guide Through Deuteronomy

BY CARL BARRETT

Foreword by Gregory Jantz

Series: Monday Blues to Sunday Pews

RESOURCE *Publications* · Eugene, Oregon

GOD'S GENERATION OF HOPE
A Guide Through Deuteronomy

Copyright © 2024 Carl Barrett. All rights reserved. Except for brief quotations in critical publications or reviews, no part of this book may be reproduced in any manner without prior written permission from the publisher. Write: Permissions, Wipf and Stock Publishers, 199 W. 8th Ave., Suite 3, Eugene, OR 97401.

Resource Publications
An Imprint of Wipf and Stock Publishers
199 W. 8th Ave., Suite 3
Eugene, OR 97401

www.wipfandstock.com

PAPERBACK ISBN: 979-8-3852-3114-0
HARDCOVER ISBN: 979-8-3852-3115-7
EBOOK ISBN: 979-8-3852-3116-4
VERSION NUMBER 11/20/24

Scripture quotations are taken from the Holy Bible, New Living Translation, copyright ©1996, 2004, 2015 by Tyndale House Foundation. Used by permission of Tyndale House Publishers, a Division of Tyndale House Ministries, Carol Stream, Illinois 60188. All rights reserved.

Contents

Foreword by Gregory Jantz | *vii*
Acknowledgements | *ix*
Biography | *x*
'Hope Found Me!' | *xii*
"The Almighty Search" | *xiv*
"The Cries for Hope" | *xxx*
Preface | *xlii*
Introduction | *xlviii*
"A Legacy of Hope!" | *liv*
The Book of Deuteronomy | *lxiii*

Chapter 1	'Godly Development'	1
Chapter 2	'Godly Direction'	5
Chapter 3	'Facing Giants'	8
Chapter 4	'Godly Obedience'	12
Chapter 5	'Godly Listener'	16
Chapter 6	'Godly Hearts'	19
Chapter 7	'God's Chosen'	22
Chapter 8	'Godly Remembrance'	25
Chapter 9	'Just Believe!'	28
Chapter 10	'God's Expectations'	32
Chapter 11	'Always & Forever'	37
Chapter 12	'Godly Worship'	42
Chapter 13	Other "gods!"	47
Chapter 14	'Godly Dedication'	51

Chapter 15	'Godly Helper'	56
Chapter 16	"All the Time!"	60
Chapter 17	'Godly Accountability'	64
Chapter 18	'Godly Duties'	68
Chapter 19	'God's Refuge'	74
Chapter 20	'Our Opposition'	78
Chapter 21	'Godly Parents'	83
Chapter 22	'Detestable Deception'	87
Chapter 23	'Christlike Integrity'	93
Chapter 24	'Godly Influencer'	97
Chapter 25	'Dishonest People'	100
Chapter 26	'Today, for God!'	103
Chapter 27	'Godly Vision'	107
Chapter 28	'A Living Blessing'	110
Chapter 29	'Personal Commitment'	116
Chapter 30	'Return to Me!'	121
Chapter 31	'Godly Repetition'	126
Chapter 32	'Godly Proclaimer'	131
Chapter 33	'Godly Acceptance'	138
Chapter 34	'Godly Legacy'	145

In Summary: "A Message of Hope!" | 153

"The Reason for Hope" | 161

"Our Foundation in Hope!" | 168

"Hope in Action" | 174

Warning Signs: "Misguided Hope" | 184

"Seek Hope" | 194

"Cling to Hope!" | 203

"Walk in Hope" | 211

"Freedom in Hope" | 220

"Whatever, Never Lose Hope"! | 227

The End! "Hope is on the Way!" | 234

Bibliography | 247

Foreword

Dr. Gregory Jantz

Hope—a powerful and elusive concept. Hebrews 11:1 identifies Hope as the anchor of faith. First Peter 3:15 calls us to be ready, at all times, to give an answer for the Hope we have in Christ. Hope is front and center in Carl Barrett's study of Deuteronomy, *God's Generation of Hope*. Carl sees great Hope when, those he calls "intentional followers of Christ," place an emphasis on training up the next generation. His inspiration comes from the Old Testament book of Deuteronomy, where Moses urges the next generation of Israelites to remain faithful as they enter into the Promised Land. We have a similar challenge today, to encourage the next generation to be faithful and, as Carl says, "it all begins with the older – more experienced – generation stepping up to the plate and embracing the role of godly leadership."

Carl has a deep concern for the struggles of the younger generation crying out for godly influencers to counter the ungodly forces in our culture. Through personal experience, he's witnessed the devastation affecting younger generations; his statistics and research are heart-wrenching. Yet, he still maintains his firm belief in our Hope, and this book is a call for parents and those older and wiser generations to pass along the truths of God's Word by being Christlike models, mentors, and teachers. His study of Deuteronomy is a call for us to create in our lives a Christlike legacy, a "conscious decision to leave a godly path for others." If you're ready to embrace this challenge and commandment from God, Carl's book will help provide a valuable roadmap.

As a professional therapist, I've witnessed what happens when people transition from childhood to adulthood without Hope. The trauma and suffering permeate not only the individual but also those around them. Yet, God's love, grace, and mercy are more powerful and, as Carl says,

FOREWORD

"individuals are more resilient to stress, pressure, and all the weights of the world when they have 'Living Hope.'" He goes on to say, "Our children and younger generations need to see the power of that Living Hope we have in Christ, which will entice and motivate them to want more of Him in their own lives." Isn't that what you want for your own children, grandchildren, and children you know? *God's Generation of Hope* is written to also entice and motivate *you* to become stronger Christians, parents, teachers, and leaders so you're better able to influence the next generation for good, for God.

Over forty years ago, I began to treat stubborn mental health and substance use issues in a different way. That new way became known as the "whole-person" approach. This whole-person approach recognizes people are made up of multiple factors – emotional, relational, physical, and spiritual – and by addressing these factors together instead of in isolation, healing, and recovery can be greatly enhanced. In his book, Carl beautifully embodies this concept, understanding "many of our children throughout our communities are mentally, emotionally, physically, and more importantly, spiritually out of balance." Carl understands the imbalance he sees in children today will be what is treated in adults tomorrow. His book is a call for all of us to stop this damaging cycle.

While this book speaks, certainly, to parents, it also emphasizes the importance of not only physical family but spiritual family. He calls us to be ready to give an answer for our Hope in Christ, especially to the children – biological and otherwise – whom God has placed under our care and influence. Deuteronomy comes down, in Carl's view, to the power of choice – who we will serve, how we will live, and what legacy we will leave. Carl understands that our choices today will help pave the way for generations to come.

Dr. Gregory Jantz is the founder of The Center • A Place of HOPE in Edmonds, Washington, voted a Top Ten facility for Depression Treatment in the United States. Dr. Jantz pioneered "Whole Person Care" in the 1980s and is a world-renowned expert on depression, anxiety, eating disorders, technology addiction, and abuse. He is an innovator in the treatment of mental health, utilizing a variety of therapies, including nutrition, sleep therapy, spiritual counseling, and advanced DBT techniques. Dr. Jantz is a best-selling author of over 45 books and a go-to media authority on mental and behavioral health afflictions, appearing on CBS, ABC, NBC, Fox, and CNN.

Acknowledgements

I want to personally thank my Publicist, Don Otis, for his assistance in elevating our mission and vision to programs across the country. I also want to thank Janet Parshall at Moody Radio, Bob Dutko and Chris Ayotte at Crawford Broadcasting Group, and Chuck Crismier at Save America Ministries for their support in promoting our books. There are so many radio programs, regionally, that have been so supportive, which has motivated me even more to continue this mission.

I also want to thank Dr. Gregory Jantz for his support and inspiration. I cannot thank my family and close friends enough for their encouragement. Because of these people, our goal is to continue to write books that will help others know that God's word has a message of motivation and hope each day of our lives. It is truly a daily journey that can lead to spiritual growth!

Biography

Carl Barrett is the Founder and Executive Director of *Monday Blues to Sunday Pews Ministry*. In partnership with other Christ-based organizations, they aim to raise more funds to serve the needy, support mission fields and spread the word of God worldwide by distributing more Bibles. As the author of impactful books such as God Values Our Daily Steps, God's Guide to Freedom, God's Holiness vs. Man's Lawlessness, and God's People Count, Carl's influence extends beyond his ministry. He also leads the First Impressions Team at Central Tyler Baptist Church in Tyler, Texas. His unwavering dedication to spreading the message of God's love and grace is a testament to his inspiring mission.

He has served as a Personal Development Mentor for the Texas Juvenile Justice Department, a teacher and chaplain in multiple state prisons and detention centers, a CASA Representative (Court Appointed Special Advocate) in various counties throughout Texas, and an instructor for the National Fatherhood Initiative.

Carl Barrett's educational journey is a testament to his unwavering commitment to learning and personal development. His academic achievements, including a BSBA from Madison University and studies in biblical and theological studies at Texas Baptist Institute, Critical Issues in Christian Apologetics at Biola University, and An Introduction to C.S. Lewis at Hillsdale College, reflect his dedication. His studies at Dale Carnegie, Development Dimensions International, and Personal Dynamics Institute have equipped him with a deep understanding of human relations development, motivational leadership, and the empowerment of engagement. His commitment to personal development is a source of motivation and encouragement for all who follow his work.

Carl's aspiring passion is to help people apply the truth of God's word to their lives so they can live it out for the glory of God—as representatives of Jesus Christ on this earth. He would tell you that it starts in our

BIOGRAPHY

homes—then throughout our neighborhoods, community, church home, and abroad. *Our bio as Christlike followers is essential to our Lord and the building of His Kingdom in our everyday lives!*

'Hope Found Me!'

I've inherited a new life that is not my own,
Full of God's blessings that must be shown,
With loved ones I know whose lives truly matter,
To believe in a Hope when life seems shattered,
He lets me know that He hears my cries,
And helps me to see life through His eyes,
He picks me up when I feel I can't go on,
Renews my strength and reminds me—' I'm not alone, '
He helps me not to look back and dwell on those days,
That can get me down and forget all His ways,
Because when I lean on Him and trust in His Word,
I gain more confidence in all that I've heard,
Now I can see clearly that all He says is true,
Just believe in My Word, and I will see you through,
But never forget to pass on My goodness,
So others can experience My lovingkindness,
This is so vital in keeping My Word alive,
If you would share with others how they can thrive,
In a life where they can rest in My peace and joy,
And realize the enemy's work is nothing but a ploy,
To prevent us from helping the younger and weak,
For without My great Promise, your future is bleak,
So believe in what I did on that old rugged cross,
And you will realize your life is not a total loss,
When you feel as if life is not on solid ground,
Your faith in Me assures you've now been found,
So invest your new heritage with a future heir,
Leave them a legacy that will help them to bear,
No matter the darkest days that will surely come,

'Hope Found Me!'

Just seek, cling, and believe in the Holy One,
No matter what comes, I will help you to cope,
With all of life's battles, remember—I'm your Hope!

"The Almighty Search"

Upon the birth of a newborn child, the beginnings of a new family, the rise of a new generation, and the path of a new creation in Christ, Almighty God is urgently looking for those who are pursuing Him first in everyday life—versus the ways of man and this world. Since the beginning, our Heavenly Father has been in an all-out search for dedicated and wholehearted servants who can bring His purpose and plan to a world too often marred by unspiritual behaviors. This "Almighty Quest" is one of the most crucial in today's world because, sadly, these times of godlessness are damaging and affecting the lives of so many innocent young children and families in homes across the globe.

Let there be no doubt: God is actively seeking 'high and low' for those who will join Him in fulfilling a long-term plan that aligns with the promises of His Holy Word. This Heavenly design and arrangement are not just for a few but for all genuine and committed believers. Just think, it will unite us in a family as one in Jesus Christ, our Lord, and Savior—if we are in line with God's most divine instruction and counsel. Always remember this key fact: Throughout our life's journey, there is a guarantee that we can rely upon, and it's this: "Our Heavenly Father's guidance is not just a promise but a steadfast reality that we can cling to in the midst of life's uncertainties, providing us with a strong sense of security and stability in His plan. It's a 'beacon of Hope' that will always light our way during our darkest days."

Here's a vital message for us as we move forward: The means of this holy calling is for 'all' faithful followers to lead others in moving this plan forward to future generations—so we're all in unison with God's ultimate desire—from the beginning to the very end. Please keep this in mind: "His commitment to guide each of us is a source of Empowering Hope that will help us overcome the trials of today's world, lifting our spirits and encouraging us to continue His work." Who in the world would decline this great opportunity?

We will see that the beauty of this Master plan lies in its inclusivity—because it's a wide-open invitation to all who are ready and willing to embrace God's ways of righteousness and holiness for the betterment of others today, tomorrow, and in the future. This all-encompassing goal is for all His devout ones, including you and me. And there's an incredible reward for each and every person who wants to be a part of this plan—regardless of today's tumultuous times. This reward is not just a promise but a reality: "He will provide us with the Hope we need in everyday life so that there will be no barriers or hindrances to accomplishing His sovereign objective." However, as we embark on this life journey, the primary question remains: "Who is ready and prepared to join His eternal initiative and reap this reward?" Please understand the severity of this grand plan because you and I are a crucial and valued part of it.

However, this plan will only include those who want to join God and come to the aid of current and future eras for His glory! This is imperative because we will see that in today's trying times, God's children in every home across this great land need His divine support and guidance more than ever. And in His guiding ways, God expects His faithful followers to possess hearts genuinely dedicated to Him—no matter the troubles we endure.

God's word reminds us in 2 Chr 16:9, 'The eyes of the Lord search the whole earth to strengthen those whose hearts are fully committed to him." But there's also a warning at the end of this passage: "What a fool you have been! From now on, you will be at war." God's message in 2 Chronicles 16:9 is a potent reminder of His omnipresence and His attributes of mercy, grace, love, patience, goodness, care, and providence.In a new paragraph, please add this below:

But also in this profound passage, we see that the great and righteous King Asa, at the end of his life, started to depend on otherworldly influencers rather than relying upon the help of Almighty God. It's as if he forgot those past victories as a leader under God's ever-present guidance. We must always remember this key point: "Victory comes when we stop looking at the ways of man and this world for our solution in all of life's circumstances, and we start looking and trusting in God's promises, provisions, and providence!" In all of life's challenges, it is easy to falter in our faith and hope and seek solutions from the eyes of human perspectives because they appear more tangible than God's most divine supernatural guidance. This is a classic example of living more by sight—than faith!

No matter our life's struggles, it's crucial to never lose sight of this essential reminder each and every day of our lives on this side of Heaven: 'Our Almighty Yahweh is always there, ready to embrace and guide His children through their most challenging trials in a world that so often strays from His holy ways.' But do we truly comprehend the significance of this message from our Creator to each of us? Can we see the underlying information in this profound passage that our Heavenly Father is trying to convey to His children?

You see, our Holy God and Heavenly Father is not a distant observer in our times of distress, despair, and discouragement. He's a Loving and Caring Parent, always ready to demonstrate His strength and help us overcome the most brutal battles in our personal lives and throughout our homes. His guidance is a source of comfort and a beacon of hope and inspiration in today's unstable and uncontrollable times. In this journey, we will see that no matter all our troubles in life, we need Hope more today than ever!

Do we truly understand that God is not a passive observer but an active Seeker of those who prioritize Him? He constantly seeks those who will trust in Him, not in the ways of man and this world. He is fervently seeking those who reject self-reliance and choose to depend on Him. In His relentless pursuit, Almighty Yahweh desires to work through leaders who are obedient servants willing and ready to accomplish His will. In doing so, we're helping others to fulfill their ultimate destiny that aligns with God's long-term plan.

However, as the scripture in 2 Chronicles reminds us, our battle against the ways of the enemy and the world is ongoing and relentless, trying to prevent us from achieving God's plan. The passage concludes with a significant warning: 'What a fool you have been! From now on, you will be at war.' In other words, there will be dire consequences if we don't commit our lives to God wholeheartedly. This is not just a suggestion—but a crucial aspect of our faith. Why? Because wholehearted living demonstrates that we love God fully (there is no division), serve Him sincerely, rely on and trust Him entirely, obey Him faithfully, focus on Him exclusively, and express and extend His love and hope to others.

Though our hearts are prone to wander, God graciously gives us new hearts that help us follow Him wholly if we're on board with His guiding principles. Trust me, this type of committed living will transcend to so many others in our path for years! Indeed, wholeheartedness is an attainable goal within our spiritual grasp—if we place our fundamental values on seeking God first and foremost in our daily lives. Do we all realize that God's word calls you and me to be sincere and authentic in our genuine commitment to Him—not only for the benefit of ourselves and others—but for His glory?

The great Apostle Paul even reminds us in Philippians 3:12–21 of our human frailty and ongoing struggle with sin—while holding onto our Hope of transformation through Christ's redemptive work on the Cross. As genuine disciples of Christ, this tension should drive us to press forward continually in the pursuit of wholeheartedness to God alone. Even in our busy and fast-paced world as parents in the household of God, it can be challenging to stay focused and committed to Yahweh. However, the Bible abounds with wisdom and guidance about the immense value of wholeheartedness in our relationship with God—because it can have a powerful spiritual domino effect on so many within our reach.

With that, let's not forget this crucial lesson: 'Our complete dedication to Almighty God with all our hearts, souls, minds, and strength not only affects us—but also has the potential to impact others around us profoundly. This responsibility underscores the influence we can have on those in our sphere of effect.' This is the point we must always keep in mind. 'If we're not aligned with God's guiding principles daily, where we trust and believe in all His ways, there will be repercussions in our personal lives that can spiritually affect those close to us for years to come.'

Paul reminds us in Gal 6:7-10, "Don't be misled—you cannot mock the justice of God. You will always harvest what you plant. Those who live only to satisfy their own sinful nature will harvest decay and death from that sinful nature. But those who live to please the Spirit will harvest everlasting life from the Spirit. So, let's not get tired of doing what is good. At just the right time we will reap a harvest of blessing if we don't give up. Therefore, whenever we have the opportunity, we should do good to everyone—especially to those in the family of faith." This strongly emphasizes the urgency and necessity of aligning our lives with God's principles.'

These compelling verses in Galatians are a sobering reminder that our choices and alliance with God's teachings have long-term spiritual effects on us and those we hold dear. Almighty God constantly reminds us in His Holy Word that if we fall into the 'arms of flesh' moreso than His Arms of love, mercy, and grace, it can have disastrous results throughout our succeeding generations! As the 'supposed' mature students of God's word, do we need to continue going over the basic teachings of the Bible in our own lives (Heb 6:1)? If we're not retaining and learning God's lessons for our own good, how can we help our younger generations, biblically, in their trying times to come?

Moreover, when I read this profound passage in the Old Testament (2 Chronicles) on how the 'Eyes of our Heavenly Father's' presence, mercy, grace, love, care, and provision are there for His children, it also reminds me of a striking parallel for a vital role in the family of God's household today, and it's this—Parenting! This led me to ponder: "Are the eyes of the heart of every parent genuinely and passionately placed on the hearts, minds, and souls of their own children for their spiritual well-being? Are family leaders treating and teaching their young ones like our Heavenly Father treats, teaches, and cares for us as His children (Isa 54:13)? Are today's parents as reliable, accountable, and present for the spiritual welfare and good of their children—as our Lord is for us?"

With that, all parents and guardians in households abroad must consider these challenging and most essential questions: "Are we loving, disciplining, and discipling our young ones in a manner that reflects godly actions in our everyday lives? Are we demonstrating gentleness, patience, and self-control in Christlike ways? Are we caring for our children with the same goodness and lovingkindness as Yahweh does with us? As devout Christian parents, are we providing for our children in the biblical manner God desires?" We must ask ourselves: "Are we physically, emotionally, and most importantly, spiritually ever-present in our young ones' life journey? How engaged are we in our young ones' lives for their biblical protection and spiritual prosperity?"

Here's the central point of the matter: 'Are we, as the wiser generation, investing the godly inheritance and heritage we've possessed as Christians—into the lives of our young ones for their future survival?' In other words, are we teaching our children the most important guiding principle they need to know for their state of spirituality, which is God's word? Are we living such godly lives that it points them to our Living Hope—Jesus Christ? But, most importantly, are we emphasizing the importance of passing these Truths on to their future heirs so the power of God's word will carry over for decades and centuries? Or—are we in the danger zone of not being wholeheartedly committed to God in this vital role—appointed to you and me by our Heavenly Father?

This is of the utmost importance because we will see that parenting is one of the most essential roles in homes today! How? Parenting doesn't only affect our children's generation, but the Bible teaches us that this job has spiritual and biblical fruit that can further others' future state of spirituality. And here's the ultimate goal: "The next generation of faithful and wholehearted godly servants will raise and train up the next generation after them, who then would train up the next. While all along the way, God's praise would spread throughout each generation until His Son's return." If not, generations and souls could be lost, and it could be our own!

We must recognize that Almighty God actively seeks out selfless and sacrificial parents—who are integral to His divine plans for the future. Just think, by faithfully and obediently adhering to His biblical requirements, we (parents) become the catalysts for transformative change in our children's lives. Consider this PowerPoint and critical takeaway: "With the power of the Holy Spirit working through us—and His Holy Word as our daily compass, we can help save a lost soul, restore, refresh, and revive lives within the family of God. We can be part of a godly plan that can transform generations, start a new beginning in Christ, and assist in keeping His Word fresh and alive for years to come."

"You see, our role as His household managers can keep the door open for His Spirit to complete His work in us, that can spread to others—and will surely impact His future Kingdom and, most importantly, glorify God's Most Holy Name. If you put this in biblical perspective, this is one of the most essential positions on earth, with the potential to significantly impact lives in our homes, schools, churches, communities, and globally!"

Parenting is undeniably one of the most challenging roles but also the most spiritually rewarding. This position may not offer monetary compensation, but it provides a direct line of accountability to our Heavenly Father. In this highly appointed position, there's no sick leave or vacation at any given time. This job requires a person to fulfill their obligations no matter if they're having a bad day. You might even have to do this job for the rest of your life on this side of Heaven for various reasons. When we're talking about family homes across this country and worldwide, it is one of the most critical jobs in the eyes of God.

As a parent and family leader, are you aware of this most critical role expected of you and me from our Heavenly Father? As a guiding light, God's word reminds us in Mal 2:15, "Didn't the Lord make you one with your wife? In body and spirit, you are his. And what does he want? Godly children from your union. So, guard your heart; remain loyal to the wife of your youth." This scripture underscores the importance of the husband and wife, united in producing godly offspring because they can carry over God's mission for years to come! Consider the profound influence of parenting in this way:

"Scripture beautifully portrays God as a loving parent, thereby elevating the role and position of human parents in God's eyes. Parenting is not just a duty but a High calling from our Heavenly Father that allows us to develop many of His divine characteristics that can be shared and taught in our young ones' lives. As parents, we are entrusted with the sacred powers of procreation, to be used only within the bounds of Marriage, as ordained by our Holy God. As stated throughout God's word, we must constantly recollect our blessed duty, which is to rear our children in love and righteousness, to cater to their physical and spiritual needs, and to teach them to love and serve one another according to His commandments."

The Psalmist even reminds us in Ps 127:3, "Children are a gift from the LORD; they are a reward from Him." We must understand that our children are gifts from God, so we must take those gifts and invest in them so they will grow to spiritual maturity. Never forget this: 'God instructs us to place value on teaching all children and the young ones to know Him, love Him, respect Him, obey Him, and tell others about Him. Plus, all the blessings He can offer us in the future.' Think about this: 'In all of those moments of teaching and disciplining our children for our Heavenly Father, they offer the opportunity for parents to teach a child that God disciplines us because He loves and cares for us and that, as parents, we do the same for our children—for their spiritual well-being' (Heb 12:1-12).

This is a matter of urgency for all family leaders in homes today. Why? Because as Christian parents, our top priority is clearly outlined in Psalm chapter 78. This passage, one of the most significant in God's word, emphasizes the importance of teaching our current descendants the fundamental principles of God's word from the early stages of their lives. This is not just a high calling but a pressing challenge for today, tomorrow, and the years to come, as long as we're here as His Citizens of Heaven on Earth!

As God echoes His commands to the parents, leaders, and others throughout our homes in Ps 78:1-8, His word is a powerful force we can apply to benefit our younger generations. "O my people, listen to my instructions. Open your ears to what I am saying, for I will speak to you in a parable. I will teach you hidden lessons from our past—stories we have heard and known, stories our ancestors handed down to us. We will not hide these truths from our children; we will tell the next generation about the glorious deeds of the Lord, about his power and his mighty wonders."

"For he issued his laws to Jacob; he gave his instructions to Israel. He commanded our ancestors to teach them to their children so the next generation might know them—even the children not yet born—and they, in turn, will teach their own children. So, each generation should set its hope anew on God, not forgetting his glorious miracles and obeying his commands. Then they will not be like their ancestors—stubborn, rebellious, and unfaithful, refusing to give their hearts to God." This is a powerful reminder of our crucial role as Christian parents in shaping the next generation, instilling in them the values and teachings of our genuine saving faith, love, and hope.

To expound on this more profoundly, even the great Apostle Paul, a beacon of wisdom and guidance, reminds us in 1 Tim 3:4-5,11 of a guiding rule for fathers and mothers in today's homes. "He must manage his own family well, having children who respect and obey him. For if a man cannot manage his own household, how can he care for God's church? In the same way, their wives must be respected and must not slander others. They must exercise self-control and be faithful in everything they do." This is a compelling reminder of the importance of our roles as parents and the respect and obedience we should command from our children, guided by the teachings of the Apostle Paul from Almighty God.

Let's truly grasp the weight of this passage, which will resonate deeply with many Christian parents: "Parents who do not diligently manage their spiritual and biblical affairs in their own homes are ill-prepared to serve the Lord beyond their four walls." This is not just a reminder but a call to action. It's a call to all Christian parents to fulfill our duty and oversee our family homes in a manner that glorifies God. If not, our family lives, and future heirs are in jeopardy of being led astray so far from the presence of a Holy God—they may never come to the hope and faith they will need to survive!

This is of extreme importance because in today's times of trouble within the American Family Homes, our *Heavenly Father is seeking responsible earthly fathers, mothers*, and leaders in the homes to be devoted to Him '*first*'—so He can equip and empower them to be adequate parents through His wisdom, knowledge, and guidance. Our Almighty God even reiterates the importance of our role as Christian parents in managing spiritual affairs in our homes throughout His word. Why? So, we will see the importance and need for our prompt, godly response that will surely help our future descendants. This is critical because our biblical responsibility is to ensure we're all in one accord as a family unit with God's long-term plan!

However, in these final days of spiritual and biblical deafening times, we are confronted with many parenting challenges within our homes, as we will see in some distressing statistics from various research companies in the upcoming pages. As an Instructor for the National Fatherhood Initiative, Mentor and Chaplain in the Prison Ministry, and representative for CASA (Court Appointed Special Advocate), I've witnessed a prevalent issue in homes that gives rise to numerous problems: 'Children are growing up with only one parent or no parents in our turbulent times, plus, some are growing up in an environment where there's no care, love, or control.' This is a grave concern as it can result in a lack of structured guidance and consistent discipline.

Moreover, it's disheartening to see our society gradually veering away from the biblical approach to raising God's children, one generation at a time. We'll see that there is no wholehearted commitment to our Lord. At best, it's only part-time, which is not pleasing to a God Who desires and requires every part of our being for the benefit of others and His glory! This is crucial because our children and young ones face many obstacles in today's society and culture that are challenging and spiritually threatening their lives. The need for immediate action is not just critical; it's paramount!

You and I will witness some disturbing facts about what's taking place in our homes and the lives of our young ones in the next chapter. While

"The Almighty Search"

it may seem bleak in these challenging areas within the American Family Homes of today, as parents and leaders, we hold the power to steer our homes toward biblical parenting under God's divine guidance. Let's not despair and instead place our Hope in the One Who can guide us in the right direction. It is within our grasp—if we align our priorities and choices with our Heavenly Father. It all begins with the older—more experienced generation stepping up to the plate and embracing the role of godly leadership to address these pressing issues as soon as possible. The call to embrace godly parenting is not just a suggestion; it's a necessity.

Unfortunately, it will be apparent that no one is teaching our young ones the righteous ways of God because, regrettably, parents and family leaders are increasingly ignoring God's guiding principles. Today, it's easy to find parenting advice from anyone who wants to help parents become good parents. However, that's not enough in today's times of unspiritual behavior. We don't just need good parents; we need '*godly parents*' more than ever who are on the same page as God's Holy Word. Don't we all realize we're in severe times of spiritual and biblical leadership in the homes across this land? Will a generation of wise and devoted Christian parents and leaders rise to the call of Almighty God and turn this all around for the good? The potential for a generation of spiritually strong and morally upright children is not just a distant dream; it's within our reach—*if we dedicate our all to God first and foremost.*

This book, "God's Generation of Hope,"—will reveal spirit-stirring and heart-wrenching realities about how today's society and culture negatively impact our children and the younger generations. We'll see eye-opening facts about how the enemy is using so many external forces to attack the inside of our homes today, trying to prevent parents from investing their godly heritage into children's lives—and leaving a legacy of our 'Living Hope' for future descendants. But the key to our younger one's future survival is based on this truth— "If parents and the wiser generation do not build their family lives on the foundation and Hope of Jesus Christ with their children, lives will continue spiraling out of control in every way, shape, and form."

Throughout this journey and search, you and I will see the importance of the Living Hope portrayed in our lives as parents and leaders. Why? To help us overcome the daily trials many families face in their homes today—that are pressing and pushing them to the edge. We will see the emphasis on the power of Hope, which is meant to inspire and uplift those close to us, providing them with the strength to endure and persevere through their most intense warfare.

You see, challenges in life are inevitable, and hope provides a boost of motivation and faith that great things are to come under the guidance of a

Sovereign God. This great expectation (Hope) also fends against depression and other negative attributes that stunt our spiritual growth. We will discover that individuals are more resilient to stress, pressure, and all the weights of the world when they have the Hope of Jesus Christ.

But there's a forewarning! We will also see a lot of repetition in this book because, just like God's holy scripture, so many things need to be repeated to us so we can ascertain and retain the actual message, remember the importance of its meaning, and establish it not only in our own lives—but also for the benefit of our loved ones. God repeats His word to us—because He wants to get our attention and draw our focus to something vitally important that is aligned with His long-term plan. In this case, through the guidance of the Holy Spirit, God wants His children to take heed of His instructions so He can counsel, strengthen, encourage, comfort, and reassure us of what He guarantees will come to fruition, which will be for our good (Rom 8:28)!

As we've seen so often throughout the Bible, the heart of God's message to us is repetitive. Why? "God repeats his words with us because, as children, it takes us a long time to catch on (like the Israelites). The power of God's Word is recurring and routine because His Word is habit-forming, and God repeats His words to us so that we will begin to develop patterns of behavior like His Son, Jesus Christ!" He does this because our Loving and Caring God has our best interest at heart for today, tomorrow, and the future. Also, He wants us to catch on to the power of His word so the Truths can be taught to everyone around us so we can all be a part of His Kingdom (as one)! This reiteration emphasizes the role and responsibility of each of us in spreading God's message, making us feel valued and integral to His Master plan.

But here's a key takeaway: "When we hear God's word, we should pray and accept it with the right motive and desire to fulfill His will—with no reluctance." We must clearly acknowledge and receive the power of God's repeated message so that, in time, it will hit home in our hearts, minds, and spirits, transforming us and transmitting to others. This life-altering conversion is a source of empowerment and hope, leading us to apply and obey His word more frequently. And this not only affects us individually but, more importantly, others around us in powerful ways! It helps us to grow with meaning and purpose for God's glory in our daily lives! This is so vital! Why, you ask?

In today's world of uncertainty, unholiness, and unrighteousness, the most important thing we can do as Sanctified Christian Parents and Leaders is strengthen and sustain our Hope in the Lord, which will impact and influence the younger generations. This emphasis on hope serves as a source of reassurance and comfort, as we need to be committed to passing this on to our heirs so they can learn how to overcome those most challenging days on this side of Eternity. Trust me; this is one of the most essential things we can do every day of our Christian lives for the benefit of our children, and that's—teaching, training, preparing, and equipping our future descendants of the ways of God. We need to be mentoring the hearts, minds, souls, and spirits of our young ones today more than ever.

Unfortunately, in this all-out search, we're also going to see some striking and alarming parallels in many Christian parents of today who are like the first generation of the Israelites from the Exodus—and that alone should not be very comforting to any right-minded believer! Remember what that first generation of Israelites struggled with? It was disobeying the very commands of God!

So, obedience to our Almighty God cannot end with one generation—because God wants a continuity of obedience to bleed over to all future eras—where they will know Who their Real Hope in life is! This powerful attribute (Hope) is the binding tie our children need to get them through the storms of life every day of their lives. But it starts with the loving and caring parents in the homes—teaching our young ones 'Whom' they can rely upon when their trying times come.

But here's the alarming fact: If parents and the mature generation don't comply with God's teachings in their 'own lives' as a daily guide for their children's state of spirituality, they will find themselves and their families very vulnerable to the enemy's ways. That's because they are not connected to God's empowering grace, which can help us overcome our most internal and external disturbances. This is critical because if we fail, as the first generation of Israelites did, it's because we put our biblical and spiritual guard down and were easily misled in our choices in life, which will affect our children and families in tragic ways.

Look at God's word as our valid confirmation and guide. Throughout the Bible, there are numerous examples of parents whose actions, priorities, and choices serve as models of virtuous parenting—or lack thereof. This tells us that it's not just about biological procreation but also about faithful and biblical parenthood, where parents are instructed to divinely raise their children in wisdom and righteousness by the power of God.

Take Hannah, for example. In her desperate longing for a child, she vowed to God that if He granted her a son, she'd dedicate him to the Lord's service. When her prayer was answered, she didn't renege on her promise, thus exemplifying integrity and a level of commitment and loyalty she made to her Lord. This form of divine guidance led to the birth of the prophet Samuel, who was pivotal in Israel's history.

"The Almighty Search"

Then there's Zechariah and Elizabeth, who, despite their old age, faithfully followed God's command and brought John the Baptist into the world. Even in the face of seeming impossibility, their obedience displayed a profound trust in God's sovereignty. You could even look at the examples of Mary and Joseph (the parents of Jesus). Mary knew that Jesus would be identified with God, but because this was a gift from Yahweh, they assumed their responsibility as earthly parents and reared Him as their own on earth. We can even look at the faithfulness of Abraham and Sarah as the start of God's ultimate commitment to lead His children to the Promised Land through future descendants!

Unfortunately, there are poor examples in the Bible that I would like to think many parents of today would not want to be exemplary of in their lives. Look at the prodigal son's rebellion—directly resulting from his father's negligence of discipline. This led to reckless living and, eventually, regret and repentance (Luke chapter 15). Also, King David's inability to discipline his son Absalom resulted in a bitter power struggle that tore their family apart (2 Sam chapters 13-18). Even the high priest Eli failed to rebuke his sons for their irreverence towards God. This resulted in their untimely deaths and the loss of priesthood for his lineage (1 Sam chapter 2). We can even look at the story of Samson and his parents when they neglected to instill in him the seriousness of his Nazarite vow, leading to his downfall.

In so many cases, we've witnessed firsthand that in God's word, the parents' role as influential leaders has been carried over for generations—in either fruitful or unfruitful ways that have impacted many lives. And here's a given fact for us today as parents: 'That level of persuasive influence still exists.' Think about this: "If parents demonstrate more of the flesh in front of their children, it can shape our young ones in so many unspiritual ways. But if they illuminate more of the Holy Spirit daily, this godly model can be more influential and productive for their spiritual well-being." It all comes down to our choices and priorities in everyday life—in other words, what's important—the ways of God or the ways of the world in our children's lives.

With that, have you ever seriously considered parents' influence on children and younger generations today, which can continue for decades? Do we truly realize the measure and extent of our lives as godly parents and family leaders and how they can trickle down to our children in lasting ways? Below is an article posted on Dr. Donald Ekstrand's 'The Transformed Soul' site, entitled "The Influence Parents Have on Their Children."

Dr. Ekstrand has served as an adjunct professor of Christian Studies at Grand Canyon University. He has served as a Pastor and in various ministries and works associated with Dr. Francis Schaeffer, Billy and Franklin

Graham, and Josh McDowell. This article is a beautiful illustration of the biblical influence of the parent-child relationship.

"First, God creates them by mixing their parents' genes, so children *inherit* some traits from their parents. Then, the parents create the *environment* in which the child is raised. In doing so, parents heavily influence a child's intelligence and personality by interacting with them. Remember that our children are like *sponges*, which means parents can significantly affect their behavior. Children model everything a parent does and incorporate what they see into their own lives."

"With this in mind, parents must set the proper examples for their children because negative examples can harm their development. Since parents are role models for their children, it is from them that children adopt specific values and life skills. As parents, this power of positive role modeling is in your hands to shape your children's future."[1] With these key points, on a personal note, I want parents to realize this proven fact: "Our children not only contain our internal DNA but also take in our external core values and priorities of everyday life. In other words, our daily model of actions and words can become a part of them. So, when their impressionable stage of life kicks in, our behaviors could set a habitual pattern of a "good or bad course in life." Just look at the examples we discussed earlier from the Bible!

This is urgent because it will become clear that there's a missing tie between the parent-child relationships across the United States. There are startling and staggering statistics about our young ones' struggles in life today that prevent them from starting that new beginning so many are longing for. We will see that today's teens need biblical guidance more than ever—because many are seeking for spiritual answers in their daily lives. Make no mistake, parents: "Our children and younger generations are searching for hope and help like never before."

We will see that millions of our adolescents today hunger and thirst for a fresh start that will lead to a better outcome—because of all the evil temptations surrounding them. I believe with all my heart that many of our young ones today know these wrong desires are not for their good. This is where parents step in as the godly examples in the early stages of their lives, empowering them to make the right choices. These are pressing times of pressing matters for God's little ones that require and demand the wiser ones to impress our younger ones with the ways of godliness for their benefit.

Please understand the urgency and gravity of this issue because this is a matter of spiritual survival for our young generation. Recent research

---

1. Dr. Ekstrand. D.W. "The Influence Parents Have on their Children."

"The Almighty Search"

from The Barna Group solidified these facts: After *the age of 30, the likelihood of people responding to the gospel for salvation was less than 4%.* As dedicated and loving Christian parents, this should rattle our spiritual cage to the core of our souls and spirits today. Think about the power of this statistical fact below and the immediate action it demands!

As many as 96%+ of people after the age of 30 may never come to the point of salvation—all because someone did not take the initiative to share the Good News with them at the early stages of their life! As parents and wiser generations, we must bear this heavy responsibility because we have the power to make a difference! If not, something is wrong—and maybe that's part of the problem with today's younger generation. Why? Sadly, parents and the older generations are apparently not passionate, bold, and confident enough to pass on the goodness of our Heavenly Father and Lord to our future descendants!

So, this leads me to ask—regarding this extensive number of young people who may never experience salvation—"If the biblical principles of Christ were taught to this vast number of people at their early stages, could that one major component of the Gospel be the game-changer in their lives?"[23] Could that early stage of biblical training have been the one dynamic thing they needed to cling to as their Hope and faith, which could have saved them eternally? Let's be inspired by the potential of early biblical training in young people's lives because it can be a life-changer. Parents, we will see that we cannot afford to delay!

The takeaway is this: "If parents and the wise generations do not hold to the Truths of God's word and live by it for the sake of the younger ones' future, they could be depriving that one child of eternal life. But also, the opportunity for that one person to impact other people's lives for the glory of the Lord." If parents and family leaders don't pass on the ways of God to the younger ones, we could be the ones who are halting the Gospel and Great Commission in a person's life! Are we feeling any conviction now?

All of this is so pressing because we must understand that the younger generations are the missing age gap in church and can be the firm foundation of godliness in the coming years. If you think about it—" *They're the Hope for Spiritual Survival in the Future—on this Side of Heaven!"* We can only establish their means of Christlike sustainability if we support them in the guiding biblical principles of God's teachings at their early stages.

Parents, don't we realize by now that God not only desires but commands us to pass on the stories from the Bible and our personal experiences

---

2. "Spiritual Maturity Process Should Start at an Early Age."
3. "Signs of Decline & Hope Among Key Metrics of Faith."

of His mighty acts from generation to generation? Why? Because it demonstrates where our saving faith, genuine love, and real hope truly lie for today, tomorrow, and the future. We can only help each lineage understand the importance of obeying God and His word by telling and teaching them daily (morning, afternoon, and night)—so they will know the significance of passing it on. If these godly guidelines are not ingrained in our future descendants', they could fall into the patterns of a society and culture that is already off course with godly teaching today.

As Christian parents and leaders, we are uniquely positioned to make a profound difference in the lives of the younger generations. They have the potential to carry the torch of God's word for years to come. We must instill in them the understanding that one Christlike act at a time can impact lives in the future. This realization should fill us with hope, inspiration, and motivation to act on God's charge today.

Ultimately, it comes down to making the right spiritual choices and aligning them with the godly priorities our Heavenly Father has laid out for us in the Bible. Our choices and priorities are crucial in raising and teaching our children. We must take this responsibility seriously, as it is a key part of our faith formation journey—for parents and all our young ones for years to come.

Undoubtedly, with all the chaos and evil temptations in today's culture, we can quickly get off course in guiding our children in everyday life. However, once we're clear on our biblical priorities and responsibilities, we can make better spiritual choices that will guide our godly decisions, which can be more spiritually productive for us and our young ones as a family. That is why family leaders must be grounded in today's most crucial primary concern—and that's: "Leading our younger generation down a more spiritual and biblical path that is aligned with God's word."

As we embark on our life journey on this side of glory, as a parent and family leader, are our hearts aligned with God's purpose and plan not just for ourselves—but for our loved ones' spiritual well-being in the days and years to come? The Apostle Paul even reminds us in Eph 6:4, "Fathers, do not provoke your children to anger by the way you treat them. Rather, bring them up with the discipline and instruction that comes from the Lord." This underscores the significant role we play in shaping our children's spiritual journey.

Just imagine the life-altering power of applying the timeless wisdom of God's word in our children's lives. This could revolutionize our family homes across the nation. How? Consider this: The United States is among the top ten countries in the world with the highest percentage of families. With approximately 84 million family homes and an average of 3 children per household, that's over a quarter billion people, 75% of our total population.[4] The potential is immense, but the reality is that we need more parental laborers in homes across America today. In other words, the harvest is great, but the laborers are few (Matt 9:37, Luke 10:2). The need for more of us to step up and take on this crucial role is urgent and cannot be overstated. Parents, please listen—we need your commitment and dedication to guide our children on a spiritual and biblical path.

Since the dawn of God's creation, we have all been shaped by a parent, guardian, or family leader for better or, sadly, worse. Regardless of our life experiences (good or bad), don't we all aspire to make a lasting and positive impact in the lives of the younger generations, leading them to Christ—our Living Hope? Instead of dwelling on the negatives in our past, God calls us to embrace our new life in Christ and use His empowering grace, mercy, love, and new hope to enrich the lives of others for the future. Today, as devout disciples and leaders of Christ, we have the divine opportunity to influence a generation of children and young ones for years to come, a chance for personal growth and spiritual fulfillment. This potential for 'positive change' should inspire hope and encouragement in us all, knowing that our efforts can lead to a brighter future for our children.

You and I have the empowering responsibility to impact a child significantly and the next generation for God's glory. Our Lord implores you and me to make this a top priority and choice in our daily lives—one that can drastically impact a young one in magnificent ways, and it's this: "My primary concern as a 'Mature Child of God' is to come to the spiritual and biblical aid of the younger generation!" This is as vital today as ever because the truth is that many of our young children desperately need the 'Living Hope' in their lives.

You may be in a church or community where all seems fine and dandy with the youths, but don't be delusional and oblivious to the real facts that are widespread. Your hearts, minds, and spirits will be shaken by what's happening in so many homes across America. The situation is urgent and dire, and we must respond with love and Christlike actions before it's too late. The time for us—as parents and leaders is to act now—as our young ones are crying out for help and hope today—more than ever!Add this scripture below:

Ezek 34:11, "For this is what the Sovereign Lord says: I myself will search and find my sheep."

---

4. "Estimates on American Families and Living Arrangements."

"The Cries for Hope"

Millions today ask, "What is happening in this country and world with all the prevailing storms of disobedience against Almighty God." But I have a more fundamental question for the millions concerned: "What in the world is happening with families in America today?" Something within the walls of American homes is significantly amiss, and it's affecting people's attitudes and behaviors in every community across the United States. Most tragically, it's detrimentally impacting our children and the younger generations' lives in so many ways. We need to address this pressing issue immediately, as it's crucial for the spiritual survival of our future eras. The state of our family homes is a matter of grave concern, and it's up to us to make a change.

No matter what report I read regarding our adolescents' pressing issues of today—and concerns within the homes across this great land, each one saddens me more and more! As I review studies, articles, and research from the Barna Group, Pew Research Center, American Bible Society, Children's Ministry Statistics, Lifeway Research, The Christian Post, Christianity Today, Crosswalk, Gallup Poll, American Medical Association, and Centers for Disease Control and Prevention clearly demonstrate that something is off-kilter and wrong in today's family homes between parents and children, and it's not being addressed.

In these bullet points below, we will see some of the main reasons why American Family Homes are going through intense battles with the enemy. I must forewarn the concerned Christian parents; these are disheartening realities! They illustrate that our younger generations' constant fights in everyday life speaks volume on why so many are having major bouts with mental health, which has increased a myriad of physical, emotional, and discouragingly spiritual detriments. *Something 'Spiritually' needs to take place in homes around the four corners of this country—so they can be reined*

"The Cries for Hope"

in and managed to the point of biblical control. Please take time to digest these major issues internally!

- Recent reports show that addiction to social media and technology amongst teenagers has doubled and continues to increase year over year, which has increased depression, anxiety, low self-esteem, eating disorders, and suicidal thoughts.[5]
- With that, social media and technology have become the natural babysitters and providers in our younger ones' daily lives because of parental neglect!
- "New reports confirm that there's an ongoing and extreme distress among teens who are having significant battles with identity crises. In other words, *they are trying to identify with something other than what God created them to be.*"
- The elevation of isolation and loneliness leads to more helplessness and hopelessness among teenagers.
- The rise of irreligious associations.
- The rapid increase in bullying and hatred.
- Unhealthy patterns with sex, drugs, and alcohol.
- Exposure to on-screen violence.
- Teenagers continue to struggle with increased levels of materialism, narcissism, anger, jealousy, inferiority issues, and peer pressure!
- 97%+ of adolescents' time is spent with other things in their daily lives that mislead them in unspiritual ways. This is a powerful and sad number!

Folks, our young ones of today are being misled into a plethora of spiritually threatening problems. Are we aware of this concerning and ongoing matter? "God, please raise awareness among today's parents and family leaders that our children need help and biblical guidance more than ever!" Why? Regrettably, the staggering statistics and research below clearly identify why there are so many issues in American Family Homes regarding the spiritual foundation of the parent-child relationship!

- A Barna report conducted less than two years ago highlighted this severe point: 'Only 2% of 'all' parents of preteens hold a Biblical Worldview.

---

5. De Angelis. Tory. "Teens Are Spending Nearly Five Hours on Social Media."

"The Cries for Hope"

- "Shockingly, few parents *intentionally* speak to their children about beliefs and behavior based upon the Bible." [6]

- Sadly, most parents subscribe to a hodgepodge of ideas and philosophies when teaching their children things about life—rather than the Truths of God's word.

- Reports show that the view and truths of God's word have declined from one generation to the next over the past twenty-plus years. And they continue to get worse!

- There has been a steady increase in church dropouts and a decline of hope and faith across all generations in the U.S. Regrettably, it is reported that the new generation Alpha will continue this distressing and downward pattern. [7]

- The share of Bible users continually decreases *as age groups move from old to young.*

- Recent reports show that 80% of Christian parents say, "They feel inadequate to teach their children Biblical principles." How can this be? Maybe parents are not genuine students of God's word! Something is wrong!

- Only 9% of Christians read God's word daily, based on a report from the American Bible Society in 2021. Many experts and theologians feel that this number is even lower!

- Only half of Christians genuinely engage with the Word of God. This means <5% of proclaimed Christians apply the Real Truth to their everyday lives.

- "*Marginally attached* Christians are the ones moving from their faith." In other words, lukewarm believers who are not dedicated wholeheartedly to the faith and Truth of God's word will eventually fall away, and this detrimental fact will impact an entire family!

- A 2021 Gallup Poll survey revealed that between 60% and 80% of young people from church-attending families leave the church as soon as they leave home. Why? Their upbringing of faith and hope in the family was not well-grounded in the Truth of God's word.[8]

---

6. ,5,6,8 Pierce. Jerry. "Only 2% of Parents of American Preteens Have a Biblical Worldview."

7. "Signs of Decline & Hope Among Key Metrics of Faith."

8. Jones. Jeffrey. "U.S. Church Membership Falls Below Majority for First Time."

"The Cries for Hope"

- A 2021 Christian Post article stated that fewer than 10% of Generation Z youth say they're committed to reading the Bible regularly. Only 10%, folks! What is the other 90% doing? This generation has stated that they have a precarious relationship with the Bible. How disheartening! Could biblical and spiritual guidance in their early stages have made a difference?[9][10]

  - This is a critical point of concern because many experts feel that this Generation is the one that can shape the future of our country! If only 10% are dedicated to the guiding words of God, then we're in trouble!

- Reports show that 51% of practicing Christian parents are "very" concerned about their children's spiritual development! If that number were a consistent trend across the United States, it would equate to more than 22 million teenagers! It is evident that something is biblically and spiritually missing in the parent-child relationship in homes today! This is so alarming! [11]

- And reports show that there are only 37 minutes of 'quality time' daily between the parent-child relationship during the work week. This is <3% per day! The operative word here is 'quality time.[12]'

  - Please grasp this Truth: "Quality is time in the Word of God." How can Christian parents form our young one's faith formation journey with 37 minutes daily? Are you kidding me?

When we look at all these severe points of reality, it does not take a rocket scientist to assess the problem within America's homes today. It's this: The practice of Christianity is softening, and parents are not setting the biblical example of God's guiding principles daily. The disturbing fact is that a decrease in God's teaching is trending downward one generation at a time. How in the world do we expect our future heirs to survive spiritually without a foundation built on God's word?

The facts speak for themselves: "The biblical worldview in the Eyes of God is vanishing one era after another." With that in mind, we must hold onto this biblical fact: "When the protection of God's Mightiness is absent in our homes, it enables the enemy to slide into our family lives with storms of frequent evil. When this happens, it will lead to a more significant elevation

---

9. Morrow. Jonathan. "Only 4% of Gen Z Have a Biblical Worldview."
10. Gryboski. Michael. "Only 9% of Gen Z Youth Are Bible-Centered."
11. "Americans Who Read Their Bible Have Far More Hope."
12. Renner. Ben. "American Family Spend Just 37 Minutes of Quality Time, Daily."

of church dropouts from the body of Christ, a falling away from the Way, Truth, and Life, which has increased with each era.

This is why we're seeing a perpetual decline of faith and hope in the Truth of God's word amongst family homes across America. Unfortunately, this is all due to a lack of wholehearted commitment to God and not seeking Him first and foremost in our daily lives! Instead of repeating the same unspiritual mistakes in our homes today, why aren't parents embedding the repetition of God's word in their children's lives each day? Where is the line of biblical accountability?

When you heighten all of this with no 'quality time of spirituality' within the homes between the parents & children, our times of despair and discouragement are inevitable. Parents, can't we see that when there's no spiritual and biblical discipline and structure in the homes, and with the escalation of our young ones' ongoing challenges, *it is no wonder why millions of God's children cry out for help today more than ever?*

As I assess and digest these realities, I wonder why 70% of Christian parents are concerned that their children will stay true to the Christian faith. Really! With all these departures from God's guiding principles, it should be no surprise that we're seeing issues in today's family homes! It is pretty easy to look at these disturbing facts and realize what the core of the problem is. These astonishing stats tell me this: 'It is pretty evident that Christian parents are oblivious to the teaching of God's powerful word in their children's lives, which can make all the difference in their spiritual stability in life!'

"Lord, it is evident that the younger generations have been misled from Your ways of holiness and righteousness to the ways of the world—because it is clear that parents have not only let their children down but, most importantly, You! We need to get back to the roots of Your Word where the power of Your Spirit is alive in us, and we're acting upon those convictions in our daily lives that lead us to Your wholesome counseling and comfort—not just for our sake, but for our children and the younger generations' future state of spirituality. I believe there are so many crying out to you for help as their '*Source of Hope,*' as in the days of the yesteryears, which were recorded in your Holy Book in Nehemiah chapter 8. For millennials, your children are seeking you—because during their most intense times of struggle, they cry out for help!" As a close friend of mine who is an author and leader of women's ministry powerfully stated, "We need to wake up church and pray for a spiritual awakening and revival in the family"![13]

---

13. Gryboksi, "Only 9% of Gen Z Youth are Bible-Centered."

"The Cries for Hope"

The psalmist David declared in Ps 18:6, "But in my distress, I cried out to the Lord; yes, I prayed to my God for help. He heard me from his sanctuary; my cry to him reached his ears." Undoubtedly, a cry from someone in the wilderness (such as David) points out the dangers of a dire situation, the truth about it, and the damage it could cause in their lives. When that child of God has finally exhausted all their worldly resources, they will eventually come to that point when they have no other option than complete surrender and submission to the One Who was always there from the beginning to help!

Like David, many of our children are trying to expose the vast corruption surrounding them because they know it will somehow harm their lives, so they cry out for help and guidance. Unfortunately, in many cases, they don't know where or 'Who' to turn to when these harsh battles confront them. Is there a responsible Christian parent or leader who can help guide them in the ways God desires? All of this leads me to ask, "What is the cause of these depressing matters with our young children today?" Well, here comes the gut punch!

Parents, when we open our life's portal in the homes to the vices of the enemy, the world, and our sinful desires, we come to an unsafe position in our Christian life that can lead to severe damage! If we don't put on the Whole Armor of God (Eph 6:10–18), be a Listener and Doer of the Word (Jas 1:19–22), and take every thought captive that is not obedient to Christ our Lord (2 Cor 10:5), our current home life and the future path will not get any easier! Why?

Because the enemy has mastered a plan that captures us when our Christian foundation is cracked open to his lying and deceiving ways, he attacks us when we're in our lowest valleys, weakest moments, and most defenseless spiritual state—he knows precisely how to blindside us! And make no mistake, he can even attack us when we're at our highest point in life, and we think everything is going great! Always recall what Peter tells us in 1 Peter 5:8: the enemy prowls like a lion looking to devour his most likely prey!

This is why we must be spiritually and biblically on guard with a mind, heart, and spirit that is sober, alert, and ready. Don't you love it when you feel like you've taken three positive steps of Christlikeness forward—but then the enemy gets you off course, and now you find yourself taking four 'fleshly' steps backward? I am not sure about you, but it is frustrating when this happens in my spiritual walk because I feel like I've let the Lord down. You see, the enemy loves to put up as many barriers in life as possible that create those personal and family setbacks—that will prevent us from starting a more maturing walk with our Lord daily. And when this affects us individually as parents and leaders, it can trickle down to our young ones!

By now, you should see the significant element that our children and the younger generation need more than ever for the turbulent and trying times ahead: 'Hope!' And here's the key! If parents and the mature generations of today do not leave a path of holiness and hopefulness for our younger ones, they can easily fall into the traps of the deceiving ones' ways. This is critical because of the steady increase of hopelessness, which is running rampant in our younger ones' lives today more than ever—all because of the intensified work of the enemy!

It is so vital that parents get on the same page with the teachings of God's word in our children's lives at the beginning stages—because if they don't, we will see that we could be headed towards an internal calamity! In time, we will come to grips with this fact: "Accountable parents and family leaders must take on and tackle these challenges in the family unit for correction immediately! Because regrettably, for many, if their course in life does not get corrected and placed on the straight and narrow, it could lead to the point of no return."

If we don't rein in these current family issues ASAP, which are gradually separating the families from God's purpose and plan, our future generation will never learn how to seek and cling to our 'Hope in the One'—Who can sustain them during their most challenging times. This is so critical because, sadly, in today's culture, the household of God's children is going through aggressive internal wars due to an external force that parents are allowing to enter the front door of the family homes. Now, this open invitation enables him to sneak into every nook and cranny!

Parents, without the wisdom and knowledge of God taught in the homes, our children and younger ones will never know what direction in life to choose when their times are tough! When the younger generation loses all spiritual sense of Who their true identity is with, they will eventually cry out for help because of their internal confusion. In the depths of these cries, how can parents and leaders get more engaged with these ongoing issues in family homes today and truly recognize these ugly realities within their own walls?

Here it is: "Our children need biblical and spiritual structure and discipline more than ever. Many young ones long for Christlike role models, mentors, and teachers! In order to get these matters under control, there must be godly leadership, accountability, and guidance, which should be spearheaded by the parents and family leaders in the homes. And trust me, parents, when these principles are enveloped with the guidance of God's word and the Holy Spirit—woven with Christlike obedience, discipline,

"The Cries for Hope"

humility, grace, mercy, and love—you will see those wrong priorities and bad choices start to dwindle."

Yes, parents can set the precedence of spiritual and biblical living in God's household today! However, according to God's guiding principles, it takes commitment and willingness to be aligned with the right choices and priorities. It will require Christlike love, patience, goodness, kindness, faithfulness, gentleness, and self-control. And in God's perfect timing and leading, watch joy and peace come to the surface in the family lives!

We desperately need this in our homes today because, let's face it, parents: The bottom line is that our children and the younger generation are hooked on things in life that will lead nowhere spiritually. So, what accountable and caring parent(s) will emerge from the shadows of today's darkened culture, take this "raging bull by the horns," and get these matters under control—one child at a time?

When our young ones have no clear godly direction and are perplexed by life's confusing ways, and they are at that crossroads in life, don't we realize that without God's guidance, they will sadly continue to turn to those evil vices that will lead them away from the spiritual blessings God has in store for them? And you ask why? Regrettably, parents have not been as engaged as they should be in their children's spiritual lives (as we've seen in the earlier data).

This is critical because, in many cases, these external evil forces, over time, can lead to an internal issue where defiance will surface against family, friends, the community, church, authorities, and most importantly, God! Does that sound familiar? Think of the first generation of Israelites! Simply put! If godly parents and disciples of Christ don't try to defuse this ticking time bomb immediately, we will experience more tension, depression, discouragement, disappointment, frustration, and division in the stressful times ahead.

More than ever, we need to get close to our children and the younger generation. We need to pray for a discerning spirit so we can listen to their hearts and determine if they are in a stage of the wilderness and confused at their crossroads in life. Somewhere along the path, so many adolescents of today have been misguided in their life's journey. And in most cases, they got off course at the early stages of life because of the lack of biblical guidance.

The wiser generation of God's people should see the signs, respond in Christlike ways, and help them to get on the path of righteousness. Remember, crying out to God is an admission of one's coming to the end of oneself and placing Hope in God alone—a beautiful portrait of surrender and submission. The only way we'll know is by spending quality time with them, where we can see the warning signs and truly know if they are crying out for help!

Undoubtedly, our children and younger generations are confronting desperate times that call for desperate measures in today's world. And they need to know that when we place those desperate measures on the value of our Hope in Christ and all His promises, it will demonstrate a complete desire for Him alone, where we can lean on Him—no matter the intensity of the troubles. He hears our cries from His throne and will always be there to assure us that His promises will get us through—if we would only believe in His guiding ways!

If parents don't apply themselves to our children's apparent issues in today's culture, we will continue to ask," Why are there issues with today's teens?" Make no mistake about this statement: "If parents spend less than 3% of quality time, spiritually and biblically, with their children, they will never be able to ascertain their genuine cries for help—and know how to lead them to the Source of 'Living Hope'!" Parents, please forever hold onto this: Without a structured and disciplined teaching of God's Holy Word in our young ones' lives, there will always be waves of emotional confusion, trouble, distress, and times of disorder. Our God is a God of order, not confusion!

As an Instructor for the National Fatherhood Initiative, I discovered that almost 80% of families in America are dysfunctional. What does this mean? A dysfunctional family is characterized by "conflict, misbehavior, or abuse." What does this lead to? Relationships between family members are tense and can be filled with neglect, yelling, screaming, and all types of verbal, if not even physical, abuse. I can personally attest to this fact because I grew up in a very dysfunctional family myself—but I survived by the Grace of God! But disturbingly, some family breakdowns do not stop there.

I also learned in my years of mentoring and teaching in the Prison Ministry that approximately 90% of homeless teenagers come from fatherless homes. Think about the power of that sad statistic! When there's an absence of a spiritual leader in the house (fathers), and the Mom and nurturer take on multiple roles to provide for her children, it leads to a lack of godly structure within the family where the enemy can gradually start to work out his plan. As an Instructor, you hear stories like this one below from various individuals, which is disheartening—because so many adolescents across this country and the world have the same message.

"As a young man growing up, I have very little recollection of who my parents were. Because of this lack of knowledge and a weakened family structure, I had almost no confidence in my abilities. I saw no means of hope and did not know which way or who to turn to in life. It took me

"The Cries for Hope"

many years to realize that all the bad things occurring in my life were due to a seriously dysfunctional family. Whose fault was this? Because the anger fueling inside of me wanted to blame someone!"

"However, I honestly had no idea that deep down inside, there were some good qualities that I did possess. Weirdly, I inherently felt they were there, and I sensed they could be of meaningful use because something felt right and good. However, I did not know how to bring them to the surface, mold them, and shape them to help me build on something more positive in the future. Because of this state of helplessness, I cry out 'WHY' almost every day of my life! I do not even know who I am crying to! Unfortunately, the wrong things in life continue to feed my starving soul!"

"I did resent and have anger toward my parents (what little I knew of them) for years because aren't they the ones who were supposed to teach me about living life, what are good and bad choices, right from wrong, how to be empathetic, loving, and endure through the tough times in life? If we don't get it from our family, we are left to learn on our own, which can take much longer in this severely off-course society and culture. If you are someone who had a family who cared and kept their promises, well, consider yourself blessed and lucky! As a confused young man, I am still searching for answers, and yes, my internal cries are constant!"

Folks, these types of stories are by the millions and will only increase if someone within the family structure does not take leadership and ownership—one child and generation at a time! More young ones are crying out around the world than we can even fathom! We can only truly know and hear their internal cries for help by spending more quality time with them in the Word of God. They need to know today more than ever that there is a Hope Who can bring them from their darkest days into His eternal Light!

This story leads me to wonder: "Do we truly realize that many of our children throughout the communities are mentally, emotionally, physically, and most importantly, spiritually out of balance?" And make no mistake about this—at one point or another in their lives, millions of them will come to a crossroads where they will cry out for someone to help them in their times of despair. However, will they know "Who to seek and turn to" when tribulation confronts them?

Once again, as a volunteer in the community and a mentor and teacher in the Prison Ministry, I witnessed too many incidents where children cried out for help, but the parents did not see the warning signs. Why? There was no quality time between the parents and children on a daily scale. It was apparent that the parents' priorities in everyday life were focused more on other things—than their children's spiritual security for the future.

"The Cries for Hope"

All of this makes me ponder a most poignant question: "Are Christian parents today remotely aware of what is happening to their children's state of spirituality?" Do we genuinely know if they are crying out for help? Have we noticed the drastic changes in their lifestyle that would raise our internal red flags to complete spiritual awareness? Most importantly, and you'll hear this a lot, as godly parents, are we laying that foundation of biblical teaching that can clearly guide our young ones to the Living Hope when their times of confusion and distress are extreme? Parents, are the spiritual eyes of our hearts, minds, and spirits in tune with our young ones?

This is imperative because the facts are this: "The gap is widening and growing farther apart from the Way, Truth, and Life, one era at a time!" "Are we, as parents and guardians, neglecting our spiritual call as the wiser generation of obedient followers of Christ?" Because honestly, based on earlier reports, it looks like many parents are walking away from their family's biblical responsibility. Many parents need to spiritually wake up—because as the chasm widens, the cries of our children are growing louder and louder as each generation approaches. 'Lord, please grant the parents and wiser ones with your divine wisdom and guidance—so we can help lead our children today and in the future to the Source of Hope!'

Always remember—that our "Almighty and Righteous God is a jealous God, and *nothing should ever be competing with Him that could drive you, me, and our young ones away from His holy presence.*" Will there be times when we stumble, fall, and fail (Ps 37:24-26)? The short answer is Yes! However, our mighty Lord upholds us with His hand. And in that tight grip, we will indeed discover throughout this journey that Hope is our trump card when desperate times call for desperate measures—because it's the True anchor for our soul (Heb 6:19). This mainstay represents our stability, security, and steadfast faith in God, no matter what comes our way! Parents, we will come to believe that this Cornerstone can be the pivotal point that can help us pave a solid path for our children's future!

With that, this is a call-out to parents! We have all inherited a genetic line that is inept to the ways of God because of our sinful nature—it is spiritually cracked and too often misguided. Paul reminds us in Romans chapter 3, "No one is righteous, no not one, and we've all fallen short of God's glorious standard." Consider this powerful takeaway and lesson, parents: "We already have an internal battle and war raging within us, so why would we become a stumbling block to our children's spiritual survival?" What do I mean?

If we don't have our own personal relationship with the Lord in order (as family leaders)—and we continue to compound our loved ones with the ugly things of our external life, like drugs, alcohol, verbal and physical abuse, sexual immorality, impurity, lustful pleasures, idolatry, hostility, quarreling, jealousy, outbursts of anger, selfish ambition, foul language, dissension, division, envy, wild parties, and other sins like these, we are not doing our children justice according to God's word" (Galatians chapter 5). Once again, when our flesh consumes our lives more than the Spirit in front of our children, it will only lead to more spiritual unrest and elevations of more cries for help!

That said, each responsible Christian parent must take precautionary steps to allot our time to certain things in life. Most importantly, we must ensure that they are spiritually productive. Why is this important? With all of the previous facts we've witnessed, we should know that whatever we choose to shape and form our everyday lives can affect and mold our children and the younger generations in either "Christlike" or "ungodly" ways. It comes down to the right choices and priorities in our lives as God's household leaders!

By now, Christian parents should be fully aware of this crucial point: Everything we say and do matters externally because it teaches our children a lot in everyday life (Read Colossians). Our level of engagement and active involvement with our young ones can set the trend for who they will become—and 'Who' they can always rely upon. The key for Christian parents is our own internal relationship with Jesus Christ. Why? Because our 'true identity' of our inner being matters—it can set the tone for something good, pure, righteous, and holy in the younger ones' lives!

Our children must see the parents and family leaders clinging to the 'God of Hope' and His goodness so they will know—"Who they can hold on to when the going gets tough!" Remember what Jesus' half-brother, James, tells us in the first chapter of his epistle: "It's not a question or matter of 'if,' but *'when' troubles come*. And when they come, will our young ones know Who to seek and cling to—will they truly be ready?" Have we taught them well? This journey of Hope will test each of us on this fact: "What path have we genuinely laid for our young ones' state of spirituality in the future?"

Preface

Stop and think seriously about this fundamental question for a moment! "How will you and I be remembered for our life on this earth?" Whether we like it or not, we will leave "some type of legacy" that others will remember—or easily forget. Will it be for a fleeting second, minutes, hours, days, months, or years? It may only affect one person or many, but eternally bear this in your heart, mind, and spirit: "You and I have a God-given choice and responsibility to leave a memorable and positive mark of Christlikeness that will carry over for generations—'NOT' forgettable and negative." Will it label you and me as a "Kingdom Builder"—or 'Kingdom Breaker?' After we're gone, will the remnants of our spiritual & biblical lives affect others in powerful, positive, and life-changing ways? Think about that!

Continuously remember this: "A Christlike legacy is intentional and a conscious decision to leave a godly path for others. It is taking the godly heritage we've inherited for our future life and then investing the breadth and wealth of that experience and knowledge into other people's lives, especially our children, so they can continue to share this with others for decades, if not centuries. We should diligently work at it daily—for all our loved ones in lasting ways."

Consider the profound influence of our Christlike legacy: It's about leaving behind the essence of our true identity, marked by our Living Hope—Jesus Christ, who has transformed our lives. This legacy should be so powerful that it continues to nurture the spiritual well-being of our loved ones and others in the years to come. Many of us will be blessed and privileged to witness this legacy lived out through our children and their descendants—and what an absolute blessing to see the torch of Christianity carried forward for God's glory! This vision should fill our hearts with joy and inspire us to action today!

Remember, the path to a godly legacy for our future heirs, starting with the parents and leaders of the homes, is our sacred duty as God's devoted children. We must always bear in mind that we will be held accountable by our Almighty God as their teachers. The key lesson and source of encouragement for you and me is this: If we align our priorities and choices with God's will, many of us will witness the eternal benefits of our spiritual investment in our children's lives (as stated above). This is a blessing not just for us, our children, and their descendants but also brings glory, honor, and praise to our Heavenly Father! What a powerful way to ensure that God's Future Kingdom is being built through you, me, and our heirs!

Make no mistake about this statement: "In life, we're either pursuing one of selfish gains—or one classified as a modeled Christlike servant." The beauty of the latter is this: "It possesses a strong desire and passion for the well-being of our loved one's and others state of spiritual survival." And in today's time of internal and external struggles and battles, it is so crucial that we choose this model of Christlikeness for our future heirs' benefit. Why?

Think about the weight of the Great Commission in our lives as reverent disciples of Jesus Christ (Matt 28:19–20). It reveals the heart of God, Who desires all people to be saved and to come to a knowledge of the 'Real Truth' (1 Tim 2:4). It compels us to share the Good News until everyone has heard it, including our children, and through them their children. Always retain the importance of this biblical fact: 'Jesus commands us to be about the business and building of His Kingdom—not the ways of the world.'

God desires you and me as accountable parents and leaders to serve Him by taking the initiative to influence and impact others for His glory (as stated earlier). This includes our immediate family, friends, brothers and sisters in Christ, neighbors, and anyone within our proximity. This is imperative because our actions in "all that we say and do as proclaimed Christians" while alive on this earth—that God has endowed us—are of the utmost importance for current and future generations now more than ever.

As iterated so often in this journey, let's not overlook the seriousness of the situation: 'God's desire is for every generation to obey Him, so this discipline is passed on to the next generation for their means of survival.' This is a call for immediate action, as I firmly believe that there are Christian parents who hold genuine hope for their children's future state of spirituality—and their succeeding heirs!

Parents, here's the path we must pave for our loved ones: 'Following God's commands in every word, living according to His guiding principles by establishing a firm foundation on the validity of the Bible and aligning our actions and choices with His will and plan.' Let's remember: Obedience is our highest call of moral duty because it is the absolute belief that God is the Supreme Authority and the Source of Truth & Hope!'

As we progress parents and family leaders, we will become fully aware of the importance of this three-fold principle that needs to be instituted in our homes today: 1) Have a daily position that is more grounded in God's word and 'all' His ways—2) Possess priorities that are more Christlike focused, and—3) Incorporate a predisposition in everyday life that is more led by God's Holy Spirit.

If we implement these basics into our family lives, the persuasive acts of evil swirling in our midst would be less invasive, which could prevent some of those unnecessary cries in the wandering wilderness. Think about that! If the Triune God (Father, Son, and Spirit) is actively working and at the center of our family's homes, the enemy will have less power to ease into our personal lives with his sly and sleazy acts, which bring so much torment.

After all, James (half-brother of Jesus) reminds us powerfully in the fourth chapter of his epistle: Jas 4:7-8, "So, humble yourselves before God. Resist the devil, and he will flee from you. Come close to God, and God will come close to you. Wash your hands, you sinners; purify your hearts, for your loyalty is divided between God and the world."

As parents, we hold a significant role as spiritual leaders in our children's lives. We can be the biblical example of ensuring that our children are more loyal to our Lord and King—versus the ways of the world. If there is ever any division, we must do as Paul instructs us in 2 Corinthians 13:5, and that's self-examine our spiritual life and ensure that our saving faith is genuine—*and our real hope lies in the promises of Christ. And most importantly, we're committed to Him in every part of our life!* That said, here's a powerful takeaway as we move forward: "If parents are wholeheartedly loyal to the Lord daily, it will set the precedence and example of an excellent guiding principle in our children's lives!"

When our children and the younger generation see that parents are placing their love, faith, and hope in Christ, no matter the difficulties, it will illustrate that we're 100% committed to our Lord as the primary source for all things—because He's Lordship in every area of our lives. This is not just a theoretical concept but a practical application of biblical principles in parenting. When we do this, the Fruit of the Spirit will come to the forefront sacrificially and selflessly in our lives for the well-being of our loved ones and others (Gal 5:22-25).

Paul reminds us in Ephesians chapter 6 that children are to obey their parents, but here's the key in that segment: "Parents are to raise their children according to God's discipline and instructions in the Bible!" This is not a suggestion but a biblical mandate for parents. When parents adhere to God's guidelines, children will learn the right type of respect for authority and have a better chance of spiritual success in the future. And when parents put their godly obedience into action, the Christlike attributes and virtues of *faith, hope, and love* will surface like never before!

You and I will see that we need these three holy virtues in our everyday lives for the sake of our children's future. Why? These attributes powerfully work upon each other in our personal lives and can bless our Heavenly Father. When we initiate and implement these beautiful qualities as our Christlike model in everyday life, they will permeate and influence our children's lives in lasting ways. This is critical for many parents today because when these three powerful elements (faith, hope, and love) are alive and at work in us for their spiritual good, it can help us avoid so many heartaches in the future regarding our children's state of spirituality. Not just for our current eras—but also for their future descendants!

But guess what? No matter all the bad and ugly facts, there is Good News in today's unrest—because there's a bright Light at the end of the tunnel. We will recognize that our only 'Living Hope' lies in a solid foundation built on Jesus Christ, our Savior and Redeemer for the future! However, if we don't engage with our young ones' lives, embrace them with the love, mercy, and grace of Almighty God, and enforce godly change for the good, the enemy will do his best to thwart all of God's plans. We must be on guard for the sake of our entire household in these trying days ahead!

Since the outset of this book and throughout this incredible journey, we will realize the importance of the family unit in the eyes of a Holy God—our Heavenly Father—and the Creator of life. And it's this: "The family unit working as one for the cause of Christ—just like the body of Christ—the church." Yes, it's that important to God because we will realize that Yahweh designed the family as the first source of biblical training and preparation for life, which entails spiritual inspiration, encouragement, and motivation. It should lead to a spiritually productive and fruitful life for the cause of God's purpose and plan that can only multiply with Him at the center of our family lives!

As we've seen so far, the concept of family is essential in the Bible, physically and theologically. Why? The physical family is the essential building block of human society, and as such, it should be nurtured and protected because that is what God requires. But more important than that is the new creation God is making in us, which is to be more like His Son, Jesus Christ. It should be comprised of a biblical & spiritual family devoted to all His ways for the sake of our children, who were gifted to us. This journey of building a spiritual family is not just a duty but a source of joy and inspiration as we see our children and grandchildren grow in faith, hope, and love.

Preface

Think about it: The defining characteristic of this spiritual family is love for one another because love binds us all together in perfect harmony, as one united in Christ (Col 3:14). God's word reminds us in John 13:34-35, "So now I am giving you a new commandment: Love each other. Just as I have loved you, you should love each other. Your love for one another will prove to the world that you are my disciples."[14] Over time, you and I will assess whether our love and faith are genuine as caring Christian parents. If they are, we're building up a family on the foundation of Hope in Christ alone—that will carry over into His glorious Kingdom!

At the end of our lives on earth, what will the storybooks say about us as Christian parents and the elderly generations in the coming years? Will they see a model of faithful servants who used their God-given gifts as a tool and sacrificially left a mark of godliness and hope for the betterment of society? We can all ask ourselves, "What will be the foundation of my legacy? Are they composed of earth's superficial things—or Heaven's everlasting beauties?"

Did we genuinely leave an impression of the Living Hope for our future heirs, who is Jesus Christ? In other words, as the days, months, and years intensify with so much hopelessness in this world, no matter what comes, our future descendants will know there is a 'Real Hope' that will get them through the trials and battles to come. Never forget: "This reassurance of the 'Living Hope' is a promise and a source of comfort and security in an uncertain world."

Only time will tell if we left our permanent and unfading mark of our Lord and Savior for the future to talk about—and the path we laid for our descendants. Have we defended our faith, hope, and love so passionately and honorably that the news of our testimony has spread? Because without our solid path of godly and holy living, generations could be lost where there is no spiritual sense of hopefulness. The choice is up to you and me before it's too late!

Family leaders, never put this out of your minds and hearts—"Everyone was meant to be here on earth, living out their purpose according to their unique gifts and calling from God!" After all, He created us in their image so we would be like them (Father, Son, and Spirit). Think about that; we have the undeniable opportunity to pass on many of God's divine characteristics to others, especially our younger ones, that can help them so beneficially in the times ahead.

So many of us have heard this story, but it's worth sharing as a reminder to all of God's serving parents in the time He allows us as leaders

---

14. "What Does the Bible Say About Family."

Preface

and mentors on this earth. "Have you ever imagined what it would be like to be present at your funeral, to hear what your friends and family say about you? The pastor, friends, and relatives all say nice, publicly acceptable things about you. But then, your children begin to reminisce about you. Your legacy is whatever they say or remember about your life and your influence on people. At that point, many people would listen and reflect somberly on their lives and may realize they've wasted their years."

"If you see yourself in that place, be encouraged! Because you are still here, alive and breathing, and can make a difference starting today—your life story has yet to be entirely written. You still have that precious gift of time on your side to create a life of faith, hope, and love that friends and family can celebrate one day. This dedication to Christlike selflessness can have a powerful influence on many of our loved ones today and in the future. Just take a moment and think: "Your life of Christlikeness can be a beacon of inspiration for others." [15]

Our responsibility to live and leave a legacy as authentic Christians for the benefit of our future descendants is not a distant dream but a pressing need of the present time. In a world where the forces of evil are growing stronger, it is imperative that the younger generations understand the power of our 'Living Hope'—Who He is and how He can guide them through life's most challenging battles. This is why Christian parents must ensure that Jesus Christ and His word are firmly established in their own lives so they are ready to share and teach their children about the Hope we have in all His promises. The goal is for these seeds of faith to take root and flourish in the family for future generations (Read Psalm chapter 1).

The profound impact and importance of parents obeying the guiding principles of God's word—and teaching them to our future descendants will become more evident than ever because it can be a conclusive life-changer—if we comply 100%. But the ultimate reason for our obedience is simple: 'When the Bible tells us so—God's word is sufficient'! Are we ready to accept the call and challenge to make a Christlike impact on the spiritual survival of the younger generations? Only time will reveal our answer. Let us persistently remember: 'It is our biblical duty and responsibility to pass on these values to ensure the spiritual survival of future generations.' It will genuinely display our commitment to our Lord and Savior for His glory!

---

15. "Are You Leaving a Godly Legacy."

Introduction

One of the most influential and renowned publications is Time Magazine. It has reached people worldwide for decades—after all, it's almost 100 years old! However, an article from about ten years ago is one that I found to be one of the most compelling reads ever. While many would consider this magazine more liberal, their assessment of this one article was fascinating in its outcome.

The article was entitled "Who's Biggest? The 100 Most Significant Figures in History." "Who's bigger: Washington or Lincoln? Hitler or Napoleon? Charles Dickens or Jane Austen?" I would even add Thomas Jefferson or Benjamin Franklin? Galileo or Socrates? Joan of Arc or Martin Luther? Michaelangelo or Leonardo Da Vinci? "That depends on how you look at it. When we set out to rank the significance of historical figures, we decided not to approach the project the way historians might—*but through a principled assessment of that person's individual achievements.*"

I will not list all 100 individuals, but it consisted of people like Plato, Shakespeare, Aristotle, Alexander the Great, Albert Einstein, Christopher Columbus, Ronald Reagan, Thomas Edison, John F Kennedy, King Arthur, Thomas Aquinas, Isaac Newton, and Sigmund Freud. As you can see, this is an esteemed list of historical people who significantly influenced people's lives across multiple fields.

But in this Time Magazine article, guess who is number one on the list and has had the most influence on people's lives *through His achievements throughout history*? It was—and is Jesus Christ! That powerful assessment led me to ponder—"If Christ's achievements were that influential and even published in a secular magazine, why are we not seeing the power of His spiritual effect lived out through each generation of 'proclaimed' Christians today?" [16] Our Savior of the world has definitely impacted so many lives throughout the centuries—it cannot be denied! As genuine followers of

---

16. Skiena and Ward. "Who's Biggest?" Time Magazine.

Introduction

Jesus Christ, is the power of our salvation in Him impacting the homes, communities, and abroad? In other words, are we working out our salvation with such diligence, reverence, spiritual fear and trembling, and responsibility that it shakes and rocks the foundation of our homes and communities in glorious ways; especially those close to us! Our Christian lives should be so transparent and widespread that no one can deny it!

This amazing article gave me more thought and led me to reflect on Jesus Christ's effect on so many people over the past two thousand years. Isn't it amazing that the most renowned poets, painters, and writers have not been able to resist conducting some of their work about our Lord, Jesus Christ, over the past centuries?From artists like Rembrandt, Leonardo DaVinci, Raphael, and Michelangelo—to poets like John Milton and John Donne to authors such as Oswald Chambers, A.W. Tozer, Watchman Nee, John Bunyan, and Jonathan Edwards (to name a few).

And I would be remiss to mention C.S. Lewis on the impact his books and Chronicles of Narnia movies have had on many. Did you know the Chronicles of Narnia series grossed over 1.5 billion dollars worldwide? While many would say that this series of books and movies are not Christ-based, they undoubtedly have biblical allegories in their underlying message that could indeed plant a seed of curious minds on Who this Lion Aslan is, how he created the world of Narnia with his voice, which is very similar to the Genesis account of how God created the earth.

In addition, Aslan dies in the place of a sinner and rises from the dead, defeating an age-old curse. Through this sacrificial act, redemption is bestowed upon Narnia because of Aslan's death and resurrection. Clearly, this is Lewis' retelling of the salvation story of Christ's substitutionary death and resurrection. The movies and books underscore and portray evil as bad, and children can quickly identify the evil in the books as unattractive. They can, at the same time, find Aslan and his righteous qualities very attractive. Regardless of your opinions, the series of movies and books can surely plant seeds of a belief in something more powerful and good than evil in the world.

Even in our modern era, TV and movie producers cannot stop producing the life story of Jesus and His effect on people for two thousand years. The movie, "The Passion of the Christ," is among the top 5 most profitable movies ever, and it's the highest-grossing independent film of all time. We see more TV programs airing the life of Christ and His impact on people like never before. Why all the sudden buzz about Jesus Christ—our Redeeming Savior—and the Light and Hope of the world?

Yes, we know that in the end times, there will be an escalation of people who are ungrateful, unloving, unforgiving, full of self-desires, and,

Introduction

sadly, haters of God and our Lord. But powerfully and on the contrary, these times of anguish we're experiencing today lead millions worldwide to long for something more truthful, positive, and encouraging. Why? Because they are weary and tired of feeling hopeless and helpless, and the only true answer lies in our Living Hope, Jesus Christ! So many people are so deep in despair that they cry out for Someone Who can lead them from their pit of suffering—to a better life. They are indeed looking for a void that needs to be filled in all of their emptiness!

Undoubtedly, Jesus's influence on people's lives has never been surpassed—He has truly inspired so many positive changes in the lives of millions (if not billions). And here's the key: "People who encounter the power of our risen Savior are transformed. Their outlook on life is altered from the bad and ugly to the good, which is more positive." And here's another critical point for parents and wiser ones: "Our children and younger generation need to see the power of that Living Hope we have in Christ, which will entice and motivate them to want more of Him in their own lives."

When I pondered more on this article and the impact this one magazine has had on society and culture over decades, it made me think about the #1 selling book of all times, the Bible. Billions of people have held the precious Words of God in their very hands over time. However, His message to that one person seemed to stop—and it did not transmit to other people's lives throughout history. We've even seen this evidence in God's word and in our modern time through the earlier data, which is disheartening.

This makes me wonder even more. If the Bible is the top-selling book of all time, and if Jesus Christ has influenced more people's lives than these most significant historical figures, why do we not see the fingerprints and impact of our Savior and Redeemer carried over from one generation to another through *His body of believers today*? We have apparently lost sight and focus on the 'Only True Hope' that can sustain us through these days full of trials and temptations.

Don't we realize that when Christ died on the cross and rose from the dead, it gave power, life, and hope to future generations who choose to accept the path of Jesus Christ by faith? Because of His atoning sacrifice, He can transform a new beginning in each generation if they would only surrender to Him and submit to following all His ways. It can lead to a life full of spiritual and positive change that can impact others in ways full of peace, joy, comfort, and contentment.

You see—that one life, death, and resurrection made the difference for the then, the now, and the future! He's the Only Hope we have! Jesus's willingness to give up His own life for the sake of others should serve as a model for Christians to follow today. Why? This should motivate us to live

Introduction

honorable lives of service and love that will impact and influence our loved ones in godly ways for years to come.

Remember this! Every generation matters to Jesus—there are no favorites! I hope and pray that each responsible Christian has a burning passion for ensuring that their respective family members, friends, and future descendants will inherit the Kingdom of God. With that, have we invested so much of His teachings into their lives that we know it's taken form, and the guarantee of their inheritance is evident in their everyday life? It cannot be denied!

If accountable Christian parents and leaders apply the Lord's teachings to their personal lives, they will flow down to others in powerful ways for years to come. Through this commitment, we can witness our Lord and Savior impacting so many lives that can be shared with future generations. The beauty of this passing on will give each era a genuine Hope—until the day of Christ's return! What a glorious sight to see transformed lives where Christlike faith, hope, and love are illuminated for the world to see!

Indeed, as Christian parents, we know that our Father and Creator desires and expects us to pass on His ways to our descendants and others so they can carry over the Hope of His promises from one generation to another. We have a significant role in shaping future generations, and he delights in us when we follow all His ways, but the key is that we also delight in Him, so we possess a heart's desire that aligns with His purpose and plan. God has given you and me the ability to choose His ways (Read Deuteronomy chapter 30), and He truly is pleased when our decision aligns with His will. Trust me; it is gratifying to our Loving Father when we ensure that we're living and leaving our mark of Christlikeness that will carry forward for the benefit of others—to His future Kingdom.

The great King David reminds us in Psalm 145:13-21, "For your kingdom is an everlasting kingdom. You rule throughout all generations. The Lord always keeps his promises; he is gracious in all he does. The Lord helps the fallen and lifts those bent beneath their loads. The eyes of all look to you in hope; you give them their food as they need it. When you open your hand, you satisfy the hunger and thirst of every living thing. The Lord is righteous in everything he does; he is filled with kindness. The Lord is close to all who call on him, yes, to all who call on him in truth. He grants the desires of those who fear him; he hears their cries for help and rescues them. The Lord protects all those who love him, but he destroys the wicked. I will praise the Lord, and may everyone on earth bless his holy name forever and ever."

Our Heavenly Father rejoices when you and I call upon the name of the Lord and follow His only begotten Son in faith, and in return, as His

Introduction

faithful servants, we can help current and future generations in Christlike manners when they see the Living Hope demonstrated in our daily lives. He takes absolute pleasure in our passing His goodness and greatness to future eras because it keeps His word fresh and alive in the lives of His future children. Our daily example of faithful living will enable our heirs to see the results of the power of Christ at work in our personal lives. It will give others hope for today, tomorrow, and the future.

Yes, our hope is in God's only Son coming back soon to save us from this world, which is escalating into a state of hopelessness. But, as genuine followers of Christ, do we truly realize the magnitude of what God expects from you and me as His Citizens of Heaven on Earth and managers of His household? It should possess a heart, mind, and spirit that reflects God's character, embodying His love, humility, and compassion for all. It should be a heart that seeks not its own glory—*but the flourishing and well-being of godliness in our lives that is passed onto everyone in our path—over the course of our time on this side of Heaven.* This type of heart finds joy in selflessly serving others, lifting up the broken, and bringing hope to the hopeless (read the four chapters in Philippians).

Today's wiser generation of believers has a major task with a High calling from our Lord! And that's to prepare ourselves, future heirs, and other generations for that day we've hoped for so many years. The Israelites cried and had hope that one day, they would be delivered from the bondage of Egypt (their enemy) and set on the path to freedom, and they were. They would see the promise of a land where they would come together as one under the authority of a Holy God, uniting with Him in fellowship and praise. Unfortunately, we have seen the eternal ramifications when God's chosen ones did not submit to all His ways!

Once again, here's a reminder for you and me today. "As obedient and responsible leaders of Jesus Christ, have we (personally) made that indelible mark of Christlikeness on our descendants' lives and others? In time, we should know beyond a shadow of a doubt that they possess that same Hope we possess, which will help them endure and persevere during these tumultuous and tempting times?"

I want to think, hope, and pray that each Christian parent wants to give their future eras a snapshot of a 'Heavenly Hope' that can make all the difference in their lives for years to come. Why is this so important? That type of Hope can shift their mindsets from the ways of the world—to the ways of our Lord, Jesus Christ (Rom 12:1–2, Col 3:1–4, and Phil 4:8–9). It points them to the One Who can be ever-present in times of trouble—because He's our Refuge and Strength—at all stages of our lives (Ps 46:1)!

Introduction

Remember, the only way future generations will know about the goodness of God and our Lord, Jesus Christ, is through the genuine followers and leaders of Christ who obediently follow His guiding principles. God has called His body of maturing believers to rise above the natural norm, entrusting us with the task of guiding the coming generations. We are to be the living example of fruitfulness, impacting God's Kingdom in our children's and the younger generations' lives like never before. Let the power of God's grace, mercy, and love be so alive in us internally that it impacts everyone externally. Our time is now to be the shining light of Hope for future generations!

Because it is in Him (our Hope, Jesus Christ) that we obtain the empowering strength to accomplish more than we might ask or think—when we allow His faith, hope, and love to be lived out. And in time, it will influence generation upon generation. That is why we must always yield to the power of the Holy Spirit, the ultimate source of empowerment, so He can enable us to shape our future based on the Hope of our Lord and Savior. Why? So, it will impact the world and future eras in ways that will provide them with a focus on an eternal home of rest, peace, and joy!

We must believe it's worth the effort for God's glory because so many teenagers are crying out for help and Hope today—more than ever! Parents and leaders, I cannot stress this enough:" We can make a difference in our young ones' lives today—for their spiritual good!" As you should know by now, it comes down to our choice of what's essential for the well-being of our younger ones' spiritual lives in the years to come! Now's our time to make that impact, and remember, our actions today can shape the spiritual landscape for generations to come!

"A Legacy of Hope!"

Today, parents and family leaders must realize this most urgent pressing matter, and it's this: As God's 'chosen ones', He began a good work in us, and it will continue throughout our lives until we see our Light and Hope of the world, Jesus Christ, "face to face" (Phil 1:6). When Christ died on the cross in our place, and we accept by faith that act of atonement—God's work in you and me has begun. We now possess the indwelling Holy Spirit, the same Spirit that had the power to raise Christ from the dead—is now in you and me.

And with its transformative power, this Spirit can enable you and me to be more Christlike in our everyday lives—when we submit to His empowering grace. This is a serious part of our sanctification stage because the evidence should be seen in our spiritual growth and maturity, *spreading and shaping other people's lives for years to come!* Remember, it is our God-given responsibility and calling right now to make that lasting impression in other people's lives—especially those close to us, which include all our young ones. And we don't do this for ourselves—but for God's glory!

Parents, can't we see as the torchbearers of faith that we must grasp the significance of leaving a lasting legacy of hope and godliness? This legacy, which future societies and our loved ones will speak of for generations, can revive, restore, and renew lives that is honoring to our Heavenly Father! As believers in Jesus Christ, let us desire and passionately strive to be remembered as the embodiment of God's goodness and greatness. Why? Because this godly path has the potential to sow seeds of hope in countless lives, including our future descendants, inspiring them to live a Christlike life.

As we consider our legacies, it's crucial to remember that money, possessions, and even a good family name are not the ultimate goals. These things, however significant, are temporary and will eventually fade away. What truly matters is the fruitful and righteous life we can leave behind, a legacy that can continue to nurture the spiritual well-being of others long after we're gone, which is more of the image of Jesus Christ our Lord.

The value and everlasting power of leaving a Christlike legacy is immeasurable—it is a testament to the life and teachings of Jesus Christ that we can pass on to the next generation. While attending church, serving in various ministries, reading God's word, and discussing the Lord are all significant milestones. However, the true essence lies in living out our authentic saving faith and love for the Lord, obedience to His word, and unwavering hope in what's to come. Our children and others must witness these precious and invaluable stones as evidence in our daily lives (Josh 4:6–7).

A secular article from Forbes magazine entitled "Leaving a Legacy No Matter How Much Money You Have" put it this way. "Our legacy is a combination of the way we live every day and the impact it has on our friends, our family, our community, and the world, as well as how we prepare others for life without us."

"Leaving a legacy is a way to let others appreciate our love and consideration for them in lasting ways. It will influence other lives because they will see that, as accountable people, we took the time to plan ahead for the impact that our absence would have on them."[17] Isn't this article spot on, even for Christians? Think about the power of this statement—"When we are no longer here, we should aim for the world and our loved ones to remember our acts of Christlikeness!"

You may never know about that one life-changing story until you get to Heaven, and that's this: "Your legacy of the footprints of Jesus Christ could be the only source of hope for someone not raised on the guiding principles of God's word. As noted earlier and a reminder on this most important matter, your memorable impression of godliness (while on earth) could be their only means of the Good News at a crucial point in that one person's life." It could be a family member, friend, neighbor, or even a stranger who was at a critical point in their life, *but they remembered your acts of Christlikeness (Heb 13:2)!*

Think about it—our living legacy could be a soul-saver for someone today, tomorrow, or the future—it could be a person's only Hope in life to cling to! This is a crucial responsibility for parents, the elder, and wiser generations to embed in their hearts and minds today, and it's this: We all can significantly impact our children's lives and the younger generation with godly guidance from this point forward—if we choose to honor and glorify God!

17. "Leaving A Legacy No Matter What."

"A Legacy of Hope!"

With that, parents cannot miss this valid point: "We must teach and train our children the importance of Christ from their beginning age of consciousness—because it's a milestone that will benefit the entire family lineage for years to come!" Why is this so important? It is evident by now that parents can have a major influence and lasting impact on their children in numerous ways. How?

When our hearts, minds, and spirits are built on the power of God's word, and we're in tune with His Spirit, our children and the younger generations will see that Christlike lifestyle in and through us, which can help develop their godly path in life. But the key is for the wiser generations to implement and incorporate the 'right spiritual tools' in their own lives, which will help our young ones build a more secure future grounded in the power of Hope, which is Jesus Christ!

To bring this point to reality, look at this momentous testimony below on the impact and influence previous eras had on a younger generation when they were raised on the power of God's word! At one point in this young lady's life, she had no hope because she did not see the value of her life in God's eyes. But that all changed! This story will show us that a prior generation of believers can affect people globally in powerful spiritual ways—through their descendants—when they teach them the importance of scripture. This life-altering stage can change an individual, family, home, and community worldwide.

"Hello, my name is Britnee Owens—formerly Britnee Wilson. I grew up in Tyler, TX, with an awesome mom and dad and lived near my wonderful grandparents. My grandparents on my dad's side raised my father in church, and he has been a faithful follower of Jesus for my entire life. My grandparents on my mom's side were generational chain breakers. They both decided to stop the unhealthy patterns of sin that the generations above them were trapped in and instead chose Jesus Christ and His Word as their guide in life. And this led them to raise my mother in church and in God's Word."

"My mom and dad had me in their young 20s and were deeply discipled in the Word shortly after having my brother and me. My parents took invaluable time to fill our hearts and minds with God's Word, both for me and my younger brother, from when we were babies all through our childhood and teenage years. I remember driving to school as a little girl each morning, and my mom would point out something to us on the way to school and teach us something about God and His nature. She would teach us songs that helped us memorize Scripture (which I can still sing today)."

"She would encourage us to read our Bibles each morning before school and ask what God taught us. My parents invested God's Word and

His love into me for my entire childhood, and it helped shape me into the woman of God that I am today. God's Word being taught and spoken over me kept me from many ways of the world. It kept me from listening to insecurities and lies about myself. The love that my parents gave me demonstrated God's love for me, and it gave me hope and helped me stay firm and steadfast in the faith—because I knew that I was loved and that my life had value in the eyes of my Heavenly Father."

"Even in conversations with my paternal grandparents today, they vividly recall learning the ways of Christ from their own parents and grandparents. If I were to talk to my great-great-grandparents, I'm certain the traces of Christ would have been blazed hundreds of years ago. They would tell us that their unwavering commitment to invest in their children's lives and beyond was to impact the world for God's glory. And the facts are this: "It has left an unerasable and unforgettable mark of Jesus Christ on generations."

"Because of my family's dedication to teaching me the ways of God in the Bible throughout my life, my own personal family and I have been able to take the Gospel of Christ to other continents worldwide. And now, we see people give their lives to Jesus Christ as their Lord and Savior—they now have a newfound hope! This generational chain of commitment and investment to ingrain the Words of God into my life is now paying dividends for God's Kingdom and changing lives worldwide."

This high-powered story shows a solid path of Christ's footprints that have bled over from one generation to another in one family! All because a generation of parents from years past made a loyal, faithful, and obedient commitment to the Lord to invest their godly heritage and inheritance into their descendants' lives, which was this: "They wanted to leave a legacy of hope that could help change society and culture in the years to come through their heirs—for God's glory!" This is an excellent portrait of genuine obedience, faith, love, and hope at work for the Lord, where lives can be restored and renewed. What a beautiful tale of God's Future Kingdom being built—through their future heirs! Is this your family story for today, tomorrow, and the years to come?

Here are some serious thoughts and heart-provoking questions for the wiser generation to ponder today: Do you know beyond a shadow of a doubt that once your story ends on this earth, you have left an unforgettable trace of Christlike hope for the good of your children and others that will carry over? Are we impacting our current society and culture in the same manner as seen in the story above? Are we preparing our loved ones for the future where their inheritance is secured? Are we passing down the Word of God to future generations as our Lord commands? As faithful parents, are we helping build God's Kingdom through our future descendants?

Undoubtedly, parents play a pivotal role in shaping the spiritual lives of the younger generations—if their life's direction aligns with God's will. Our Christlike attitudes and behaviors can be the binding tie of genuine hope with our children's spiritual lives—if Christ is at the center of our lives. However, it will come down to 'priorities and choices.' In other words, if family leaders do not establish a firm foundation of seeking the Lord first, our children will never gain sight of our Living Hope. It must be a repetition of seeking His guidance conveyed and portrayed daily.

The best way to teach our children today, which can be passed on for generations, is to leave a legacy that points them to the Living Hope, Jesus Christ (1 Pet 1:3). This is not just a duty but a privilege because, as we've seen so far throughout this journey, the younger generations need Hope more than ever! As stated earlier, God tells us that children are His gift to us, and we are to invest our godly heritage into their lives so they will have a 'legacy of Hope.' Doing so will help them endure and persevere in the tumultuous times ahead, where His Word and Spirit are perpetually at work for His glory.

Once again, here's a key point and reminder for today's older and more mature generation: "What are we doing 'now' to form our minds, hearts, and spirits in productive and fruitful ways for the good of our children and young ones (Rom 12:1–2)"? This is so critical. Why? As the shifting and dangerous cultural winds come our way—that is already off course to the ways of God—too many parents are oblivious to what is happening in their own homes. How? As we've seen in the awful statistics earlier, there's a lack of godly discipline in the American Family homes today. Because of this detriment, they have become spiritually numb to the unprotected and corrupt areas of their children's lives that are being overlooked—but need to be addressed now!

Parents need to stop disregarding what's happening in their homes today—*that prevents their children from growing in Christlike ways*. Instead of pointing their young ones to the ways of culture because they fit and accommodate their worldly comfort zone of convenience, they need to point them to Christ by living according to the right priorities and choices that align with God's word. It is time for the wiser ones to 'walk the talk' and set the example of Christ for our younger ones to model in the future! Isn't the all-embracing and profound story and testimony above an excellent example? Their focus was fixed on the teachings of God's ways into their children's lives at an early stage—versus not conforming to the ways of the world.

Again, Paul reminds us in Col 3:14–17, "Above all, clothe yourselves with love, which binds us all together in perfect harmony. And let the peace that comes from Christ rule in your hearts. For as members of one body, you are called to live in peace. And always be thankful. Let the message about Christ, in all its richness, fill your lives. Teach and counsel each other with all the wisdom he gives. Sing psalms and hymns and spiritual songs to God with thankful hearts. And whatever you do or say, do it as a representative of the Lord Jesus, giving thanks through him to God the Father."

Once again, King David reminds us in Psalm chapter 145 of a compelling goal for parents, and it's this: "Caring godly parents will leave a legacy of Christlikeness to their children and grandchildren that can be passed on for generations to come." To put this in a more robust perspective, think about this! If Christ is our daily benchmark (Eph 5:1), what kind of legacy did Jesus leave? Should our Lord's example be the role model we follow—for the benefit of our future heirs? Is His standard of exemplary worth imitating for the well-being of others? Following Christ's example not only benefits our future generations but also brings us joy and fulfillment.

You see, Jesus, God's only Son, faithfully passed on His teachings from His Father to others, leaving a permanent remembrance of the people whose lives He changed. In return, these recipients were faithful to His teachings so they could be taught to others and be carried on through future generations. It was an intentional and perpetual cycle that would carry on for God's glory.

Our new life in Christ should start with you and me by leaving a legacy that enables our young ones to cling to that Hope during their difficult stages on this side of Heaven—because, trust me, they will need it sooner or later! As parents and family leaders, we bear the responsibility of being the primary source of the Gospel for our younger generation in their lifetime. Once again, we may be their only source of the Living Hope—Jesus Christ. This must be ingrained in our hearts, minds, and souls daily for their spiritual well-being in the future!

The Apostle Paul tells us in Rom 5:3–6, "We can rejoice, too, when we run into problems and trials, for we know that they help us develop endurance. And endurance develops strength of character, and character strengthens our confident hope of salvation. This hope will not lead to disappointment. For we know how dearly God loves us because he has given us the Holy Spirit to fill our hearts with his love."

Paul even reminds us in 1 Tim 4:8–11, "Physical training is good, but training for godliness is much better, promising benefits in this life and in the life to come. This is a trustworthy saying, and everyone should accept it. This is why we work hard and continue to struggle, for our hope is in the living God, who is the Savior of all people and particularly of all believers. Teach these things and insist that everyone learn them."

"A Legacy of Hope!"

Finally, profoundly in Deut 11:18-19, "So commit yourselves wholeheartedly to these words of mine. Tie them to your hands and wear them on your forehead as reminders. Teach them to your children. Talk about them when you are at home, when you are on the road, when you are going to bed, and when you are getting up."

To substantiate the importance of the parent-child spiritual relationship, there were some key findings and results on what happens when most children come to know the Lord in a 2019 Children's Ministry Statistics article. You're going to see that this report is amazing! At the core of this research, it all starts early, with the parents at the forefront of impacting their children's lives. When this happens, and Christ is at the center of a structured family life, we have a better chance of spiritual survival through our children, which can be passed on from generation to generation.

The top two findings in their report show that 1) childhood is when most people find Jesus, and 2) parents have the most impact. To put their data into a more robust perspective, over 80% of children come to know Christ before the age of 20. So, does our biblical teaching matter at the early stages of our children's lives—and the younger generations' spiritual development for the future? An absolute and unequivocal—Yes! [18]

"The best learning I had came from teaching." Corrie Ten Boom.

"Teaching kids to count is fine, but teaching them what counts is best." Bob Talbert.

"Thinking that education is something different from discipling our children is a sure sign that we have been 'educated' by the state. Education is discipleship." RC Sproul Jr.

"An education without the Bible is no education." Clive James

When we take time to educate and train our children from the outset of their early stages, we're building blocks and steps in their lives that will ensure them a better chance of enduring the battles and temptations of life. In some translations, the word 'Train up' is used, commonly meaning Bible reading, attending church, and memorizing scriptures. Truth be known, God is saying, "Watch Me in My love, mercy, and grace—and model the ways of my Son, Jesus Christ, in daily life so that they influence and impact current and future generations."

The Apostle Paul reminds us of the importance of putting our salvation at work and in motion for the good of others and for God's glory. The key is when our genuine saving faith, love, and hope are active in us through the power of the Holy Spirit—it will signify these key points: 1) We're pursuing the obedience of God, 2) We're progressing through the

---

18. Kummer. "How Do Kids Come to Know Christ?"

process of sanctification, and 3) We're devoted to God's work to completion and fruition for the benefit of His Kingdom, and His glory! Note some of these powerful passages below as a beacon in our own lives that can surely enlighten others in our path:

Phil 2:12-13, "Dear friends, you always followed my instructions when I was with you. And now that I am away, it is even more important. Work hard to show the results of your salvation, obeying God with deep reverence and fear. For God is working in you, giving you the desire and the power to do what pleases him."

Gal 6:9-10, "So let's not get tired of doing what is good. At just the right time, we will reap a harvest of blessings if we don't give up. Therefore, whenever we have the opportunity, we should do good to everyone—especially to those in the family of faith."

Isa 54:13, "I will teach all your children, and they will enjoy great peace."

Prov 22:6 says, "Direct your children onto the right path, and when they are older, they will not leave it."

Deut 4:9-10, "But watch out! Be careful never to forget what you yourself have seen. Do not let these memories escape from your mind as long as you live! And be sure to pass them on to your children and grandchildren."

Parents, when our children and younger ones come to know the Lord at an early stage of their lives—this is what can occur: 1) They are more likely to stay true to their faith, 2) Serve the Lord wholeheartedly, 3) Possess a genuine love that leads them to obey God's word, 4) Have complete respect for who God the Father, Christ the Son and the Holy Spirit is, and 5) Be a devoted follower that is willing and committed to living and passing on their "real hope" to coming generations. Is there a spirit-minded Christian parent today who would not want this in their children's lives for the well-being of their future?

As we enter the book of Deuteronomy, we will see the greatest commandment from our Almighty God: "Love the Lord with all our hearts, souls, minds, and strength (Matt 22:34-36)." When God's children fulfill this command, they will come to believe and have hope in His greatest promise and it's this: "Do not be afraid or discouraged, for the Lord will personally go ahead of you. He will be with you; he will neither fail you nor abandon you."

Don't we realize that we have the greatest gift, eternal life, because of God's wondrous grace? And if we love the Lord with all our heart, soul, mind, and strength, we take rest, peace, comfort, and hope in that excellent promise today, tomorrow, and in the future, which is, "I will never leave you or forsake you." Parents, our children need to see the evidence of this greatest commandment, precious gift, and enduring hope of promise lived out in our daily lives for their state of survival! Why? Because it's their biblical and spiritual roadmap for the times ahead. Just think, as parents, we have the wonderful opportunity to help lead our current and future eras to that blessed day when we can all stand before our Lord—as one family—and hear those precious words from our Savior: "Well done, my good and faithful servant(s)."

Hope is: Helping–Others–Prepare for–Eternity!

The Book of Deuteronomy

'The Next Generation'

Let us now embark on a beautiful journey through the Book of Deuteronomy, the last book of the Pentateuch. This book is often quoted in the New Testament, foretelling the history of the nation of Israel and laying the foundation for the gospel message. It calls upon men and women to trust in God and to obey His Word, but most importantly, it points to our Living Hope, the salvation that Jesus Christ, Israel's Messiah, will bring.

Moses called upon the second generation of Israelites to enter into a covenant relationship with God, just as the first generation had done. The Book of Deuteronomy is a book of duty and obligation to many. However, faith, hope, and love are also included in this book. We have to remember today, just like the Israelites then, that obedience is prompted by our genuine love. And that love displays our faith and hope in the One Who can sustain, provide, and protect us today as He did thousands of years ago.

The power of this final book written by Moses could be easily outlined in the following bullet points, which is all life applicable to us today in teaching the power of God's goodness and greatness to our children, grandchildren, and beyond:

- Choose life in a Holy God by loving Him and all His ways.
- Move when God moves in our life for a purpose and plan that glorifies Him.
- God blesses us so we can bless Him through worship and praise. He's faithful to us, so we should also be loyal to Him by complying with the truths of His promises.
- Listen, Understand, and Obey the Laws of God.

- Remember God's provision and protection of "Faithfulness and Goodness" throughout life's journey.
- Purge the corruption of sinful acts and inject God's purity into our daily lives.
- The succession of a godly lineage for the future is embedded by the guidance of God's word and Spirit.

This marvelous book underscores the importance of knowing and applying God's word in our lives. As God's chosen ones, we must realize that the Christlike actions we initiate and implement in our lives can help teach and lead a generation of people for years to come. As we progress, we will truly see the importance of these life-changing applications that must be taught to our future descendants. And here's the reason why!

After leaving Egypt, the first generation of Israelites left us reminders of their selfish acts and unbelief that we don't want to be associated with or remembered as God's chosen ones. We witnessed their examples of disobedience, whining, complaining, discontent, and an absolute turn-your-face against God's way in their life's journey. The root of this defiance was due to their *'lack of'* faith in God's guidance, love for His commands, and hope in all His promises and provisions for a blessed and future land.

Unfortunately, their choice to rebel against God and all His teachings would be their demise. They would eventually die in the wilderness and never see the richness of God's promises. But here's a PowerPoint for us today: Only Joshua and Caleb from the first generation would advance into the Promised Land because of their obedience and faithfulness to Almighty God. They chose to obey God because they had faith in His word, love for His commands, and hope for what was to come in the future! They trusted in God's message—no matter what!

However, the Second Generation would be given the opportunity to respond in ways that could glorify God. Regardless, it would come down to their choice to either continue the ungodly ways of their predecessors or be future successors by incorporating the ways of God into their family's lives. I can only imagine what was going through the minds of some of these Second-Generation Israelites.

Knowing that their relatives from that first generation would not see the Promised Land—due to their defiance against God, *there was now hope for this new generation because of God's unbelievable faithfulness, graciousness, patience, lovingkindness, and mercy on them.* What's truly amazing about this storyline is this: "Our God is definitely a God of second chances, regardless of our ignorance." However, the key hinges on His people making the right choice, which will boil down to either blessings or curses, life or death, or prosperity or disaster.

So, it would be the Second Generation of Israelites—the younger ones who were prepared and qualified to lead and enter the Land God had promised their ancestors years before. But here's the critical point: "Can this new generation learn from their parents' bad mistakes?" Were they ready to obey the Lord? How ready were they to take up the responsibility given to them by Almighty God and move the nation of Israel forward? What lessons would they have to learn that would gain God's approval?

And here's the takeaway for you and me as family leaders: "What can we as parents of today learn from this storyline (the good and the bad) for the godly benefit of our younger ones' future success?" "Are we preparing our younger ones today for the difficult days and years ahead? "As we look at the contrast between these two generations of Israelites, one group was branded as "unfavorable and forgettable" and another as more "memorable." So, here's a key question for you and me: "Do we know which one of these categories we would fall into today as godly parents?"

That first generation of Israelites reacted more out of the flesh than responding to God in the manner He desired—they were more focused on their self-ambitions than the ways of God. This statement is crucial for us all today as family leaders: "How we respond to each life circumstance can label us for the current and future generations in powerful ways. Our words and deeds, great or small, have more effect on people than we realize—and the results could multiply throughout society for years to come—it comes down to making the right choice."

A great example is the first generation of Israelites, whose choice was the opposite of God's will. Their path in life was more about them and their selfish desires! This leads me to ask," Is leaving a memorable path of Christlikeness even a priority in our daily lives as parents for our future descendants?" The failings of that first generation of Israelites should be an eye-opener for the Christian parents of today. Why?

All Christian parents mustn't waste our God-given opportunity to influence our children and younger ones with the portrait of the Living Hope (Christ) for their well-being! This is vital because millions today are being misled in ways opposite to God's plan for their future state of spirituality, as noted so often in this book. And you and I, as the wiser generation, are implored by the Lord to help shape them in godly ways so they will have a better chance of survival and reach their promised land.

As discussed earlier, our choice of words and deeds can impact lives more than we can ever fathom or comprehend, for they could lead to blessings or curses. Today, you and I must grasp this and live by it: "Our genuine saving faith in how we convey or portray it in everyday life can impact the generations to follow." As devout Christians, we all have the choice to make a difference of godliness in people's lives today and in the future!

Many know that in the Book of Deuteronomy, we see the power of choice (as noted a few times earlier). The Israelites were commanded to choose between life or death, blessings or curses, and prosperity or disaster. This was not a command with a physical undertone but one of spiritual principles because obedience was at the root of their choice. Tragically, the first generation of Israelites failed to obey God wholeheartedly, while God, in all His goodness, was always faithful and true to His word. And no matter what, God would seek and find a generation of people willing to commit themselves to Him first and foremost so His long-term plan could be fulfilled!

Think about this: For that new generation—the phrase *life and prosperity* would indicate that by choosing to follow in obedience and faithfulness to the two covenants Moses had laid out in Deuteronomy chapter 5 through 30:14, Israel can expect to live a life of abundance. By following the covenant of God, Israel will have community health that could carry forward to future generations. However, would they choose a wholehearted commitment to the One Who would always provide, protect, and sustain them throughout their journey, or fail as the first generation did? Once again, if they fail, there will be consequences. [19] This same truth applies to you and me today!

The Israelites, who were in bondage for over 400 years, were delivered by Almighty God. They were allowed to move with God if they had absolute trust in His ways. However, as we all know, the first generation made many mistakes, leading to one failure and embarrassment after another. But in all of God's grace, mercy, and love, His promise would stand true to the very end. Yahweh promised that He would be beside them, behind them, and in front of them, and He would never forsake them. He would be their Sustainer, Protector, and Provider no matter what. He lived up to His word, but that first generation did not commit to Him wholeheartedly!

Amazingly, God had promised them victory, and the land He commanded them to go in and take was already theirs; all they had to do was trust and obey His word, but they could not even do this—with all the unbelievable promises He had in store for them. Because of that first generation's failure, God would use a generation of people more willing to fulfill His will and plan! We must embed this in our hearts and minds: "God will

---

19. "Deuteronomy 30:15-20 Meaning."

never lead us where His grace cannot provide for us, or His power cannot protect us."

Indeed, that first generation of Israelites had seen the mighty hand of God at work during their long, ill-fated journey in the wilderness. Yet, like many people today, they walked by sight, not faith, and their unbelief and disobedience displeased God. The Bible reminds us in Heb 11:6, "Without faith, it is impossible to please God." The first generation's failure to believe in Yahweh and the promise of His word kept them from entering the Promised Land—and this truth has never changed.

This invaluable last book of the Pentateuch has a powerful personal application for us today. How? God's word quotes passages at least forty times from Deuteronomy in the New Testament, only behind Psalm and Isaiah as the most. This book reveals much about the character of God. It conveys to us the importance of this message, "If we truly love God, we will obey His word." Deuteronomy tells us that God is the only God; He is Jealous, Gracious, Just, Faithful, Loving, and Merciful, yet He is angered by the sin in our lives. Why? Sin separates us from a Holy God Who has a life full of milk and honey in store for you and me!

Just like Israel, as God calls us closer to Himself, He requires us to comply with His will. He desires us to fear Him out of complete reverence, love and serve Him, faithfully obey His word, walk in all His ways, and pass on His Goodness to future generations! In Deuteronomy chapter 6, this passage provides guidance and instructions on the urgency of parents teaching and preparing their current and future descendants in the Torah (the law of God). Just look at the compelling passage below, our guide for parents today!

Yahweh tells us in Deut 6:1-9, "These are the commands, decrees, and regulations that the Lord your God commanded me to teach you. You must obey them in the land you are about to enter and occupy, and you and your children and grandchildren must fear the Lord your God as long as you live. If you obey all his decrees and commands, you will enjoy a long life. Listen closely, Israel, and be careful to obey. Then all will go well with you, and you will have many children in the land flowing with milk and honey, just as the Lord, the God of your ancestors, promised you."

"Listen, O Israel! The Lord is our God, the Lord alone. And you must love the Lord your God with all your heart, all your soul, and all your strength. And you must commit yourselves wholeheartedly to these commands that I am giving you today. Repeat them again and again to your children. Talk about them when you are at home, when you are on the road, when you are going to bed, and when you are getting up. Tie them to your hands and wear them on your forehead as reminders. Write them on the doorposts of your house and on your gates."

In this passage lies the central theme of this remarkable book, Deuteronomy. It sets precedence and illustrates the daily pattern we're to construct in our daily lives and as teachers to our future descendants—so they will understand the importance of passing them down to their children. *If we truly love God and all His ways, we will emphasize and iterate His words—constantly repeating His teachings and guidelines.* Always remember that when we live a repetitious life as God's faithful servants, continually displaying genuine love for the Lord and His word, it will solidify and magnify godly hope in spectacular ways to everyone we know!

God's words in this profound passage are clearly addressing the situation of generations beyond those who wandered in the wilderness under Moses. The viewpoint here is that all Israelites participated in the Exodus for generations to come and were a part of the Lord's mighty redemption. Amazingly, all generations of Jews constitute a portion of the Exodus generation. The life application for us today, as genuine believers, is that we all are partakers of God's message (His Holy Word), and the parallel teaching is for us to pass on the torch of this Good News to each generation.

When we do this, we don't just follow His guiding principles; we live by them. We walk in His ways of righteousness and holiness, and in doing so, we live by His laws and regulations. This manner of living leads to great flourishing throughout our homes, churches, and communities. Such a godly and righteous walk is not just a response to the laws of God; it's a manifestation of our absolute commitment and mutual engagement with His purpose and plan because of our faith in Jesus Christ—our new life and Hope!

God wanted His children (the nation of Israel) to *love, serve, obey Him,* and recognize that He alone is their *God. Doing so would establish a closeness with Yahweh, where* they would realize that God's blessings and promises were faithful, accurate, and genuine. However, they would have to understand some key points, and they were: "Substituting their worldly ways with the ways of God! And they had to stop listening to others who were contrary to the path of God—because it only leads to a path of destruction!" These same principles apply to you and me today and our future heirs because we must remember this: "God can raise up a generation for His glory, but it's up to you and me individually to ensure we're part of His plan so His fruitfulness will dwell and bleed over for years to come."

The Psalmist reminds us in Ps 102:18-28, "Let this be recorded for future generations so that a people not yet born will praise the Lord. Tell them the Lord looked down from his heavenly sanctuary. He looked down to earth from heaven to hear the groans of the prisoners, to release those condemned to die. And so, the Lord's fame will be celebrated in Zion, his praises in Jerusalem, when multitudes gather together, and kingdoms come to worship the Lord. He broke my strength in midlife, cutting short my days."

"But I cried to him, "O my God, who lives forever, don't take my life while I am so young! Long ago, you laid the foundation of the earth and made the heavens with your hands. They will perish, but you remain forever; they will wear out like old clothing. You will change them like a garment and discard them. But you are always the same; you will live forever. The children of your people will live in security. Their children's children will thrive in your presence."

This wonderful set of passages portrays a deliverance that shall not be lost or forgotten— but should be carefully recorded by God's people for *generations to come*. Why? For the instruction and encouragement of all succeeding generations. The great theologian Charles Spurgeon made these powerful comments about this passage in Psalm chapter 102: "Registers of divine kindness ought to be made and preserved: we write down in history the calamities of nations - wars, famines, pestilences, and earthquakes are recorded; how much rather then should we set up memorials of the Lord's lovingkindness!" "Nothing is more tenacious than man's memory when he suffers an injury; nothing more lax if a benefit is conferred. For this reason, God desires, lest his gifts should fall out of mind, to have them committed to writing."[20] Parents, think about this charge; it starts with us!

What a beautiful promise to pass on from one generation to another as converted believers in the Holy One! But as stated earlier, the choice hinges upon you and me as accountable Christian parents and the wiser generation(s) who care for the future of God's glory being manifested through each generation until His Son, Jesus Christ, returns! Remember, our genuine lives of hope will display Christlike love, obedience, and faith for every person on our path from the beginning of our lives to the end. And that type of undisputed life will impact others for years!

I hope and pray that all responsible Christian parents and leaders of today recognize this fact: "God's grace, mercy, and love should motivate and entice us to strive more for His glory—not just for ourselves, but for the benefit of our loved ones!" It truly is a matter of hope for survival! Even though Moses would not enter the Promised Land, he did not forgo his responsibility as the leader of God's children—he completed his task until the end of his life.

20. Enduring Word. "Afflicted, But Full of Trust."

I have some final questions—vital for parents and all family leaders today: 1) Are we developing and directing our young ones in the godly manner our Father desires? 2) Are we obediently adhering to all of God's truths in our daily lives—living by them so the younger generations will see that they have a fighting chance against the giants in this world through our active lives as Christians? 3) Are we repetitiously ingraining God's guiding principles in our future heirs' lives so they will remember God's goodness and blessings and set their focus on Christ alone?

If so, they will always know and believe in Who their Helper and Refuge is. Remember, you and I have been chosen for a purpose and plan, and God will hold us accountable! As we move forward in this powerful book, these stepping stones throughout each chapter of Deuteronomy will help us all understand how imperative it is for parents and the mature generation to develop our lives in Christlikeness for the well-being of our future descendants. Enjoy this journey that can lead to fruitful living—one generation—and one child at a time!

Deut 6:25, "For we will be counted as righteous when we obey all the commands the Lord our God has given us."

Chapter 1

'Godly Development'

Deut 1:1–8, "These are the words that Moses spoke to all the people of Israel while they were in the wilderness east of the Jordan River. They were camped in the Jordan Valley near Suph, between Paran on one side and Tophel, Laban, Hazeroth, and Di-zahab on the other. *Normally, it takes only eleven days to travel from Mount Sinai to Kadesh-barnea, going by way of Mount Seir. But forty years after the Israelites left Egypt, on the first day of the eleventh month, Moses addressed the people of Israel, telling them everything the* LORD *had commanded him to say.* This took place after he had defeated King Sihon of the Amorites, who ruled in Heshbon, and at Edrei had defeated King Og of Bashan, who ruled in Ashtaroth. While the Israelites were in the land of Moab east of the Jordan River, Moses carefully explained the LORD's instructions as follows."

"When we were at Mount Sinai, the LORD our God said to us, 'You have stayed at this mountain long enough. It is time to break camp and move on. Go to the hill country of the Amorites and to all the neighboring regions—the Jordan Valley, the hill country, the western foothills, the Negev, and the coastal plain. Go to the land of the Canaanites and to Lebanon, and all the way to the great Euphrates River. Look, I am giving all this land to you! Go in and occupy it, for it is the land the LORD swore to give to your ancestors Abraham, Isaac, and Jacob, and to all their descendants.'"

At this point of the journey, Israel was camped on the great plains of Moab, able to see across the Jordan River into the land God had promised to His nation. Undoubtedly, the Israelites had come through a long and challenging journey from Egypt—made all the more prolonged and difficult because of their unbelief and the death of the adult generation that first came out of Egypt. At this pivotal point in Israel's history—on the threshold of the

Promise Land and ready to adopt a true national identity, Moses spoke to Israel in this book of Deuteronomy.

As we begin this remarkable journey, we will discover that Deuteronomy is Moses' last words and final warning to Israel before his death. This marvelous book was a series of sermons preached by Moses to God's nation with a heavy and passionate heart. You see, Moses' heart was burdened because he knew that he would not enter the Promised Land of Canaan with Israel. His disobedience to God at Meribah (Numbers 20:1-13) meant he would not see Israel's exodus from Egypt through to completion.

Undoubtedly, Moses' heart was heavy because he knew that if this new generation of faithful servants did not obey the law and guidance of God (like the first generation failed to do), then God's covenant would work against them and curse them. So, the LORD passionately pled through an emotional and heartfelt Moses in Deuteronomy, pleading for Israel to *choose life* (Deut 30:19).[1] If they did not develop by God's guidelines, their future efforts would be futile!

A journey that should have only taken 11 days took approximately 40 years. The distance was not the issue; it was their hearts! In God's eyes, moving a mass of people across the wilderness was not the principle of the matter; it was going deeper, teaching His children the importance of obedience. This journey was painful in so many ways, but through it all, God only cared about one key component—their spiritual heart.

Deuteronomy is truly a book of notes for reminding—and also a book of preparation and development. We can never outgrow our need for remembrance, as Peter said in his second Epistle 1:12. Deuteronomy was a helpful book of reminder and preparation even for Jesus, our Lord, Savior, and Hope of the world. In His temptation in the wilderness, He quoted from it three times in answering Satan. If it was important to Jesus, it should be equally and just as vital to every responsible Christian today. Constantly meditating on key scriptures in our Christian Walk's weakest areas helps us develop a fruitful strategy against the enemy—led by the Holy Spirit.

Our Messiah is the daily example we should follow! In Matthew 4:4, Jesus quotes Deuteronomy 8:3 when He says, "We do not live by bread alone; rather, we live by every word that comes from the mouth of the LORD." Also, in Matthew 4:7, Jesus quotes Deuteronomy 6:16 when he responds to Satan's challenge to throw himself down from the temple. In Matthew 4:10, Jesus quotes Deuteronomy 6:13 when he rebukes Satan during his temptation in the wilderness. Even in Matthew 19:17-19, Jesus quotes Deuteronomy

---

1. Enduring Word. "Moses Remembers the Journey of Israel."

5:16–20 when he tells the rich young man to keep the commandments in order to enter eternal life.

Throughout each chapter of this book, we will discover that our life lessons are apparent when our hearts are "rightly focused" on the truths of God's word. He puts us through the wringer for a reason—and that's to get our attention and draw us closer to Him to address an area where we need refining and developing. The one key takeaway for you and me is this: Yahweh does not want us to be so focused on all our personal issues that we forget His goodness and all His ways. If we focus too much on ourselves, we will never possess godly development! Remember, just like the Israelites, God wants us to rely upon His wisdom, guidance, and obedience to His Word, for that is the only way we can develop more godliness in our daily lives. We will see if this second generation of Israelites can learn from this life lesson as we progress.

You see, just like the Israelites, our Heavenly Father has to constantly remind us because He wants us to remember the abundance of His mercy, grace, and lovingkindness. Just like that second generation of Israelites, He's spared us for a purpose and plan throughout our journey of life, regardless of the self-imposed issues that lead us away from His loving arms. He constantly reminded the Israelites of all He had done for them and was going to do, but still, so many failed to recognize His lovingkindness. Sound familiar?

God understands how everyday life and our internal turmoil can get in the way of our progress, so in His divine way, He can give us a better glimpse and understanding of an area that needs developing in our daily lives. Like the Israelites, we go through the purifying stages for a reason. God wants us to be holy, so he will purify those who choose to do His will. Once again, throughout this book, you will see a lot about choices! This is so important because when our choices align with His will, it awakens our spiritual life, which is so refreshing.

In the passage at the beginning of this lesson, Moses was not laying out an itinerary, but he was summarizing the nation of Israel's development. When God gave them His covenant at Mount Sinai, they would need knowledge and responsibility by His command to move with God and follow Him to the Promised Land. God iterated to them countless times how He wanted them to live their lives. They were His people, and He was their God, and He wanted them to represent Him by being set apart from the unrighteous ways of the other nations. This can only be done under the tutelage of a Sovereign God, through the power of His word and led by the Holy Spirit.

Since we are created in the image of God, we are the representatives of many of His characteristics throughout our life's journey. The Bible teaches us that God cares about our spiritual development because, in our growing stages, He desires to see more of His Son, Jesus Christ, in and through us. Paul powerfully reminds us in 1 Tim 4:8–10, "Physical training is good, but training for godliness is much better, promising benefits in this life and in the life to come. This is a trustworthy saying, and everyone should accept it. This is why we work hard and continue to struggle, for our hope is in the living God, who is the Savior of all people and particularly of all believers." This passage should be a daily objective for all followers of Jesus Christ who genuinely want to develop more godliness in their lives!

As we embrace and embody Christlikeness, we should strive for righteousness and holiness—like it's second nature. When we mature this way, we start to see the sanctifying work of the Holy Spirit in our daily lives, and we stop trying to self-realize our lives in our own eyes. When we continually develop under the daycare of the Holy Spirit and the word of God, we ensure that Jesus Christ is at the center of our faith. If not, we fail the test and are not developing in the way God desires (2 Cor 13:5). So, here's our benchmark: "When the world sees the ways of Christ developing in our daily lives inwardly and outwardly, we are on the road to God's purpose and plan"!

2 Tim 3:14–17, "But you must remain faithful to the things you have been taught. You know they are true, for you know you can trust those who taught you. You have been taught the holy Scriptures from childhood, and they have given you the wisdom to receive the salvation that comes by trusting in Christ Jesus. All Scripture is inspired by God and is useful to teach us what is true and to make us realize what is wrong in our lives. It corrects us when we are wrong and teaches us to do what is right. God uses it to prepare and equip his people to do every good work." This powerful passage is our bedrock for real-life biblical application for you, me, and future generations! It will ensure that we're on the path of developing more godliness in our daily lives!

Chapter 2

'Godly Direction'

Deut 2:2–3, 7, "Then at last the Lord said to me, 'You have been wandering around in this hill country long enough; turn to the north. For the Lord your God has blessed you in everything you have done. He has watched your every step through this great wilderness. During these forty years, the Lord your God has been with you, and you have lacked nothing."

The time had finally come for the Israelites to move after going around in circles for 38+ years. God now tells them clearly to move north because they had been wandering in this wilderness long enough. They had no clue which direction to go until God told them, for He was fed up with them wandering in a state of confusion with no clear direction in life because of their foolishness.

But amazingly, in verse 7, through all their disobedience, defiance, and rebelling against God, it should be a great encouragement to the next generation that if God provided for the rebellious Israelites in the desert, would He do any less for them as they were preparing to enter the land? What a merciful, gracious, and loving God! They knew their time had come, and God, no matter what, would be with them through it all! However, the key will lie in their obedience to go in the direction God leads them!

Today, many Christians are just going around in circles in their own "wilderness experience." We may struggle financially, materially, physically, emotionally, and sadly spiritually—and the burdens may press us to our knees. The flesh cries out for relief, but the believer is forced to wait on the Lord, find God's peace and joy during trouble, and mature in their walk with Christ through it all (James chapter 1).

Paul encourages those who "have this treasure in fragile jars of clay": "We are hard pressed on every side, but not crushed; perplexed, but not in despair; persecuted, but not abandoned; struck down, but not destroyed. We always carry around in our body the death of Jesus, so that the life of Jesus may also be revealed in our body" (2 Cor 4:7–10). The reason for these trials, Paul says, is "to show that this all-surpassing power is from God and not from us" (verse 7).

As discussed in my past books, the wilderness is an unpleasant place, fleshly speaking. We naturally want prosperity, health, and an easy-going life. But the same God who created the beautiful garden also created the wilderness. There will be times of trial and pressure, and our faith will be tested. You may be in the wilderness and wonder if God sees and knows your situation.

Always remember that our Omnipotent, Omnipresent, and Omniscient God sees and knows our every situation. The God of grace will meet us anywhere on our road in life, and at just the right time, when we come to Him with the right heart, He will set us back on our feet and lead us in the right direction.

If we're in a bad spot in life, we will only know the right direction by listening to God's voice, where He can lead us down His path of righteousness and away from the desert. But we will not discover that road if we're not reading and applying His word to our lives and submitting to the guidance of the Holy Spirit.

Remember what Paul tells us in 2 Cor 5:7 and Rom 10:17, "We walk by faith, not by sight," and "Faith comes by hearing the word of God." Always remember this: "Hearing the word of God is when we receive it, accept it, apply it, and obey it." The gut punch is in Heb 11:6–7, We cannot please God without Faith. "When we accept His truths, believe in them wholeheartedly, and trust His will and plan as His godly ones, we can rest assured that we're on His path—because He directs the path of the godly and righteous (Ps 37:4, Prov 16:9).

In today's fast-paced society and culture, we often get behind the steering wheels of life and have no clue where we are going. And when we seem lost, especially for most men, we try to figure out the directions ourselves. However, in almost all cases, we go around in circles, which can lead us to a farther distance from our original destination. Spiritually, we spend ineffective time searching for our destination and purpose in life when we don't involve God in our plans. Remember, God wants us to seek Him first so He can assist and lead us productively.

In Matthew 6:33, Jesus reminds us, "Seek the Kingdom of God above all else and live righteously, and he will give you everything you need." The bottom line is this: "We are to seek the things of God as a priority over the

'GODLY DIRECTION'

things of the world." In doing so, He will supply our needs that align with His plan and the right path in life.

God offers His believers a free GPS, "God's Protective Services." All He requires from you and me is to stay close to Him through His word, submit to His Spirit, be a diligent listener, humble doer, faithful servant, display His Fruit of the Spirit (Gal 5:22–23), and possess a disciplined prayer life. When we incorporate these components into our daily lives, we can feel His presence, as if He's taking the journey with us in the front seat. We can hear His voice through His word and Spirit and know the directions of life we must take. The more we follow our Lord daily, the more of His love, peace, patience, joy, faith, and grace we will experience.

But when we allow society and culture to overwhelm us in the driver's seat, the obscurities of life can blind us and lead us down the wrong path. We must stop letting all the interferences and interruptions of life guide us to a detour opposite God's GPS. Instead, stay on His directive course daily and do not waver. Don't allow any variations (imbalances) in this life's course to lead you astray from God's path. We need to position our spiritual senses to His pathway!

Prov 20:24 says, "The LORD directs our steps, so why try to understand everything along the way?"

Ps 32:8–9, "The LORD says, "I will guide you along the best pathway for your life. I will advise you and watch over you. Do not be like a senseless horse or mule that needs a bit and bridle to keep it under control."

Chapter 3

'Facing Giants'

Deut 3:1–3," Next, we turned and headed for the land of Bashan, where King Og and his entire army attacked us at Edrei. But the LORD told me, 'Do not be afraid of him, for I have given you victory over Og and his entire army, and I will give you all his land. Treat him just as you treated King Sihon of the Amorites, who ruled in Heshbon.' "So, the LORD our God handed King Og and all his people over to us, and we killed them all. Not a single person survived."

Og was a huge giant who could strike much fear in the Israelites. Plus, they had to know that king Og was the ruler of over 60 fortified cities. I am sure this intimidated God's children and set unbelievable fear in their hearts and minds. The Israelites had a big problem going up against the mighty army of Og, king of Bashan. God's children did not stand a physical chance, but they had one massive asset in their corner—Almighty God!

There was a huge problem the Israelites had to face, and that was not only a well-trained army but also the enormous king, Og. This king was a Rephaim, who was a group of people who were large and great warriors. It is said that king Og's bed was almost fourteen feet long and six feet wide, so he was undoubtedly a large man who tried to set fear in the Israelites. But here's the point: Even though Og's army attacked God's children, in all of God's sovereignty and faithfulness, He handed over Og and his army to the Israelites.

Despite king Og's incredible size and strength, God gave Israel's army the victory, and they would possess the land of Bashan. Once again, God prevailed and was faithful to His promises. What a beautiful illustration that there is no obstacle or barrier too large for God; there is nothing impossible for Him (Matt 19:26). God does not quake before giants, and neither should

His children. All things are possible through the One Who gives us strength (Phil 4:13).

As children of God and followers of Christ, we will all encounter spiritual giants in our lives. When Israel was moving forward in God's direction, the physical giants appeared to scare them away, and they did. But as we read in Numbers chapter 14, the fear of mere mortal man and, most importantly, disobedience against God's faithfulness and promises would lead to their ultimate punishment. God wanted His children to have absolute faith in all His provisions and securities in life because that is all that matters in His eyes.

Many believers feel that the power of God in a person's life should keep them from all trials and conflicts. But for us to build up our Christ-like character, we must take on the giants in life so God can give us more strength, reveal more of His Son, and, in the end, honor and bring glory to His name. Think about this: "If we do not endure troubles in our life's journey, we will never learn the power of perseverance, which helps build our patience, commitment, determination, purpose, diligence, tenacity, and real-life biblical application. It is needed for our sanctification process, which should lead to progression!"

Paul reminds us in Romans 5:1–5, "Therefore since we have been made right in God's sight by faith, we have peace with God because of what Jesus Christ our Lord has done for us. Because of our faith, Christ has brought us into this place of undeserved privilege where we now stand, and we confidently and joyfully look forward to sharing God's glory. We can rejoice, too, when we run into problems and trials, for we know that they help us develop endurance. And endurance develops strength of character, and character strengthens our confident hope of salvation. This hope will not lead to disappointment. For we know how dearly God loves us because he has given us the Holy Spirit to fill our hearts with his love."

Perseverance through genuine saving faith is a vital aspect of Christianity because it is the evidence that our faith is from an Almighty God, not man. Persevering faith is not effortless or automatic but requires human responsibility. Christians must maintain their intimate relationship with Jesus Christ through the perseverance of faith because it is vital to our growth in Him. Christians must trust in God and keep their vision on Him when faced with giant hardships in this life.

No matter the size of our problems, we're in good hands with God on our side. When God's people trust Him, God demonstrates His Almighty power and glory by giving us those little victories, often the ones we take for granted. If we need to tap into the power and promises of God, we need to trust Him, and we show our trust by obeying Him, and our love for Him is reflected in our obedience. Obedience to God proves our love for Him (1 John 5:2–3) and demonstrates our faithfulness to Him (1 John 2:3–6).

As noted earlier, faith is necessary to please God (Heb 11:6), and if our faith is genuine, we will live a lifestyle characterized by righteousness, modeling Jesus Christ. We obey His commands, not because we must, but because we love Him so much that we believe in Him, regardless. We are enabled to obey because, once we believe in Christ and are saved, we are now a new creation remade, and His Spirit indwells in us. We are not the same people we once were. As Paul wrote in 2 Cor 5:17, "If anyone is in Christ, he is a new creation; the old has gone, the new has come!" Most importantly, when we obey our Father, Christ is seen through us, and He's glorified! And that is the home run!

We so often fail against the more significant barriers in life because we lack the wisdom and knowledge of what God's word tells us. Second Peter's first chapter reminds us of this: for us to grow in God's knowledge, we must pay attention to the scriptures and apply them to our lives so our faith will increase. That will lead to a life of moral excellence, which leads to us knowing God better. Knowing God leads to self-control, which leads to patient endurance, and this type of endurance leads to godliness. This leads to having a genuine love for others, which enables us to be more productive and useful in the knowledge of our Lord Jesus Christ.

If we tolerate spiritual giants in our lives, they will consume us and take over our lives. They will cross our godly boundaries in every way possible and threaten us with absolute fear, anxiety, and worry. But we keep forgetting that we have the support of God and His powerful Spirit in us. Therefore, we should confront our giants in this life with force because God did not give us a spirit of fear but one of power, love, and self-control (2 Tim 1:7).

We all know the extraordinary story of David and Goliath. As Goliath tried to set fear in the Israelites and move closer to them, David, who had more fear of God than man, came forth with the power of God! David didn't just hold and protect his ground; he ran in the enemy's direction. And he didn't just attack his giant; he finished him off. If we don't kill our spiritual giants in life, our giants will kill us. So, we need to eliminate those spiritual giants in our lives so we can move forward with God productively. Why? Because spiritual giants will hinder our Christlike growth.[1]

Examples of spiritual giants that can be debilitating and stunt our growth in Christ are 1) A negative mindset and heart, 2) worldly distractions, 3) evil desires (Gal 5:19–21), 4) unholy relationships, 5) being too

---

1. Laurie. Greg. "How to Conquer a Giant in Your Life."

cynical and judgmental, 6) unforgiveness, 7) a weak prayer life, 8) a lack of reading and applying God's word to our lives, 9) stifling the Holy Spirit when He convicts and counsels us in an area that needs to be addressed, 10) pride (all about self), 11) a worrisome, anxious and impatient spirit, and 12) not resting in the promises of God's word where we can find and experience peace, joy, comfort and daily guidance.

If we address the 12 weak areas above that are preventing us from victory, we will have a better chance of overcoming the barriers in life. Remember, our victory is already established in Christ, and when we surrender and submit to His empowering guidance, what an experience it will be when we can enjoy those wins in our lives!

We all must realize that the Apostle James tells us we will face hardships in life, and when they come, we're to consider them as opportunities for joy and growth. Sometimes, these giants seem like insurmountable obstacles that can bring absolute defeat to our personal lives. We all will deal with temptation and the tests of time in this journey that we call life. But every giant in our path is conquerable if we face them in faith and realize that God is bigger than any problem that will come our way.

Always remember the great promise from God's word about temptations that may hinder our walk with the Lord, found in 1 Corinthians 10:13: "The temptations in your life are no different from what others experience. And God is faithful. He will not allow the temptation to be more than you can stand. When you are tempted, he will show you a way out so that you can endure."

Phil 4:6–7, "Don't worry about anything; instead, pray about everything. Tell God what you need and thank him for all he has done. Then, you will experience God's peace, which exceeds anything we can understand. His peace will guard your hearts and minds as you live in Christ Jesus."

Josh 1:9, "This is my command—be strong and courageous! Do not be afraid or discouraged. For the LORD, your God, is with you wherever you go."

And here's a beautiful and powerful scripture to memorize daily: 2 Corinthians 6:10, when you feel that those giants in life are more than you can bear. "Our hearts ache, but we always have joy. We are poor, but we give spiritual riches to others. We own nothing, and yet we have everything."

Chapter 4

'Godly Obedience'

Deut 4:1-6," And now, Israel, listen carefully to these decrees and regulations that I am about to teach you. Obey them so that you may live, so you may enter and occupy the land that the Lord, the God of your ancestors, is giving you. Do not add to or subtract from these commands I am giving you. Just obey the commands of the Lord your God that I am giving you. "You saw for yourself what the Lord did to you at Baal-Peor. There, the Lord your God destroyed everyone who had worshiped Baal, the god of Peor. But all of you who were faithful to the Lord your God are still alive today—every one of you. "Look, I now teach you these decrees and regulations just as the Lord my God commanded me so that you may obey them in the land you are about to enter and occupy. Obey them completely, and you will display your wisdom and intelligence among the surrounding nations. When they hear all these decrees, they will exclaim, 'How wise and prudent are the people of this great nation!'

What a powerful passage on the importance of obeying God's word "completely and wholly." This passage clearly tells us that any human in their finite mind cannot take or add anything to God's word, for His word is faithful, complete, and good! These instructions, decrees, and guidelines from God are perfect in all their fullness, and to take anything away would make them incomplete. God's word is not designed as a defective blueprint or roadmap—but one full of guidance, which provides all the details that benefit our everyday lives. Today, we need it more than ever as we take on our own spiritual warfare(s) in life.

The Israelites are about to embark on some massive battlegrounds, and they will need God to help them through these confrontations to enter the Promised Land. However, their prerequisite is complete obedience to

'Godly Obedience'

God, which they've often struggled with. Without their obedience, they would lose God's support. So, Moses reminded Israel of their past rebellions against God in the wilderness. As they were ready to enter the Promised Land, he wanted them to think about their need for complete obedience in light of their many past rebellions.

One of Satan's great strategies is to make us remember what we should forget—and forget what we should remember. He is a master of us not believing we need to repent and come clean with God. If we don't come clean with our past sins and continue to rebel against God, we can easily repeat them, falling into the same sinful patterns and traps that the enemy wants. Paul reminds us in 1 Cor 10:12, "If you think you are standing strong, be careful not to fall."

After all, we are creatures of habit! It's like we're living in a wandering cycle of one sin after another. The only way to eliminate that cycle is to obey God's guidelines wholeheartedly and allow Him to purify us. The Israelites' physical life and death relied upon their obedience to God. And for us today, in the larger sense, spiritual life and death depend on our complete obedience to God's word.[1]

You see, our Almighty God's decrees (His holy word, the Bible) are His truths then, now, and forever! Never forget this living and biblical fact that still exists today: "Any law or regulation from God has a purpose that is designed to guide us in living a lifestyle that aligns with His will and plan. And if we adhere to them, they will illustrate our complete devotion to God alone!" Remember, Yahweh is the same yesterday, tomorrow, and in the future, and so are His words. We identify with our Almighty One (through His Son) when we follow His guiding principles in life, and we don't deviate from them one bit. Always remember, if we drift from God's living word, we will find ourselves conforming more to the ways of the world and man! And that opens the door to more disobedience!

And here's the golden key to the passage at the outset of this lesson above: God tells us that if we obey His word "completely," we will display more of His wisdom and intelligence in today's unbelieving world! And when they see us as believers in Christ who follow God's word like His children should, the dark world will see something special in how we conduct ourselves! And more than ever, we need His divine wisdom and intelligence! If you need God's wisdom, ask for it, as James tells us in the first chapter of his epistle. But when we ask, it must be genuine and serious with real intent that we will be loyal to our Lord alone!

---

1. Enduring Word. "A Call to Obedience."

Many New Testament apostles remind us how to conduct ourselves in this world as devout Christ-followers. Their God-inspired words of application are crucial in our lives because the unbelievers will see one of two things: *"More of the world—*or *More of Christ in our daily actions!"* Once again, what we choose in our life's path is up to us individually—because we're either going to desire more of the world—or more of God!

Paul, John, and Peter remind us of some significant passages we can apply in our everyday lives: In Eph 5:1-2, "Imitate God, therefore, in everything you do, because you are his dear children. Live a life filled with love, following the example of Christ. He loved us and offered himself as a sacrifice for us, a pleasing aroma to God." 1 Tim 4:12: "Let no one despise you for your youth, but set the believers an example in speech, in conduct, in love, in faith, in purity." Tit 2:6-7 "Likewise, urge the younger men to be self-controlled. Show yourself in all respects to be a model of good works, and in your teaching, show integrity and dignity." John 13:15, "For I have given you an example, that you also should do just as I have done to you." 1 Pet 2:12: "Keep your conduct among the Gentiles honorable, so that when they speak against you as evildoers, they may see your good deeds and glorify God on the day of visitation." Phil 3:17: "Brothers, join in imitating me, and keep your eyes on those who walk according to the example you have in us."

The Christian life is lived by faith and obedience to the One True God who saved, empowered, sealed, and kept us by His power—we are held forever! The daily life of faith grows and strengthens as we seek God in His Word and continually build up the body of Christ! When we comply with His word and are in step with the Spirit, we're illustrating a walk by spiritual faith, not physical sight, glorifying God in all things! The sign of a completely obedient Christian is demonstrated by their willingness to submit themselves humbly and lovingly to their Lord Jesus Christ. He rules in and through them, which is evident in their pattern of life, embodying righteousness and holiness.

Why do we do this? We obey the Word because we love the Word (Jesus Christ). The Psalmist reminds us in Ps 119:167, "I obey your statutes, for I love them greatly." And we love the Word because we love God, and it's shown in and through us when the world sees Christ in our words and actions! Jesus also reminds us in John 14:15, "If you love me, obey My commandments." Our genuine love for the Lord should drive us to obey Him in everything we say and do that aligns with His holy scriptures.

1 Pet 1:13-16, "So prepare your minds for action and exercise self-control. Put all your hope in the gracious salvation that will come to you when Jesus Christ is revealed to the world. So, you must live as God's obedient children. Don't slip back into your old ways of living to satisfy your

own desires. You didn't know any better then. But now you must be holy in everything you do, just as God who chose you is holy. The Scriptures say, "You must be holy because I am holy."

1 John 5:3-5, "Loving God means keeping his commandments, and his commandments are not burdensome. For every child of God defeats this evil world, and we achieve this victory through our faith. And who can win this battle against the world? Only those who believe that Jesus is the Son of God."

Chapter 5

'Godly Listener'

Deut 5:1-4," Moses called all the people of Israel together and said, "Listen carefully, Israel. Hear the decrees and regulations I am giving you today so you may learn them and obey them! "The Lord our God made a covenant with us at Mount Sinai. The Lord did not make this covenant with our ancestors but with all of us who are alive today. At the mountain, the Lord spoke to you face to face from the heart of the fire."

This passage in chapter 5 is vital because it deepens the importance of complying with God's laws. In verses six through twenty-one, "He repeats" the ten commandments from Exodus chapter 20 to this generation of people. Why is this so crucial? God's children needed to understand the urgency of paying attention to His regulations and obeying them faithfully.

God uses repetition to draw our attention to His word and remind us that He is consistent in all His instructions. When God repeats His decrees to us, He emphasizes the importance of His message so we will listen, take heed, and see the reliability in His words of truth.

We are creatures of habit and so often allow the ways of the world to cloud our view of God's word. So, God repeats His words to us because, just like the Israelites, it takes us a long time to catch on. His Word is habit-forming, and over time, they can develop patterns of Christlike behavior in our lives, one that God desires in you and me.

God's children had entered into a covenant with Yahweh! So, Moses commanded them to not only listen and hear but also learn and follow them. It was necessary now for the present generation to hear these terms as their fathers had done. Israel was bound to the covenant they agreed to in Ex 24:1-8, yet the covenant was made with the previous generation, which perished in the wilderness. It was vitally important that the present generation understand and embrace the covenant if they were to enjoy its blessings—" because it is one of the living, not of the dead." Think about the spiritual application of this.

This principle pertains to us as believers up to this present day. Every generation must learn the truth of God for themselves because we all have our own personal convictions. It is not sufficient to "know" truth merely as something believed and practiced by a past generation. It is not just following traditions and rituals but knowing that you're following His truths and living them out (individually) for a reason! A great example of this application is when Jacob had his experience with God himself. He could not live out the blessings of God by relying on the experiences of Isaac and Abraham, but he had to deal with God one-on-one.

When Jacob experienced God, he wrestled with Him until daybreak. This struggle symbolizes Jacob's internal battle with self. God wanted to enter into a bonding relationship with Jacob, but He couldn't do so until Jacob admitted his weakness of self-reliance, deceit, and trickery. Ultimately, through this personal encounter with the Lord, the lineage of the savior of the world would come in the line of Jacob's son, Judah.

Listening to God's word is when we "personally" absorb and accept His plan for our lives willingly and wholeheartedly. And when we observe, learn, and interpret the scripture to 'understand' its "accurate text better," we can know how it applies to our lives today. When the power of His word goes to work, through the power of the Holy Spirit, we are enabled to obey them and put them into action (Heb 4:12–13, 2 Tim 3:16–17). And when we do this, we open the door to God's blessings in our personal lives—in His timing!

What is a genuine godly listener? They are spiritually grounded in the Truths of the Bible and always listen to God's voice—because that is their primary interest in life. They seek the abundance in all that God's word can provide and produce (Col 3:16) with a desire to learn more from God than the ways of man. They intently and intensely yearn for more of the Lord's divine teachings—versus the ways of the secular world.

They live by the words of the Apostle John, "God's words are not burdensome because loving God means to obey His Word, and His Word is not hard to follow." They acknowledge this key point: "Keeping God›s law is not too difficult or beyond our ability because He supplies us with the strength we need to comply with it (2 Peter chapter 1). This is accomplished when our hearts, minds, and spirit are in sync with the faithfulness of His word."

A godly listener longs to adapt to the lessons of God so they can be adept (competent) in His loving ways. They home in (focus) on His wisdom and knowledge so they can discern the ways of God—and those that are not. Their key attributes are seeking the truth of His word and how it applies to their life. They don't make decisions or plans without taking them to God first—and they do not react rashly but respond patiently with prudence (Prov 16:3).

Their lives are built so solidly on the truth of God's word that they don't shift with the winds of culture and society—but pursue ways of improvement in their daily Christian Walk. They know how to remove the distractions of the world (Rom 12:1–2)—sift out those areas of falsehood and deceptions (test the spirits 1 John 4:1)—examine their genuine faith in the Lord (2 Cor 13:5)—and discard those weak interactions of life that can disable their listening skills (Isa 40:31).

They realize that they are not perfect but continually strive to be more in tune with the holiness of God—versus out of sync and disconnected with God—especially when the unholiest ways of the world try to take over their lives. Their motive to be godly listeners is driven by their love for God and His word, putting it into practice and exemplifying each element of the Fruit of the Spirit, which builds up their overall relationship with their Lord, Jesus Christ.

We cannot be practical doers of the word without genuinely listening to God's accurate message. In the first chapter of his Epistle, James reminds us to be doers of the word, not just listeners. So, if our hearts are in tune with the actual message from God, we will not only be in harmony with it, but we will obey it and do exactly what it says. The evidence of that action will be measured by the effectiveness of our time in His word and listening to His will for our lives. The results will be this: "The unbelieving world will see the fruits of our labor and know that our ears lean more toward an Almighty God—than the ways of the world."

Prov 2:1–5, "My child, listen to what I say and treasure my commands. Tune your ears to wisdom and concentrate on understanding. Cry out for insight and ask for understanding. Search for them as you would for silver; seek them like hidden treasures. Then you will understand what it means to fear the Lord, and you will gain knowledge of God."

Matt 7:24–26 says, "Anyone who listens to my teaching and follows it is wise, like a person who builds a house on solid rock. Though the rain comes in torrents and, the floodwaters rise, and the winds beat against that house, it won't collapse because it is built on bedrock. But anyone who hears my teaching and doesn't obey it is foolish, like a person who builds a house on sand."

Chapter 6

'Godly Hearts'

Deut 6:4–9 "Listen, O Israel! The Lord is our God, the Lord alone. And you must love the Lord your God with all your heart, all your soul, and all your strength. And you must commit yourselves wholeheartedly to these commands that I am giving you today. Repeat them again and again to your children. Talk about them when you are at home and when you are on the road, going to bed, and getting up. Tie them to your hands and wear them on your forehead as reminders. Write them on the doorposts of your house and your gates."

This passage is central to Deuteronomy because it sets the pattern that helps us relate God's Word to our daily lives. Loving God means that our mind, heart, soul, and all we have within us honor Him and reflect that He is truly Lord over our lives! These commands were expounded to teach God's children how to implement them when the nation entered the Promised Land.

The power of this passage in Deuteronomy starts with a resounding exclamation: Listen, O Israel! He instructed them to listen closely to everything He said and be careful to obey—because then and only then will all go well. Not only is He reminding them of Who God is and what He's done and will do, but He is also to be the Lord of their lives; nothing else is to come before Him.

The Hebrews were knowledgeable in making religion a part of their life because religious education was life-oriented, not based on information. They used their life experiences and the circumstances of their daily lives to teach about God. Today, the key to teaching children is in the best guide we possess, and that's God's word. If we want our children to follow the Bible, God must be a part of our life experiences so that they can see how faithful we are to Him through all life's circumstances. Seeing God in every aspect of daily life requires wholehearted commitment, discipline, and diligence.

There was always the danger that the Israelites' conquest would lead them to believe they could enjoy the good things of God *without submission to His word and ways of holy living*. Does that sound familiar to us today? When we are in our comfort zone, do we get so complacent and content with the earthly things in life that, over time, we take our eyes off the goodness and grace of God?

Our rule of thumb for today is found in Rom 6:1–7, "Well then, should we keep on sinning so that God can show us more and more of his wonderful grace? Of course not! Since we have died to sin, how can we continue to live in it? Or have you forgotten that when we were joined with Christ Jesus in baptism, we joined him in his death? For we died and were buried with Christ by baptism. And just as Christ was raised from the dead by the glorious power of the Father, now we also may live new lives. Since we have been united with him in his death, we will also be raised to life as he was. We know that our old sinful selves were crucified with Christ so that sin might lose its power in our lives. We are no longer slaves to sin. For when we died with Christ, we were set free from the power of sin."

The importance of His holy scripture should be on display in our daily lives—with the guidance of the Holy Spirit. Why? Because He points out our flaws and errors, and His purpose is to lead us to all Truths. It's the only guide that can complete us spiritually because His words are absolute, authoritative, influential, sufficient, and will supply all our needs; it will accomplish all that it has provided and promised (Isaiah 55:11). Of course, none of this means that our lives will be perfect and smooth sailing, but it does mean that we can lean on Him for all things and know He is faithful to the end!

We can only think, meditate, and relate to God's teachings when He has our undivided attention and whole hearts. If we are half-hearted in our approach to the holiness of His word, we can and will get easily distracted by the things of this world and lose complete focus on His guidance. But, on the other hand, if we constantly think about the depths of His message, we must possess a whole heart dedicated to Him 100%! That is why God requires us to think about His word in the mornings when we wake up, throughout the day, talk about it with everyone, write it on the outer and inner walls of our home, discuss it around the tables, and end our nights on the breadth of His decrees.

While going to church, fellowship with believers, and sending our children to Christian schools are building blocks, it is the solid foundation of the Bible that cements all of God's lessons and practical teaching into

'Godly Hearts'

our daily lives; they are the effective learning skills we need to sustain and survive in a world of self. And that life application can only be attained if we delve our whole heart into His pool of refreshing and reenergizing truths.

Ps 1:1–3, *"Oh, the joys of those who do not follow the advice of the wicked, or stand around with sinners, or join in with mockers. But they delight in the law of the* LORD, *meditating on it day and night. They are like trees planted along the riverbank, bearing fruit each season. Their leaves never wither, and they prosper in all they do."*

A whole heart is best described as righteous (not perfect) but pure and striving for God's holiness. It has been broken, molded, refined, and purified to the state of an undeniable yearning for more of the Lord daily. It is faithful through the tests of time, overrun with obedience, love, humility, and repentance—fashioned in a way that displays godliness in their daily activities. Their life of integrity and accountability are enveloped inwardly and outwardly due to their development stages of God.

God's word reminds us in Jer 24:7, "I will give them hearts that recognize me as the Lord. They will be my people, and I will be their God, for they will return to me wholeheartedly." This type of heart represents one that has returned to their Lord, and they allow Him to govern them in all areas of their lives. They are acknowledged for a heart that is spiritually good and fruitful.

Their Christian conversion and commitment to the Lord are authentic because their changed heart points to the sufficiency of God's grace. They possess an inner strength inclined to the voice of His word and Spirit—and not to the ways of the world. They are now prone to more acts of holiness vs. unholiness. It's not accidental; it's intentional and becomes second nature in their daily lives!

Matt 22:37–40, "Jesus replied, '"You must love the LORD your God with all your heart, all your soul, and all your mind.' This is the first and greatest commandment. A second is equally important: 'Love your neighbor as yourself.' The entire law and all the demands of the prophets are based on these two commandments."

Psalm 119:2 says, "Joyful are those who obey his laws and search for him with all their hearts."

Chapter 7

'God's Chosen'

Deut 7:7-9, "The Lord did not set his heart on you and choose you because you were more numerous than other nations, for you were the smallest of all nations! Rather, it was simply that the Lord loves you, and he was keeping the oath he had sworn to your ancestors. That is why the Lord rescued you with such a strong hand from your slavery and from the oppressive hand of Pharaoh, king of Egypt. Understand, therefore, that the Lord your God is indeed God. He is the faithful God who keeps his covenant for a thousand generations and lavishes his unfailing love on those who love him and obey his commands."

God's children of Israel were set apart by His choosing and were called to live as His holy people. The Israelites were to be distinct from the pagan world and unto God for His particular use and to bring Him glory and honor. They were to be exclusively the LORD's and wholly separated from the unholy practices of idolatry.

Israel was holy in their position, and thus, they would be blessed in their conduct because they were to behave differently than the godless nations. However, Israel was difficult to love because of her stubbornness and continuous rebelling acts. Still, God's empowering love, grace, and mercy are displayed even more because of their rebellion and defiance! Even in their sinfulness, this enables God to showcase His great glory!

The LORD did not set His love on or choose the nation of Israel because they were more numerous. The elect meant the LORD set His love on them as His special ones. God chose them because He was keeping His promise to their ancestors—after all, God is always faithful and true to His words to the very end. The key is that the Israelites' motivation for such total obedience should be steadfast in this: "They knew God loved them." That same motivation should apply to us as Christians today. If we know beyond a shadow of a doubt that God loves us and we're His chosen one—our loyalty of obedience to His word and all His ways should be seen in our actions.[1]

Chosen means someone who is God's favorite and preferred by Him as the best or most appropriate. From another biblical perspective, it is those whom a sovereign God has handpicked to perform His holiness in a world opposite God's purpose and plan. He has selected you and me to fulfill His will—where we use our God-given gifts as His children to build up the body of Christ and His Kingdom for the future. God has sent a personal invitation to His chosen children—who have been separated from the unholiness of this world to participate in His magnificent plan. Still, God will not force us because the choice is up to you and me if we want to be a part of this exclusive family (Deut chapter 30).

There should be an excellent inspiration for our obedience to the Lord by knowing and walking in God's unconditional and everlasting love. Believing God loves us and living with that belief as a conscious and absolute fact, we should find it much easier to obey Him and *"destroy anything that is damaging our loving relationship with the One who chose us before creation."* As His chosen ones, we should inherently possess a desire to continue in sanctification and love the privilege we have in spreading His cause of the Gospel.

However, even as our love deepens for the Lord and we grow closer to Him, we still feel like we're in the minority as believers in Jesus Christ and, at times, in a stage of defeat. In today's world, and as we approach the end of time, that feeling will intensify—I feel it more and more each passing day. We will be consumed by so much hatred and evilness that we must set our thoughts on the realities of Heaven rather than the things of this earth, as Paul states in Colossians chapter 3. Even Peter reminded the believers in his first epistle that they would endure social and economic persecution because they were the minority and would feel like strangers.

But a powerful passage in 1 Pet 1:2 should be embedded daily in our hearts, souls, and minds. "God the Father chose you long ago, and the Spirit has made you holy. As a result, you "have obeyed Jesus Christ" and are cleansed by His blood." Some translations say sanctification, and that's the key. As we grow more in Him, we will see that we're separated from the world for an exceptional cause in these end times. But it all hinges on our obedience to Him in that cause. So, there's a special privilege for holiness in our lives as we follow the ways of our Lord. We are called to live intentionally as God's chosen ones.

1. Got Questions. "Why Did God Choose Israel to Be His Chosen People?"

As His spiritual elect, we continue to walk and talk with Him every day, not every other day, but daily. In that relationship, when we're carrying heavy burdens, we faithfully go to Him and surrender them all. As His own, we not only read His word but also assess its meaning and apply it to the weakest areas of our lives. This helps us to be more assertive and overcome obstacles in our daily Christian Walk. And in our closeness with Him, we strengthen our confidence and boldness in what He's telling us, which is absolute Truth.

As God's special, we long to use our God-given gifts to build His Kingdom and establish unity in His body. We focus more on others and less on ourselves, preventing ourselves from being a stumbling block but helping the weaker in faith. We possess hearts of humility, grace, mercy, and love. God's elect doesn't show favoritism but loves everyone unconditionally and sacrificially. We aim for Christlikeness, so He is honored and glorified each step of the way. We don't expect anything in return but to return to Him the glory and praise He deserves and is worthy of. It's part of our calling and duty as His family of choice.

Eph 1:3–8, "All praise to God, the Father of our Lord Jesus Christ, who has blessed us with every spiritual blessing in the heavenly realms because we are united with Christ. Even before he made the world, God loved us and chose us in Christ to be holy and without fault in his eyes. God decided in advance to adopt us into his own family by bringing us to Himself through Jesus Christ. This is what he wanted to do, and it gave him great pleasure. So, we praise God for the glorious grace he has poured out on us who belong to his dear Son. He is so rich in kindness and grace that he purchased our freedom with the blood of his Son and forgave our sins. He has showered his kindness on us, along with all wisdom and understanding."

I cannot even fathom and wrap my finite mind around this most profound passage above. God has chosen you and me to be a people for Himself, marked for doing great things of righteousness and holiness—and He selected you and me as His unique ones before the creation of the world. And in these days of tumultuous times, it gives me rest and comfort because it gave my Father pleasure in doing this for me! As God's elect, we're held to a different standard from the ways of the world, and it should lie in our faithfulness and obedience to His word—unwavering, which is what He prefers and expects in His children!

Chapter 8

'Godly Remembrance'

Deut 8:12–15, "For when you have become full and prosperous and have built fine homes to live in, and when your flocks and herds have become very large, and your silver and gold have multiplied along with everything else, be careful! Do not become proud at that time and forget the LORD your God, who rescued you from slavery in the land of Egypt. Do not forget that he led you through the great and terrifying wilderness with its poisonous snakes and scorpions, where it was so hot and dry. He gave you water from the rock!"

In this chapter, God calls His children to remember all He had done for them and obey His decrees without reservation. He even throws up the warning flag because He knows His children all so well. It's not if, "but when will you be satisfied" because God faithfully keeps all His promises. They must be devoted to remembering they are His gifts, His chosen holy ones. It was not something they earned, but He wants them not to forget the Giver of the gifts, His promise and commitment, and all His provisions over time. A good antidote then and now is a continual attitude of gratitude to God!

When everything is fine and our lives are filled with abundance, we can easily forget the LORD Himself and fail to remember that it was all His working of provisions and blessings—on our behalf. It is easier to say from our lips that "God did it" or "It's all the blessings of the LORD" than to truly mean these words in our hearts. When God takes the measure of a man or woman, He does not put a divine tape measure around our heads to see how much we know and believe, but He puts it around our hearts to see how much we genuinely obey and love Him! Because a proud heart is on "fleshly autopilot" doing its own thing, going its way, forgetting that everything they have is from Almighty God. They have reached their comfort zone of self-complacency and found contentment in what they think is theirs!

Paul reminds us in 1 Tim 6:9–12, "But people who long to be rich fall into temptation and are trapped by many foolish and harmful desires that plunge them into ruin and destruction. For the love of money is the root of all kinds of evil. Some people, craving money, have wandered from the true faith and pierced themselves with many sorrows. But you, Timothy, are a man of God, so run from all these evil things. Pursue righteousness and a godly life, along with faith, love, perseverance, and gentleness. Fight the good fight for the true faith. Hold tightly to the eternal life to which God has called you, which you have declared so well before many witnesses."

What a powerful passage reminding us of "what we truly need" versus what some may want or feel they need in their lives. Because today, we're either pursuing the wealth of this world or the righteousness and wisdom of a Holy God. Our faith is not passive; it's an ongoing and active faith that requires obeying God—knowing and feeling all that He's provided is enough and good—and no matter what, it is well with our soul!

Children of God who remember His goodness recall fresh in their minds and hearts where He brought them from and where He's placed them in life today. They are mindful of who they were in the old and who they are today, tomorrow, and forever in the new. They don't get trapped in the past snares, but they've broken free because of their newness in Christ. They are more in tune with their state of spirituality than the life of materialism.

Their remembrance of what God has fulfilled in their lives leads them to a state of ongoing thankfulness all the time, not just part of the time. They discovered that their identity in the old self is gone, and they are now seen as children representing Jesus Christ. Their spiritual state of remembrance is established with more of the divine and eternal nature versus a mortal mindset. Their remembrance of God's goodness is like second nature in their minds and hearts.

Remembering God's faithfulness and promises is part of our daily discipline and duty. It can only be accomplished when we're rooted in the depths of His word and allow His Spirit to lead us down the paths of beautiful memories. Unfortunately, that is not always the case. Below are some danger signs that could be evident if we are not disciplining our spiritual lives with structures of fruitful remembrance.

- When we lose our peace and joy (Rom 14:17, 15:13).
- We start to complain and groan too often in life (Phil 2:14).

- We always feel disgruntled and angry; we possess a stinking attitude (Jas 1:19–20).
- We become discontented—feeling spiritual discomfort (Heb 13:5).
- We think and act more worldly. We want to taste more of our flesh than God (Rom 8:8).
- We feel distant from our Lord (Psalm chapter 13).
- Our prayer life and time in His word have diminished (Phil 4:6).
- We lost a heart of praise and thankfulness (1 Thess 5:18).
- We discourage more than encourage; we've lost the words of grace and love (1 Thess 5:11, Col 4:6)).
- We are more consumed with the negative than the positive (Prov 25:26).
- We break down more than build up. We forget Who we're building for (2 Tim 1:7)!
- We focus more on self than God (Phil 4:8).

God is gracious, kind, and good to us even when we don't deserve it. However, He also knows that we have many spells of spiritual memory loss—He knows we are forgetful. So, He gives us memorials through the power of His word and His Spirit. We must build more godly testimonials daily and talk about them with anyone and everyone, as we've witnessed in so many passages throughout the Book of Deuteronomy. We can never forget God's goodness.

Remember, our God-given means of remembrance should be active in our lives, so we must immerse them in our minds and hearts daily. As discussed earlier in this book, look at the power of Moses' message to the Israelites in Deuteronomy chapter 6. Memorize this powerful message in the core of your soul and spirit and live by it.

Eph 1:3, "All praise to God, the Father of our Lord Jesus Christ, who has blessed us with every spiritual blessing in the heavenly realms because we are united with Christ."

Jas 1:17–18, "Whatever is good and perfect is a gift coming down to us from God our Father, who created all the lights in the heavens. He never changes or casts a shifting shadow. He chose to give birth to us by giving us his true word. And we, out of all creation, became his prized possession."

Chapter 9

'Just Believe!'

Deut 9:1–3, "Listen, O Israel! Today, you are about to cross the Jordan River to take over the land belonging to nations much more significant and more powerful than you. They live in cities with walls that reach the sky! The people are strong and tall descendants of the famous Anakite giants. You've heard the saying, 'Who can stand up to the Anakites?' But recognize today that the Lord your God is the one who will cross over ahead of you like a devouring fire to destroy them. He will subdue them so that you will quickly conquer them and drive them out, just as the Lord has promised."

The Anakites were gargantuan men (humungous). Many scholars say they could be anywhere from seven to nine feet tall, and Goliath came from this group of men. These enormously large men would use their grand stature to frighten the Israelites because they knew their physical appearance alone would startle God's children. They also possessed a reputation for being bad people who would bully and belittle those who were much smaller and felt inferior.

In the book of Numbers (chapters 13 and 14), Moses tries to convince the nation of Israel that Yahweh is with them and that no giant of any size can overcome Almighty God. Dreadfully, it is apparent that the Israelites still do not believe, and they succumb to the fear of man.

In this chapter, God reminded His children of their past and all the victories He had provided (through God's empowering grace). But they needed to understand that He was still not done with them—for more obstacles were coming their way in a fleshly manner. These giants would use their immense size to intimidate the Israelites more than their noble cause. Their size alone could strike fear and frighten anyone, especially God's children because the Israelites knew about these huge men from the scouting report. Now, it has become a reality right before their eyes.

As discussed in an earlier chapter, for our daily reminder, there was no way the Israelites could accomplish this victory in their strength—and based on the physical stats on paper, they did not have a chance in the world. So, God commanded them to do something beyond their ability—humanly speaking. He desired for them to *"believe in Him for all things"*!

He wanted His children to know what this battle would be like, so Israel had to understand the impossibility of the fight on their own, but most importantly, they also had to realize that there would be a certainty of victory in the LORD. They had to *believe (wholeheartedly)* and have absolute faith in God's promise that He was with them and would hand the enemy over to them!

It was a battle far too big for Israel but not too big for the LORD. Israel had to come to grips with these two facts: 1) That in themselves, the job was impossible, and 2) but in God, they could not lose (I can do all things through Christ which strengthens me, Phil 4:13). God was calling Israel to a partnership; and work with Him to win the battles (2 Cor 6:1). What a wonderful truth we must remember daily! He simply asks us to believe it is possible, and He will take care of the rest. But it seemed evident that the big Anakites had stolen their peace and joy! This is a personal statement: When I see big obstacles before me, I think of this powerful acronym: B-I-G, Believe-In-God!

We cannot serve God and ourselves simultaneously (see Luke 16:13). Living for God means we make a final decision and choice about Who is in charge and control—in other words, we believe in Him and His words no matter what. When our flesh attempts to reaffirm its rights, we take it back to the cross, allow it to die there, and never retrieve it. If we truly believe in our Lord for all things, when sin tempts us, we have already made a decision because we seek God's will over our own. Gal 1:10 asks, "Obviously, I'm not trying to win people's approval, but of God. If pleasing people were my goal, I would not be Christ's servant."

True believers in Jesus Christ do not spend their lives trying to please anyone but God himself. They are never ashamed to proclaim the name of Christ in any given circumstance (Rom 1:16–17). Within them, there's a hunger and thirst to tell others about their belief in the One Who made all the difference in their life. They boast of their victories (big and small) through God's grace versus their own accomplishments. They persistently stand in the gap for the Lord, knowing where their loyalty lies.

Genuine followers of Christ never aim to seek man's confirmation for anything in life, only God's stamp of approval. They embody a boldness and confidence that positions them to stand up for their faith against anyone of falsehood. Their belief is so steadfast that they exemplify every element of the Fruit of the Spirit (Gal 5:22-23) with all the mercy, grace, and love God can abound.

Living for God may be challenging when times of difficulty arise, but it is not joyless. Paul wrote his most joyful letter while suffering persecution in Rome (see the Book of Philippians). Yes, we will still face temptation and hardship in this life on earth, but when the glory of God is our focus, living for Him becomes the source of our joy rather than a struggle (Ps 100:2; Neh 8:10, 1 Cor 6:20; 1 Pet 4:16). Simply put, a true believer is a person who has chosen to live for Christ as Lord of their life over anything else—nothing can barge in and disrupt their faithful relationship with God.

So, here's the personal challenge for you and me. Are we, as Christians, showcasing a daily life as true believers in Jesus Christ? It should consist of the following:

- A newness and freedom of life in Christ—not one of bondage; because we're a new creation! 2 Cor 5:17
- Faithful obedience to the application of God's word in our lives versus the fleshly disobedient ways of man. 2 Tim 3:16-17
- A strong desire for more ways of the Spirit than the flesh, exhibiting Christlike humility, grace, repentance, and forgiveness. Romans chapter 8
- Pursuing a life of righteousness and holiness. 2 Timothy chapter 2.
- Possessing a reputation of godliness, not godlessness—A God Builder! 1Tim 4:8
- Embodying the Fruit of the Spirit (Love, Joy, Peace, Patience, Kindness, Faithfulness, Gentleness, Goodness, and Self-Control). Gal 5:22-23
- Growing in all areas of Christlikeness and not living a stagnant life. 2 Peter chapter 1.

Paul reminds us in Colossians chapter 3 that Jesus has given His faithful followers the power to live for Him now, tomorrow, and in the future. And in that new life, we have a hope rooted in our 100% confidence in everything He says—will come to fruition! True believers in their Lord and Savior will act out their genuine saving faith all the time and never live a life of hypocrisy. The game-changer is this: consistently staying close to His word daily and living by it with absolute zeal and boldness. That type of believer is found in 1 Peter.

1 Pet 1:6–8: "So be truly glad. There is wonderful joy ahead, even though you must endure many trials for a little while. These trials will show that your faith is genuine. It is being tested as fire tests and purifies gold—though your faith is far more precious than mere gold. So when your faith remains strong through many trials, it will bring you much praise, glory, and honor on the day when Jesus Christ is revealed to the whole world. You love him even though you have never seen him. Though you do not see him now, you trust him, and you rejoice with a glorious, inexpressible joy."

Chapter 10

'God's Expectations'

Deut 10:12-13, "And now, Israel, what does the LORD your God require of you? He requires only that you fear the LORD your God and live in a way that pleases and loves and serves him with all your heart and soul. And you must always obey the LORD's commands and decrees that I am giving you today for your own good."

At the beginning of this chapter, we see where God told Moses to chisel out two stone tablets like the first ones and make a wooden Ark—a sacred chest to store them in. He told Moses to come up to Him on the mountain, and He would write on the tablets the exact words that were on the ones he smashed. Then God told Moses to place the tablets in the Ark.

Why did Moses break the first tablets of the law? It was not only out of his anger but a powerful and visible representation of the nation of Israel breaking the law of God. So, God commanded that they restore the law by bringing forth two new tablets. God's writing on the new tablets was consistent with His first writings, indicating that His holy word is the same yesterday, today, and forever: never changing. This type of holy consistency and commitment is the life He requires from you and me. But this is also a beautiful depiction of God's mercy in allowing another set of tablets written for their guidance, even in their ignorance!

God wanted His written words to be the starting point and stirring for Israel's right walk with Him, for it was the only way. What a powerful picture of the inspiration of God's word; though God did not literally write the Scriptures with His own hand, He did perfectly guide the minds and hands of the writers so that the Scriptures are "God-breathed" (2 Tim 3:16).

The Ark of the Covenant was the most instrumental symbol of faith and God's presence. Placing God's laws (His very word) in the Ark illustrates

'God's Expectations'

Yahweh's expectation from the Israelites and us as His children to get right with Him. We cannot come before His presence unless we have a genuine saving faith of absolute reverence and respect. Even during our own times of rebellion, we must entirely focus on applying His word in our lives. [1]

In the passage above, Moses reminded the Israelites what God expected from them. If you think of the approximately 613 OT laws, they were created to cause His children to think of Him constantly and His desires for them. Through the guidance of His word and Spirit—God helps us to keep our focus on Him and His expectations as His children daily; the rest is up to us. Ps 119:105 reminds us, "His word is a lamp to our feet and a light to our path." Step by step—there's no better guide.

During their journey in the wilderness, the Israelites were reminded to be prepared to move every time God moved. If not, they would be left behind. God expected His chosen ones to move when He moved, the same expectations He requires from you and me today. So, how can we, as believers, incorporate more of His ways in our daily lives that constantly remind us to think about God's expectations?

Just like His words and promises never change, His desires and commands for each of His children are clear, consistent, and straightforward. God encourages us to seek the Lord, live in a way that pleases Him, fear the Lord out of complete respect and reverence, love Him, and serve Him with all our hearts, souls, minds, and strength. When our lives are not in tune with God in all areas of our lives, the busyness of this fast-paced world can threaten to carry us away without a moment's notice. When this happens, we can easily forget God's supplying grace.

If we could only realize how kind, gracious, loving, patient, and good God is in all His requirements of us, maybe we would quit our moaning, groaning, whining, and grumbling ways and begin to serve Him with complete, wholehearted Joy. This is true in what John writes: "For this is the love of God that we keep his commandments. And His commandments are not burdensome" (1 John 5:3). If anything, His words bring us joy, peace, and comfort, but they also supply us with internal strength!

Jesus never promises us that obeying Him will be easy, but here's the key—our spiritual effort, willingness, self-discipline, and pure motives to serve our Lord are not a burden for those who faithfully love Him and fear Him. Pleasing Him will become second nature, a significant achievement in this earthly life that we can be proud of! It does not mean we've reached perfection, but we're progressing through the sanctifying process.

---

1. Enduring Word. "Recovering After a Fall."

Even in those moments of voidness, when we feel like we do not please the Lord with all we have, we should examine our lives, approach His throne with a humble and contrite heart, and ask: "Lord, what do you want from me? Grant me your wisdom and knowledge, and lead me down your path of righteousness!" James (Jesus' half-brother) reminds us in Jas 1:5–8 below, emphasizing the power and enlightenment that come from seeking God's wisdom:

"If you need wisdom, ask our generous God, and he will give it to you. He will not rebuke you for asking. But when you ask him, be sure that your faith is in God alone. Do not waver, for a person with divided loyalty is as unsettled as a wave of the sea that is blown and tossed by the wind. Such people should not expect to receive anything from the Lord. Their loyalty is divided between God and the world, and they are unstable in everything they do."

Always remember that what God expects from you and me is that we wholeheartedly dedicate ourselves to Him—nothing less. That is the meaning of the parable of the talents in Matthew, chapter 25. This profound chapter encourages us to live with a deep sense of responsibility and love that aligns with God's expectations of His faithful children. It challenges us to use our talents wisely as we prepare for the end times. If you read this beautiful parable, you will see that we are rewarded because of our faithful commitment to God.

As devout followers of Christ, we must utilize our talents (not just our gifts) for the glory of His name and Kingdom! After all, these are blessings from Almighty God, and we should invest them in eternal things. That is a perfect way for us to return in favor of those blessings at the foot of His throne. Tragically, so many talented people jeopardize their rewards in Heaven because they do things out of selfishness—in other words, they do it more for the honor of man, not God. Their hearts and motives are not godly, which is not pleasing to Yahweh. These types of people have lost sight of God's expectations!

It is so essential for all believers to realize that when we delight in the Lord first, He will give us the desires of our hearts. The Psalmist reminds us in this passage that if our #1 goal in life on this side of Heaven is to please the Lord greatly, He will ensure that our desires align with His so we can do things that gladden His heart. Remember, God will give rewards in heaven at the judgment seat of Christ based on our faithfulness in service to Him (2 Cor 5:10).

The rewards will show the reality of our sonship with the Lord of our lives (Gal 4:7). God will give us rewards in heaven in order to fulfill the law of sowing and reaping, as recorded in Gal 6:7–9, and make good on

'God's Expectations'

His promise that our labor in the Lord is not in vain (1 Cor 15:58). These rewards in heaven are the completion of our earthly story. They will be eternally satisfying (Ps 16:11). Don't we all long for those words from our Savior, "Well done, my good and faithful servant?"

Remember the passage in Heb 11:6, "And it is impossible to please God without faith. Anyone who wants to come to him must believe that God exists and that he rewards those who sincerely seek him." Without faith, it is impossible to please God; in fact, we cannot even begin to approach the Lord, understand His expectations, and experience a personal relationship with Him without it. Faith is the precious vault in Heaven in which the believer's life is lived.

We are called "believers" because we continually put our faith, trust, and confidence in God. The Christian life begins with faith, and it perseveres us until the end. When we accept the evidence in God's Word (Rom 10:17) and reach out in response to experience fellowship with Him, we begin to live by faith, which is what He expects—because this type of faith pleases God. [2]

When we align our daily lives with the expectations of God, we, as His children, don't expect anything in return, for He gets all the glory, honor, and praise—not us! A child of God who knows God's requirements is a dedicated student of the Word and is consistently complying with His Truth and the Spirit. They prepare for the seconds, minutes, hours, and days ahead, anticipating what will come. Their plans align with God's will because they have a "real" hope that many do not even possess today.

So, what does God expect from you and me?

- First, be sure we've accepted His Son, Jesus Christ, as Lord and Savior by faith (Rom 10:9, Eph 2:8–10).
- Second, upon that acceptance and once we possess the indwelling Spirit, we must start living out our genuine saving faith through complete obedience and love for His word and start our growth phase (1 John 4:15, Rom 8:15–17, 1 Cor 2:12, Eph 4:30).
- Third, be a listener and doer of His word—apply it, grow in it, and live by God's very breath daily. The Holy Spirit can help us put our faith into action so that the Fruit of the Spirit is displayed in our personal lives (Jas 1:22, Gal 5:22–23).
- Fourth, when we get out of line, we must repent with a humble and selfless heart and allow the Holy Spirit to work out His convictions in

---

2. Got Questions. "Without Faith, It is Impossible to Please God."

our lives— while He counsels and comforts us through the sanctifying process (Acts 3:19, 2 Pet 3:9).

- Fifth, utilize our God-given gift(s) to build up the body of Christ and His Kingdom. Be a devout bondservant for the Lord (1 Pet 4:10, Jas 1:17, 1 Cor chapter 12)!
- Sixth, be the epitome of God's love, mercy, and grace with everyone (1 John 4:8, 2 Cor 5:7, 2 Cor 13:14, 2 Cor 9:8, Matt 5:7, Eph 4:32, and Col 3:12).
- And seventh, possess a vibrant prayer life and embody genuine worship and fellowship (Phil 4:6, John 4:24, Ps 95:6, and 1 John chapter 1). When we do this, we will have a heart set and mindset of thankfulness and constant praise, which honors and glorifies our Heavenly Father!

Prov 23:17–19 says, "Don't envy sinners, but always continue to fear the Lord. You will be rewarded for this; your hope will not be disappointed. My child, listen and be wise: Keep your heart on the right course."

Phil 1:20–27, "For I fully expect and hope that I will never be ashamed, but that I will continue to be bold for Christ, as I have been in the past. And I trust that my life will bring honor to Christ, whether I live or die. For to me, living means living for Christ, and dying is even better. But if I live, I can do more fruitful work for Christ. So, I really don't know which is better. I'm torn between two desires: I long to go and be with Christ, which would be far better for me. But for your sakes, it is better that I continue to live. Knowing this, I am convinced that I will remain alive so I can continue to help all of you grow and experience the joy of your faith. And when I come to you again, you will have even more reason to take pride in Christ Jesus because of what he is doing through me. Above all, you must live as citizens of heaven, conducting yourselves in a manner worthy of the Good News about Christ. Then, whether I come and see you again or only hear about you, I will know that you are standing together with one spirit and one purpose, fighting together for the faith, which is the Good News. "

Mic 6:8 says, "No, O people, the Lord has told you what is good, and this is what he requires of you: to do what is right, to love mercy, and to walk humbly with your God."

Chapter 11

'Always & Forever'

Deut 11:1-8, "You must love the Lord your God and always obey his requirements, decrees, regulations, and commands. Keep in mind that I am not talking now to your children, who have never experienced the discipline of the Lord your God or seen his greatness and his strong hand and powerful arm. They didn't see the miraculous signs and wonders he performed in Egypt against Pharaoh and all his land. They didn't see what the Lord did to the armies of Egypt and their horses and chariots—how he drowned them in the Red Sea as they were chasing you. He destroyed them, and they have not recovered to this very day!"

"Your children didn't see how the Lord cared for you in the wilderness until you arrived here. They didn't see what he did to Dathan and Abiram (the sons of Eliab, a descendant of Reuben) when the earth opened its mouth in the Israelite camp and swallowed them, along with their households and tents and every living thing that belonged to them. But you have seen the Lord perform all these mighty deeds with your eyes!" "Therefore, be careful to obey every command I am giving you today so you may have the strength to go in and take over the land you are about to enter."

God is straightforward with all the details and facts His children need to know. He reminds them to love their Lord and "always" obey His requirements because that type of consistent loyalty and respect will lead to blessings that can last "forever." But the Almighty One also made a powerful statement in verse 2 when He said He was not talking to their children; God was talking to them directly (the elder ones)! He laid ownership and accountability on each of them individually to ensure they would pass on His greatness and goodness to their future descendants. Doing this would demonstrate their steadfast faithfulness and obedience to God and all His ways.

He reminded His children of all He did for them during their wandering days—His provisions, protection, and fulfillment of His promises. So, when He made this claim at the end of verse 7, "You have seen the Lord perform these mighty deeds with your own eyes," it clearly shows that they were responsible for raising their children on the facts of all the things God had provided and promised His children. It was to be passed down from generation to generation. This applies as much to us today as it did to the Israelites thousands of years ago! As we've seen in this book, this type of godly responsibility should be perpetual in our lives as His wiser ones to the younger generation—it should be never-ending!

God's chosen ones had powerful reasons to believe in God and obey His commands. Why? Because they had witnessed everything God reminded them of in His wondrous acts throughout that barren desert. Moreover, He demonstrated great love and care for His children through their deepest woes and heightened trials. But God knew His children all so well, for even after all they had witnessed, they still struggled with their faith and obedience to Almighty God.

So, God commanded Israel to love Him in all His ways and show it by how they lived their lives as His own. However, their love for the Lord would not only be reflected in their personal lives—but it would also be revealed if they shared and passed it down to their heirs! Unfortunately, that was not the case 100%! It makes me wonder if they truly understood the depths of God's love—because His love is not entirely up to humans' impulses or feelings—it is both unconditional and conditional. This means He accepts us as we are, no matter what we've done. What a merciful, gracious, and loving God we serve!

To expound, God's unconditional love involves His total acceptance, but conversely, His conditional love requires discipline. Our Heavenly Father disciplines us for our good because of His love for His children, as we can see from the author in Hebrews chapter 12. In this powerful chapter, God proves His love by disciplining us. Yes, it can be painful, but afterward, there can be a quiet harvest of right living for those trained in His righteous and just ways. This process helps us to be more in tune with His will and purpose for the long run. Remember, God expresses His love perpetually to us in His grace, mercy, holiness, and sovereignty from beginning to end.

However, He does require a response from you and me, and it should be the type of reciprocating love (return in favor) with absolute trust in His ways and a complete reverence and respect for Him as Lord of our lives—which entails 100% compliance with His holy word. When we genuinely commit to this type of love for our Lord, it will illustrate our absolute faith and obedience to Him all the time—through every trial, loss, and suffering until the end. This type of godly love will resonate and carry over to our children and others. But here's the gut punch: "We either choose to love the LORD "in all His ways"—or not."

In other words, we cannot pick various laws from His word to follow and choose not to follow the rest of them. That will not lead to the productive life He desires in you and me. Over time, our choices will be seen in one of two areas: "The fruitfulness of Christ in our lives, or unfruitful ways like the first generation of Israelites." Our commitment to His word and all His ways must be an 'always and forever' compliance—not partly, but wholly!

Most of history is more concerned with what man has done and all their accomplishments. So, when humans make their mark in the history books, we are taught to remember what they did—it is part of our ongoing education and learning. In many cases, each of us ensures that these impactful stages of humanity will always be remembered by our children and carried on for their good. Why? Many parents genuinely believe that these teachings in today's institutions will benefit them somehow, improving their future sustainability.

But God wants us to look at "His magnificent history and storylines," so we will remember the miraculous things He did for His children then—and what He's doing for you and me today. Seeing the validity and truth of His word can impact our belief in the One true God more and more with each passing day. But we can only know and believe it by being in the depths of His word and living by it daily. We learn far more and benefit sufficiently by looking at what God has accomplished throughout the lives of His children in the Bible and even in our own lives to this day.

Remember, God wants us to fix our thoughts on His realities, not men (Col chapter 3). I can only imagine what this world would be like if we constantly embedded in our minds, hearts, and souls all God has done and will do—as He confirms in His word. He wants us to channel those reminders of His goodness over time to the world until our Lord returns.

Few of us have seen dramatic miracles like the ones the Israelites experienced, and it may be challenging for us to obey and remain faithful—because we're waiting for our own supernatural phenomenon to happen. But we have the truest document of all, which proves all the facts: His Holy Word. The Bible tells us in John 20:29, "Then Jesus told him, "You believe because you have seen me. Blessed are those who believe without seeing me." Are we living by that very truth? Once again, when our hearts are in the depths of His Word, we get a snapshot of His miracles. It should reassure us that He's always with us (Isa 41:10, Zeph. 3:17). The lessons we learn from the past that are recorded in God's word, which should be our guiding principles of Truth for today, can provide us with a hope that should strengthen our faith in the Lord daily.

In Isaiah, we see the power of God coming to the aid of His chosen children. When they felt hopeless while in exile, God assured them that He would bring the nation of Israel back to their original homeland in His timing. Can you imagine what was going through their minds after all those years in captivity? "Freedom, thank God, freedom at last"! However, God's redemption and restoration are always done with His divine justice and righteousness. He never saves or redeems at the *expense* of His justice and righteousness.[1]

This Godly process was crucial because they would be ashamed of their former idolatrous ways when God's children were redeemed with His holy justice. This is spiritually good when someone is ashamed and embarrassed over their sin. To put this into a more robust perspective for believers today—there is something severe and spiritually wrong when a child of God is shameless or beyond embarrassment and is not remorseful. God even promised He would give Judah the gift of shame and embarrassment over sin again. This should permeate to the core of our soul and spirit as "genuine repentant believers!" Remember this about genuine repentance—you should not return to the ways that separated you from a Merciful and Everlasting God!

We must remember that God's righteousness and justice are the pillars and foundations of His governing rule. His justice sets all things right, and His righteousness establishes that right relationship with Him through His Son. A beautiful parallel is when we truly accept Christ as our Lord and Savior; He should be 100% Lordship over our lives. You see, through the redemptive act of Jesus Christ, God provided a way for the unrighteous to be vindicated (redeemed)—through "genuine saving faith" in Jesus Christ (always & forever).

God imputed righteousness and justice to us as an expression of His mercy so that we can re-enter the realm of His righteousness (our position in Him) and holiness (our godly character) and be saved from the consequences of sin, which is eternal death. And that type of glorious freedom is perpetual! Take heart and joy in the power of that freedom because it will last the rest of our lives! And that word is the Good News that was preached to you.

In Psalm 103, we are encouraged to praise the Lord as we are reminded of our Heavenly Father's lovingkindness, compassion, mercy, grace, and

---

1. Enduring Word. "Isaiah Chapter 1, Indictment and Invitation."

incredible patience toward us. This comes from His great and loyal love for His children. God's love is never-ending; it never gives up, is never broken, and lasts always and forever—it is guaranteed because of what Jesus Christ did on the cross for you and me! The only requirement is to believe and accept this atoning act by faith because it can grant us eternal life.

Ps 103:11–18, "For his unfailing love toward those who fear him is as great as the height of the heavens above the earth. He has removed our sins as far from us as the East is from the West. The Lord is like a father to his children, tender and compassionate to those who fear him. For he knows how weak we are; he remembers we are only dust. Our days on earth are like grass; like wildflowers, we bloom and die. The wind blows, and we are gone as though we had never been here. But the love of the Lord remains forever with those who fear him. His salvation extends to the children's children of those who are faithful to his covenant, of those who obey his commandments!"

Always remember what the author in Hebrews reminds us in Heb 13:8–9, "Jesus Christ is the same yesterday, today, and forever. So do not be attracted by strange, new ideas. Your strength comes from God's grace, not from rules about food, which don't help those who follow them." Our Lord is unchanging in a changing world that is decaying and dying by the day, and we can rest in that promise. This powerful passage helps us look backward and forward so that we can know He is reliable today, tomorrow, and in the years to come. His promise is dependable, good, unwavering, and trustworthy for the rest of our days.

Matt 24:35 says, "Heaven and earth will disappear, but my words will never disappear."

Isa 40:8, "The grass withers and the flowers fade, but the word of our God stands forever."

1 Pet 1:25, "But the word of the Lord remains forever."

If you ever lack faith and get discouraged in this world of craziness, here are words of comfort that should always and forever be embedded in our hearts, minds, and souls to show you the guarantee of His promises that will endure for all times—2 Tim 2:13, "If we are unfaithful (faithless), he remains faithful, for he cannot deny who he is." His words are true to the very end!

Chapter 12

'Godly Worship'

Deut 12:4-5, 7-9, «Do not worship the Lord your God in the way these pagan peoples worship their gods. Rather, you must seek the Lord your God at the place of worship He himself will choose from among all the tribes—the place where His name will be honored. There, you and your families will feast in the presence of the Lord your God, and you will rejoice in all you have accomplished because the Lord your God has blessed you. Your pattern of worship will change. Today, all of you are doing as you please because you have not yet arrived at the place of rest, the land the Lord your God is giving you as your special possession."

In this chapter, God tells His children to destroy the pagan altars and idols and use His place of worship for its primary purpose: genuinely glorifying and praising His Holy Name! Almighty God did not want anything remaining that would tempt them and lead them astray in their times of worshipping Him. So, He commanded them to discard anything that was getting in the way of honoring Him above all other things. And that still stands true for you and me today!

God wanted their wholehearted commitment of reverence and respect to Him because He desired to be the first place in their hearts, which is the same for you and me. Worship was not left to the opinion of the individual Israelite; they had to worship God at His prescribed and desired place and among other worshippers of God. Worship is not a "do as you please" or "all about me" activity or motive. It's about Him, reflected in our loving relationship with a Holy God.

We may think it's not easy to find honorable places where God wants us to worship Him, but they are out there. Believe it or not, there are some genuine bible-believing, truth-teaching, God-honoring, Christ-loving, and

'GODLY WORSHIP'

Spirit-filled bodies of Christ out there for you and me. Are they perfect? Absolutely not, because humans are not perfect. Keep in mind that the enemy has a tactic and strategy, and that's this: he does not want us to find places of honoring and praising our Heavenly Father because He hates it when we worship our Creator and God as a body, and he despises unity in Christ—because the enemy thrives on division and destruction.

But there is a place where God wants you and me to worship because He does not want us in isolation, which can make us easy prey for the enemy. Instead, God wants us in fellowship with our brothers and sisters in Christ (united in His power)—bonding, building, and growing His church in Truth! It's a place where we give our all to Him.

In Acts 2:42–47, Luke reminds us, "All the believers devoted themselves to the apostles' teaching, and to fellowship, and to sharing in meals (including the Lord's Supper), and to prayer. A deep sense of awe came over them all, and the apostles performed many miraculous signs and wonders. All the believers met together in one place and shared everything they had. They sold their property and possessions and shared the money with those in need. They worshiped together at the Temple each day, met in homes for the Lord's Supper, and shared their meals with great joy and generosity—all the while praising God and enjoying the goodwill of all the people. And each day the Lord added to their fellowship those who were being saved."

Godly worship allows us to express our love and devotion to Him freely and to open the floodgates of our hearts, minds, souls, and spirits to His presence. It is our time to value and treasure what God has provided in our lives—because He is worthy of all our praise! It is an act of exalting and magnifying God in a place of utmost honor and reverence. Godly and biblical worship is acknowledging the greatness and goodness of God both publicly and privately. Whether public or private, worship can include physical expressions of praise, honor, and humility—raising our hands and hearts in unison.

Many today could begin to worship God in Spirit and Truth (John 4:24) if they would only "destroy" the wrong ways of worshipping the Lord. It's not about what the church can offer you on Sunday, "but what you can offer Him in complete service for His benefit." Some give their hearts to so many other things, and there is very little to give to the LORD, which can lead anyone to lose that spiritual sight of what godly worship is all about. He wants our whole hearts to praise and honor Him and nothing less.

What is tragic is that so much of what is called worship in today's church isn't genuine worship. It is self-focused, man-focused, and personal-experience-focused instead of God-focused. And here's the scary fact—so much of today's worship is measured by how we feel instead of how God should be honored, praised, and glorified. Sorrowfully, some churches tamper with sensuality, which is more of a control by the flesh than the spirit (1 John 2:15–16).

It is so important that we understand the meaning of sensuality because, in the Bible, sensuality is usually listed with other evils that include sexual promiscuity and perversion. Also known as "lewdness" or "debauchery," *sensuality* can be defined as "devotion to gratifying bodily appetites; free indulgence in carnal pleasures." The word *sensuality* comes from the root word *sense*, which pertains to our five senses. The Greek word most often translated as "sensuality" means "outrageous conduct, shocking to public decency; wanton violence." Sensuality is a total devotion to the gratification of the senses, excluding soul and spirit.[1]

These are simply caution signs for us as followers of Christ because sensuality can abuse our God-given gifts if we get too caught up in "self." Sensuality has no place in the life of a child of God. Peter reminds us more about this in his first epistle, 1 Pet 4:3 (ESV), "For the time that is past suffices for doing what the Gentiles want to do, living in sensuality, passions, drunkenness, orgies, drinking parties, and lawless idolatry." Paul reminds us in Romans 8:4 that Christians "do not walk according to the flesh but according to the Spirit."

We must remind ourselves that true worship is not about us showcasing our talents for the good of man and self but displaying our innermost thoughts and feelings with such adoration and reverence to our Lord—as if we are at the foot of His throne singing our praises as depicted in Revelation! The sound of sacred music from our hearts through our lips should be so full of genuine spiritual emotion that God can hear our heartfelt voices—no matter the sound of all the instruments. When our hearts are more in tune with Him, our pattern of true worship shifts from us to Him!

Godly worship is not about our physical posture but the posture of our hearts and spirit. It is driven by a pure, righteous, humble, and repentant heart emptying its soul of self and laying itself down at the feet of His throne. It consists of a mind-centered focus on Jesus Christ, expressing sincere gratitude; it is selfless, not selfish. To truly worship God, we must understand who He is and what He has done, and the only place He has fully revealed Himself is in the Bible.

True worship is an expression of praise from the depths of our hearts toward a God who is understood through His Word. If we do not have the Truth of the Bible at work in our lives, led by His Spirit, we do not know

---

1. Got Questions. "What Does the Bible Say About Sensuality."

God, and we cannot truly worship and honor Him. It is a divine nature that pours from the inside—out.

As Spirit-filled believers in Jesus Christ, we should know if our worship and praise are selflessly honoring God our Father. How? Our minds and hearts must be set on the Lord, and our entire being must be engaged and embraced in humble and reverent submission to Him alone. True worshippers respect the Bible as God's Word, strive to live by its principles, and do not waver from its teachings. Always remember, the highest form of praise and worship is obedience to Him and His Word, not participation in this wicked world, but in the breadth of His holiness.

Rev 5:9-14, "And when he took the scroll, the four living beings, and the twenty-four elders fell down before the Lamb. Each one had a harp, and they held gold bowls filled with incense, which are the prayers of God's people. And they sang a new song with these words:

"You are worthy to take the scroll and break its seals and open it. For you were slaughtered, and your blood has ransomed people for God from every tribe and language and people and nation. And you have caused them to become a Kingdom of priests for our God. And they will reign on the earth."

"Then I looked again, and I heard the voices of thousands and millions of angels around the throne and of the living beings and the elders. And they sang in a mighty chorus:

"Worthy is the Lamb who was slaughtered—to receive power and riches and wisdom and strength and honor and glory and blessing." And then I heard every creature in heaven and on earth and under the earth and in the sea."

They sang: "Blessing and honor and glory and power belong to the one sitting on the throne. And to the Lamb forever and ever. And the four living beings said, "Amen!" And the twenty-four elders fell down and worshiped the Lamb."

Singing should be congregational, but it should never be performed for the credit of the congregation. Some may say this church has 'Such remarkable singing,' 'They have such great talent in this church,' or 'This place is quite renowned for its music!' However, while the compliments of humans can puff up our pride, this is a poor achievement if this is our mindset and disposition of our hearts. Our singing should be such that God hears it with pleasure, like a sweet aroma flowing from the body of Christ to His Heavenly realm.[2] Never forget this key takeaway: "It's not about the genre of

---

2. Enduring Word. "The Worship God Commands."

music; it's all about the genuineness of our words of praise and honor from our hearts to His ears."

Isa 25:1, "O Lord, I will honor and praise your name, for you are my God. You do such wonderful things! You planned them long ago, and now you have accomplished them."

Ps 150:1–6, "Praise the Lord! Praise God in his sanctuary; praise him in his mighty heaven! Praise him for his mighty works; praise his unequaled greatness! Praise him with a blast of the ram's horn; praise him with the lyre and harp! Praise him with the tambourine and dancing; praise him with strings and flutes! Praise him with a clash of cymbals; praise him with loud clanging cymbals. Let everything that breathes sing praises to the Lord! Praise the Lord!"

Remember, genuine worship of praise, honor, exaltation, magnifying, and fellowship is when our hearts and minds are centered and focused on the power of God moving in and through us by His Spirit—so He gets the glory, not anything or anyone else. We were created in God's image to be like them (the Trinity, Gen 1:27). We are designed to worship and glorify Him alone. Why? Because He's the only One Who is worthy of our praise!

Dan 2:20 says, "Praise the name of God forever and ever, for he has all wisdom and power."

Chapter 13

Other "gods!"

Deut 13:1-4, 18, "Suppose there are prophets among you or those who dream about the future, and they promise you signs or miracles, and the predicted signs or miracles occur. If they then say, 'Come, let us worship other gods'—gods you have not known before—do not listen to them. The Lord, your God, is testing you to see if you truly love Him with all your heart and soul. Serve only the Lord your God and fear Him alone. Obey His commands, listen to his voice, and cling to Him." "The Lord, your God, will be merciful only if you listen to his voice and keep all his commands that I am giving you today, doing what pleases Him."

God's children were told and warned not to listen to false prophets or anyone who falsely led them to worship other gods (like money and materialism). Whether they were a close friend or relatives, God would not allow any teaching away from the Truth of His word and commands. Moses warned the people of the danger of false prophets in their midst because they would surface in their lives sooner or later.

But the heart of these first four verses is God allowing such deceivers in their lives; He wanted to ensure His children's hearts would prove faithful to Him through all the tests. He would determine if they were devoted to the Almighty God where their faith and trust were steadfast in Him—or would fall prey to a sign or experience. For His children to do what was right in His eyes, they had to demonstrate their faithful allegiance to Him. They must never allow family, ethnic, or national ties to be any more significant than their bond with the Lord and His Truths!

The first two guidelines in the Ten Commandments are: 1) You shall have no other gods before Me, and 2) You shall make no idols. There is a primary reason why God set the precedence with these first two commandments. He knows of all the temptations surrounding us in life that can lead us down a path of unrighteousness and away from His holy presence. Nothing is more damaging to our faith than allowing other gods (idols) to creep into our lives and take over God's relationship. They can seem innocent and are something we feel is needed for entertainment or pleasure. But that subtlety can lead to a severe course of action in our lives, leading to a spiritual detour and a danger zone—drifting us away from God's primary position in our daily lives.

Opening the door to other falsehoods can easily disable our walk with the Lord and establish all types of obscurities that will create spiritual blindness. This path of "other gods" taking priority in our lives will lead us to go in the opposite direction of God's way. One of the leading causes is self, which consists of two hideous elements: pride and greed. The dangerous roots of self are when we get consumed with everything we need from this world, which almost always takes our focus and eyes from our Holy God!

We must be cautious in these end times and pay close attention to God's word and all His Truths because the Bible clarifies why God sends a strong delusion in the end times (2 Thes 2:10–12). Simply put, God sends a strong delusion to those who choose not to believe the gospel of Christ. If we are not grounded students of the word of God, so many of us can easily get swayed away to a life of self-pleasure. But as believers, we must not allow anything or anyone to distort our thoughts and hearts from the accurate word of God's message (Col 2:8).

This is a scary place to be—when one knows the Truth of His word and refuses to obey it. They are now subject to lies, deceptions, and all types of falsehood from human minds and lips. It can lead to a path of destruction in following other little gods. Paul reminds us in Rom 1:21–22, "For although they knew God, they neither glorified Him nor gave thanks to Him, but their thinking became futile, and their foolish hearts were darkened. Although they claimed to be wise, they became fools". When people reject the Truth and spin His message around to fit their lifestyle or comfort zone, God will harden them and turn them over to a deluded mind. Therefore, today, more than ever, we must be grounded and rooted in the Truth of His Word as our daily guide—breathing and living it!

The enemy is out to deceive us and lead us down paths of unholiness—preventing us from growing in the ways of Christlikeness. So, he puts those little things in our life that seem good and okay, but suddenly, we turn more to these other gods in our spare time than we do to Almighty God. A good measuring stick is this: When we spend more time with other pleasures of life than God in our daily activity, it can lead to hazardous areas, and we should feel a strong prompting from the Holy Spirit when we're spiritually disoriented. If not, we need a genuine self-examination to ensure our real saving faith is in Jesus Christ (2 Cor 13:5, Ps 139:23–24).

I am not talking about the works of man and having a mindset of legalism, but I am talking about the motives and desires from a heart that has a solid spiritual predisposition with the Lord as first place in their life! Always remember, while other gods or idols want to take away our time of holiness, God graciously gives us the freedom to enjoy time with Him as often as we like each day. This is vital because He wants to keep us close to Him so we can perform more acts of His holiness and godliness. It comes down to our daily choices and priorities as His children today! What is more important to us in this life?

As noted earlier, the dangerous and harmful root of "other gods" stems from self. But the foundation of keeping the Lord first in our lives is genuine affection—a love that will never allow anything to sneak into our lives and take God's place in our hearts, souls, and minds. God promises blessings for those who model godly values for their children (Deut 7:9). Just as children learn to run to idols by watching their parents do so, they can also learn to turn away from idols by observing their parents giving God His rightful place in their daily lives. In other words, He's their refuge (place of security and retreat).

When we make the Lord our hiding place (Ps 32:7), He fills our hearts' deepest needs like nothing else can. And when we have no gods but the One True God in our lives, He is faithful to shelter us with His love and protection (Ps 36:7; 144:2; Mal 3:17–18). Ps 103:17 says, "The LORD's love is with those who fear him, and his righteousness with their children's children." We must give the Holy Spirit free rein to smash any idols our hearts have erected. When we allow Him to remove anything that has established itself as an idol, we can then be filled with His joy and peace (Gal 5:22; Eph 6:18).

God has placed "eternity in man's heart" (Ecc 3:11), and a relationship with Jesus Christ is the only way to fulfill this longing for eternal life. Our idolatrous pursuits will leave us empty, unsatisfied, and, ultimately, on the broad road most people take, which leads to destruction (Matt 7:13).

So, take Jesus' message to heart in His Sermon on the Mount in Matthew chapter five. He first told the people to realize their need for Him, which means emptying their tank of self. From there, when He's our #1 priority, we will see throughout the Beatitude that He fills our tank with more of Him than us. It is no longer I, but Christ in me (Gal 2:20).

Jesus tells us that we cannot serve two masters (Matt 6:24)—we will love one and hate the other—think about the power of that choice! Paul powerfully reminds us in Galatians chapter five that only two forces constantly fight each other and cannot co-exist—they are the flesh and the spirit—one controls our lives more than the other. Do you know for a fact which one is mastering your life today? Every idol or pagan practice we allow in our lives over time will squeeze out any space for the Lord. Always look at an I-D-O-L in this sense: an Individual-Doing-Oppositely-Lord's way.

Proverbs 4:23 says, "Guard your heart above all else, for it determines the course of your life."

Exod 23:13 says, "Pay close attention to all my instructions. You must not call on the name of any other gods. Do not even speak their names."

Deut 6:14–15, "You must not worship any of the gods of neighboring nations, for the Lord your God, who lives among you, is a jealous God. His anger will flare up against you, and he will wipe you from the face of the earth."

Chapter 14

'Godly Dedication'

Deut 14:22-23, "You must set aside a tithe of your crops—one-tenth of all the crops you harvest each year. Bring this tithe to the designated place of worship—the place the Lord your God chooses for his name to be honored—and eat it there in his presence. This applies to your tithes of grain, new wine, olive oil, and the firstborn males of your flocks and herds. Doing this will teach you always to fear the Lord your God."

Just like when God chose the nation of Israel to be His special people, and they were to be set apart for His glorious use, He also had specific guidelines for them to set aside a special portion of their blessings unto Him. Doing this would require them to conduct themselves as unique and distinct amongst the rest of the world with a wholehearted commitment to God's ways and His requirements—but their actions and choices had to align with God. While the pagans and non-believing world gave their time and efforts to false gods, Almighty God would set the standard of holy giving unto Him through their tithes, first and foremost.

Throughout the Bible, God has made the purpose of tithing very clear, and that was by showing His children the importance of putting God first in their lives through their selfless, sacrificial, and faithful tithes. No matter their harvest level (great or small), God expected them to tithe and bring their gift to the chosen place, where His name would be honored. Since the beginning of God's detailed guidelines, He has given clear direction and understanding of where He would be so they could prepare their hearts and give to Him willingly.

In God's instructions, He wanted to teach His children that they should always fear the Lord their God. In other words, fearing God means having such an admiration for Him that it dramatically impacts how they should live by putting Him above all things. The fear of God is respecting Him, obeying Him, submitting to His discipline, and worshiping Him in absolute awe and reverence. It is such a deep-rooted godly dedication that His children want to lovingly give their possessions to the One Who has blessed them immensely. And that same type of devout emotion and response applies to you and me today.

Paul reminds us in 2 Cor 9:6–8, "Whoever sows sparingly will also reap sparingly, and whoever sows bountifully will also reap bountifully. Each one must give as he has decided in his heart, not reluctantly or under compulsion, for God loves a cheerful giver. And God can make all grace abound to you, so that having all sufficiency in all things at all times, you may abound in every good work."

In the heart of this passage, we see the definition and description of a cheerful giver. To expand on this even more, a cheerful giver is enthused to give joyfully and willingly because they want to follow the example of their Lord, Jesus Christ. Their sole purpose is trusting God for all things in their life and being faithful to the One Who has always been faithful to them.

They don't worry or get anxious about the things in this life but aspire to please God by dedicating their all to Him with no reluctance, sorrow, or feelings of being forced. They are so confident in this drive of holiness because they know beyond a shadow of a doubt that God is their staying power to sustain them through it all! It's a blessed honor and duty—like it's second nature!

A dedicated person to God "alone" knows they have been chosen by their Father to live a Christian life, and they understand the grace of God. When we give generously and with a willing heart, God assures us He will watch over and provide for us (Isa 58:9; Ps 41:1–3; Prov 22:9; 2 Cor 9:8, 11). We need to remember that it's not just our treasure that we are to give back to God cheerfully. As King David pointed out, everything we have is from God (1 Chr 29:14), including our talents and our time. As our days are numbered (Ps 139:16), our time indeed belongs to God. And any gifts we have are also from Him; therefore, "As each has received a gift, use it to serve one another, as good stewards of God's varied grace." (1 Pet 4:10).[1]

As believers in Jesus Christ, just like the Israelites, we are also chosen people who are special to God. God's word reminds us in 1 Pet 2:9, "But you are not like that, for you are a chosen people. You are royal priests, a holy nation, God's very own possession." But also, in the heart of Colossians chapter 3, Paul is telling the holy people of Colossae how Christians are expected to live their new life in Christ.

---

1. Got Questions. "How Can I Become a More Cheerful Giver."

'Godly Dedication'

When we've taken off our old nature, and we're anew, our focus shifts from the ways of the world to the realities of Heaven and how we are to please our Lord. What we do first with the blessings from God will genuinely demonstrate "what or Who we value most." Are we giving our best unto the Lord as a ritual—or as a heartfelt duty and habit that has become like a second nature of love and loyalty? Are our hearts in the right place? If they are, our tithes and offerings are from a genuine and willing heart, expecting nothing in return.

Godly dedication is devoting all we are and all we possess to God. I am not saying to give all your money and possessions away, but allow God to lead you in doing whatever His will is in your life. In doing so, it positions us in His dwelling place of holiness. It is a wholehearted seeking of God and doing what he tells us to do at all costs. It is so enveloped in a desired dedication that it changes everything about a person's life. They no longer possess a heart for the world but one purposely loyal to the Lord alone. This type of zeal leads us to give Him what He deserves and all He desires from you and me.

By doing this, we are building a close-knit relationship with God and choosing what is more essential in our daily lives. True dedication to God comes by dwelling in his word and not just reading it but doing what He says. A faithful follower of Jesus Christ discards all the earthly things lurking within them that are unpleasant to the Lord. Instead, they clothe themselves with tenderhearted mercy, kindness, humility, gentleness, love, and patience. They let the fullness of God's word take root in their lives, so it fills them with songs of praise, teaching, counseling, and helping others through the wisdom of God. And in all they do, they're true representatives of Christ, honoring God the Father! As a result, they have a new focus on not building a life for their own good—but helping to Build a Kingdom for the good of God.

Dedicated believers of God long for a sanctified life that brings them closer to Him, and in that closeness, they desire the same things God does. Through it all, they realize that He is their backbone of strength no matter what—nothing can replace it. That devout relationship has an absolute resolve to their Lord daily with diligence and perseverance—applying His word with a single-minded drive of loyal allegiance to Him alone.

Nothing gets in their way because they are not timid but tenacious! They realize it's a committed daily task for the rest of their lives. In the depths of their heart, a person solely dedicated to the Lord is unwavering, unswaying, untiring, and unshakeable; they are in it for the long haul. Their spiritual boundary line is cemented in the Lord because He is their top priority. This type of unity yields a proper perspective for that person in their focus on earthly things, and that's this: "What we have truly belongs to Him." We dedicate them back to Him, for He is worthy!

A solid guide for a steadfast and faithful follower of the Lord incorporates these components below in their daily life as a means of dedicating their all to Him, and they don't waver from them one bit.

- Devote time with the Lord throughout the day for prayer, repentance, reverence, thanksgiving, praise, and honor while glorifying Him in all that we say and do. (Deut 6:5, 2 Chr 7:14, Ps 51:1-3, Ps 100:4, Rom 14:8, Col 3:17, Prov 3:9, 1 Cor 6:19-20, 1 Cor 10:31, Phil 1:20, 1 Tim 4:4-5, Mk 1:35, Matt 6:6, 1 Chr 16:11, Ps 119:18, Rom 10:17).
- Prioritize our spiritual life over our earthly life. Don't get involved with the ways of the world, but instead with the ways of God (Matt 6:33, Galatians chapter 5, Rom 12:1-2).
- Draw closer to God through time in His word and the application of His Truths into our lives. Know and grow in His wisdom and knowledge (Read the book of James).
- Act upon God's will for our life (1 Thess 5:12-28, 1 Thess 4:1-12, Romans chapter 12, 1 Timothy chapter 2, 1 Peter chapter 2, Colossians chapter 3, Col 4:1-6).
- Share His mighty acts in our lives with others. Be a living testimony for the Gospel—and for the cause of Christ (Ps 61:1-2, Ps 119:46, Rom 1:16-17, Eph 6:20, 1 John 5:11, 1 Pet 3:15, Rev 12:11).
- Get engaged and involved in a body of believers for times of unity and worship to a Loving and Merciful God (Ephesians chapter 4).
- Exhibit acts of the Fruit of the Spirit in our daily lives, both inside and outside our homes (Gal 5:22-23).
- Utilize our gifts to build up the body of Christ and His Kingdom (1 Pet 4:10, 1 Corinthians chapter 12).
- Honor the Lord by dedicating all our heart, time, talents, temple (body), and treasure for His purpose and will (Ps 144:4, Isa 58:13-14, and Col 4:5, Matt 25:14-30, 1 Cor 6:18-20, Matt 6:21, Prov 3:9, Isa 29:13, Prov 3:5, 3:9, 4:23, 23:26, and Psalm 51:10).
- Don't grieve the Holy Spirit, but allow Him to convict, counsel, and comfort us while leading us to all Truths. (Acts 2:38, John 14:15-26, Rom 5:13, Rom 8:26, 1 Cor 3:16-17, Gal 5:22-23, Eph 4:30-31).

'Godly Dedication'

Col 3:1–4, "Since you have been raised to new life with Christ, set your sights on the realities of heaven, where Christ sits in the place of honor at God's right hand. Think about the things of heaven, not the things of earth. For you died to this life, and your real life is hidden with Christ in God. And when Christ, who is your life, is revealed to the whole world, you will share in all his glory."

Chapter 15

'Godly Helper'

Deut 15:7–11, "But if there are any poor Israelites in your towns when you arrive in the land the Lord your God is giving you, do not be hardhearted or tightfisted toward them. Instead, be generous and lend them whatever they need. Do not be mean-spirited and refuse someone a loan because the year for canceling debts is close at hand. If you refuse to make the loan and the needy person cries out to the Lord, you will be considered guilty of sin. Give generously to the poor, not grudgingly, for the Lord your God will bless you in everything you do. There will always be some in the land who are poor. That is why I am commanding you to share freely with the poor and with other Israelites in need."

An essential part of God's children entering the Promised Land was helping the poor among them. God wanted Israel to be generous givers to those in need—and this was a vital step as they were preparing to enter and possess the land God promised. When Yahweh commanded them to share freely, it was their choice. However, that willing and voluntary choice also depicts their true intentions and desires from the heart. God gave them the free will to choose to help the needy or not. Doing it of their own volition without being forced or asked would demonstrate that a person genuinely desires the same things as God!

So, at the end of every seventh year, any debts were canceled, and creditors had to forgive any loans to their fellow Israelites, called Shemitah. Its purposes were mainly the recovery of agricultural land and breaking the cycle of perpetual debt. Still, another critical point was to provide a source of strength for the poor, which was important to God. Why? Because He wanted an attitude of gratitude with an open heart and an open hand from His blessed children—He did not want them to forget their fellow man.

If they did, as we see in the passage above, God knew that it could lead them to be mean-spirited and possess a heart of refusing to help, which stems from selfishness. But, as Paul reminds us once again in 2 Cor 9:6-7, God loves a cheerful giver. God didn't want the Israelites to give generously to the poor; He wanted them to do so with a grateful and willing heart—and if they were unselfish and kind, God would bless them. This type of heart and mind does not expect anything in return because it's grounded in the truth of realizing what God expects from them. And this is what our Lord requires from you and me.

Today, it's easy for us to rationalize whether most poor or homeless people have brought this upon themselves or that this is their chosen life. When our flesh has this type of reasoning, we can close our hearts and hands to people who are "really" in need. But we must never forget one thing: we are not called to reinvent God's reasoning for ignoring the poor. Instead, we are called to help and respond to their needs—no matter who or what led to their condition.

However, we must make this cause of helping the poor a matter of prayer, asking the Lord to show us what He wants us to do. Then, he will give us wisdom and a discerning spirit to recognize a genuine need. One verse that nicely summarizes our expected charity for the poor is found in the first Epistle of John. "If anyone has material possessions and sees his brother in need but has no pity on him, how can the love of God be in him? Therefore, dear children, let us not love with words or tongue but with action and in truth" (1 John 3:17-18).

A godly helper possesses a unique set of spiritual skills and a genuine passion of lovingkindness for the well-being of God's children; they are more concerned about others than themselves. Their yearning for the care of God's creation of humankind is yielded to the guidance of the Holy Spirit in their decision-making, not the ways, minds, and hearts of man. They understand what it means to be a servant of the Lord, which is a heartfelt response to the needs of others with spiritual maturity. A godly helper is suitable in the eyes of God because He knows their motives and desires are in the right place.

When a helper for the cause of Christ surfaces, we see someone who knows where real life, help, and the truth comes from—the One Who is our Source of Love, Hope, and Faith. God created us all in His image, on equal ground, so why would another human look down on another as if they are better? A genuine godly helper does not possess an attitude of being cynical and critical but one that is caring and sharing and longs to please God first! How? Because they have the power of God's love at work in their lives. Look at some of these powerful quotes below that are truly life-applicable for you and me today.

"What does love look like? It has hands to help others, feet to hasten to the poor and needy, eyes to see misery and want, and ears to hear the sighs and sorrow of men. That is what love looks like."[1]

– Augustine

"Have you ever noticed how much of Christ's life was spent in doing kind things?"[2]

– Henry Drummond

"The Christian is a person who makes it easy for others to believe in God."

– Robert Murray McCheyne

Deut 22:4 says, "If you see that your neighbor's donkey or ox has collapsed on the road, do not look the other way. Go and help your neighbor get it back on its feet!"

If we conducted an in-depth study of the biblical definition of a helper from God's perspective, we would learn that society has this powerful word wrong in their finite minds and hearts. The profound difference between God's definitive meaning and this culture's stereotype is quite contrasting. Even most churches have it wrong.

When our God says Helper, it's a profound revelation of expertise offered in God's kind of love. It is one of divine sacrifice with acts of selflessness and humility! After all, think about it: One of the definitions and attributes of the Holy Spirit is that He's our Helper! Even God Almighty says He is our Help and Shield in times of need. To take this to the triune level, even Christ "helps" us as our Advocate to the Father. In the power of God's word, we will discover that when God says "helper," He refers to someone with great spiritual skills dedicated to godly service! Does this define you and me as genuine "godly helpers"?

A helper for God's people shares freely, willingly, and voluntarily. The New Testament equates sharing with genuine faith. In explaining how faith is to be lived out in good works, James says true religion is "to visit orphans and widows in their distress and to keep oneself unstained by the world" (Jas 1:27).

Always remember that helping others in a sharing and caring Christlike manner originates from an attitude of the heart that matters to God (Matt 6:2–4). Sharing with others reminds us that we are not to set our affections on things of this earth nor store up treasures that have no eternal

---

1. Christianity. "Thirty-Six Powerful Christian Love Quotes."
2. "The Greatest Thing and Others."

'Godly Helper'

value (Col 3:2; Matt 6:20). Sharing also keeps us humble, frees us from the love of money, and teaches us to die to ourselves (Rom 6:6; 1 Tim 6:10). We are most like Jesus when we freely share ourselves with those He brings into our lives.[3]

Matt 5:13-16, "You are the salt of the earth, but if salt has lost its taste, how shall its saltiness be restored? It is no longer good for anything except to be thrown out and trampled under people's feet. You are the light of the world. A city set on a hill cannot be hidden. Nor do people light a lamp and put it under a basket, but on a stand, and it gives light to all in the house. In the same way, let your light shine before others so that they may see your good works and give glory to your Father who is in heaven."

Hebrews 13:15-16 says, "Through him, then let us continually offer up a sacrifice of praise to God, that is, the fruit of lips that acknowledge his name. Do not neglect to do good and to share what you have, for such sacrifices are pleasing to God." Add this verse in the next paragraph below:

Heb 13:1-3, "Keep on loving each other as brothers and sisters. Don't forget to show hospitality to strangers, for some who have done this have entertained angels without realizing it! Remember those in prison, as if you were there yourself. Remember also those being mistreated, as if you felt their pain in your own bodies."

---

3. Got Questions. "What Does the Bible Say About Sharing?"

Chapter 16

"All the Time!"

Deut 16:16–17, "Each year every man in Israel must celebrate these three festivals: the Festival of Unleavened Bread, the Festival of Harvest, and the Festival of Shelters. On each of these occasions, all men must appear before the Lord your God at the place he chooses, but they must not appear before the Lord without a gift for him. All must give as they are able, according to the blessings given to them by the Lord your God."

In this passage, each man was to give *according to the blessings they had received from the LORD*, which were proportionate to what God had given them. This would illustrate their honorable participation as godly children, heeding God's words. It was apparent that God had blessed them because He instructed them in the scriptures to "not" appear before the LORD empty-handed.

The LORD blesses His people according to His own will. Of course, some people have more, and some have less, so each person must decide in their hearts the level of generosity they are willing to offer that will honor God. But we must remember that Almighty God knows our true motives and desires. God reminds us in His word, Prov 21:2, "People may be right in their own eyes, but the LORD examines their heart." In Luke 16:15, "Then he said to them, "You like to appear righteous in public, but God knows your hearts. What this world honors is detestable in the sight of God."

As you can see in this chapter in Deuteronomy and the preceding ones, you would think there is a lot of repetition when it comes to the importance of God's guiding principles on a person being a selfless servant. This was so important in the eyes of God because, once again, a high-spirited contributor to the Lord's work gives, with constant pleasure, "knowing God is good all the time!" They offer with a heart that is aligned with the heart of God because they don't expect God to reciprocate, for they are aware of all His blessings in their life every day.

This is a primary reason why God set aside Jewish festivals or feasts, which were literally "appointed times" and designated days ordained by God to be kept in honoring His name. Why? To continuously remind His children how He led them out of slavery and bondage, on the path to freedom and into the Promised Land. He established these times of remembrance because He knew they would forget over time. These times of celebration are essential not only to Israel but also to the overarching message of the Bible. Why? Because they foreshadow or symbolize an aspect of the life, death, and resurrection of the Lord Jesus Christ. They all had a message of remembrance then and of spiritual significance for us today.

During these most important feasts in Israel, every Jewish man was to go to the place of the Tabernacle and celebrate the designated festival with the whole nation of Israel. God established various events throughout the year as times of remembrance, but at the same time, God wanted all His children to remember His blessings "all the time, not just three or seven times a year." In Psalm chapter 103, David reminds us, "Praise the Lord and 'never forget' all the good things He's done for us."

Each feast was to be a holy assembly where each Israelite (God's chosen people) set aside an established time for God when they would read and understand His laws and then apply them in their lives. But this was not meant to be a half-reminder but to remember God's goodness and gracious blessings all the time. God provided His children with constant reminders of His greatness so they would realize that His promises would stand true throughout their life's journey to the Promised Land!

These festivals were a joint effort of God's people set aside to remind themselves of Yahweh's means of supplying all their needs in life when they needed it the most. They would draw the nation together for celebration and worship as they recalled what God had done in delivering them from their years of bondage. However, the observance of these festivals also taught them the reality of sin, judgment, forgiveness, and the need to thank God and trust Him rather than hoarding possessions.

We must constantly remind ourselves of all those little blessings God brought forth in our lives so we will never forget them deep in our hearts and minds. The big stuff we can easily remember because they are significant to us, such as going on a vacation, holiday get-togethers, a fresh new start in life, promotions, a day of purchasing something brand new, parties, and special events with friends and family, and the list goes on and on. Each of these personal moments' springs forth a level of joyful memories that can carry on in our memory bank for years to come.

So, in the midst of life's hustle and bustle, we need to remember all the little and big things our Lord has done for us—how he got us through the storms of life and provided for us when we needed it the most. God has an appointed time for us to remember everything He's done for you and me throughout our lives—and that's every minute of every day because that type of remembrance will bring more contentment, joy, and peace to our lives (Read Psalm chapter 1).

When we give back to God our heartfelt praise expresses our appreciation for all the ways He has blessed us throughout our life's journey. We're saying, "God, we're grateful and thankful for all You've done in our lives, and we love You and want to honor You." It should be a spiritual prerequisite engrained in the depths of heart, soul, and mind with such a conviction and yearning that it cannot escape us internally without acknowledging our Heavenly Father!

I love this profound statement from John MacArthur. "The more you focus on yourself, the more distracted you will be from the proper path. The more you know Him and commune with Him, the more the Spirit will make you like Him. The more you are like Him, the better you will understand His utter sufficiency for all of life's difficulties. And that is the only way to know real satisfaction."[1]

When we remove our thoughts from all worldly distractions and focus on God first, it shows the disposition of our Christlike hearts. When people dedicate their lives to the Lord, they aim to please Him with a willing, humble, contrite, giving, selfless, and gracious spirit because they recognize and acknowledge God's lovingkindness! It's the foundation of that ongoing relationship with our Lord, which leads to continuous praise, fellowship, and worship.

When we consistently set aside time to magnify the Lord, we keep Him in focus and at the center—as our primary source of preference and reference. Yes, we have times of weekly corporate worship that reinforce God's rightful place over all our affairs. However, it's not a once—or twice-a-week plan; it should be constant—all the time—every beating moment of our daily lives!

The more we exalt God through daily worship from the heart, the smaller our problems seem, and the more manageable life becomes. We can accomplish this type of life when we're diligently in prayer, fervently in the word of God, constantly meditating on His word, always yielding to His ways, and yearning for more of His holiness in our daily lives.

---

1. "John MacArthur Quote."

"All the Time!"

When we apply the truths of Romans 12:1–2 to our lives, we can attain a life of sacrificial holiness (not perfection). Yes, there will be challenges on this side of Heaven, but in that closeness with our Lord all the time, we have a much better chance of spiritual survival—than without Him by our side. This type of spiritual commitment illustrates that we're giving the Lord all our heart, soul, mind, and strength!

Giving back to our Lord should reflect our genuine connection with Him, how much we truly know Him, our heights of honoring and praising Him, and the depths of our trusting Him—every minute of every day. Christians who give back to God sacrificially want to be a part of His business, and this illustrates their real priorities in everyday life. It's not a part-time commitment but an "all-the-time dedication."

Eph 1:3, "All praise to God, the Father of our Lord Jesus, who has blessed us with every spiritual blessing in the heavenly realms because we are united with Christ."

Psalm 103:1–2 says, "Bless the Lord, O my soul, and all that is within me; bless his holy name! Bless the LORD, O my soul, and forget not all his benefits."

Chapter 17

'Godly Accountability'

Deut 17: 2–3, 5, "When you begin living in the towns the Lord your God is giving you, a man or woman among you might do evil in the sight of the Lord your God and violate the covenant. For instance, they might serve other gods—which I have strictly forbidden then the man or woman who has committed such an evil act must be taken to the gates of the town and stoned to death."

This chapter's overarching theme is simply this: "God wanted evil to be purged from the nation of Israel, from His chosen ones." The Israelites struggled to live up to God's standards throughout the Old Testament, so He had to enforce severe ramifications for those who would not comply with His decrees. God wanted to be the King of His children, the nation of Israel. So, He implored (moderately speaking) them to follow His ways mainly since He chose them as His own. God established standards that would keep them in line with His will and plan because they had difficulty with moral rules.

In this passage above, a person was not put to death based on the witness of one; it was on the witness of two or more—and it was a spectacle or display in the town when someone was put to death. The primary purposes of this regulation were: First, the townspeople would witness the pelting of stones upon the guilty with the intent that they would flee from evilness and adhere to God's ways. Two or more had to witness the act of the guilty party to prevent division and from anyone giving false testimony—they had to be of one accord. Second, the accusers would cast the first stones, making them think twice about accusing the guilty unjustly.

As you can see in these powerful illustrations, God wanted His people to be responsible and held accountable for finishing what they initially

'Godly Accountability'

started. Our loving Father provides a way of living a life for Him that embodies godly accountability—because He's given us every resource for living a life that's pleasing to Him. But, just like the Israelites, we seem to have difficulty sticking with the plan as His Citizens of Heaven on Earth. He gives us His word and Spirit to help us achieve His goal from start to finish. Paul reminds us in Philippians chapters 1 and 2 that God, who began a good work in us, will continue this work until it's completed.

Godly accountability is essential to our Lord because we were made in His image and share many of His characteristics. However, how we handle and live out those attributes is critical. The scriptures tell us to live an honorable and pleasing life to God, which glorifies His name. God's word tells us to walk by faith, not by sight, which will indicate if our daily steps are more in tune with Him or the world.

When we are joined to God by our side (Amos 3:3), we are not prone to go in the opposite direction in everyday life. This is vital because if the Lord is attached spiritually to us, we can possess the same desires that will keep us aligned with His will and plan. When we're in that closeness with Christ, we can rightly serve Him as honorable representatives and imitators on this earth (Col 3:17, 1 Cor 11:1, and Eph 5:1).

As genuine followers of Christ, we "Do Not" need to have this mindset and heart: "Do as I say, not as I do," which is a statement of the flesh. Instead, we should possess a mind, heart, and soul, demonstrating this: "What I say is what I do because Jesus is my example." We can only accomplish the latter by living a life yielding to the power of God's word and His Spirit!

Paul reminds us in Romans 3:23 that we have all sinned and fallen short of God's glorious standard. With that in mind, we need the power of His Spirit and words alive in us so we can be raised up from our ashes to the point of being Christians who are godly and accountable to the One Who can set our paths straight. When we truly understand and acknowledge our Lord as the Righteous One and aim to model His life, it displays our level of maturity as Christians who are liable and responsible, realizing that we are answering to Someone who knows every little thing we're up to.

When we do this, we expose genuine Christlike humility, love, obedience, and faith to the One who can help us because we know we are in a constant battle against the enemy. We must realize that Satan knows our weaknesses, and he knows when we are vulnerable. And we cannot afford to live a life as irresponsible believers because if we do, we can become immune to a life that God did not intend for you and me.

From that point of giving our lives to Jesus Christ, we now have the indwelling Spirit living in us, chipping away all those ugly knots. He's shaping, molding, refining, remaking, and redefining us as the new creation He wants us to be daily. Peter reminds us in his second epistle that God's given us every resource to live a godly life—in other words, we have no excuse. Simply put, we have everything we need to live a life that pleases our Holy God.

And here's the power punch. He's allowing us to share in His divine nature through these resources to live a life that honors and glorifies His name. The key is our application of His resources in our daily lives, which should depict our role as Christians who hold ourselves accountable to God alone. This type of godly accountability desires to please the Lord in all their ways of life and never grieve the Holy Spirit.

Below are some key bullet points that will signify if we're "true accountable Christians" in our daily lives.

- We recognize the atoning sacrifice of the price Jesus Christ paid on that cross for our sins. Living by this truth conveys and portrays our spiritual sense of God's grace, mercy, and love. It is then we become-dedicated and loyal Christians (Rom 5:8, Eph 5:2, and Heb 9:28).
- We're not just reading the word but applying it to our lives to attain more of God's wisdom to discern right from wrong, good vs evil. We repent and stray from sin to grow spiritually (Ps 1:2, Ps 119:11, Jas 1:22–25, Phil 4:9, and 2 Tim 2:2).
- It reminds us to model humility and acknowledge that none of us are perfect, but we continue to strive for His glory and eternal rewards (Rom 3:23, Isa 64:6, Phil 3:12–15, Phil 3:14, and Jas 4:6–10).
- We're Kingdom Builders, not destroyers or Kingdom Breakers. We encourage more than discourage to build up the body of Christ.
- Constantly displaying the Fruit of the Spirit: love, joy, peace, patience, kindness, goodness, faithfulness, gentleness, and self-control (Gal 5:22–23, 1 Thess 5:11, Heb 3:13, and 10:24).
- We use our God-given gifts for His glory, honor, and praise (1 Pet 4:10, Jas 1:17, and 1 Corinthians chapter 12).
- We live in complete reverence and respect for our Lord because we know we will give a personal account to God for every action and motive behind those actions (Deut 13:4, 1 Pet 1:15–16, Heb 12:28, Prov 1:7, Prov 9:10, and Titus 2:12).

Rom 14:10–13, "So why do you condemn another believer? Why do you look down on another believer? Remember, we will all stand before the judgment seat of God. The Scriptures say, 'As surely as I live,' says the

'Godly Accountability'

LORD, 'every knee will bend to me, and every tongue will declare allegiance to God.'" Yes, each of us will give a personal account to God. So, let's stop condemning each other. *Decide instead to live in such a way that you will not cause another believer to stumble and fall."*

Chapter 18

'Godly Duties'

Deut 18:1–3, 5: "Remember that the Levitical priests—that is, the whole of the tribe of Levi—will receive no allotment of land among the other tribes in Israel. Instead, the priests and Levites will eat from the special gifts given to the Lord, for that is their share. They will have no land of their own among the Israelites. The Lord himself is their special possession, just as he promised them...For the Lord, your God chose the tribe of Levi out of all your tribes to minister in the Lord's name forever."

The Levite Priests had specific duties, such as teaching people about God and His laws, exemplifying a godly life, caring for the Tabernacle and its furnishings, and distributing offerings; they also served as judges (Deut 17:8–13). But because these assigned men of God could not pursue any other interests outside their God-given assignments, Yahweh established plans within the nation of His people where they would not take advantage of them. With that, the Priests were to be supported by gifts and offerings of God's people, and He expected His children to accept their roles in these godly functions and comply with His commands to take care of their needs.

This was important because the priests had an enormous duty and responsibility once they accepted the role of God's ministers. He required the Priests to live holy lives and to be blameless before Him because if they were innocent before God, no man could point at them with any criticism. God called these men to distinguish between the holy and the profane, the unclean and the clean amongst His children, and be the godly examples of righteousness and holiness. What a high calling!

As noted, for them to perform these godly tasks, Israel must support the Priests in functioning adequately and providing spiritual leadership to God's people, which was vital in staying close to God. By God's grace and

'GODLY DUTIES'

appointment, the Levitical Priests were undoubtedly privileged—for they were His dedicated servants! They proved their wholehearted loyalty to God as His servants, which was evident after the incident of the golden calf in Exodus chapter 32.

But for these remarkable servants to care for God's nation, they had to *accept God's duties willingly and diligently*. To expound on this tribe's specific godly duties, the high priest could deliver mandates to guide the nation and was the only one permitted to enter the Most Holy Place, which contained the Ark of the Covenant, the symbol of God's very presence. God held the priests to the most stringent standards of behavior and ritual purity! This clearly illustrates to you and me that, as His appointed ones (today), we're called to a higher standard of righteousness and holiness that must align with His will for our lives.

What a perfect dovetail from Godly Accountability's last chapter to our Godly Duties! God chose and accepted you and me as His own long before the foundation of this world for a reason and purpose (Eph 1:3–5). He adopted us into His family through Jesus Christ and predestined our lives to be His special possessions to serve Him in various ways. Once we're in His caring hands, God secures us by sending the Holy Spirit as a preserving seal to lock in our faith, as an authenticating symbol to validate our sonship and Lordship, and as protection to keep out destructive forces. But just like the Levite Priests of the nation of Israel, Almighty God does this to prepare us to fulfill a godly duty that is part of His long-term plan. Why is this important?

First, we must understand what godly duty is: "It refers to the specific tasks or actions that a believer is *expected to perform as part of their job as servants of our Heavenly Father and Lord Jesus Christ*. To elaborate on this even more, our day-to-day activities should entail our godly duties as His faithful children. Why? Because they are required to fulfill our roles as His servants as part of a future objective (it's not a part-time position). To put this on an understandable level, godly duty is recognizing that we all are responsible to God first and then others, including our children and family members.

It is performing unselfish acts daily, whether great or small, that blesses, encourages, motivates, and builds up others—it makes the community and world a better place to live. How? It enriches and elevates everyone within our reach! It is powerfully productive when that person takes ownership of their God-given duty as His servants—because it demonstrates that they are not only receiving the power of God's word but also accepting it, applying it, and obeying it. It also illustrates that this selfless believer recognizes their gifts from God and is willing and diligently ready to put them into action.

This level of obligation and commitment should reveal a conclusive and settling fact, and it's this: "The world should see the undeniable duties of the Lord active in our daily lives. Others should visibly see the substance of Jesus Christ as our Living hope in how we conduct our Christian faith and love. You see, once we welcome Jesus into our hearts as Lord of our lives, we have the indwelling Spirit at work in us, and there should be nothing ambiguous or gray in our Christian life as loyal and faithful servants who are set out to fulfill their God-given tasks. Remember, we were accepted, redeemed, and sealed for a purpose: to fulfill an assignment that aligns with our Lord's Great Commission."

Remember what Paul tells us in his first letter to Timothy: "We were saved and redeemed by Almighty God to live a life of holiness." And even the author in Hebrews chapter 12 reminds us that without living a holy life, we cannot see God. Why is this so important, you ask? Once we accept our duties from God and serve Him wholeheartedly, it signifies that we're His possession. As His righteous ones, we're on that path of sanctification towards the end result of holiness. Once again, we're not talking about perfection, but we're striving for that goal Paul referenced in Philippians chapter 3—pressing on towards our eternal goal.

Also, Paul reminds us in Phil 1:6, an essential passage that correlates with our God-given duties as God's servants, "And I am certain that God, who began the good work within you, will continue his work until it is finally finished on the day when Christ Jesus returns." This is so important because when we recognize our God-given duties as followers of Christ, it is a vital stage of our growing phase as His servants—it's part of our sanctification process that should lead to progress.

And here's the key takeaway for you and me. To find our God-given duties, we must go to the pages of God's Word, pray for God's guidance, and yield to His Spirit for clarity. Many believers know what God requires of them but are frustrated by their continual failure to perform what they know they should do. When we are repetitiously in the word of God, observing, learning, interpreting the message, applying His commands, and obeying them, we start to attain more of God's wisdom and knowledge and acknowledge our gifts and talents. Then, we hold ourselves accountable for all the things God has endowed in our lives as His Citizens of Heaven on Earth! We put them into motion!

This beautiful passage in Philippians reminds us that God's work in us is a continuous journey, emphasizing His steadfastness and our role in His divine narrative. It's a testament to God's Faithful Completion and His unending commitment to us until our Lord Jesus Christ returns. Much like an artist chiseling away at a sculpture, God refines, molds, and perfects us daily so we can perform our God-given duties with honor and praise to Him alone.

When we know beyond a shadow of a doubt what our duties are as His chosen ones, it's a comfort and peace to understand our purpose in this life as His special possession. We're His appointed laborers, messengers, representatives, and ambassadors who desire and drive to live for God daily. Peter reminds us in 1 Pet 4:10, "God has given each of you a gift from his great variety of spiritual gifts. Use them well to serve one another." We are now more aligned with the characteristics of God, and the world has noticed that trademark in our daily lives.

So, I beg the question: "Does the world see the label of a committed Christian in our lives—one who holds themselves responsible for the tasks God has set before them for the state of spirituality?" Does our community of believers see a person so entrenched with their godly duties as God's special possession—they know we're obligated, loyal, respectful, aligned, committed, and faithful to the One Who has given us a charge and mission to pass on His Good News to others? Is God's stamp of approval so visible in our lives inwardly and outwardly—everyone knows that our first chore on any given day is solely dedicated to fulfilling God's will and plan in our daily lives. Why is this so important?

The seal of God symbolizes three primary themes: ownership, authenticity, and protection. It signifies that we belong to God, who has chosen us as His children and redeemed us by His grace for a purpose and plan today, tomorrow, and the future. But just as important, it also testifies to the genuine nature of our saving faith, backed up by the power of the Holy Spirit at work in our lives for others and, most importantly, our Lord.

The word *sealed* in the New Testament comes from a Greek word that means "to stamp with a private mark" to keep something secret or protect or preserve that sealed object. In other words, from a spiritual perspective, that person is distinct from the unbelieving world because deep inside, they should possess a spirit that blocks out the world's evilness, stops the darkness from taking control of their lives, and shuts down any falsehoods trying to creep in. *Remember, a believer and follower of Christ should be identified by God's seal of approval, not by the world's standards.* We are more in tune with our duties as God's servants than anything else. It is noticeable to everyone!

For example, we must be responsible for our actions toward others (Luke 10:30–37). We are accountable for how we treat our families (1 Tim 5:8). We are responsible for studying God's Word and applying and living by His truths (2 Tim 2:15). We are implored to pass on His goodness and greatness to the next generation of believers. We must pray, serve, and care for others in need, which is God's command. We are called to forgive others and use words of grace. We are to edify, encourage, and build up the body of Christ. We are accountable for how we steward money (Heb 13:5). We are even called to carry other people's burdens (Gal 6:2). In other words, walk alongside them with all of the mercy, grace, and love He abounds in our lives for that person's well-being! When others are weak, we can help lift them up and strengthen them through the power of God.

Godly duty is a delight and desire to love and obey God's work in our lives—it is not how much we do—but how much we love. If a servant does not do his work willingly out of love, it is not acceptable in the eyes of God—there is no driven purpose. Our God-given duties for our Lord should be so enfolded by God's love, mercy, and grace that they are not burdensome to us—because it's a privilege and honor to serve Him because He's saved and called us for that reason!

Once we receive and accept God's will and purpose in our lives, our godly duties are not passive—but actively aggressive. It should produce a life of fervent prayer, fasting, obedience, repenting, and surrendering to His higher purpose and calling. As we will see later in this journey, acceptance recognizes that the God who spoke His very words in existence still controls our lives, and the world should recognize this fact in us by the power of His word and Spirit! Accepting our godly duty is an all-out passion for serving the Lord with all our heart, soul, mind, and strength—no matter what comes our way.

When God's children are confronted with personal struggles, we may not want to receive the challenge of our godly duties, but we should be prepared to accept, embrace, and enforce them. Why? We have absolute confidence and trust in Whom we can rely upon when our times are so intense we want to throw in the towel and not serve (danger zone). However, in the end— after one victory at a time, He gets the glory and honor, and it brings Him great pleasure to see these results in our lives.

God expects you and me to accept our duty as His servants on this earth with confidence and boldness. In a famous passage in Josh 24:15, God's word tells us, "As for me and my house, we will serve the Lord." What does this mean? We serve Him with all we have, our heart, soul, mind, and strength every minute of every day. During the tests of time, we face them with the type of faith that is fervently rooted in the power of God! There is no relenting or regretting; we aim to show others Who possesses the inside of us.

We're called to do what He says and exemplify His greatness and goodness in all that we say and do! Paul reminds us in Phil 2:14-15, "Do everything without complaining and arguing so that no one can criticize you. Live clean, innocent lives as children of God, shining like bright lights in a world full of crooked and perverse people." We're implored to glorify God daily so others will see the thrill of living for Him. We should feel urged to show His authority in our lives with gladness and joy as Christ-followers in this society and culture of today!

So, the kind of service that makes God look valuable and thrilling in our lives is the kind that serves God by "constantly receiving and willingly 'accepting' from God all the resources He's provided." Utilizing our God-given gifts to glorify Him, such as in 1 Peter 4:11, "Do it with all the strength and energy that God supplies. Then everything you do will bring glory to God through Jesus Christ." When we apply God's teachings in our daily lives, God is seen as glorious when all our serving is moment-by-moment, receiving and accepting the riches and excellent resources He's provided. This can be accomplished through an ongoing and consistent connection with our Lord.

Our level of acceptance of God at work in our lives—through the power of His word and Spirit will illustrate our genuine connection with Him, His authentic seal of godliness in our daily life, and our valid Christ-like identification. It will reveal a humbling belief and consent that we are loved and accepted unconditionally, even though we are unworthy. That honest relationship will expose the lack of our self-worth and realize our need for Him.

In this level of growth and obligation, we see His hands of discipline as acts of lovingkindness because deep inside, He wants us to accept His training as a godly guide in everyday life (Hebrews chapter 12). We understand and have a greater sense of hope to get us through life's difficulties because it is no longer about self—but Him in us performing those godly duties that will assist in building His Kingdom (Gal 2:20).

That type of connection will result in this: We will "Serve the Lord with gladness," as the Psalmist says in Psalm 100:2. Also, in Phil 2:12–13, "Dear friends, you always followed my instructions when I was with you. And now that I am away, it is even more important. Work hard to show the results of your salvation, obeying God with deep reverence and fear. For God is working in you, giving you the desire and the power to do what pleases him."

Chapter 19

'God's Refuge'

Deut 19:8-10, "And if the Lord your God enlarges your territory, as he swore to your ancestors, and gives you all the land he promised them, you must designate three additional cities of refuge. (He will give you this land if you carefully obey all the commands I have given you—if you always love the Lord your God and walk in his ways.) That way, you will prevent the death of innocent people in the land the Lord your God is giving you as your special possession. You will not be held responsible for the death of innocent people."

As Israel expanded throughout the Land, there would be more cities of refuge as part of the distribution of the Promised Land. These cities of refugees, discussed in Numbers chapter 35, are where someone accused of murder could flee to protect himself from the dead person's relatives. The leaders of these refuge cities were to hold a trial and determine the facts of the case. FYI—a list of the cities of refuge is found in Josh 20:7-8.

After judgment had been handed down and it was determined that the manslayer or murderer was not guilty (Num 35:24), he was to remain in that city of refuge. Therefore, anyone who accidentally killed someone would "only" be protected in those designated cities. If he left the city any time before *"the death of the high priest,"* he would no longer be protected— it would be his fault if he were killed. What a great example that shows us that when someone makes an unfortunate decision, it can lead to death— because they fled their ultimate place of safety.

The Psalmist provides us with strong words of reassurance of Who our Shelter is in Psalm chapter 46, "God is our refuge and strength, always ready to help in times of trouble. So, we will not fear when earthquakes come, and the mountains crumble into the sea." What would be your immediate

'God's Refuge'

reaction if you heard the mainstream news spreading the word that our nation was about to experience an earthquake or nuclear blast that would crumble this nation's existence? Would it be absolute fear, worry, and anxiety, or trusting God? Who or what would be your hiding place?

In this powerful Psalm, the writer tells us that no matter the utter destruction coming our way, there should be within each one of us a total belief that God can save us. We often worry about life's physicality but forget about the most important thing: our spiritual position in Christ. A beautiful reminder of those who genuinely seek refuge in the Lord is found in Proverbs 18:10, "The name of the LORD is a strong fortress; the godly run to him and are safe." The operative word in this passage is that the "godly runs" to the Lord!

Knowing God as our refuge enables us to trust Him more freely, and we need not fear situations or people who threaten our well-being, whether physically or spiritually. No situation we will ever face is out of God's control, so the best place to be is always right with Him in His sheltering arms of love, grace, peace, and understanding.

A question that often arises is, "How do I make God my refuge?" It's easy to picture a physical refuge protecting us from some danger, but how can we make God—whom we can't see—our refuge? David is an excellent example of someone who knew God as his refuge. At different points in his life, David was on the run from people who literally wanted to kill him, but he always found safety in God (Ps 62:7–8). An easy way to make God our refuge is to ask Him to be our Protector and Shield. David said, "Pour out your hearts to him," and that's what David always did. He poured out his heart to God about what was happening in his life and asked God to intervene. When we turn to God for help or protection, we begin to know Him as our refuge.[1]

This is important! God becomes our refuge when we trust His Word more than we trust the culture, social media, mainstream news, or even our own feelings of anxiety. The world tells us to "listen to our hearts," but God says our hearts will deceive us (Jer 17:9). God's Word is the only place we find security and protection. Why? Because it is the only source of Truth and faithful promises that will be fulfilled. Take joy in what God reminds us of in His word. Instead of doubting, we can live with "absolute" confidence that God will be with us through it all! He is our spiritual haven during all our storms in life.

Sadly, many believers today are struck with high levels of a worrisome spirit because of all the falsehoods, trials, and temptations surrounding us.

---

1. Got Questions. "How God Is Our Refuge?"

When we get enwrapped and engulfed in human theories of propaganda and spreading news contrary to God's word, it can lead us to an unstable and imbalanced spirit that is not spiritually healthy. But, as steadfast followers of Jesus Christ, our foundation is in the Rock of Ages, not shifting sand, because one of the most incredible positions of refuge is our relationship with Jesus Christ, which is eternal security.

Do you ever feel insecure about your salvation and inheritance in Christ? Today, so many question the assurance of their salvation and their eternal protection. But here's the key: The steady progression of our spiritual walk and obedience to His word is evidence of our linking identity in Christ. While we can also have reassurance by dwelling amongst our believing brothers and sisters in Christ and the Church, we should have confidence that we are saved based on God's promises—because God is the embodiment of all Truth, which means He cannot lie.

When we come to Christ and possess Him as our blanket of protection, not just for today but for the future, we're secured in His promises once and for all. We don't need to wonder and ponder because God does not change. He's faithful and true to His word forever. We should have the assurance from Christ's Word that our salvation will never be questioned because, as His loyal followers, we know He has us in the palm of His nail-scarred hands.

Our lifeline and means of escape are based on the perfect and complete salvation God has provided for us through His Son, Jesus Christ. Once a believer is anchored under the blood of Christ, there is an overwhelming sense of joy—and a peace that surpasses all our understanding. Once we are sealed, it is fastened and fixed forever. But the only way we can ensure this salvation of security is by running to Christ and accepting Him as Lord and Savior of our life. Because if anyone flees and goes in the opposite direction, calamity awaits, leading to a path of destruction that no one wants.

When we surrender and submit to our Lord and run to him for help and trust, we have reached the point of giving it to Someone Who has more power and authority than we do individually. Always remember, His place of refuge is where we find spiritual healing, strength to face perpetual difficulties, and learning to be gracious, merciful, forgiving, and loving to those who hurt us. What a place of security and comfort to rest in!

Our Heavenly Father and Lord remind us that they will never leave or forsake us throughout the Old and New Testaments. That's His promise to you and me, no matter how dire our circumstances may seem. But here's a gut punch and challenge for you and me: "Those who are genuinely centered in the will of God will also commit to the Lord that no matter what, they will not leave or forsake Him!" That's a spiritual commitment that cuts to soul and spirit. *Think about it—He is always there for us, so are we always there for Him?*

Hebrews 6:18 says, "So God has given both his promise and his oath. These two things are unchangeable because God can't lie. Therefore, we who have fled to him for refuge can have great confidence as we hold to the hope that lies before us."

Eph 4:30, "And do not bring sorrow to God's Holy Spirit by how you live. Remember, he has identified you as his own, guaranteeing you will be saved on the day of redemption."

Chapter 20

'Our Opposition'

Deut 20:1-4, "When you go out to fight your enemies, and you face horses and chariots and an army greater than your own, do not be afraid. The Lord your God, who brought you out of the land of Egypt, is with you! When you prepare for battle, the priest must come forward to speak to the troops. He will say to them, 'Listen to me, all you men of Israel! Do not be afraid as you go out to fight your enemies today! Do not lose heart or panic or tremble before them. For the Lord, your God is going with you! He will fight for you against your enemies, and he will give you victory!'"

Before Israel crossed the Jordan and entered the Promised Land, they were a small nation of people that would go up against armies and nations larger and stronger than them. However, God reminds us in Deut 9:1-3, "Listen, O Israel! Today, you are about to cross the Jordan River to take over the land belonging to nations much greater and more powerful than you. They live in cities with walls that reach to the sky! The people are strong and tall descendants of the famous Anakite giants. You've heard the saying, 'Who can stand up to the Anakites?' But recognize today that the LORD your God is the one who will cross over ahead of you like a devouring fire to destroy them. He will subdue them so that you will quickly conquer them and drive them out, just as the LORD has promised."

God's army was rarely in an exceptional position (strategically) against their enemies, but this was part of God's plan where He could display His almighty power and glory. You see, so often in battle, the Israelites would visibly see more horses, chariots, and opposing forces than them—how intimidating this must have been. But regardless of the visible danger in front of them, they were "commanded" by God not to fear! Even to this day, the nation of Israel is even smaller than it was in the Old Testament days, surrounded by opposing nations that seem much superior to them. But God's promise, provision, and protection for His chosen nation still stands today and will until the end! No opposition can come up against our Almighty God!

When the Israelites went into battle, they were never to fear their opposition. Why? Because the strength of the military did not determine the outcome, but by the One Who said, 'I am with you, do not be dismayed—I will never leave you or forsake you'! Even when they could see more horses, chariots, and people before their physical eyes, the Almighty One gave them a more significant and superior reason not to fear but to have absolute faith in His provisions and promises. Remember, like then— and even today— God is always faithful to His children by His words.

When He exclaimed— "The Lord God is with you," this was to be taken for what it meant from our Sovereign God! Yahweh expected them to have trust and confidence in His words; after all, they witnessed firsthand God's proven ability to be faithful throughout their journey in the wilderness. This passage from Paul in Romans 8:31 is always a good reminder for us when confronted by the opposition: *"If God is for us, who can be against us?"* One who has God on their side makes for an unbeatable partnership.

And just like the Israelites, we often experience overwhelming opposition daily. It does not matter where we may be; sometimes, we feel outnumbered and helpless because the opposing ones against us seem insurmountable. Why? It's evident as Christians today that our position as followers of Jesus Christ is a threat and opposition to the unbelieving world.

As our times on this earth come to an end, it is becoming more evident that the opposing ones starkly contrast with the true believers in Jesus Christ because of their clashing and conflicting ways. Remember, God tells us not to love or follow their life patterns. Why? Because we're to be set apart from the world and strive for His holiness—we are on a completely different path than the unbelievers.

It should be no surprise that we're in a battle—not against man's flesh but the spiritual forces of evil and darkness (Eph 6:12). These opposing forces today can dishearten and demotivate our charge in serving the Lord, which shows just how weak we are when we attempt to do things in our strength. When these types of forces confront us, many believers stray away in fear because they feel inadequate to stand upon the Truth of God's word. We cannot afford to allow the opposing forces to get the best of us when we have the Lord on our side.

One of the main reasons we feel weak against the enemy, which is too often, is because we've drifted away from God and lost that connection of power through His Spirit and Word (Heb 2:1–4). Living without Christlike structure or discipline leads to a daily life that is not in spiritual order and will always be in disarray. That is the enemy's strategy because He does not want us on our knees in prayer, our hearts and minds in the word of God, and our spirits in sync with the Holy Spirit. The enemy knows how to lead us astray and distract us in everyday life, leading to a weakened and defeated spirit when evil forces are in front of us. But you and I can counter this tactic from the enemy by applying this passage below, which is from Jesus's half-brother.

Jas 4:7–10, "So humble yourselves before God. Resist the devil, and he will flee from you. Come close to God, and God will come close to you. Wash your hands, you sinners; purify your hearts, for your loyalty is divided between God and the world. Let there be tears for what you have done. Let there be sorrow and deep grief. Let there be sadness instead of laughter and gloom instead of joy. Humble yourselves before the Lord, and he will lift you up in honor."

Jesus Christ tells us in John 14:15 that *if we genuinely love Him, then obey My commandments.* This is important because that type of supernatural obedience aligns our real love in the heart of His word; our affections are no longer misplaced, and we don't get the sense of discouragement or confusion. We now sense the power of endurance, perseverance, joy, peace, patience, and self-control, which can lead to more wisdom, confidence, and boldness in standing up to the opposition.

When we make God's guiding principle more second nature in our lives versus the habitual ways of the world, we will always have a scale tilting more with the abundance of the Lord on our side than the forces out to destroy us. And here's the Good News when God is on our side!

- God can strengthen, defend, and deliver us from the power and wickedness of the enemy (2 Tim 4:17–18).
- Our enemy may be strong, but God is stronger (1 John 4:4).
- God, in all His faithfulness, enables us with the same mighty power that raised Jesus Christ from the dead! (Eph 1:19–20).
- Our enemies are defeated through Christ's victory on the cross (Col 2:15).
- "For the battle is the Lord's!" declared David (1 Sam 17:47), and this should be our cry as we engage in spiritual warfare.

Remember, focusing on the wrong enemy weakens our cause because our fight is not against flesh and blood, as mentioned earlier. Our spiritual position is strengthened when we know our battle is already won, and that's when we solely depend more on the King and Lord in our daily lives! Because Christ is the Victor yesterday, today, and forever! That is why it is so vital for believers to pray for a discerning spirit. Why? So they can possess a better understanding of God's wisdom in His word so they will know where the root of lies and deceptions are coming from. Our #1 enemy on this side of eternity will do everything he can to deceive us to the point of failing.

Will there be times when we sense failure in life? Yes! When we have that sense of failing, our first reaction may be to run or give up, but by God's grace, we get back up again and start over. When it comes to sin, we can all avoid and flee from it because we are reminded of what Paul tells us in Phil 4:13: "For I can do everything through Christ, Who gives me strength." Even with our abiding love, faith, and devotion to God, we can and will fall in this life.

But guess what? God is not shocked and caught off guard, so He sent His Son to die for our sins. We must continually remind ourselves of this; we cannot face our opposition alone. We must keep our eyes on the Savior and Redeemer who can bring us through all our fights in life. We must heed (trust and obey) His word and lay aside the sin that can inevitably lead us to spiritual failings.

The author in Hebrews 12:1–4 reminds us, "Therefore since we are surrounded by such a huge crowd of witnesses to the life of faith, let us strip off every weight that slows us down, especially the sin that so easily trips us up. And let us run with endurance the race God has set before us. We do this by keeping our eyes on Jesus, the champion who initiates and perfects our faith. Because of the joy awaiting him, he endured the cross, disregarding its shame. Now, he is seated in the place of honor beside God's throne. Think of all the hostility he endured from sinful people; then, you won't become weary and give up. After all, you have not yet given your lives in your struggle against sin."

In this journey, God has marked out a course for us, including the good, the bad, and the ugly. But when we cling to the Savior, even our failures can be turned into successes by the One who controls everything and strengthens us in our weaknesses. Our ultimate victory in Jesus is assured, but complete victory will only come when we are out of this world of temptation and safe in the arms of the Lord in Heaven. What a glorious day that will be. But in the meantime, we are still called to be His Light in this darkened world and Citizens of Heaven on Earth.

A constant reminder for us in our daily life—when we're in a battle against the enemy, we should lie in the power of Jesus Christ's words to Paul when he was struggling with that thorn in his flesh. In 2 Cor 12:8–10,

Christ tells Paul profoundly, "Three different times I begged the Lord to take it away. Each time, he said, "My grace is all you need. My power works best in weakness." So now I am glad to boast about my weaknesses so that the power of Christ can work through me. That's why I take pleasure in my weaknesses and in the insults, hardships, persecutions, and troubles that I suffer for Christ. For when I am weak, then I am strong. "

Don't forget this important daily reminder: Even though it is God's will for His children to grow stronger in faith and to labor to advance His kingdom on this Earth, God does not remove the opposition in our life's journey. In other words, if you and I respond appropriately and more spiritually, the opposition will drive us to greater reliance on the Lord—with an incredible determination to do what He has called us to do, and that's to be more Christlike!

Always remember, no matter the opposing forces, they will never have as much power over us as the power of God, Who is inside us. Therefore, through the daily application of His word and guidance of His Spirit in our lives, we need to learn how to use this power to our advantage because He's always by our side, ready to defend our cause. Those little victories in our lives bring so much glory, honor, and praise to our Lord!

Even in our most minor battles with those temptations confronting us in today's society and culture, another passage for us to take comfort in is found in 1 Cor 10:12-13, "Therefore let anyone who thinks that he stands take heed lest he fall. No temptation has overtaken you that is not common to man. God is faithful, and he will not let you be tempted beyond your ability, but with the temptation, he will also provide the way of escape, that you may be able to endure it." Always remember what the Psalmist tells us in Ps 46:1, "God is our refuge and strength, always ready to help in times of trouble."

And we cannot forget one of the greatest examples of all when Jesus was tempted by the enemy in the wilderness, Matt 4:1-4 reminds us profoundly, "Then Jesus was led by the Spirit into the wilderness to be tempted there by the devil. For forty days and forty nights, he fasted and became very hungry. During that time, the devil came and said to him, "If you are the Son of God, tell these stones to become loaves of bread." But Jesus told him, "No! The Scriptures say, 'People do not live by bread alone, but by every word that comes from the mouth of God.'"

Chapter 21

'Godly Parents'

Deut 21:18–21, "Suppose a man has a stubborn and rebellious son who will not obey his father or mother, even though they discipline him. In such a case, the father and mother must take the son to the elders as they hold court at the town gate. The parents must say to the elders, 'This son of ours is stubborn and rebellious and refuses to obey. He is a glutton and a drunkard.' Then, all the men of his town must stone him to death. In this way, you will purge this evil from among you, and all Israel will hear about it and be afraid."

There is no evidence that this type of punishment ever took place. Still, the critical point in God's word is this—He's telling us rebellious acts or disobedience would not be accepted or tolerated in the homes. Of course, there had to be checks and balances, but purging this type of rebellion from the community was required to protect God's children from any evil having a domino effect throughout the nation of Israel.

God clearly shows us in these passages that He does not tolerate corruption among His children. Why? Because any sin separates us from the will of God. So, in all of Yahweh's grace, mercy, and love, this purging of evilness was for their good, but most importantly, it was part of His divine plan for future generations. However, a pivotal point in this passage then and for us today is that the parents were responsible for their children's actions, so God wanted them to teach His ways of holiness and godliness at the early stages of their lives.

While this did not necessarily pertain to a young child, it dealt with a child at the age of accountability. This is an interesting topic for many parents today. So, I beg the question. What is the age of accountability? Many Jewish customs have a set age of 13. But no scripture in God's word gives a specific age. So, a better way to look at the age of being held responsible is from this perspective below:

When someone is at a certain "age" or a particular period in their life, *"clearly understanding their condition and 'knowing how they should react or respond' in support of that situation, is a telltale sign of their keen awareness."* In other words, *when their consciousness level of awareness and knowledge is engaged, it helps them choose between right and wrong or good and evil. This tells us that it's on a case-by-case basis in many situations.* Let's face it: Everyone's stage of maturity varies by person. That is why it is so vital we start embedding the principles of God's word into our children's lives as soon as possible!

Outside of our relationship with Jesus Christ—and husband and wife (man & woman), no other bond is as important as the one between parents and children. To put this into a spiritual perspective, the first four of the ten commandments are how we relate to God, but the final six pertain to us as true believers—who love and abide by His laws. *And here's the point: the first commandment of the six that relates to us individually is "Honor your father and mother. Then you will live a long, full life in the land the Lord your God is giving you."* (Exod 20:12)

This is the first commandment with a promise attached, which is essential for us to understand today. God promised that for the Israelites to live a life of peace for generations in the land, they would be required to respect authority and build families on the solid foundation and principles of God's teachings. This was important because honoring parents means we act to show them the courtesy and respect they deserve.

But always remember what we covered at the beginning of this book: "In many cases, our children look to us as their role models, and they will reciprocate (do the same in return) in how their parents taught and treated them." If we teach them the importance of the right type of respect and reverence at an early stage of their lives, embodied with God's love, mercy, and grace, they will not only respect their parents in the right and loving way that establishes godly unity—but also fear God out of the due reverence and respect He deserves.

As the mother who bore a child into life's existence and the father as the spiritual leader—they are to be revered and honored as one by the children. We are to obey them based on the teachings of God's word, which is an example of putting God first. When we apply the core fundamentals of this commandment to our daily lives, we will also discover that God is teaching us to respect all authorities outside the walls of our home (Rom 13:1).

'Godly Parents'

And here's the gut punch: "If we are not obeying at home in all of God's ways, more than likely, we will not obey any other authorities outside our home." We only draw the line when any authority teaches ways opposite to God's word. But even in these situations, we still clothe ourselves with tenderhearted mercy, humility, kindness, gentleness, and patience (Col 3:12–17) and show Whom we represent and honor above all.

Parents are essential in the eyes of God, as we see throughout the scriptures. Even when we struggle to get along with our parents, we are still commanded to honor them. God wants us to exemplify Christlikeness and the Fruit of the Spirit (Gal 5:22–23) in this most important relationship, for it can build Christlike generations for years to come. When we honor our fathers and mothers with diligence and persistence, especially when it is not easy or comfortable, *it proves that we are God's* children of promise, His chosen and precious children of our Heavenly Father. In doing this, we exhibit our actual possession and position in Him. (Eph 6:1–3)

In the power of our obedience and love for God's commandments, He promises a life of joy, peace, and security that other children or family members may not get the opportunity to experience. What do I mean by this? As an Instructor for the National Fatherhood Initiative, an alarming statistic still rattles my spiritual cage to this day. And that's this: 90% of homeless children come from a fatherless home. That is why we need more structured families grounded in the Truths of God's word with Christ at the center.

So, keep this in mind: As godly families, we can powerfully portray how we can be God's light in someone's dark world. Always remember that honoring our parents is about respecting *God and His word* because God instructs us to do this. Keeping and obeying our Father's commandments builds deeper and broader channels in our hearts for respecting and loving *Him, first and foremost*.[1] Plus, it sends a message to others that we're representing God's teaching in our lives as parents and children.

God said in Gen 1:26, "Let us make human beings in Our image, to be like Us. They will reign over the fish in the sea, the birds in the sky, the livestock, all the wild animals on the earth, and the small animals that scurry along the ground." So, God created human beings in his own image. In the image of God, he created them; male and female, he created them. Then God blessed them and said, "Be fruitful and multiply. Fill the earth and govern it."

In these powerful passages, being a parent takes its original pattern and precedence from God Himself. The new life of a child that a mother bears into this world started with the intimate love between a husband and

---

1. "Honor the Parents God Gave You."

wife, which began with God's unconditional love for you and me. Think about the power of God's love for each of us individually, which should be carried on through all our descendants for generations to come.

So, are we, as parents, teaching our children the example of God's love in the union of familyhood? Are we embodying the role of accountable godly parents in our homes—raising, nurturing, and teaching our children the same way God taught His chosen ones, the Israelites, through their life's journey? What is our benchmark of guiding principles that we are incorporating as examples of God-fearing parents so we can pass down generations of godliness for years to come? Ownership starts with the parents, so our children have something to live by as a guide for their heirs.

Today, biblical accountability is needed more than ever before. Why? Because there's a falling away from the structure and discipline of God's teachings in many lives. As believers, we must take responsibility for our actions as individuals in our homes, schools, churches, community, and abroad as parents. We should earnestly and desperately seek conscious choices in our daily lives with the help of the Holy Spirit. When we ask for God's help and heed His advice, it shows the world that our dependence in life is leaning more towards the One who can lead us more pleasingly in teaching and guiding our children according to God's plan. It is the only chance of generational survival we have!

As stated earlier, and I cannot say this enough, how we rear our children in ways pleasing to God can reciprocate (respond and return) in favorable, beautiful, and glorious ways for years to come. Please remember, "Fathers and mothers are God's constituted home authority" (Proverbs 1:8; 6:20–22). They are appointed in spiritual positions to bring their children up, look after them, nurture and train them along godly paths, and admonish (rebuke) them away from ungodly ones. Fathers and mothers who do not discipline their children are themselves undisciplined and disobedient to God's will. Paul sums it up beautifully below in the book of Ephesians.

Eph 6:1–4, "Children, obey your parents because you belong to the Lord, for this is the right thing to do. "Honor your father and mother." This is the first commandment with a promise: If you honor your father and mother, "things will go well for you, and you will have a long life on the earth." Fathers, do not provoke your children to anger by the way you treat them. Rather, bring them up with the discipline and instruction that comes from the Lord."

Chapter 22

'Detestable Deception'

Deut 22:5, "A woman must not put on men's clothing, and a man must not wear women's clothing. Anyone who does this is detestable in the sight of the Lord your God."

In this short and profound passage, God commands men and women not to reverse the original sexual role He assigned and appointed in their respective lives. He wanted His children to distinguish between the two sexes He supernaturally created, and anyone who failed to observe this law and disobeyed God's decree was considered an abomination to the Lord. We must remember that since the creation of the world, God has a purpose in making you and me uniquely and intricately male and female for a grand purpose and plan, which will glorify Him.

This was not only because cross-dressing was a feature of paganism and idolatrous worship in the ancient world but also because of the terrible cultural price that is paid when it is pretended that there is no difference between men and women that God designed since the beginning. This is distasteful in the eyes of God because "cross-dressing" is done to deceive or to present oneself as something that he/she is not.[1] Our true identity in life should reflect our Perfect Savior and Redeemer, Jesus Christ!

Deception is the main trickery of the enemy because Satan's primary weapon is deceit. He is described as the "serpent of old, called the Devil and Satan, who deceives the whole world" (Rev 12:9). Satan uses many techniques to deceive us to sin, and transgenderism is one of the epic proportions and on the rise worldwide. The enemy is the father of lies and wants

---

1. Enduring Word. "Various Laws in Deuteronomy."

to lead anyone from the Truth of God's purpose and plan in the lives of His children. God longs for us to bring glory and honor to His name, not shame.

We must understand that Almighty God does not make mistakes, for He is Sovereign and All-Knowing and never leads His children down a path of confusion—but of righteousness and holiness. The Psalmist reminds us in Ps 18:30, "God's way is perfect. All the Lord's promises prove true. He is a shield for all who look to him for protection." Believing and staying steadfast in the Truth of God's word is not a crutch to the weak; it is a stronghold of Truth and protection for anyone who feels vulnerable during specific trials. When we surrender our weaknesses to Him and submit ourselves humbly to His will, He will uphold, strengthen, and guide us in all His glorious ways.

However, if we fall prey to Satan's tactics and become doers of any paganist or unholy culture or ways opposite God's word—we have now been deceived and snared in this state of delusion by the enemy's work. If this happens, we will find ourselves *'not doers of God's Holy word'* (Jas 1:22). God's true children must put His guiding biblical principles into action daily because His word and commandments have all our answers in everyday life. As His children, we need to be steadfast in 'all His Truths,' not just those that fit our self-satisfaction, comfort, and a lifestyle of worldly contentment.

If we ignore God's word or counsel, it will lead us to deception, destruction, and more sinful acts. That is why God tells us to be careful and pay attention to His guiding ways (read 2 Peter chapter 1). Why? Because when we're out of compliance, we will be more vulnerable (susceptible) to leaning toward our own ways in this life versus the ways of God. Then, it becomes a domino effect that can lead our lives out of control and further away from His teachings. That's why it is so vital that we act upon our personal convictions ASAP. The book of James (Jesus' half-brother) is a powerful source for acknowledging His truths. I challenge you to read all five chapters because you will assuredly get convicted in some area of your life that needs correction.

Remember, to live a life of godly order and discipline, we must pay close attention to God's guidance daily. Why? Because in His word, He provides us with practical examples and reasoning, making it easier for us to make righteous decisions according to what God wants—but only if we apply His word to our lives. Remember what the Apostle John tells us in 1 John 5:3–5, "Loving God means keeping his commandments, and his commandments are not burdensome. For every child of God defeats this evil world, and we achieve this victory through our faith. And who can win this battle against the world? *Only those who believe that Jesus is the Son of God.*"

In the power of this passage in 1 John, Jesus tells you and me that He never promised obeying Him would be easy. In fact, He reminds us in Matt 11:22 that this evil world will hate us because we're followers of Christ. But He also gives us words of comfort and spiritual strength when He says in this same verse, "But those who endure to the end will be saved." This is why we must put forth an all-out effort in serving and following Him with all our hearts, minds, souls, and strength. Why? Because there will be no burden to anyone for following the ways of our Lord Jesus Christ—for this shows our genuine love and commitment to His word.

Yes, there will be times when our spiritual wagon of worries, doubts, fears, and anxiousness is overloaded, and it will seem that we cannot bear anymore in this world of deception and lies. However, in Matt 11:28–30, Christ reminds us, "Then Jesus said, "Come to me, all of you who are weary and carry heavy burdens, and I will give you rest. Take my yoke upon you. Let me teach you because I am humble and gentle at heart, and you will find rest for your souls. For my yoke is easy to bear, and the burden I give you is light."

We must constantly remind ourselves of this daily: "If our confident hope, foundation, and identity in Jesus Christ sway just one inkling, we will abandon ourselves to the ways and standards of this culture, which is a danger zone." This is so important in today's crazy world because a faith that wavers is disloyal to God and His teachings and cannot advance spiritually (James chapter 1). If we don't observe God's word, interpret its message, and apply it in all life's circumstances, we will grieve the Holy Spirit and hinder our growth and maturity as Christians. We cannot afford to lose our love for obeying God's teaching in all areas of our lives. Why? Because it can surely drift us away and lead to a severe disconnect from our Lord (read Hebrews chapter 2).

One of the reasons why some "so-called believers" become unfaithful and let God down is because they are no longer students of His word—but more of the world. These are what I call "Dabbling Christians." In other words, they are superficial and, if not just as bad, hypocritical. They are so deceived in their seemingly Christian Walk that there is no evidence of fruitful righteousness in their daily life. They want to tinker with the ways of the world and its unholy practices—and have a piece of Christ at the same time. Jesus tells us, "We cannot serve two masters, for we will love one and hate the other" (Matt 6:24).

When we get outwitted by the deceiving one, we lose our connection to God's teachings. Then, we no longer yield to His Spirit and listen to our fellow believers in Christ. How can this happen? Day by day, humankind is falling prey to the enemy because it is leaning more toward its own understanding, self-desires, and man's ways of teaching—versus God's word. It makes me wonder about the teachings of the Apostle John in 1 John 2:19: "They were never a part of us." If that doesn't get our attention, I don't know what will.

This is why when our Lord says, "If anyone has an ear, let him hear," He attempts to get our attention for a reason. Remember, the ones with ears "who will listen" are *those true believers* who have been given the word of God and heed it—and what a measuring stick of spiritual performance. God has given us all the godly resources we need to live a life that honors Him, but are we doing it? Are you and I more in tune as listeners of God's word where we've accepted and live by its Truths, or more in tune with the ways of the world?

Unfortunately, we live in a society that has lost its identity, who they are supposed to be in Christ, and their primary purpose in life. After all, we were created in the image of God, and we're to bring glory to His name in how we live our daily lives. Woefully, many don't desire to be a new creation in Jesus Christ because their preference is in the ways of unholy practices. They allow the enemy to obscure their vision from God's righteousness, which can lead anyone to a state of depravity.

God's word reminds us in Romans chapter 1, beginning with verse 18, that God shows His anger from Heaven against sinful acts and wicked people who suppress the Truth. Instead of worshipping an Almighty God who created them for His use, humans have chosen to live a life that does not honor God and, if anything, brings shame to His holy name. And in humans' selfish and vile decisions, God abandoned them to whatever shameful things their hearts desired.

While we all know that Satan is not omniscient like Almighty God, and he cannot force us to sin, he can place thoughts into our minds and lead us into temptation as a powerful strategy to lure us into sinful acts and away from the words of God. He can easily deceive us when our pattern of sin is more habitual, which leads us to be easy prey. He can make us believe the things that are good for us are harmful and, on the flip side, trick us into thinking the things *that we know are bad for us* are good. Always remember, Satan confuses us and makes us question anything that is for our Christlike good. He has muddled the minds of so many people in this society because they are either spiritually blind or not genuine students of God's teachings (read the Parable of the Four Soils in Matthew, chapter 13).

Undoubtedly, today, the enemy has mastered a battlefield in people's minds, creating complex societal challenges, such as transgenderism and other sexual obscurities. With this escalation heightened with each passing day increasingly, *we must prepare ourselves in Christlike ways* to treat those confused by the enemy in our homes, schools, churches, and communities. It is not if, but when it comes—because it is on the rise like a Tsunami on a destructive path of doom. As Christ-followers, we need to pray for discerning spirits where we will utilize all of God's grace, mercy, and love that He abounds. Why? Because more and more evil confrontations are coming.

Remember, we should always be spiritually sensitive, kind, tenderhearted, and empathetic toward those who are in a state of spiritual confusion and shower them with an abundance of Christlike love. Why? Because God commands it, and they need Christ in their life! We should not react by demonizing and rationalizing these situations in our fleshly minds and hearts but respond in the spirit by helping these lost souls by showing them that there is One Who leads to all Truths, and He can heal and transform anyone who seeks His help. Our genuine compassion for others should demonstrate loving care about their eternal destiny and real identity in the Savior (John 3:16). Remember, God wants anyone who has detestable acts of sin to repent because sin separates that child from His will and plan.

As God's children, we all must live by this—"He will hold us accountable for our actions as His bondservants, so don't forget there's a mission field of hurting souls that need healing all around us." This is critical because daily, there seems to be an excessive *'lack of motivation'* for selfless service and holy living in our society—it's vanished like vapor in the air.

We want to cast stones at others we think are living unrighteously— versus casting God's love (Read Romans chapter 2). When believers become too cynical, critical, judgmental, and caught up in the flesh, they can shift from the faithful to the unfaithful. This leads them to move away from doing less for God's glory because they do things their way. Never forget this: "All of these ways are simply acts of the enemy in deceiving and deterring Christians from acts of faithful service who are being misled!"

If we are not careful, we can become numb to the word of God, which leads to resisting the Holy Spirit. We then get too complacent in our own little world and allow apathy (lack of interest) toward Christ to take root in our daily lives. And that could lead to the killing field of apostasy (a falling away from the genuine faith). And it seems there are so many today who call themselves Christians and abandon the faith—really! This solidifies what John said: "They were never a part of us?" These types of people were deceived all along the way because they were never in the right tune and tone with God and all His ways.

Those with ears to hear the word of God must never abandon their eternal responsibilities in conduct in word and deed. Remember God's powerful passage in Col 3:25: "If you do what is wrong, you will be paid back for the wrong you have done." A simple plan for a sanctified Christian is this—don't ignore God's divine directions and His True Way of life so you will not be deceived so easily by the enemy!

Psalm 86:11-13, "Teach me your ways, O Lord, that I may live according to your Truth! Grant me purity of heart so that I may honor you. With all my heart, I will praise you, O Lord my God. I will give glory to your name forever, for your love for me is very great. You have rescued me from the depths of death."

Prov 13:13-21, "People who despise advice are asking for trouble; those who respect a command will succeed. The instruction of the wise is like a life-giving fountain; those who accept it avoid the snares of death. A person with good sense is respected; a treacherous person is headed for destruction. Wise people think before they act; fools don't—and even brag about their foolishness. An unreliable messenger stumbles into trouble, but a reliable messenger brings healing. If you ignore criticism, you will end up in poverty and disgrace; if you accept correction, you will be honored. It is pleasant to see dreams come true, but fools refuse to turn from evil to attain them. Walk with the wise and become wise; associate with fools and get in trouble. Trouble chases sinners, while blessings reward the righteous."

This is so important because the wiser Christians should desire godly teaching that can provide a fountain of life for others-because it can help turn anyone away from the snares of death. But it comes down to a choice. The enemy not only wants to deceive others into more sinful acts, but he will also outwit believers into thinking we don't need to help the deceived ones who are falling further away from the Truth. We must always come to the aid of all our young ones and brothers and sisters in Christ to ensure they are on the path of righteousness, not fallacy! This is a crucial challenge for all Christians today to be "Genuine Kingdom Builders!"

Chapter 23

'Christlike Integrity'

Deut 23:21–23, "When you make a vow to the LORD your God, be prompt in fulfilling whatever you promised him. For the LORD your God demands that you promptly fulfill all your vows, or you will be guilty of sin. However, it is not a sin to refrain from making a vow. But once you have voluntarily made a vow, be careful to fulfill your promise to the LORD your God."

At the end of chapter 23, we see this verse regarding making a vow to our Lord. A key takeaway for all of God's children is we should always be prompt in fulfilling our promises to our Heavenly Father. When making a vow to God, He has already set the benchmark at the highest of standards—because *God keeps all His promises*. But making a hasty vow that was impossible to attain or had the wrong motives would be considered guilty in the eyes of God. But most importantly, Solomon reminds us in Ecclesiastes chapter 5 that our words of haste could lead to sin.

Making a vow to God is serious. Why? When we do not fulfill our commitment to the Lord, its misuse could result in taking "the name of the Lord our God in vain." Sadly, so many people believe that taking the Lord's name in vain refers to using the Lord's name as a swear word. However, there is much more involved with an unproductive use of God's name. As God's obedient children, we must understand the severity of misusing our Lord's holy name.

Example: Those who call on the name of the Lord pray in His name, and they proclaim His name as part of their identity, but they deliberately and continually disobey His commands; these people are taking His name in vain. Jesus Christ has been given the name above all names, at which every knee shall bow (Phil 2:9–10), and when we take the name "Christian" upon ourselves, we must do so with an understanding of all that it signifies as His ambassadors.

If we profess to be Christians but act, think, and speak worldly or profanely, we take His name in vain. When we misrepresent Christ intentionally or through ignorance of the Christian faith as proclaimed in Scripture, we take the Lord's name in vain. When we say we love Him but do not do what He commands (Luke 6:46), we take His name in vain and are possibly identifying ourselves to be among those to whom Christ will say, "I never knew you, away from Me" in the day of judgment (Matt 7:21–23).[1] That should rattle any right-minded person to the core of spirit and soul!

The name of the Lord is holy, as He is holy, and it is a representation of His glory, His majesty, and His supreme deity. We are to esteem and honor His name as we revere and glorify God Himself. To do any less is to take His name in vain. Paul reminds us powerfully in Colossians chapter 3 that if we're truly living the new life as Christians, our sights will be more fixed on heaven and not the vile things of this earth. We are then putting the old life to death because we are now striving to become more like Christ since we are His holy people.

Always remember, when we allow the message of God's word to fill our lives in all that we say and do, we will intentionally aim to be His representatives as His own on this earth. It is driven by a yearning for more of God's way in our daily lives and an absolute yielding to the power of the Holy Spirit. When Christians genuinely model this new type of life, they are known as godly people who, by their words and deeds, can be trusted.

We should be so full of Christlike integrity that everyone around us knows it; we don't have to vow to anyone because the community knows that our "yes is a yes and our no is a no." If we are known as trustworthy people, we don't have to iterate the words "I promise." Our words should fit the bill if we're known by our godly and holy traits as trusting people through our continuous actions of godliness.

Many people stray from committing to the Lord because, in their flesh, they are afraid that they cannot keep it. Could this fear be based on a reluctance to depend entirely upon the Lord to help them fulfill a significant promise that aligns with His will for their lives (read Proverbs chapter 3)? After all, isn't His grace sufficient (2 Cor 12:9)? Are we lacking our trust in God to help us make commitments that He wants to hear from our lips and hearts daily? They should be embedded in our minds and spirits!

Examples of areas in our lives where our Lord desires our vow of commitment to Him daily:

1. Got Questions. "Taking the Lord's Name in Vain?"

'CHRISTLIKE INTEGRITY'

- Possess a repentant and humble heart. (Isa 57:15, Ps 51:17)
- Portray and convey a vibrant prayer life. (Jas 5:16)
- Keep His commandments, demonstrating our genuine love for Him. (John 14:15)
- Be students of His word, learning, growing, and teaching. (Ps chapter 119)
- Longs for us to commit to being willing and giving servants. (1 Pet 4:10)
- Dedicate our lives to spreading the Good News about Jesus Christ. (Rom 1:16, 10:15)
- Carry out the task of making disciples throughout our families, neighborhoods, and communities. (Matt 28:19–20)
- Engage with Him through times of praise and worship—for they declare our thankfulness to Him for all the blessings He's provided in our lives, which exemplify our highest form of honor and respect. (Rev 4:11, Rom 12:1)
- Commit to being quick to listen, slow to speak, and slow to get angry. (Jas 1:19)
- Pledge to be faithful to Him as He is to us. (1 Cor 1:9)
- Display each element of the Fruit of the Spirit in our daily active life. (Gal 5:22–23)
- Be responsible Christians, sanctified and set apart for His holy use. Commit to treating our bodies as the Temple of God (1 Cor 6:19–20 Rom 12:2, 2 Cor 6:14–18).

If we are not leaning upon the knowledge of God's understanding in committing to Him our all, then we must ask ourselves this: "Are we controlled by more of the fleshly desires in our lives—than our godly vows that should be aligned with His will and purpose in our daily life?" Once again, God's word reminds us in Proverbs chapter 3 that loyalty and kindness are essential qualities of Christlike integrity because they involve actions and our attitudes. While thoughts and words are of the essence in demonstrating a Christlike character, our actions reveal a genuine life that displays our loyalty to Christ in all that we do.

God's word reminds us in Jas 5:12, "But most of all, my brothers and sisters, never take an oath, by heaven or earth or anything else. Just say a simple yes or no that you will not sin and be condemned." I'm unsure which is worse, an unteachable mouth or a half-hearted commitment. That's a spiritual gut punch for all of us!

We can all take the extra step and go the extra mile in our daily commitment to God. We must aspire to live a life that glorifies Him in a more positive and trustworthy light in this darkened world—by dedicating all our words and deeds to Him for His glory! Paul reminds us in Col 3:17, "And whatever you do or say, do it as a representative of the Lord Jesus, giving thanks through him to God the Father."

Chapter 24

'Godly Influencer'

Deut 24:16 says, "Parents must not be put to death for the sins of their children, nor children for the sins of their parents. Those deserving to die must be put to death for their own crimes."

In this passage, God commanded that everyone must be responsible for their own sin(s). A father cannot be blamed and held accountable for the sins of their grown children, and the children cannot be blamed and held responsible for the sins of their parents. God's word reminds us in 2 Chr 25:4, "Parents must not be put to death for the sins of their children, nor children for the sins of their parents. Those deserving to die must be *put to death for their own crimes.*" The key here is this: We're all held accountable to God for all our words and deeds. It will not go unnoticed because one day, we will all stand before God and answer to Him for our actions, good or bad.

Judges on the earth did not have the right to put the parents to death for the sins of their children, but God in all His righteous and just sovereignty might extend the penalty of sin to include the whole family, as we see in the case of Achan's family (Josh. 7:16–26). In this storyline, recorded in Joshua, Achan did not take the commands of the Lord seriously, and the effects of his sin were not only felt by the nation but, most significantly, by his own family. Because of his disobedience, Achan and his entire family were stoned to death, and then they burned their bodies. After their death, the Israelites piled a great heap of stones over them, which stands to this day and is called "The Valley of Achor" (Trouble).

What a powerful example that shows us that if our choices and decision-making are not in obedience to the guidance of God's word, our results can have a detrimental effect on us individually, our family, and an entire community. Achan was the head of his family and, in a sense, like a tribal chief. If he prospered, the family prospered, but if he suffered, the whole family suffered. After Israel had just experienced a significant victory in Jericho, Achan was instructed to destroy all the spoils so they could be consecrated to the Lord. Instead, Achan kept some for himself. This one act of rebellion by one individual led Israel to be defeated by a weaker enemy. Why? Because God was angry at the entire nation because of one man's disobedience.

Achan had the excellent opportunity to be labeled as a godly influencer for the nation and within his own family, but instead, he was marked as a "Troubler for Israel." Only one person acted in disobedience, but all of Israel was held responsible. Why would God fault the whole nation for the sin of one man? Because Israel was one people in the Lord under His divine guidance. And today, God's children are one body in Jesus Christ. We belong to each other, we need each other, and our actions affect one another (1 Cor 12:12). Achan's sin profoundly impacted the whole community, as our sin today affects the entire body of Christ and even our close ones in tragic ways. [1] That is why we must be a godly example for everyone we are in contact with. Why?

Because a godly influencer is always under the controlling power of God—they are set apart for God's holy use and ready for action. They constantly seek His wisdom for the best course, obey His specific commands, exemplify a humble and willing servant, and possess a discerning spirit to dissect right from wrong. As the Lord of their life, they inspire others to God's plan with biblical discipline, structure, and obedience because of the godly application in their life. If we are moving toward God under these guiding principles and leadership skills, more than likely, someone will probably follow us (like one weaker in faith or a young one). However, it is evident that Achan did not possess these types of spiritual skills and ultimately missed his target of being responsible for his actions.

Our Christian responsibility is "Living a consistent and committed Christian life for our Lord!" The Bible teaches us repeatedly that we're personally responsible and accountable to our Almighty God; we are liable to Him "ultimately" for the life we choose to live. The utmost sadness would be for death to knock at our door and find us failing to live a consistent and committed Christian life for our Savior. But also, just as important, not being a stumbling block for the weaker in faith and leading them down a path of destruction as Achan did. We must actively employ and deploy God's business in our lives so it will affect others all around us in glorious ways.

1. Got Questions. "The Valley of Achor."

'GODLY INFLUENCER'

For us to have a positive and spiritual influence on our children's choices in the future, it hinges on how we raise them in their developing stages of life. A society of confusion and chaos can make all the difference in the world because one of two things will happen: they will choose wisdom or foolishness. Parents' godly impression in their homes, churches, and community can be a huge determining factor in their children's choices by teaching them the ways of God. They must understand that God's word has all life's answers, not men's. We all must deepen our understanding of His teachings, message, and meaning by studying the breadth of the Bible together and living by it daily.

Not only can we significantly influence our immediate family, but by knowing and growing more in God's grace, we can also affect others in our neighborhoods, schools, churches, and abroad. How? When others see the delight of God in our lives by choices that show His active presence at work in us, it can be a game-changer in someone's life, one with eternal results. When others and our own flesh and blood see godly order in our lives, it clearly illustrates where the origin of our roots lies (and that's in our Lord). Our "true" work for the Lord, while done in His strength, will accomplish all He wants it to. Every good work that we do as humble, faithful, obedient, and loving servants is noticed by our Master and will be rewarded. He reminds us in His word that He will give to every one according to what they've done (Rev. 22:12). And what a great motivation in this is that we have God's promise that our work "is not in vain." "It is the Lord Christ you are faithfully serving"! (Col 3:24).

Just a simple daily reminder: A godly influencer is looking out for the best interest of others, not just themselves. They are submissive, selfless, obedient, and steadfast to the Lord's calling in their lives, for the benefit of others. They have an established goal for the future of God's Heavenly Kingdom, not their earthly possessions in the now. Their sights and perspectives are set on something a lot higher.

1 Pet 3:13–17, "Now, who will want to harm you if you are eager to do good? But even if you suffer for doing what is right, God will reward you for it. So don't worry or be afraid of their threats. Instead, you must worship Christ as the Lord of your life. And if someone asks about your hope as a believer, always be ready to explain it. But do this gently and respectfully. Keep your conscience clear. Then, if people speak against you, they will be ashamed when they see what a good life you live because you belong to Christ. Remember, it is better to suffer for doing good, if that is what God wants, than to suffer for doing wrong!" The godly influencer sees the bigger picture through God's lens!

Chapter 25

'Dishonest People'

Deut 25:13-16, "You must use accurate scales when you weigh out merchandise, and you must use full and honest measures. Yes, always use honest weights and measures so that you may enjoy a long life in the land the Lord your God is giving you. All who cheat with dishonest weights and measures are detestable to the Lord your God."

In the heart of this passage, God's word tackles the problem of dishonesty. Moses says, "You must use accurate scales." In other words, it had to be precise, without error, detailed, reliable, and convincing for all people involved. Moses prefaced this powerful set of passages with the "aim to be right and on the mark." Anything off-kilter was unacceptable because it could lead to a despising heart, which is "measured as detestable in the eyes of God!"

But also look at the power of God's word when He says, "Yes, always use honest weights and measures so that you may 'enjoy' a long life in the land your God is giving you." If a genuine child of God is committed to His commands and laws 100% and is full of His Spirit, they will never take advantage of anyone because there is no room for deceit within them. Why?

Because these types of honest and godly people *yearn to please the Lord*—they want to possess a guiltless heart with a spirit full of joy, peace, and contentment—aimed at glorifying God! They don't want to be associated with those who take shortcuts and attempt to get ahead by their own evil deeds. This is all due to a person's heart that is in tune with the integrity of godly living by His holy standard—and nothing less!

But contrary to the godly ones, these godless people neglect His guidelines. They have a heartless desire because their selfish acts *benefit them more than others. They want to gain more of this world's materialistic and*

'Dishonest People'

financial things—rather than the spiritual, fruitful, and goodness of God's ways. Sadly, the godless motives and desires are set on a standard 'well below' the Lord's!

Unscrupulous traders had two kinds of "weights" and "measures"—large ones for buying and small ones for selling. This should be an easy tip-off that their ulterior motive was all about themselves—because their self-desire is that the scales would tip more towards their personal gains versus the "right thing to do according to God's principles." They wanted to be the benefactor, not what was honorable in God's eyes.

However, in the Eyes of God, when conducting business with a neighbor or anyone, there could not be two different scales, but one that was fair, honest, and agreed upon. This sets the precedence for honesty and integrity, qualities of a genuine dealer who looks out for the best interests of all parties involved.

As believers of a Holy and Just God, we must never forget that Christ-like honesty in all our business dealings is an essential feature of our daily walk with God and is a requirement for a right relationship with him. However, and what's awful in this life, we will meet people who testify to God's goodness and kindness from their lips but continue implementing unethical business practices in their hearts. What a distasteful and poor representation of our Lord, and it will never benefit any gain for His Kingdom.

For Christians, it's a profound disappointment to deal with anyone dishonest. It does not matter where we go nowadays; unethical practices are prevalent everywhere. From the homes to the communities to the state and federal level, but tragically, even in churches. What leads to such levels of dishonesty? Romans chapter 1 captures the core of why unscrupulous acts are at work in every area of life, which leads to an inevitable downward spiral into sinful traits. It's because they completely ignore God's ways. After all, they feel their way is the best avenue in life.

Rom 1:18, 28–32, "God shows his anger from heaven against all sinful, wicked people who suppress the truth by their wickedness. Since they thought it foolish to acknowledge God, he abandoned them to their foolish thinking and let them do things that should never be done. Their lives became full of every kind of wickedness, sin, greed, hate, envy, murder, quarreling, deception, malicious behavior, and gossip. They are backstabbers, haters of God, insolent, proud, and boastful. They invent new ways of sinning, and they disobey their parents. They refuse to understand, break their promises, are heartless, and have no mercy. They know God's justice requires that those who do these things deserve to die, yet they do them anyway. Worse yet, they encourage others to do them, too."

Caution: When people reject God and His word, they start developing ideas of what's more appealing and meaningful to their lives for enjoyment. That opens the door to every type of wicked behavior and evil act that will separate anyone from the will of God. The deeper they go into this tunnel of no return, the more God will eventually allow them to live their chosen life of destruction (Read Romans chapter 1). He will give them over to their desires, leading to the consequences of their sinful behavior. Yes, it could be the point of no return unless they repent and turn to Christ!

Always remember this: The enemy is prowling like a roaring lion looking for someone to devour in all his deceitfulness (1 Pet 5:8). If we open the door of dishonesty in any shape or form, it can lead to other sins and down the path of unrighteousness. When this happens, it can lead to the evil gateway of the lust of the eyes, the pride of life, or the lust of the flesh. When any of these three detriments take control of our lives, we can easily get snared into areas of covetousness, jealousy, sexual desire, arrogance, and vanity—compounded with the ongoing works of the enemy and the evilness of this culture, which is dominated by sin and disobedience. Who in their right mind would want to be entrapped by these unholy vices?

In Eph 4:25-28, Paul reminds us, "So stop telling lies. Let us tell our neighbors the truth, for we are all parts of the same body. And "don't sin by letting anger control you." Don't let the sun go down while you are still angry, for anger gives a foothold to the devil. If you are a thief, quit stealing. Instead, use your hands for good hard work, and then give generously to others in need." In this chapter of Ephesians, we are challenged to live as God's children of light and not allow the enemy to influence us and consume our hearts with darkness. When this happens, it can affect the individual and break down the unity of the body of Christ. And that will never be tolerated in the eyes of God.

However, God loves it when we change from following ways that lead to death to His ways that lead to life. God wants us to possess a contrite and humble spirit that is willing to change and to have a reverence and love of His Word, which reveals the essence of His truth and honesty in us. John 17:16-17, "They do not belong to this world any more than I do. Make them holy by your truth; teach them your word, which is truth."

'Genuine followers of Jesus Christ' become pure and holy through their sanctification stages in life by believing, applying, and obeying God's word daily. When they do this, it has the power to transform minds and hearts, leading them to make things right in God's eyes, which honors and pleases Him. Yielding to His word and Spirit will always lead us to the right path, not the one of destruction.

Chapter 26

'Today, for God!'

Deut 26:16-19, "Today the LORD your God has commanded you to obey all these decrees and regulations. So be careful to obey them wholeheartedly. You have declared today that the LORD is your God. And you have promised to walk in his ways, and to obey his decrees, commands, and regulations, and to do everything he tells you. The LORD has declared today that you are his people, his own special treasure, just as he promised, and that you must obey all his commands. And if you do, he will set you high above all the other nations he has made. Then, you will receive praise, honor, and renown. You will be a nation that is holy to the LORD your God, just as he promised."

In this passage, we see vital statements such as, "You must obey all of His decrees," "and be careful to obey them wholeheartedly." God needed to iterate the words to His children "to be careful" because the tendency of their fallen flesh seemed to be the first thing that would sneak in and lead them to do the opposite of God's ways.

Throughout the scriptures, it was apparent that God's children would forget His commandments and forsake obedience when the flesh took over. God wanted their obedience to be motivated and empowered by an internal desire to serve and love Him first and foremost! This cannot happen when the flesh is consuming our lives. That is why God always persuades His children to have a heart 'wholly' committed to Him!

For over twenty chapters in the book of Deuteronomy, Moses reminded Israel of God's decrees—and now he strongly urged them to keep His commands. Why was this so important? Because the Israelites were God's people—His own possession, and they needed to start obeying God as His own—by showing it and acting as if they belonged to Almighty God. He always wanted His chosen ones to be distinctly set apart from the rest of the world, exemplifying His holiness—one day at a time!

In the opening of this passage, the precedence is established, "Today." It is the present time and distinct from yesterday or tomorrow. There's no better direction or guideline to be outlined in God's word when He declares "Today" because God has promised us guidance and direction for today's present time—for yesterday is gone, and tomorrow may never come!

James reminds us powerfully in Jas 4:13-17, "Look here, you who say, Today or tomorrow we are going to a certain town and will stay there a year. We will do business there and make a profit. How do you know what your life will be like tomorrow? Your life is like the morning fog—it's here a little while, then it's gone. What you ought to say is, "If the Lord wants us to, we will live and do this or that. Otherwise, you are boasting about your own pretentious plans, and all such boasting is evil. Remember, it is a sin to know what you ought to do and then not do it." God is telling you and me that He wants us to act in ways honorable to Him today, not tomorrow or next week. *The time today is now, the present!*

Time and time again, the Bible emphasizes the importance of 'today.' So often in Deuteronomy, God tells us, "Today I am giving you a choice between life or death, prosperity or disaster." More compellingly, have we ever stopped to think about the prayer Jesus taught His disciples? Especially in the line where He says, "Give us the day, our daily bread!" Not yesterday or tomorrow, but give us this day! There's nothing more profound about the importance of today than in the very prayer Christ taught His followers.

William Shakespeare coined the old idiom, "Life is too short, so live your life to the fullest…every second of your life, just treasure it." [1] Live life to its fullest is a cliché often said to encourage people who are feeling the blues, depressed, lonely, or self-pitying in their present circumstances. They need to live out every moment of life to its furthest limitations.

Even the Greek philosopher Epicurus promoted the philosophy of living life to its fullest extent. In his philosophy, the path to true happiness lies in the pursuit of pleasure. The English idiom "eat, drink, and be merry, for tomorrow we may die" is often ascribed to Epicurus. Although Epicurus introduced the idea of eating, drinking, and being merry in his philosophical writings, the actual wording appears in the Bible, as do many other idioms. [2]

In 1 Corinthians 15:32, Paul reminds us, "And what value was there in fighting wild beasts—those people of Ephesus—if there will be no

---

1. Quote. "Life is Too Short, Shakespeare."
2. Shakespeare Quote. "Eat, Drink, and Be Merry."

resurrection from the dead? And if there is no resurrection, "Let's feast and drink, for tomorrow we die!" What did he mean by this? There is a powerful underlying tone in what Paul tells us in this passage.

Paul faced physical death almost every day as a servant of Jesus Christ. However, from a spiritual sense, the way Paul lived his life 'all-out' for the gospel was evidence of the truth of the resurrection and his committed life as a Christian. He was such a steadfast example of his position in Christ; others would look at him and say, "There is no way that a man like this would live a life of such dedication 'each day' unless there was truly a reward awaiting him in Heaven." Regretfully, most of us are so concerned about living comfortable lives here on earth that our lives give no evidence of the resurrection of our Lord and Savior.[3]

So many of us get wrapped up in making plans for tomorrow, next week, next month, next year, and so forth. Trust me, there's nothing wrong with making plans, but make sure God is part of your 'daily' planning process. Always remember these passages in Psalm chapter 37, "Commit everything you do to the LORD." "Trust him, and he will help you." "The LORD directs the *steps of the godly*. He delights in every detail of their lives."God is telling you and me that every day (especially today), He delights in every detail of our lives. But remember, He's addressing the godly ones, those in line with His will and plan!

Once again, James tells us in his fourth chapter that we need to remind ourselves that life is short and only God knows our timetable that He's endowed us on this earth. If we live our lives to the fullest for God's glory today and then repeat that every day—it will not matter when our time is up! Why? Because when we live out the Lord's formula for today, *we're living out our spiritual lives 'through His fullest' daily!* Does this make you want to cry out, *"Fill my cup, Lord, I lift it up, Lord, come and quench this thirsting of my soul?"*

As believers in Jesus Christ, we must strive to live intentionally, with our thoughts fixed on the realities of Heaven and not this earth. We must examine our lives daily and ensure that our hope and faith are rooted in Christ—always yielding to the guidance of His word and Spirit. We must use the Fruit of the Spirit as our measuring stick; each element lived out in our lives today (Gal 5:22–23).

We must live as Christ taught us in the Beatitudes, which depicts the ideal disciple and his present and future rewards. The person whom Jesus describes in this passage has a different quality of character and lifestyle

---

3. Enduring Word. "Our Resurrection."

than those still "outside the kingdom" (Matt chapter 5). Today, we need to live our lives with the mindset based on the scriptures below.

Neh 8:10 says, "The Joy of the Lord is my strength."

Phil 4:7 reminds us, "I have the peace of God, which surpasses all understanding".

Joshua tells us in Josh 1:9, "Be strong and courageous! Do not be afraid or discouraged. For the LORD, your God is with you wherever you go."

2 Tim 1:7 says, "For God has not given us a spirit of fear and timidity but of power, love, and self-discipline." We need to be full of joy about our eternal lives in Christ today, for a great reward awaits us in Heaven.

Matt 6:32, "So don't worry about tomorrow, for tomorrow will bring its own worries. Today's trouble is enough for today."

Romans 14:17–18 says, "For the Kingdom of God is not a matter of what we eat or drink, but of living a life of goodness and peace and joy in the Holy Spirit. If you serve Christ with this attitude, you will please God, and others will approve of you, too."

2 Cor 6:1–2, "As God's partners, we beg you not to accept this marvelous gift of God's kindness and then ignore it. For God says, "At just the right time, I heard you. On the day of salvation, I helped you." Indeed, the "right time" is now. Today is the day of salvation."

Ps 118:24 says, "This is the day the LORD has made. We will rejoice and be glad in it."

Hebrews 3:7–8 says, "That is why the Holy Spirit says. Today, when you hear his voice, don't harden your hearts, as Israel did when they rebelled, when they tested me in the wilderness."

Phil 4:4–5, "Always be full of joy in the Lord. I say it again—rejoice! Let everyone see that you are considerate in all you do. Remember, the Lord is coming soon!"

Chapter 27

'Godly Vision'

Deut 27: 1–5, 8," Then Moses and the leaders of Israel gave this charge to the people: "Obey all these commands that I am giving you today. When you cross the Jordan River and enter the land the Lord your God is giving you, set up some large stones and coat them with plaster. Write this whole body of instruction on them when you cross the river to enter the land the Lord your God is giving you—a land flowing with milk and honey, just as the Lord, the God of your ancestors, promised you. When you cross the Jordan, set up these stones at Mount Ebal and coat them with plaster, as I am commanding you today. Then, build an altar there to the Lord your God, using natural, uncut stones. You must not shape the stones with an iron tool. You must clearly write all these instructions on the stones coated with plaster."

Moses has now proclaimed the message to the Israelites, and he's done talking; it's now time for God's children to be doers of the word. What better way to remind the Israelites of the importance of putting it into action is by writing His commands down on stones where they will be visible right before their eyes. Many translations state that they were to whitewash the stones with lime, which would make the commands pop out like neon lights. Plus, they could only be written on uncut stones—not those of man, but those naturally prescribed by God. Following God's specific preparation makes His commands plain to see and accessible to everyone. There would be no escaping from the word of God, which is now visible before their very eyes.

Throughout chapter 27, we see clear words from our Holy God, who loves us so much that He does not want to curse us but bless us. These orders or restrictions "should not" be taken as threats but as life's simple reality and facts of a need to possess a godly vision as His children that is in tune with God. Throughout the holy scriptures, we see many underscores where God tells us to avoid all dangers. Yahweh constantly reminds His children to avoid anything that's not part of His will. God, in all His love and mercy, is providing us with the plain truth and a clear path for our good—but we need to ensure that our spiritual vision is not obscured. He requires one significant active role in our daily lives: obedience!

When our hearts are aligned with God, His commands should give us an extra incentive and motivation to obey Him wholeheartedly because His words are clear. That type of holy alignment demonstrates that our eyes, hearts, minds, and spirits have a godly vision in sight with His purpose and plan. As His own, we must realize that God has a divine vision for our lives, and it should be the spiritual pulse that pumps through everything we do and say by His word. When we're in the depths of His word, observing it and applying it, we gain clarity and reasoning. And just as important, we have the Holy Spirit to guide us towards ensuring that we align with God's vision—through His lenses and not our own.

It is essential for us all to understand that God created us to be a people of vision. Still, it must be a godly vision for our personal lives, our families, our friends and neighbors, our hobbies, our business affairs, the community, and most specifically, the church. A heart of godly purity is one of the most critical components of having a divine vision. Why? Because purity is morally clean, without blemish and obscurities, it is perfect and without fault. Is this even attainable? In all of God's grace, yes!

In Matthew chapter five, Jesus reminds us in His Beatitude, "God blesses those whose hearts are pure, for they will 'see' God." (Matt 5:8). Being pure in heart involves a singleness of heart toward God alone; it has no hypocrisy, guile, or hidden motives. It is marked by transparency and an uncompromising desire to please God in all things. It is more than an *external* purity of behavior; it is an *internal* purity of the soul and spirit. The only way we can be truly pure in heart is to dedicate our lives to Jesus and ask Him to do the cleansing work. David powerfully reminds us in Ps 51:10, "Create in me a pure heart, O God, and renew a steadfast spirit within me." God is the one who makes our hearts pure by the sacrifice of His Son and through His sanctifying work in our lives (see also 1 John 3:1–3).[1]

A believer with a godly vision of purity is more focused on God's realities in their daily life than the ways of the world. Because of their spiritual clearness, their faith is strengthened through everyday circumstances—for they see life through God's lenses. This leads them to rely more upon the

---

1. Got Questions. "Be Pure in Heart."

Lord than the ways of man. Their understanding of God's will and purpose in daily life is less complicated because they see God's message as user-friendly, clear, and straightforward—it's like a beacon they cannot run from. They are continuously drawn to His 'Guiding Light!'

This type of divine vision is due to this basic principle: "It's a dedicated believer who makes God's word more accessible, unlimited, and unhindered in their daily routine—because it's the completeness of their life of unbrokenness in Christ. They know He's the One Who makes us whole with spiritual clarity." This does not mean a life of perfection but one that is in unity with their Lord and Savior. Amen! Remember this passage in Amos 3:3: "Can two people walk together without agreeing on the direction?"

Throughout the last twelve verses of this chapter in Deuteronomy, the Levites would shout out to all the people of Israel curses if the people did not obey God's commands—these were like an oath conveyed to the people by the priests. But here's the key to their commitment! It would be affirmed by God's people, who would promise to stay away from any actions not prescribed by God by saying Amen, which meant "So be it"! By doing this, people assume responsibility for their actions.

And today, what better way to solidify our prayers and commitment with such a godly vision and purpose than with a profound Amen! In doing this, we affirm our faith that the Lord will answer our prayers and bring His goodwill into our lives in His perfect timing. And even though we may not know how He will respond, we trust He will do what is best for us, as He always does.

We must never forget that our prayers should be prayed according to the will of God. Then, when we say "amen," we can be confident and believe that God will respond, "So be it," and grant our requests—in His timing! We may not see it now, but because of our devout faith and godly vision, our trust is in Him—no matter the outcome. Never forget this: "Our spiritual response and obedience to God's word proves that we're followers of the True Light, that will never go dim!

John 20:29, "Then Jesus told him, "You believe because you have seen me. Blessed are those who believe without seeing me."

Chapter 28

'A Living Blessing'

Deut 28: 1-2, 7-9, 58-59 'If you fully obey the Lord your God and carefully keep all his commands that I am giving you today, the Lord your God will set you high above all the nations of the world. You will experience all these blessings if you obey the Lord your God" ... "The Lord will conquer your enemies when they attack you. They will attack you from one direction, but they will scatter from you in seven!"

"The Lord will guarantee a blessing on everything you do and will fill your storehouses with grain. The Lord your God will bless you in the land he is giving you." "If you obey the commands of the Lord your God and walk in his ways, the Lord will establish you as his holy people as he swore he would do." .... "If you refuse to obey all the words of instruction that are written in this book, and if you do not fear the glorious and awesome name of the Lord your God, then the Lord will overwhelm you and your children with indescribable plagues. These plagues will be intense and without relief, making you miserable and unbearably sick."

In the power of this chapter, we see that God is giving His children very detailed instructions on how they can be set apart and raised high above any other nation. God tells the Israelites to commit wholeheartedly to obeying His commands and follow them carefully. When God's word tells us to be careful, He is conveying to us—to be on guard and cautious of all the falsehoods surrounding us that can lead us astray. When we get off course from the blessings of God, it always hinges upon that one wrong choice.

But there is one looming word in this chapter that is the ultimate game-changer when it comes down to our choices in life, and it's: "If!" The power of this two-letter word, like a little puff of air that exits from our lips—ranks

'A Living Blessing'

high among language's most powerful and mysterious words: "Little *if* can build all the castles in Spain." The dictionary calls *if* a conjunction, meaning supposing that, but others call *if* a trigger word, one that signals and sets off the extraordinary.[1]

The word 'if' is one of the most essential words in the Bible because it speaks directly to our responsibility to God and is undoubtedly overlooked by many followers of the Lord as an action word. Most promises in the Bible have conditions, and the word 'if' speaks to those conditions. And here's the key: Our responses to God's commands will affect our relationship with Him and determine what we receive from Him—or not. Jesus always put the 'if' on man's side and never on God's side—in other words, "If a man does, God will."

You see this profound two-letter word throughout God's word linked to our spiritual response, such as "listening to the voice of God, obedience, faith, being an actual follower of Jesus, our genuine belief in His word, and our hearts." Jesus used the word 'if' all the time. Almost half of the 574 occurrences in the New Testament are in the four Gospels. But this compelling two-letter word is nestled throughout the Old and New Testaments with the directive undertone that God's children must put His commands into action! The following passages are many uses of the word 'if' in the Bible:

"Now listen to me *'if'* you are wise. Pay attention to what I say"- Job 34:16.

"Hear, O my people, while I admonish you! O Israel, *if* you would but listen to me! - Psalm 81:8.

'If' anyone has ears to hear, let him hear." - Mark 4:23, and Revelation 13:9.

"As it is said, "Today, *if* you hear his voice, do not harden your hearts as in the rebellion." - Hebrews 3:15, 3:7, 4:7.

And, "My son, *if* you will receive my words and treasure my commandments within you," "Make your ear attentive to wisdom, Incline your heart to understanding; For *if* you cry for discernment, Lift your voice for understanding"; "*If* you seek her as silver and search for her as for hidden treasures; then you will discern the fear of the LORD and discover the knowledge of God." - Proverbs 2:1, 2, 3, 4, 5.[2]

Just like the Israelites, "if" we are not progressing (sanctifying) as children of God and we continue to do the same ordinary things in everyday life, it will stunt our Christlike growth. When this is obvious, we need to

---

1. Lydon. Michael. "The Power of If".
2. Rous, Rex. "If—The Biggest Word in the Bible".

quit copycatting the ways of the world and get on God's path of spiritual blessings. Always remember that God wants to bless us in extraordinary ways, but it always hinges on our obedience!

When God made a covenant with the nation of Israel, it contained three major features: The law, the sacrifice, and choice. The idea behind the choice is that God was determined to reveal Himself to the world through Israel, His chosen ones. He would do this either by making them so blessed that the world would know only God could have blessed them so much—or by making them so cursed that only God could have done this—and still allowed them to live by His mercy.

But no matter the outcome, God's glorious love, mercy, and grace would be evident. However, the choice was up to Israel—to follow God or the way of self.[3] God clarified that the only way to receive His blessings was through complete obedience to Him and all His ways. But Yahweh had to insert the caveat and trigger "if" in His word as a warning because, like the Israelites, many believers choose based on their conditions of self-comfort, contentment, and satisfaction.

God desired to bless His nation so much—because He wanted the entire world to notice the power of His enriched blessings upon their lives. He longed for Israel to be His channel of amazing grace so the whole world would come to know Him. He wanted to bestow upon His chosen one's showers of undeniable favor that could gain the attention of the unbelieving world and attract them unto Himself. However, the curses for disobedience are more numerous than the promised blessings from God. Why? Because God knows His children and humans all so well. That's why we see more "ifs" than "I will."

We all want to experience God's blessings in our lives, but God requires a set of guidelines for us to live by, which is godly obedience driven by our abiding love and genuine faith in Him. This chapter has as many gut punches as any chapter in the Old Testament because what lay in the power of this chapter are words that we either long for or want to stray from. They are "blessings or curses" and "prosperity or disaster," which can ultimately result from our spiritual life based on our choices on this side of Heaven.

Many of us love to praise God when we recognize all His blessings in our daily lives. But when the absence of His favor feels void, we allow our spirit to become empty of Him, which can lead us to stray away from the praises He is always due. We must ask this critical question: "Are my praises to God conditional based on the number of blessings I receive?" If the Lord stripped you and me of everything we had physically, materialistically, and

---

3. Enduring Word. "Blessing and Cursing."

financially, what would be our song of praise back to Him from the depths of our hearts? Would it be, "I am counting all my blessings, oh Lord, and I am going to name them one by one, regardless of the dire conditions that face me today?" Read the story of Job!

Is our prerequisite of praises to the Lord based on our circumstances in this worldly life? Or, no matter what happens, is it well with our souls? How can we impact the Kingdom of God *if we constantly dwell in our lowest of lows?* When on the flip side, no matter what comes our way, God always wants us to put Him on display in our daily lives as the High of Highs. Paul reminds us in Philippians chapter four to *rejoice in that Lord, always!* Here's a gut punch: "Are our blessings genuinely resting on the joy and promises of God?" Remember what James tells us powerfully in the first chapter of his epistle. When troubles come, we must consider them opportunities for joy because they help us become more like Christ over time.

God longs for you and me to be such a living blessing in this world today that it will permeate and touch our family members, friends, neighbors, communities, schools, churches, and throughout. For you and me to be a living blessing for God and others, we must be a living sacrifice, giving our all to God. To be "a living sacrifice" is to be entirely at God's disposal—to be available and willing to obey God in whatever he asks or commands (Romans chapter 12). And this requires a complete submission of ourselves unto Him. And when we allow the power of God's Spirit to perform His acts within us, this comes forth:

First, when we devote our lives to the Lord 100%, and we're sold out on being a living blessing, we become doers of His word (Jas 1:22). A doer of God's word doesn't just read and hear it, but they put the holy scripture into action daily. Their faith, hope, love, and obedience are evident in their life as Christians! They keep their tank full of the Lord—it's so sustainable and full of spiritual energy that it enables them to endure and persevere in everyday life. Will there be times of weakness? Yes, but they know God's grace is sufficient! Here's the key: "Their selfless and humble acts of the Word incorporated into their lives are driven by an undeniable love for their Lord. Plus, they understand the importance of biblical application in a world that does not comprehend the Word of God.

A doer of the word leads a person to repent of any known sin pointed out by the Holy Word, rejoicing in the promises God points out by abiding in Him, growing in His wisdom and knowledge, showing His love to the world, and holding the Word of God deep in their minds, hearts, and souls with all their strength. This leads to a Christ-follower exhibiting the Truth, the Way, and the Life in their daily routine. This type of person blesses the

Lord in immeasurable ways—because they constantly bring a sweet aroma to the feet of His throne!

Second, with the rise of unholiness all around us, we can be a living blessing when we pursue Christ no matter what the day holds, Eph 1:3. When we come to grips with the spiritual blessings that we have in the heavenly realms (as followers of Christ), we recognize that our righteous relationship with Jesus helps us to realize this—we can know our Heavenly Father better. We start to see as God's chosen one; we are saved, forgiven, reconciled, restored, adopted, gifted, and have the power to do God's will. That type of personal relationship exposes a vessel of God's blessing in and through their daily lives that will impact others.

Lastly, no matter what comes our way, we can be a living blessing when we press on toward our eternal goal with joy. In Paul's letter to the Philippians, he emphasized that when God began the good work within them, He would continue His work until it was completed and when Christ returns. Paul conveys that we need to live a life that illustrates such an eager expectation and hope in Christ; *it will never bring shame to the name of our Lord.* We are called to be His Citizens of Heaven on earth and possess a living joy in serving Him with such unity through humility that our Lord is magnified. We are called to be shining lights for Christ through the darkest times and never have an attitude of complaining and arguing, but one that demonstrates Christlikeness.

This unbelievable joy shows a society and culture the power of what we truly believe in, which is the priceless gain of knowing Jesus Christ that gives us strength to press forward in life. Our blessed relationship with Him allows us to progress, knowing that we will not reach perfection, but it displays a life of faith that is so grounded in our Lord and Savior that it is inescapable for any naked eye. It is so revealing and powerful because our heavenly lives are illuminating immeasurably.

Another critical key to living out our blessed life for God is when our genuine love and thanksgiving are acknowledged and anchored in Christ, His Son—exalting Him daily. It's then that we realize His mercy and grace have abundantly provided us with a spiritual life full of undeniable praise and worship to the One Who is worthy and deserving of all we have now and in the future. And then, no matter what happens in our lives, we will always sing the Goodness of God so others will see that we're a product of His living blessing.

Genesis 12:2–3 says, "I will make you into a great nation. I will bless you and make you famous, and you will be a blessing to others. I will bless those who bless you and curse those who treat you with contempt. All the families on earth will be blessed through you."

'A Living Blessing'

Matthew 5:16: "In the same way, let your good deeds shine out for all to see so that everyone will praise your heavenly Father."

"If" we comply with God's word and apply it to our daily lives, not only will He bless us in His way and timing, but we'll also be showing the world of unbelievers that this type of life is beyond comprehension and can only come from an Almighty Creator. And this blesses Him beyond all measures. But always remember, when we choose to obey the Lord, he will bless us. Luke 5 teaches us that God blesses us and others through his power when we obey. *It should not be a matter of if—but when!*

The ultimate blessing that God has given is the new life and forgiveness that comes through faith in His Son, Jesus Christ. The material blessings we enjoy daily are temporary, but the spiritual blessings available to us in Christ encompass time and eternity! As the Psalmist said, "Blessed is he whose help is the God of Jacob, whose hope is in the LORD his God" Ps 146:5. A living blessing to God is one who displays the realms of Heaven in their daily lives! Always remember this powerful statement as God talking to you and me daily: *"I will, if you will!"*

Chapter 29

'Personal Commitment'

Deut 29: 2-6, 9-15, "Moses summoned all the Israelites and said to them, "You have seen with your own eyes everything the Lord did in the land of Egypt to Pharaoh and to all his servants and to his whole country— all the great tests of strength, the miraculous signs, and the amazing wonders. But to this day, the Lord has not given you minds that understand, nor eyes that see, nor ears that hear! For forty years, I led you through the wilderness, yet your clothes and sandals did not wear out. You ate no bread and drank no wine or other alcoholic drink, but he provided for you so you would know that he is the Lord your God…"

"Therefore, obey the terms of this covenant so that you will prosper in everything you do. All of you—tribal leaders, elders, officers, all the men of Israel—are standing today in the presence of the Lord your God. Your little ones and your wives are with you, as well as the foreigners living among you who chop your wood and carry your water. You are standing here today to enter into the covenant of the Lord your God. The Lord is making this covenant, including the curses."

"By entering into the covenant today, he will establish you as his people and confirm that he is your God, just as he promised you and as he swore to your ancestors Abraham, Isaac, and Jacob. "But you are not the only ones with whom I am making this covenant with its curses. I am making this covenant both with you who stand here today in the presence of the Lord our God *and also with the future generations who are not standing here today."*

Moses, the great leader, called God's chosen ones together again to remind them of the miraculous things they had seen with their own eyes—all that God had done and was continuing to do in their lives. The generation

'Personal Commitment'

of unbelievers had died off in the wandering wilderness; now, it was an opportunity for the new generation of faith to rise above the cause for their Sovereign God through their commitment to Him. So, Moses will reaffirm the covenant with the new generation.

God's covenant with Israel could be summed up in two sentences: 1) God promised to bless His chosen ones by making them the nation whom the rest of the world could come to know. 2) To reciprocate (do the same in return), the Israelites promised Almighty God that they would show their love for Him through their obedience—and in return, He would bless them physically and spiritually. God would never waver on His promise because He is always faithful—but before Moses even restated these words, God's children were already neglecting their part of the bargain.

Moses reiterated the words of God to warn them, once again, that if they did not uphold their commitment to Yahweh, they would experience the consequences of severe discipline like their predecessors. Would these efforts by Moses, of repeating and reminding God's children of His guidelines, finally be the game-changer once and for all? After all the mighty miracles they witnessed in their journey for almost forty years and all the reminders of God's faithfulness through His promises and provisions—could this make the difference? Unfortunately, it was evident that their fleeting moments of godly commitment were scarce—for they were 'few and far between.'

As we look at the passage above, we see that during their forty years in the wilderness, their clothes or sandals did not wear out, and though they had no bread to eat or wine to drink, all their needs were provided for by God's Almighty Hands. From the beginning of this journey, God committed to His children that He would be with them; He would be their Sustainer, Protector, and Provider, and they would experience His blessings—*but He needed their decisive commitment to be His own.* Look at some examples below on the power of God's provision throughout their journey—for they all witnessed remarkable and unmistakable miracles. How could they have overlooked these undeniable provisions from God?

- [BL1-3] Clothes and sandals do not last forty years of hard marching on rocks and hilly terrain.
- The wilderness does not provide enough food and water to meet the needs of some two million people for that extended period of time.
- A nation of slaves for 400 years does not conquer standing nations and take their land apart from an Almighty God in their corner—Who was supporting them every step of the way[/BL1-3].

Each of these *great wonders* (proof in themselves of God's power and love for Israel) has a spiritual parallel in our lives today. This shows us that God's Omnipresence, Omniscience, and Omnipotence are real—the beauty is that He's our Stronghold, Sustainer, and Source for all our daily needs. And they do not change from yesterday, today, and tomorrow— it's perpetually in movement because that's our Almighty God's commitment to you and me.

Through God's faithfulness and staying true to His word, God wanted their wholehearted commitment and for them to keep their part of the covenant. After all, they had witnessed some of God's most significant works, so there was only one logical response and reply. Right? After seeing and knowing the greatness and goodness of God's love and power, you would think it should make this new generation of faith more committed than ever to His covenant.

But that was not the case—it was never a total commitment to constant and consistent living according to God's ways. They could not keep their end of the deal because they also so easily got distracted by the ways of the pagan world, primarily due to their lack of focus on God's teachings. They continuously rebelled and refused to obey God's laws, which led to them violating the terms of the covenant. The Israelites did not have an ultimate desire, commitment, or willingness to follow God's instructions. They did what comes naturally for humankind: disobeying God and ignoring His law (Romans 8:7).

We Christians must see the urgency of our commitment to God through how we live as students of His word. We always seem to point the finger back at the Israelites, but so many of us are no better. This is not to be taken lightly or treated with a grain of salt, as if we don't wholly believe something we are told—that should be a significant gut punch! God commands us to follow His ways so we can receive His spiritual blessings—it must be a wholehearted desire and devotion to Him. We must ask ourselves, what prevents us from giving our all to Him?

So many believers today succumb to the same trap of man's ways and fall in love with all life's physical and worldly blessings. These temporal things seem to be their motivation toward happiness and enjoyment. However, when we accept Christ as our Savior and possess the indwelling Spirit within us, our sole purpose in this life of commitment to God is an ongoing progression of spiritual growth, not for the things of this world. Once again, this does not mean we will reach spiritual perfection, but we don't allow the world to get in the way and stop our progress from committing our all to Christ!

'Personal Commitment'

Committing to our Lord involves assessing our direction in life and ensuring that Christ is central to our daily commitment. We should examine our lives and check our spiritual harnesses to ensure we always attempt to draw close to God. When we draw closer to God, as James tells us in the fourth chapter of his epistle, He will draw closer to us. Then, we can attain His wisdom and knowledge and ensure we are on His path of righteousness.

When we incorporate this type of focus in our lives, we will see that our commitment is moving forward with our Lord, and we are maturing and growing in our faith! That is always a fantastic and secure position in life. This level of dedication will illustrate that God is at the top of our priority list. Below are some great bullet points that can help us commit daily to our Lord—in all His ways.

- Trust God and all His promises, and believe in your heart that He will bring all things together for the good—according to His purpose and plan and in His perfect timing (Proverbs chapter 3, Ps 37:5, Rom 8:28). Be faithful to Him as He is to us.
- Genuinely love God through our obedience to His word.
  - When we commit to God our all, it demonstrates the depths of our love toward Him and others. 1 Kgs 6:61, Deut 6:5, Matt 22:37–38, John 14:15.
- Be living sacrifices.
  - Our real relationship with God will illustrate that He comes first in everything! Matt 16:24–25, Rom 12:1–2
- Make God's ways more of a habit in life, like second nature (as stated earlier)!
  - Our excellent standing with God will be shown in how much time we give Him daily. Tit 2:12
- Surrender and submit our all to Him, Rom 6:13, Jer 29:13 Ps 103:1 Jam 4:7–10.

When we commit to God 100%, we must humbly give it all to him with absolute faith and trust in His Sovereign Power. 1 Cor 6:19-20.

Josh 24:14, "So fear the LORD and serve him wholeheartedly. Put away forever the idols your ancestors worshiped when they lived beyond the Euphrates River and in Egypt. Serve the LORD alone."In a new paragraph below, please add this.

I would be remiss not to mention the power of God's message at the end of this passage at the outset of this chapter where He states, "I am making this covenant both with you who stand here today in the presence of the Lord our God, and also with the future generations who are not standing here today."

Extraordinarily, this text conflates time and generations to embrace all Jews in the covenant, but also for those who were grafted in, which includes you and me. With that, is our personal commitment to the Lord so profound daily that it resonates with all our descendants today and will carry over for years?

Chapter 30

'Return to Me!'

Deut 30:1–5, "In the future, when you experience all these blessings and curses, I have listed for you, and when you are living among the nations to which the LORD your God has exiled you, take to heart all these instructions. If at that time you and your children return to the LORD your God, and if you obey with all your heart and all your soul all the commands I have given you today, then the LORD your God will restore your fortunes. He will have mercy on you and gather you back from all the nations where he has scattered you. Even though you are banished to the ends of the earth, the LORD your God will gather you from there and bring you back again. The LORD your God will return you to the land that belonged to your ancestors, and you will possess that land again. Then he will make you even more prosperous and numerous than your ancestors!"

In this passage, we see an open-door invitation from God that His children can return to Him "if" they obey His commands with all their hearts and souls. Through Moses, God tells the Israelites, "When they are ready," they can return to Him. In the power of these scriptures lies God's unbelievable mercy and love for His children, but He requires them to do one thing: obey Him! He has not and will not close the door on His children, but as He demanded from the Israelites, He wants our whole heart, not part of it. So, here's the big question. When will we be ready to give Him our whole hearts?

God promises that if we return with a contrite and humble heart, He tells us in Jer 24:7, "I will give them hearts that recognize me as the LORD. They will be my people, and I will be their God, for they will return to me wholeheartedly." God even reminds us in Neh 1:9, "But if you return to me and obey my commands and live by them, then even if you are exiled to the ends of the earth, I will bring you back to the place I have chosen for my name to be honored." What an Ever-Loving and Merciful God!

God's mercy, grace, and love are well beyond our finite minds. Even if God's children walked away and went in the opposite direction, down the path of destruction, He would still take them back. Here's the beautiful result! Once they returned to Him, He would provide them with an inner renewed strength to help them stay close to Him and prevent them from drifting away from His holy presence. But here's the crucial point: they must dedicate their lives to Him wholeheartedly.

While He's calling His children back to Him, He requires them to keep all His commands. Like the miracles He performed, His laws and words are not hidden from the naked eye—they are exposed and readily within our reach because they are written in the hearts and minds of the people (Jer 31:33, Rom 2:15, Heb 10:16-26). Peter reminds us, once again, in his second epistle, that God has given us every resource to live a godly life—one that glorifies and honors His holy name. God simply tells us there's no excuse because the evidence is clear!

Ever since the division of this blessed nation, the children of Israel have been scattered all around the world, but once they became a unified nation in 1948, God would be with them and bless this country in remarkable ways over the years. However, many still do not recognize Jesus Christ as the Messiah and Savior of the world. But God continues to work in ways with the hope of opening their eyes to the promise of His word and that He is not done with them yet.

One of those ways is through the 1950 Law of Return. It is the foundational law of Israel so that they would view this blessed nation by God as a Jewish democratic state. This law establishes the principle that Jews may become citizens of Israel simply by showing up in the country and declaring their intention to become citizens. It gives 'every' Jew the right to return, live in Israel, and gain Israeli citizenship.

It would be their individual choice to come back to the place that God initially promised His children. This proves that He is still working in His most mysterious ways (to this day), attempting to get their attention and let them know He is still faithful to His promises by protecting, providing, and sustaining the lives of His chosen ones. We are witnessing the power of God's word right before our very eyes today. But will they eventually open their hearts, minds, spirits, and souls to the power of God's blessed ways through Jesus Christ?

Today, when Christians drift away from God, and they are going in the complete opposite direction of His calling and purpose in their life (like Jonah), there are two words that are probably the most powerful and essential ones in God's vocabulary—and it's not rest and relaxation, but "repent and return (to Me, wholeheartedly)." When we stray from God's guidance, and we become so distant from His holy presence, it is due to a three-letter word prevalent in humans' minds and hearts, and that is sin! Sin separates us from God's will and the very presence of His divine holiness and righteousness.

Here are some caution signs that could reveal if we are distant from the Lord. 1) If we are easily irritable, 2) weak to the temptations of life, 3) more into the ways of the world than God, 4) very critical and cynical of others, 5) gossiping more than worshipping, 6) we cannot move from the old life of the flesh to the new life in Christ, 7) we harbor unforgiveness, 8) lack Christlike love, joy and peace, 9) have no desire to fellowship with other believers, because we're constantly negative and all about self, 10) we don't read the word of God (daily), 11) possess feelings of hopelessness and helplessness, 12) have a deaf ear and blind mind and spirit to the Holy Spirit's guidance, and 13) possess no yearning to apply God's word into our lives. If any of these are present in our daily lives, we must return to the Lord's throne of mercy, grace, and love ASAP!

Just like the nation of Israel, which had a long history of wandering far from God and repeatedly disobeying His holy laws—God, in His infinite love and mercy (as Jeremiah tells us in Lam 3:22), calls us to repent and return to Him. The last book of the Old Testament, Malachi, points us back to the Lord. It tells us how to get right with God by obeying His Word and being faithful.

In the power of this book, Malachi is confronting God's children with their sins because He wants to restore their lives. We see in Malachi that God loves perfectly and completely, but His love is a love of response and action. He will guide us and guard our hearts and minds if we yield to Him. However, many people who call themselves Christians today continue to distance their lives from the love of God and His Son—because they are on the wrong path of correction. However, please never forget, when we feel like our lives are shattered and beyond hope and help, God promises us that it is never too late and beyond repair!

This last book of God's Old Testament portrays a stunning portrait of Israel's continued unfaithfulness to a loving, patient, gracious, and merciful God. But what is layered throughout this book, like all of God's word, is the power of hope and forgiveness. When a child returns to the Lord with complete obedience, we will see absolute humility, repentance, faith, and love.

What an unbelievable bridge leading us from the end of the Old Testament to the New Testament, which shows us that once we're in Christ, we are transformed from the old to the new. Remember, a follower of Jesus Christ wants to dwell in His holy presence and never return to the old ways that kept them far from His love, peace, and joy. When God says Return to Me, and I will return to you, He says, "Abide in Me, and I will abide in you, for we can do nothing apart from Him" John 15:4-11. Once we are conscious of our sins, we must always return to our Savior, repent, and let them go—because we can now grow and be more like Christ! What a desired place to be each day of our lives!

Mal 3:6, "I am the Lord, and I do not change. That is why your descendants of Jacob are not already destroyed. Ever since the days of your ancestors, you have scorned my decrees and failed to obey them. Now return to me, and I will return to you," says the Lord of Heaven's Armies."

The poem below is from my second book, "God's Guide to Freedom," taken from Hosea chapter 11. The power of these words reassures us that we are His special treasure—even though we may drift far away from Him, He will allow us to return to Him in complete obedience and reverence!

"When you were a child, I loved you and called you out from the bondage that enslaved you. But the more I called out to you, the farther you moved from Me.

Because you continued to fall back into the traps of your old life — that kept you far from Me–it was I, your God, that taught you had to walk — leading you along by the hand."

"But you didn't know or even care that it was I, your Loving God, who took care of you. I guided you along with my kindness and love. It was I that lifted the heavy yoke from your neck and from the shackles that held you back. It was I, your Loving God, who stooped to feed you when you were hungry. Since you refuse to return to me, you will be forced to return to the entrapments of your old life."

"Because of this, you will experience a swirling within you like never before. The enemy will swarm you and attempt to destroy you with every evil plan they can conspire. It seems that you're determined to leave Me – your Almighty and Loving God. But why?"

"Sometimes, you call me the Most High, but you don't truly honor Me. And in it all, how can I, your Loving God, give up on you, for you are My own! How can I let you go? How can I destroy or demolish you?"

"I am your Loving God, and My heart is torn within Me, and my compassion overflows! No, I, your Loving God, will not unleash my fierce anger, and I will not destroy you! For I am your Loving God and not a mere mortal. I am the Holy One living among you. I, your Loving God, will not come to destroy you, for someday you will follow Me."

"My heart churns within Me; My sympathy is stirred — I will not execute you.

'Return to Me!'

"Even with the fierceness of My anger, I will not destroy you! I, the Lord, will roar like a lion, and when I roar, you will return — trembling with reverence! Like a flock of birds that's been freed, you will come from the bondage that enslaved you. Trembling like doves, you will return to Me, and I will bring you home again, says the Lord!"

"For I am God, and not man, the Holy One in your midst; and I will not come with terror. When you give your all to Me, you shall walk with the Lord all the days of your life! And you will dwell in My House forever, for you are My own, says the Lord!"

Deut 30:19-20, "Today I have given you the choice between life and death, between blessings and curses. Now, I call on heaven and earth to witness the choice you make. Oh, that you would choose life so that you and your descendants might live! You can make this choice by loving the LORD your God, obeying him, and committing yourself firmly to him. This is the key to your life. And if you love and obey the LORD, you will live long in the land the LORD swore to give your ancestors Abraham, Isaac, and Jacob."

If you've drifted away from God's presence, never forget that He has open and loving arms to take anyone back, no matter who you are or what you've done. *All He wants is your wholehearted commitment and willingness to follow Him and all His ways!*

Chapter 31

'Godly Repetition'

Deut 31:9-13, "So Moses wrote this entire body of instruction in a book and gave it to the priests, who carried the Ark of the LORD's Covenant, and to the elders of Israel. Then Moses gave them this command: "At the end of every seventh year, the Year of Release, during the Festival of Shelters, you must read this Book of Instruction to all the people of Israel when they assemble before the LORD your God at the place he chooses. Call them all together—men, women, children, and the foreigners living in your towns—so they may hear this Book of Instruction and learn to fear the LORD your God and carefully obey all the terms of these instructions. Do this so that your children who have not known these instructions will hear them and learn to fear the Lord, your God. Do this as long as you live in the land you are crossing the Jordan to occupy."

The faithful man of God, Moses, loved Yahweh's word with all his heart, soul, mind, and strength. He wanted to be part of God's plan to ensure His laws were passed down to future generations. As the nation of Israel was getting closer to entering the Promised Land, they would be required to do something that could change how they received and accepted God's laws 'wholeheartedly.' It could be the ultimate life game-changer.

Now that the whole assembly has been gathered and they are going to hear, once again, the laws of God, they would not hear them again for seven more years. Can you even fathom reading God's word once every seven years? There were no other means of spreading God's word than by reading God's laws by the leaders and priests of their nation. If they did not adhere to this seven-year plan, so many would forget—unless they remembered in their hearts and minds all that God had taught them. This was so critical for them thousands of years ago and even for us today!

'Godly Repetition'

The one major component that God's children will require is memorizing God's word in their hearts and minds and repeating His words from their lips so they would remember. Memorizing God's word was an essential element and an important part of their worship because if the Israelites did not remember the laws of God, ignorance and disobedience would set in, and they would break God's covenant.

But many did not store God's laws in the fabric of their souls and spirits because they lost focus and got caught up in the pagan world, which led to their forgetfulness and eventually defying God's ways. If they had reflected on God's goodness and intentionally repeated God's words to themselves, their families, and the nation, it would have become habitual and ingrained in their everyday lives.

Once again, the Psalmist reminds us in Ps:1 1-3, "Oh, the joys of those who do not follow the advice of the wicked, or stand around with sinners, or join in with mockers. But they delight in the law of the LORD, meditating on it day and night. They are like trees planted along the riverbank, bearing fruit each season. Their leaves never wither, and they prosper in all they do."

A significant part of the Levites' job was ministering the word of God to the Israelites. They were scattered throughout the nation—and every seven years, they were to have a public reading and explanation of the law of God, as was modeled so powerfully in Neh 8:1-8. The Levites played a crucial role in preserving and spreading God's word, a responsibility they should have upheld with utmost dedication and reverence.

The first we know of a public reading of the law is in Joshua 8:30. The next we hear of it is during the reign of Jehoshaphat (2 Chronicles 17:7), more than 500 years later. Then, in the reign of Josiah, there was another public reading of the law (2 Chronicles 34:30) more than 250 years after Jehoshaphat. What a gap! Of course, there might have been public readings of the law as commanded here, which are not recorded, but the fact that some are recorded probably means they were unusual, not typical. With this kind of neglect of God's word, no wonder Israel was so often in trouble![1]

Do we ever wonder why God repeated the same message to the nation of Israel (and even to us) throughout scripture? God repeats His word to His children because He knows us all so well. Just like with some toddlers, God's children often take a long time to follow instructions. If we realized that the power of His word is habit-forming and could make all the difference in a life of obedience or disobedience, we would meditate on His word more often. God repeats His words to us so that we will begin to not only

---

1. Enduring Word. "Final Instructions."

grow in maturity and become wiser—but also develop patterns of behavior like His Son, Jesus Christ!

Remember what the author tells us in Heb 4:12-13, "For the word of God is alive and powerful. It is sharper than the sharpest two-edged sword, cutting between soul and spirit, between joint and marrow. It exposes our innermost thoughts and desires. Nothing in all creation is hidden from God. Everything is naked and exposed before his eyes, and he is the one to whom we are accountable."

When God repeats His words to us, He shows the consistent credibility of His message and tells us to take ownership and be accountable to His commands. He is so patient with us, but as humans, we have an unbelievable sense of unwillingness when applying His word to our lives. Do you think, at times, we're just as stubborn, ignorant, and neglecting God's word as much as the the Israelites? Simply look at the current pattern of our society and culture. It really makes me wonder if we're making the type of impact on our young ones-that God desires by the way we live daily? If we're not repeatedly living out the word of God each day of our lives, we're falling short!

Even the apostle Peter knew that repeating things was necessary so we would remember them. In his second epistle, he tells us to pay close attention to the scriptures, for within them lies our guidance for growth, discerning from the dangers of the world, and anchoring our lives in the hope and faith in Christ, our Savior. In 2 Pet 1:12-15, he wrote, "Therefore, I will always remind you about these things—even though you already know them and stand firm in the truth you have been taught. And it is only right that I should keep on reminding you as long as I live. For our Lord Jesus Christ has shown me that I must soon leave this earthly life, so I will work hard to make sure you always remember these things after I am gone."

A leader of any team or organization who aims for success continually reviews the fundamentals of execution toward the winning objective. They assess their strengths, weaknesses, opportunities, and threats so they can improve in all areas of their performance level. They must put these basics into daily practice so they will be incorporated and ingrained in the day-to-day performance of their team members and not allow any deviations or variations along their course of action to become a detriment.

The leaders take ownership of the teams' outcome and ensure that the team stays focused, motivated, and encouraged to accomplish their goals. If implemented 100%, they will see the winning results. The same principle applies to the fundamentals of our constant living faith. If we lose focus, get bored, or get impatient with our Christian life, it will be a long road—that could lead to no return. That could be scary!

'GODLY REPETITION'

Words and repeated plans require an intentional focus and internal strength. Each repetition of God's word in our daily lives will sink into our minds and hearts and influence our attitudes, behaviors, and actions. Always remember that when we yearn for God's word daily, Christians will be more apt and prone to yield to the Holy Spirit for day-to-day guidance. Then, they start to see more righteousness revealed in their daily lives! And when this happens, what a powerful and wonderful result that honors our Heavenly Father!

Paul even reminds us in Romans chapter 12 that when we sacrificially and selflessly give our lives to the Lord, it takes the complete dedication of our thoughts and words because they represent our genuine saving faith as followers of Christ. However, if we copy the behaviors of the world, the results will lead to a life full of self, pride, and corruption. When we allow bad habits in our everyday lives, they will affect us emotionally, physically, mentally, and most importantly, spiritually.

Christians, if we enable our fleshly desires to consume us more than the power of God's word, it will never lead to a solid and structured life that is pleasing to God. However, when a Christian takes ownership of their life and enables godly repetition daily, it will disable and defuse the enemy's weapons. Always remember, there is a spiritual blessing and reward when we instill a repetition of godliness and holiness in our lives—one small victory at a time.

God is gracious to us in our weaknesses, and He understands that we quickly forget because of our weak flesh. So, He often repeats His requirements and duties in Scripture because He wants them alive and active in us daily. The truths of the Bible—God's life-breathing words are a powerful book of repetition that should be echoed in our lives as His children on this earth for us individually, but also for future heirs. Most importantly, we should never get tired of repeatedly hearing and reading the same lessons because they help prepare and equip us today, tomorrow, and the future.

Neh 8:1–6, "All the people assembled with a unified purpose at the square just inside the Water Gate. They asked Ezra, the scribe, to bring out the Book of the Law of Moses, which the LORD had given for Israel to obey. So, on October 8, Ezra, the priest, brought the Book of the Law before the assembly, which included the men and women and all the children old enough to understand. He faced the square just inside the Water Gate from early morning until noon and read aloud to everyone who could understand. All the people listened closely to the Book of the Law."

"Ezra, the scribe, stood on a high wooden platform that had been made for the occasion. To his right stood Mattithiah, Shema, Anaiah, Uriah, Hilkiah, and Maaseiah. To his left stood Pedaiah, Mishael, Malkijah,

Hashum, Hashbaddanah, Zechariah, and Meshullam. Ezra stood on the platform in full view of all the people. When they saw him open the book, they all rose to their feet. Then Ezra praised the LORD, the great God, and all the people chanted, "Amen! Amen!" as they lifted their hands. Then they bowed down and worshiped the LORD with their faces to the ground."

What a profound depiction of God's children attentively listening to the word of God. The results of this powerful moment were life-changing for the Israelites. It is vital for us today to realize and acknowledge that we cannot afford to get dulled or resistant to the teachings of God's word. So, we should listen carefully to every verse throughout scripture and ask the Holy Spirit, "How does this apply to my life?" God repeats a message to us for a reason: He wants us to return to Him with a different mindset and heart. And that reiteration of His word can make a huge difference in a decision that needs to be made today!

I cannot repeat this scripture enough. Paul reminds us in 2 Tim 3:16–17, "All Scripture is inspired by God and is useful to teach us what is true and to make us realize what is wrong in our lives. It corrects us when we are wrong and teaches us to do what is right. God uses it to prepare and equip his people to do every good work."

Always remember what God's word tells us in Isa 55:11, "It is the same with my word. I send it out, and it always produces fruit. It will accomplish all I want it to, and it will prosper everywhere I send it." In our lives, as His genuine believers, His word can only prosper when we live by the power of His word day in and day out! Refer back to Heb 4:12–13.

When we yield to the power of God's word and Spirit, daily, godly repetition will move us toward mastering a plan and goal aligned with God's will. And with Him as our Guide, we can accomplish a giant task with frequent small actions toward the goal. How? Because godly repetition creates habit-forming ways like our Savior that lead to great things for His glory!

Chapter 32

'Godly Proclaimer'

Deut 32:1-4, "Listen, O heavens, and I will speak! Hear, O earth, the words that I say! Let my teaching fall on you like rain; let my speech settle like dew. Let my words fall like rain on tender grass, like gentle showers on young plants. I will proclaim the name of the Lord; how glorious is our God! He is the Rock; his deeds are perfect. Everything he does is just and fair. He is a faithful God who does no wrong; how just and upright he is!"

What a powerful song of proclamation we see in this chapter. Not only did Moses tell the nation of Israel to listen, but he called out to all of God's creation to hear these words of praise, and once they listened, he would speak. These are profound words at the beginning of this chapter when Moses says, "Listen, O heavens, and I will speak. Hear, O earth, the words that I say!"

These intense verses are vital for us as observers and doers of God's word because He states in this passage, "Let my words fall like rain on tender grass, like gentle showers on young plants." What a beautiful depiction of God telling us as His children that He wants the breadth of His word to fall on believers who are softhearted, compassionate, and susceptible to His divine ways. When our hearts, souls, and minds are spiritually positioned in this posture, we will receive His words with such affection that we will adore them and accept them willingly.

Moses is calling on everyone in all of God's creation to proclaim the name of the LORD, for He is worthy of all their praise every moment of every day. In Moses' highly proclaimed words, he calls on everyone to show the greatness of God by the way He ascribes us to live—because God is our

Rock, and His word and work are perfect. Everything our Sovereign God does is just and fair—He does no wrong!

Undoubtedly, Moses was a great leader, prophet, and man of worship. This song comes after Moses has preached three sermons to the Israelites, and now, he will follow it up with a powerful proclamation of honor and praise in song to Almighty God! As God's children today, could we sit through three sermons and one hymn in complete worship, glory, and honor to our Lord?

Read the power of these lyrics in chapter thirty-two, and we will see the outline of Israel's history, which reminds them of all their disobedience and rebellion against an Almighty God. But most importantly, God did not want His children to repeat their acts of defiance. This song is a simple reminder for God's children to ingrain the power of His word and message in their hearts, minds, and souls—and cling to absolute faith in Him, obey His laws, and trust Him for all things.

But also to realize there is hope in Yahweh, for He ends the songs with these compelling words; "I will take vengeance on His enemies and cleanse His land and people." But this will only apply to God's chosen ones who will follow His guidelines with wholehearted trust and obedience—and stop all their foolish, repetitive acts.

As God's mediator and representative of God's nation, Moses was a witness against a rebellious and defying Israel that consistently corrupted itself by following ways far apart from God's will and plan. Because of Moses's appointed position for God, he would be the nation's proclaimer of adoration and exultation to God for Who He was, what He has done, and what He is going to do in the lives of His children. This role of a godly proclaimer was due to a man (Moses) unrelenting faith, trust, and obedience to God.

So often, in their course of action through the wilderness, the Israelites were more about their selfish desires than God's, even after their Heavenly Father bought them, freed them, and set them on His path of righteousness. Their continuous disrespect, foolishness, and "lack" of wisdom and loyalty led them to rebel against the One Who had done so much for them. Do we see any parallels in this passage and song that apply to us? Let's reflect on the consequences of their actions and learn from them.

Today, why is it so imperative for God's children to be godly proclaimers of the Truth of His word? If the world does not hear our personal profession of faith in Christ in our lives, it will depict us as people who are not loyal to all of God's ways. After all, a godly proclaimer proudly promotes the Lord as their ruler. They officially declare it publicly with an undeniable insistence that will portray an outward indication of Who reigns in their

'Godly Proclaimer'

life. Their works and words in all acts exemplify their all-out efforts for God, with no loyalty or dedication to anything or anyone else.

One who is a devout godly proclaimer of His word never wavers and sways from one side to the other or up and down like a teeter-totter. They don't shift to the ways of the world a few days of the week and back to the Lord later in the week. No, the weights and scales in their lives are spiritually balanced towards the ways of God's holiness and righteousness. The one holy nugget we need to keep as our check and balance in everyday life is in James's first chapter of his epistle, which is the wisdom of God.

Jas 1:5–8, "If you need wisdom, ask our generous God, and he will give it to you. He will not rebuke you for asking. But when you ask him, be sure that your faith is in God alone. Do not waver, for a person with divided loyalty is as unsettled as a wave of the sea that is blown and tossed by the wind. Such people should not expect to receive anything from the Lord. Their loyalty is divided between God and the world, and they are unstable in everything they do."

Another excellent example for us to follow is in the Book of Acts. Throughout this powerful book, we see repeated examples of the Apostles and the early church who embodied supernatural boldness and confidence—even in the face of suffering or persecution. They did not care what society and culture thought about them because they were representing the voice of the One Who would give them the strength to proclaim His Good News to any and everyone. They were never ashamed to proclaim the Name of the One Who saw them through the battles of life.

We find these Apostles and other servants proclaiming the gospel and speaking it with an unmatched level of loyal enthusiasm. We have read and seen their stories of planting the seeds of the Gospel, and people were persuaded to change their lives. God's appointed proclaimers reasoned from the scripture and not the ways of man. They clarified the truth and expounded on its meaning and the importance of applying it to their lives. These godly followers did not just present the message of God to the community of people, but we observed them testifying before rulers without any hesitation in spreading the Truth.

Today, we live in a society where the Truth has been watered down and even abandoned in many cases. You may have heard the term postmodernism used in conversation in recent years. One of the fundamental beliefs of postmodernism is that there are no absolute truths because it has the subtlety of a theory that involves a radical reappraisal of modern assumptions about culture, identity, history, or language. This simple definition contradicts God's word of who we are as His creation. In a culture that increasingly believes there is no absolute Truth, followers of Jesus Christ must guard, protect, and preserve it.

The only way to defend the truth is to proclaim our genuine saving faith and live it out! The most effective way to confront a culture so deceived by Satan is to know and believe the Truth of scripture and proclaim its very word with zeal. You can best defend God's Word by asserting its power and accuracy because it is sufficient for its own defense (2 Tim 3:16–17; Heb 4:12–13).

God's word reminds us in 1 Tim 3:14–15, "I am writing these things to you now, even though I hope to be with you soon so that if I am delayed, you will know how people must conduct themselves in the household of God. This is the church of the living God, which is the pillar and foundation of the truth."

In this passage, Paul describes the church as the pillar and foundation of the truth. That's why we give so much time to training (discipling), teaching, preaching, observing, interpreting, applying, evangelizing, and proclaiming the Word of God through the defined application of His word in all that we say and do—because it is valid and accurate, and there is no other way to survive spiritually.

Our church (the body of Christ) is responsible for upholding the truth in words and deeds in our homes, communities, on the streets, in God's house, and everywhere in life. When we hear and apply it, we should live by how we proclaim it from the inside to the outside. Why is this so important? Because it is through the proclamation of God's actual Truth that the Holy Spirit moves the unrepentant sinner to repentance.

This is going to be a huge gut punch. If we're not faithfully proclaiming all the Truths of God's word daily, we're not loyal to Him 100%. In other words, we're more part-timers than full-time servants as Christians. And here's the scariness of a part-timer Christian; they are not entirely dedicated to the cause of Christ because they are drifting into the zone of a lukewarm believer.

When a Christian does not enthusiastically proclaim God's message, it makes you wonder if they are even reading God's word daily. How can someone not get excited about God's divine message to them personally and not want to reveal and share this with a world that needs the truth—because we're surrounded by so much falsehood! Don't we know by now that the power of God's word, led by the Holy Spirit, can transform, conform, and reform us in all His ways of righteousness and holiness?

God's word in Rom 1:16–17 reminds us profoundly, "For I am not ashamed of this Good News about Christ. It is the power of God at work, saving everyone who believes—the Jew first and also the Gentile. This Good

News tells us how God makes us right in his sight. This is accomplished from start to finish by faith. As the Scriptures say, "It is through faith that a righteous person has life." This underscores the importance of faith, as it is through faith that we can trust in the power of God's Spirit to work in and through us.

This passage clearly tells us, as believers, that if we're not proclaiming the Good News about Christ in our daily lives, the power of His Spirit is not active in us. It's almost like saying we're ashamed of Christ because it will offend people. A leading contributor to this flawed Christian life is the 'lack of boldness,' which is the courage to act or speak fearlessly despite real or imagined dangers. When a person acts boldly, they are gifted and filled with the power of God's Spirit, and it is on full display and at work because they put it into action regardless of the possible consequences. But always remember this significant takeaway and PowerPoint: It's all about our approach of gentleness, tenderhearted mercy, and lovingkindness (Read Colossians chapter 3). It is truly a spiritual balancing act where we need the Holy Spirit's help and guidance!

Paul reminds us in 2 Tim 1:6–9, "This is why I remind you to fan into flames the spiritual gift God gave you when I laid my hands on you. For God has not given us a spirit of fear and timidity, but of power, love, and self-discipline. So, never be ashamed to tell others about our Lord. And don't be ashamed of me, either, even though I'm in prison for him. With the strength God gives you, be ready to suffer with me for the sake of the Good News. For God saved us and called us to live a holy life. He did this, not because we deserved it, but because that was his plan from before the beginning of time—to show us his grace through Christ Jesus."

Let's not forget that boldness was one of the first characteristics the Holy Spirit imparted to the disciples when He came to dwell in them after Jesus ascended into Heaven. These were the same followers of Jesus who had been hiding in fear of the Jewish authorities, seeking solace in prayer and mutual encouragement. But when the Holy Spirit descended upon them, those once-fearful disciples were transformed into fearless preachers and messengers of the Good News (Acts chapter 2). This transformation is a testament to the power of the Holy Spirit and a powerful reminder of the potential of boldness in our lives as believers.

A short time later, after Christ was no longer by their side, the disciples faced persecution from the authorities. So, what did they do? They prayed for boldness (Acts 4:29), and their prayer was answered. They were filled with the Holy Spirit and "spoke the word with boldness" (Acts 4:31). God gives us boldness and confidence when our objective is to obey and glorify His Most Holy Name. Christians, in today's off-course society and culture from the ways of God, we cannot get caught up in the fears of man! Our only fear should be placed in the absolute reverence and respect for God alone! When we have that right type of fear ingrained in our core, we will proudly, boldly, lovingly, passionately, and confidently proclaim His Truths!

Remember, Christ did not come to earth to bring peace but to divide. Jesus reminds us in Matthew 10:34-39 that one who is genuinely committed to the Lord and proclaims His ways is the one who made the right decision to pick up their cross of self and follow our Lord. Those loyal to Jesus will portray different values, morals, and goals versus the ways of the world. They will exhibit the Fruit of the Spirit and more ways of righteousness and holiness in their active life! *They know how to defend their faith and are not afraid to—because they live it out for the world to see—daily.*

Once again, as noted earlier, many apologetics hang their hat on this set of scriptures in 1 Peter chapter 3 (v 13-17). "Now, who will want to harm you if you are eager to do good? But even if you suffer for doing what is right, God will reward you for it. So don't worry or be afraid of their threats. Instead, you must worship Christ as the Lord of your life. And if someone asks about your hope as a believer, always be ready to explain it. But do this in a gentle and respectful way. Keep your conscience clear. Then, if people speak against you, they will be ashamed when they see what a good life you live because you belong to Christ. Remember, it is better to suffer for doing good, if that is what God wants, than to suffer for doing wrong"!

I firmly believe that we cannot effectively proclaim and defend our faith in Jesus if we're not genuinely living it out for His glory. But when we actively and boldly live out our genuine saving faith in Christ, our defense of the faith strengthens our confidence and hope. It gives us a sense of purpose and fulfillment, inspiring and motivating us to continue on our journey for the cause of Christ without ceasing.

You see, at the end of our life's journey, there will be those who will receive rewards for all their righteous doings on this side of Heaven—because they were not ashamed of their status as godly proclaimers. Then there are those lukewarm believers who are straddling the fence and are not even aware of what Heavenly rewards are. These types of people shun their Christlike responsibility, which could lead to the path of no return (scary). Throughout scripture, we clearly see the kind of proclaimers God intends us to be from Christ's very lips. Godly proclaimers will go through the fiery trials of persecution and personal tests—but Christ did as well, and that's our example! Read 2 Corinthians chapter 4.

God's word even reminds us in Acts 4:32, "And now, O Lord, hear their threats, and give us, your servants, great boldness in preaching your word. Stretch out your hand with healing power; may miraculous signs and wonders be done through the name of your holy servant Jesus."

After this prayer in Acts, the meeting place shook, and they were all filled with the Holy Spirit. Then, they preached the word of God with boldness because all the believers were united in heart and mind. They felt that what they owned was not theirs, so they shared everything they had with supernatural power because it was the work of God's Spirit. The apostles testified powerfully to the resurrection of the Lord Jesus, and God's great blessing was upon them all.

The importance of proclaiming the truth is carried over in Acts chapter five, where we see the sad story of Ananias and Sapphira. They were "supposed' followers of Christ, but the words from their lips were not true, which led to their demise. Remember, "What we most often proclaim outwardly is what truly possesses us inwardly." That's a gut punch! Read Matthew 15:11.

When God proclaimed the heavens and earth into existence by His very word, it was the start of something new, and it brought Him great glory because He clearly stated that it was "very good." This should be our goal as followers of Jesus Christ. Why? Once we have that indwelling Holy Spirit alive in us as His new creation, the words, and actions that come forth from us as believers should be very pleasing in the eyes of our Lord and Creator!

Eph 5:1-2, "Imitate God, therefore, in everything you do, because you are his dear children. Live a life filled with love, following the example of Christ. He loved us and offered himself as a sacrifice for us, a pleasing aroma to God."

Chapter 33

'Godly Acceptance'

Deut 33:1-3, "This is the blessing that Moses, the man of God, gave to the people of Israel before his death: "The Lord came from Mount Sinai and dawned upon us from Mount Seir; he shone forth from Mount Paran and came from Meribah-kadesh with flaming fire at his right hand. Indeed, he loves his people; all his holy ones are in his hands. They follow in his steps and accept his teaching."

Moses clearly portrays himself as a faithful man of God because he looks at the nation of Israel with a shepherd's heart of compassion for the children of God. He cannot leave the people he has led for forty years in the wilderness without blessing them. As we all recall, at the beginning of God's commission to Moses, he did everything he could to sway away from God's calling to lead His children from bondage. But Moses finally received God's word with humble submission to carry out God's purpose and plan. In this chapter, we see where Moses will bless each of the twelve tribes in unique ways before he leaves this earth.

What a powerful depiction of a man who willingly received and accepted God's marching orders before the Exodus with such faithfulness and compassion—not only for God but for God's chosen ones. It clearly shows us that anyone who receives God's message wholeheartedly will accept it humbly, for Moses was the humblest man in God's eyes! (Num 12:3). A perfect correlation we can refer to in this chapter goes back to chapter 18, entitled Godly Duties.

Accepting our key role as God's servants in fulfilling the Lord's mission should be evident in our willingness and diligence to carry it out, no matter what! Just look at Moses as our example. It was so important for Moses to receive God's message because this demonstrates his humility, faith,

'Godly Acceptance'

and love for His Lord. Someone who finally receives God's message with a willing, obedient, and humble heart surrenders to self—and submits themselves to a more powerful Source that can lead them through the process. And here's the primary takeaway—when people reach this type of heart set and mindset, they are spiritually fit, able, and ready to take on God's plan.

After Moses had preached the nation of Israel a farewell sermon, we saw in the previous chapter that he had given them a long psalm in praise and honor of God for all He had done for them—and would continue to do in their future lives. But also nestled in this psalm, Moses is telling God's children not to repeat their acts of disobedience. In other words, if you receive and accept God's word lovingly, you will obey it faithfully.

Now, nothing remains but to dismiss them with a blessing, so he pronounces a blessing upon each tribe, which should bring each one of them such a level of joy, happiness, pleasure, and fulfillment. Would these blessings bestowed upon them *be received with such a heart that it would lead to their faithfulness to God for years to come?* Or would there be envy amongst the tribes of the nation—because they felt like God was showing more favor to one versus the other?

This chapter shows the difference in the type of blessings each tribe received. Although all the tribes are part of one nation, each tribe has unique characteristics. When Jacob blessed them, and later by Moses, each tribe received a different blessing. These blessings have much to teach us as a blueprint for life because each of the twelve tribes reflects a unique path in life. God's word tells us in Gen 49:28 at the conclusion of the blessings, "These are the twelve tribes of Israel, and this is what their father said as he told his sons goodbye. He blessed each one with an appropriate message." But no matter the type of blessing they would receive, they were to act in unity as one nation under God's sovereign guidance!

After all, each of the twelve tribes' names and persons had different meanings and symbolized their various paths in life. Examples: Reuben was the first but lost his place, Simeon was the aggressor, Levi was the cleric, Judah was the leader, Dan was the judge, Naphtali was the free spirit, Gad was the warrior, Asher was the prosperous one, Issachar was the scholar, Zebulun was the businessperson, Joseph was the sufferer, Manasseh symbolized reconnection, Ephraim–transformation, and Benjamin was the ravenous one.

Throughout chapter thirty-three, we see how God blesses each tribe differently. As we see in their names and their course throughout life, we see examples such as—one is blessed with more divine responsibility, one with more authority, one with more prosperity, one with more strength, one with more knowledge, one with more intellect, one with more skill as a warrior, and one who would suffer more than others. Each blessing that they received from God reveals significant meaning in the time they were given. However, some tribes did not receive blessings from God because of their unrighteous ways of living.

So often in life, we see how God blesses others in ways that may make us jealous and think God either loves that person more or is showing them more favor. But that is not how God wants us to think as His children. We should look at it through God's lenses; He is drawing you and me together "as one" because of our unique gifts and talents. Each one of our gifts is unique as believers in comparison to another. We're here to accept God's blessed gifts with such a humble heart that we will serve Him in building His ultimate Kingdom. But when we envy others, we open the door to the enemy, preventing us from using our God-given gifts for His glory. Always remember, we're not here in this life journey to please humans, but God Himself!

While the cliques of this world may contemplate and place conditional rights on our heads, determining if they want to accept us into their little group or not, once we became believers in Jesus Christ, our acceptance by God was immediate and unconditional. However, always remember, as a faithful servant of the Lord, we are accountable for our words and deeds, and God does expect us to reflect His Son, Jesus Christ, in how we conduct our daily lives. Don't you know that we were enemies of God at one time, but once we accepted Christ into our lives, we are forever on His side and in His resting arms of love, mercy, and grace?

This type of divine affirmation is not known by humankind because, in the eyes of this world, acceptance shifts based on their criteria of materialism, lineage, money, titles, and pure pride. But with God, it is a gift bestowed on us by Himself. It is not anything we must work for; it is accomplished through accepting Jesus Christ by faith and believing all He has done for you and me (Eph 2:8–9). Christ even told us that the world would hate us because we're following the One who is hated by the world first (John 15:18–27). Powerfully, the Savior and Hope of the world has drawn the line in the sand of acceptance—and there are only two sides. Which side of acceptance are you on—the world or Christ?

The Apostle Paul had a great relationship with the Philippians, but nestled in these four chapters and the letter he wrote to them, we see not only words of encouragement and joy but also many areas of life application in our lives as accountable Christians. These profound passages below should be memorized as daily reminders that will help us hold ourselves responsible as genuine followers of Christ. These are significant passages for examining our proper position as accepted members of God's household.

'Godly Acceptance'

Phil 1: 4–6, Whenever I pray, I make my requests for all of you with joy, for you have been my partners in spreading the Good News about Christ from the time you first heard it until now. And I am certain that God, who began the good work within you, will continue his work until it is finally finished on the day when Christ Jesus returns."

Phil 1:20–24, "For I fully expect and hope that I will never be ashamed, but that I will continue to be bold for Christ, as I have been in the past. And I trust that my life will bring honor to Christ, whether I live or die. For to me, living means living for Christ, and dying is even better. But if I live, I can do more fruitful work for Christ. So, I really don't know which is better. I'm torn between two desires: I long to go and be with Christ, which would be far better for me. But for your sakes, it is better that I continue to live."

Phil 1:27, "Above all, you must live as citizens of heaven, conducting yourselves in a manner worthy of the Good News about Christ. Then, whether I come and see you again or only hear about you, I will know that you are standing together with one spirit and one purpose, fighting together for the faith, which is the Good News."

Phil 2:1–2, "Is there any encouragement from belonging to Christ? Any comfort from his love? Any fellowship together in the Spirit? Are your hearts tender and compassionate? Then make me truly happy by agreeing wholeheartedly with each other, loving one another, and working together with one mind and purpose."

Phil 2:14–16, "Do everything without complaining and arguing, so that no one can criticize you. Live clean, innocent lives as children of God, shining like bright lights in a world full of crooked and perverse people. Hold firmly to the word of life; then, on the day of Christ's return, I will be proud that I did not run the race in vain and that my work was not useless."

Phil 3:12–14, "I don't mean to say that I have already achieved these things or that I have already reached perfection. But I press on to possess that perfection for which Christ Jesus first possessed me. No, dear brothers and sisters, I have not achieved it, but I focus on this one thing: Forgetting the past and looking forward to what lies ahead, I press on to reach the end of the race and receive the heavenly prize for which God, through Christ Jesus, is calling us."

Phil 4:4–9, "Always be full of joy in the Lord. I say it again—rejoice! Let everyone see that you are considerate in all you do. Remember, the Lord is coming soon. Don't worry about anything; instead, pray about everything. Tell God what you need, and thank him for all he has done. Then, you will experience God's peace, which exceeds anything we can understand. His peace will guard your hearts and minds as you live in Christ Jesus. And now, dear brothers and sisters, one final thing. Fix your thoughts on what is true, and honorable, and right, and pure, and lovely, and admirable. Think about things that are excellent and worthy of praise. Keep putting into practice all you learned and received from me—everything you heard from me and saw me doing. Then the God of peace will be with you."

During our most difficult times, we never stop praying for the essential things in our daily lives. But still, we rest in the waiting because God has promised that He hears us (1 John 5:15)—and He is ever-present in times of trouble because He is our Provider (Ps 46:1). Even in our lowest valleys and most profound times of despair, we experience times like—the child is disabled; the house is in ashes, I've lost it all, I'm at the end of my rope, the pink slip is on the desk; what am I going to do now? The discouraging list could be endless!

However, no matter the situation, godly acceptance lets us rest in the divine tension between our continued faith in God and His sovereign plan.[1] Never forget this fact: "We cannot allow the enemy to deter you and me from our God-given areas of service as accountable Christians in building His future Kingdom." Even Job modeled godly acceptance of tragic circumstances when he said, "Shall we receive good from the Lord and not evil?" (Job 2:10). We never stop praying for that which is important to us, but we rest in the waiting because God has promised that He hears us (1 John 5:15). Even in the darkest circumstances—godly acceptance leads me to press on! [2]

Paul reminds us in Rom 12:6-8, "In his grace, God has given us different gifts for doing certain things well. So, if God has given you the ability to prophesy, speak out with as much faith as God has given you. If your gift is serving others, serve them well. If you are a teacher, teach well. If your gift is to encourage others, be encouraging. If it is giving, give generously. If God has given you leadership ability, take the responsibility seriously. And if you have a gift for showing kindness to others, do it gladly."

If we look at these gifts above, one believer can't possess all these gifts at one time. God uses our abilities as preachers, evangelists, missionaries, leaders, givers, counselors, teachers, mentors, and those who embody acts of lovingkindness, hospitality, and generosity to build up His body as one under His authority. A generous giver might fail as a leader, just like a leader might not be a good preacher of God's word. We should receive our gifts with such love, humility, and commitment that it will make us thankful that others are blessed with unique gifts and talents for the building of God's Kingdom.

1. Got Questions. "What Does the Bible Say About Acceptance?"
2. Got Questions. "What Does the Bible Say About Acceptance"?

'Godly Acceptance'

Paul even reminds us in his first epistle of Corinthians chapter twelve that believers have all received different kinds of spiritual gifts. The Holy Spirit has provided us with these God-given abilities to serve our Lord faithfully as one in building up His church and Kingdom. God is working through you and me differently for a common goal. And remember, it is the same Loving and Almighty God doing this work through all of us by His Holy Spirit— "We are all One Body with Many Parts."

When we receive and genuinely accept the truth of God's word in our lives, it will present a faithful follower of Christ who is living that new life (Colossians chapter 3). If we think about the early Christians, they had access to the Old Testament but did not have the New Testament or Christian books to study and help apply to their lives. Their stories and teachings about Jesus Christ were memorized and passed on from one person to another, spreading the Good News.

A God-fearing Christian should receive God's word with such humility, love, and obedience that they will seek His wisdom and guidance and plead for conviction while admonishing their wrongdoings. They will diligently stay connected with Him daily through His word and prayer and seek the good of others in unity. As devoted followers of Christ, we should thrive more on peace and goodwill toward others than our own well-being. Why? Because it surfaces our acts of selflessness and sacrificial model of godliness.

As God's chosen ones, He expects you and me to willingly receive and accept His Son and His word with faith and loving obedience. What does this mean? When we receive God's will with the right type of heart, mind, and spirit, we accept to choose and believe without reservation that "God causes everything to work together for the good of those who love God and are called according to his purpose for them." (Rom 8:28).

Even when Moses heard God call him and responded, "Here I am, God," . . . little did he know what God would ask of him. When God revealed the purpose of His calling to Moses, Moses was reluctant and did not receive God's message with complete resolve. The key to receiving and accepting God's word requires absolute humility (as noted so many times). Look at James 1:21 when he says, "In humility receive the word implanted, which can save your souls." "So the point of this passage is to obtain the word of God, but the only way you will receive it right is through humility."

Col 3:12–17, "Since God chose you to be the holy people he loves, you must clothe yourselves with tenderhearted mercy, kindness, humility, gentleness, and patience. Make allowance for each other's faults and forgive anyone who offends you. Remember, the Lord forgave you, so you must forgive others. Above all, clothe yourselves with love, which binds us all together in perfect harmony. And let the peace that comes from Christ rule in your hearts. For as members of one body, you are called to live in peace. And always be thankful. Let the message about Christ, in all its richness, fill your lives. Teach and counsel each other with all the wisdom he gives. Sing psalms and hymns and spiritual songs to God with thankful hearts. And whatever you do or say, do it as a representative of the Lord Jesus, giving thanks through him to God the Father."

Always remember this: 'When you're at a crossroads in this life and question God's acceptance of you as His child, it does not matter who you are or what you've done. When you accepted God's Only Son, by genuine saving faith, you were redeemed and accepted by Almighty God. When you firmly accept that Living Hope in your life and believe it with all your heart, soul, mind, and strength, and it is evident in your obedience and repentance, nothing can change that welcoming love from our Heavenly Father.'

You see, He is fulfilling His promise of eternal life, a beautiful and powerful portrayal of God accepting us as His own once we believe and accept Christ as the Savior and Lord of our lives. It's an acceptance of faith and Hope that will help us all endure and persevere in life's troubles. Never forget this: Godly acceptance is not based on our performance in our own strength—but on Christ's finished work on the cross—and His salvation at work in our lives (through the power of His Spirit) that will impact others for years! And please never forget this fact: When we receive and accept God's message, it reveals that our heart, mind, and spirit are aligned with His long-term plan. It demonstrates a response of humility, willingness, and complete dedication. And no matter what, it does not waver one inkling!

1 Thess 2:13, "Therefore, we never stop thanking God that when you received his message from us, you didn't think of our words as mere human ideas. You accepted what we said as the very word of God—which, of course, it is. And this word continues to work in you who believe."

Chapter 34

'Godly Legacy'

Deuteronomy chapter 34, "Then Moses went up to Mount Nebo from the plains of Moab and climbed Pisgah Peak, which is across from Jericho. And the Lord showed him the whole land, from Gilead as far as Dan; all the land of Naphtali; the land of Ephraim and Manasseh; all the land of Judah, extending to the Mediterranean Sea; the Negev; the Jordan Valley with Jericho—the city of palms—as far as Zoar. Then the Lord said to Moses, "This is the land I promised on oath to Abraham, Isaac, and Jacob when I said, 'I will give it to your descendants.' I have now allowed you to see it with your own eyes, but you will not enter the land."

"So, Moses, the servant of the Lord, died there in the land of Moab, just as the Lord had said. The Lord buried him in a valley near Beth-peor in Moab, but to this day, no one knows the exact place. Moses was 120 years old when he died, yet his eyesight was clear, and he was as strong as ever. The people of Israel mourned for Moses on the plains of Moab for thirty days until the customary period of mourning was over."

"Now Joshua—son of Nun was full of the spirit of wisdom, for Moses had laid his hands on him. So, the people of Israel obeyed him, doing just as the Lord had commanded Moses. There has never been another prophet in Israel like Moses, whom the Lord knew face to face. The Lord sent him to perform all the miraculous signs and wonders in the land of Egypt against Pharaoh, and all his servants, and his entire land. With mighty power, Moses performed terrifying acts in the sight of all Israel."

Moses spoke to God face to face, and they had an unbelievable relationship; they knew each other by name. Moses was so important in God's eyes, for He summarizes this chapter profoundly by stating, "There has never been another prophet in Israel like Moses." But also, in this beautiful passage, we see God's sweet grace shown to Moses.

Though he could not set foot in the Promised Land, God allowed him to see it. Standing on the peak of Nebo on the collection of Mountains called Pisgah, Moses stood on what is now the modern nation of Jordan, looking towards the majestic views of the land God promised their ancestors centuries earlier. This bittersweet moment, where Moses could see but not touch the land, underscores God's care for Moses' legacy, and He made that evident in this last chapter of Deuteronomy. Moses' undeniable Godly heritage has lasted for thousands of years and will continue until the end of time.

I can only imagine what was going on in Moses' mind as he stood on that peak overlooking the land he had sought after for forty years. What drama in this passage, but also what inward pain! I am sure there was a strong sense of accomplishment but also mixed with disappointment. As we discussed earlier, Moses had a selfless attitude. Yes, he was not a perfect man and failed God in various stages of his life, but God knew that Moses intended to fulfill God's long-term plan. And that is what mattered to Yahweh, Moses' heart, to please God!

Can you envision Moses looking out over that vast scenic view? He finally saw the end result of his life's work as God's servant—leading the children of Israel into the Promised Land—and heard God say, as clearly as he had ever heard God speak, "This is the land that I promised to my children." God's word proved to be true, and the work of His faithful servant would come to fruition for God's nation.

A man who did not seek a legacy of his own desires, but one who was called and led by His Almighty God would be entitled an epitaph of titles and accomplishments such as:

- It was not "Moses, Prince of Egypt."
- It was not "Moses, Murderer of an Egyptian."
- It was not "Moses, Shepherd in the Wilderness."
- It was not "Moses, Spokesman for a Nation."
- It was not "Moses, Miracle Worker."
- It was not "Moses, Prophet."
- It was not "Moses, the Man Who Saw a Piece of God's Glory."
- It was not "Moses Who Never Entered the Promised Land." [BL/1–8]

'GODLY LEGACY'

In the eyes of the mortal man, these may be some of the titles labeled upon Moses. However, at the end of it all, the title most significant to Yahweh was this: "Moses, the servant of the LORD." No, Moses was not a great speaker, but through the power of God, this great messenger and leader spoke three sermons to the nation of Israel that make up this excellent book of Deuteronomy. God gave this stuttering shepherd the ability to develop into a national leader and powerful orator who would provide the people of Israel hope! Moses' courage, humility, and wisdom made the Hebrews a strong nation, and he did not let this go to his head.

You see, this great prophet and best friend of God had an undeniable reverence, love, and awe of who God was and what Yahweh could do in his life in leading God's people and leaving them something that would encourage and motivate them to move forward with God's plan. In Moses' weaknesses, we see God's greatness as His chosen helper. And this same power from God's Spirit is still the same power that is active and alive in true believers today. It can provide us with the strength to do great things as leaders of our family and communities.

This makes me ponder—is this end title "Servant for the Lord" enough? We often *say* it, which sounds humble, but honestly, think about this—it is more challenging to live it genuinely. To be satisfied with simply being the servant of the LORD is a precious thing indeed. It should be a badge of honor and privilege, knowing that God has selected us to perform extraordinary feats for the well-being of others in our path throughout life's journey. Think about this—it is the happiest of all stations in our life on this side of Heaven. Why? When the Master is glorified, the servants are satisfied.

If one is truly a servant of the LORD, it can be demonstrated by a simple test: how they react when someone *treats* them as a servant. Many are pleased to be servants for people or in circumstances of their own choosing. But that isn't really being the servant of the LORD. Moses is a perfect example for us to follow as we summarize this last book of the Pentateuch. [1]Are we embodying the same humility, respect, love, obedience, and faithfulness towards our Lord as Moses did with Almighty God? Are our motives and desires aligned with the choices and priorities of life that God desires for you, your family, and all future descendants?

This last chapter will be a lengthy one for a good cause because living a godly legacy for our Lord is not one that is temporary and vanishes like a vapor—but one that lasts for generations to come. While many of us long to leave a legacy of our own personal possessions and names, I hope and pray

---

1. Enduring Word. "The Death of Moses."

that as Christians, all our words and deeds will not only move our current and future heirs to possess those blessed traits from Almighty God—but also the tentacles of that heritage will spread to other homes, communities and abroad. But most importantly, God's name is exalted above all.

Never forget this key takeaway: The urgency of our mission and calling from our Lord to leave our young ones a legacy of His goodness is clear and vital for today. Why? Because the current and newer generations are witnessing a society and culture drifting further from the truths of God's teachings, such as godly faith, hope, and love. Even if we have raised our children in a Bible-believing, churchgoing, and servant-minded environment, the rapid onslaught of godlessness in this world is a stark contrast to God's principles. This can lead our descendants to forget what they were taught quickly—if these guiding biblical principles are not consistently in front of their eyes, hearts, minds, and souls.

However, as individuals deeply connected to God's work, we can help them remember the things that impacted our lives in Christlike ways that can influence them and others for generations to come. Because a lasting legacy continues forever on this side of Heaven, it is set in stone in our spiritual life. These memorable stones are written on our hearts, and the hearts of our loved ones will visibly see them. It was due to our faith, obedience, love, and belief in Jesus Christ as the Son of the Living God and Savior of the world, for He is the legacy that will last forever.

Remember what God's word tells us in Josh 4:6–7, "We will use these stones to build a memorial. In the future, your children will ask you, 'What do these stones mean?' Then you can tell them, 'They remind us that the Jordan River stopped flowing when the Ark of the LORD's Covenant went across.' These stones will stand as a memorial among the people of Israel forever."

Each tribe was tasked with selecting a representative to take a significant stone, symbolizing God's mighty deeds. This memorial was a powerful tool for the people of Israel to pass on the stories of God's greatness, ensuring His work would not be forgotten. This underscores the importance of storytelling in preserving our faith and values, a practice we should continue today.

We must leave large memorial stones of our faithful lives as Christians, so the bedrock of our legacy is embedded and ingrained in the hearts, souls, and minds of our relatives and everyone who has crossed our path throughout our life's journey. Our personal stories, our experiences, and our faith journey are not just tools but powerful tools for instilling faith in others. We often fail in our trust in God because we forget the great things He has done through every stage of our lives. And it's often that our children's and others' faith is weak because they have never been told how great and good God is and how He can work in and through people's lives. [2]

Joshua also set up a pile of memorial stones in the very bed of the river Jordan so that when it was lowered in a season of drought, those stones could be seen and would testify of the time that God had completely dried up the Jordan. This was so important in God's word because even in our times of spiritual dryness, including those days or years in the wilderness, we must remember the great things God has done in our lives that aided us to endure and persevere during those turbulent times—so that it influences others around us with such joy (James chapter 1).

If we all desire to live a life of godliness, the one essential component we need to help us achieve this goal is the wisdom of God. To gain earthly riches, you need knowledge and wisdom to make decisions that will yield you significant gains—and the same applies to those who truly desire to store their treasures in Heaven. The Book of Proverbs is one of the best books to read, observe, interpret, and apply in our daily lives—when it comes to obtaining those 'real' nuggets of godly wisdom. Below are some great scriptures that can help us prepare a godly legacy that will leave God's lasting footprints on our Christian life to benefit others in this generation and those to come.

Prov 1:1–7, These are the proverbs of Solomon, David's son, king of Israel. Their purpose is to teach people wisdom and discipline, to help them understand the insights of the wise. Their goal is to teach people to live disciplined and successful lives and to help them do what is right, just, and fair. These proverbs will give insight into the simple knowledge and discernment of the young. Let the wise listen to these proverbs and become even wiser. Let those with understanding receive guidance by exploring the meaning in these proverbs and parables, the words of the wise, and their riddles. Fear of the LORD is the foundation of true knowledge, but fools despise wisdom and discipline."

Prov 2:1–5. "My child, listen to what I say and treasure my commands. Tune your ears to wisdom and concentrate on understanding. Cry out for insight and ask for understanding. Search for them as you would for silver; seek them like hidden treasures. Then you will understand what it means to fear the LORD, and you will gain knowledge of God."

Prov 3:1–6, "My child, never forget the things I have taught you. Store my commands in your heart. If you do this, you will live many years, and your life will be satisfying. Never let loyalty and kindness leave you! Tie them around your neck as a reminder. Write them deep within your heart.

---

2. Enduring Word. "Memorial Stones."

Then, you will find favor with both God and people, and you will earn a good reputation. Trust in the LORD with all your heart; do not depend on your own understanding. Seek His will in all you do, and he will show you which path to take. Don't be impressed with your own wisdom. Instead, fear the LORD and turn away from evil."

Prov 13:24, "Those who spare the rod of discipline hate their children. Those who love their children care enough to discipline them."

Prov 22:6, "Direct your children onto the right path, and when they are older, they will not leave it."

Prove 23:22–25, "Listen to your father, who gave you life, and don't despise your mother when she is old. Get the truth and never sell it; also, get wisdom, discipline, and good judgment. The father of godly children has cause for joy. What a pleasure to have children who are wise. So give your father and mother joy! May she who gave you birth be happy."

Some aim to leave an inheritance of all their material possessions, wealth, business, and worldly accolades with no spiritual structure. These types of people could be classified as those who want their heirs to possess the family's name, "my claim to fame," because they left a legacy of self and pride. They built their earthly foundation on shifting sand, and these treasures will perish one day and will no longer be useful.

Then, some selflessly desire to leave a godly legacy to their descendants with an ultimate objective from a more spiritual perspective, not physical. They want their heirs and the world to remember them with the title, "My claim is to His Holy Name," because they have built their structure on the solid rock of God's word and His principles. These are the spiritual treasures that can sustain life eternally.

You see, there will be those with a physical and worldly vision that lends to a temporal perspective, and then there are those with a spiritual vision that's in permanent sight for God's glory, which is Truth and reality. The only way we can ensure that we have on God's goggles and are in line with His future plans will fall back on our lives as students of God's word who put His basic teachings to work in their lives daily. This is all because their hearts, souls, and minds were more in tune with His ways and not the world.

Once again, Jesus powerfully reminds us in Matthew 6:19, "Don't store up treasures here on earth, where moths eat them and rust destroys them, and where thieves break in and steal. Store your treasures in heaven, where moths and rust cannot destroy, and thieves do not break in and steal. Wherever your treasure is, the desires of your heart will also be."

Storing treasures in heaven requires Christlike wisdom, knowledge, absolute love, faith, and obedience. This is a game-changer because those whose foundation is grounded in the Truths of God's word and all His ways have invested in the future Kingdom, not the one that will perish. A person leaves a spiritual legacy for the benefit of others because they are seeking God's will and purpose in all they do in life, which can give others a genuine snapshot of Heavenly Hope.

As God's children, we must understand that leaving a Christlike legacy has an enduring impact and influence on those left behind on this earth. It is our opportunity to help make a change in our homes, schools, churches, communities, and abroad. Those who will prioritize this are fully aware that all they have, physically and spiritually, is a blessing from God. They want the abundance of these blessings passed on to as many as possible because it can be a life-changer for someone. The passage below in Proverbs is profound and can yield a spiritual and biblical guide for everyday life if we yearn for its teachings.

Prov 13:9–22, "The life of the godly is full of light and joy, but the light of the wicked will be snuffed out. Pride leads to conflict; those who take advice are wise. Wealth from get-rich-quick schemes quickly disappears; wealth from hard work grows over time. Hope deferred makes the heart sick, but a dream fulfilled is a tree of life. People who despise advice are asking for trouble; those who respect a command will succeed. The instruction of the wise is like a life-giving fountain; those who accept it avoid the snares of death. A person with good sense is respected; a treacherous person is headed for destruction.'

"Wise people think before they act; fools don't—and even brag about their foolishness. An unreliable messenger stumbles into trouble, but a reliable messenger brings healing. If you ignore criticism, you will end in poverty and disgrace; if you accept correction, you will be honored. It is pleasant to see dreams come true, but fools refuse to turn from evil to attain them. Walk with the wise and become wise; associate with fools and get in trouble. Trouble chases sinners, while blessings reward the righteous. Good people leave an inheritance to their grandchildren, but the sinner's wealth passes to the godly."

As genuine Christians grow in their spiritual maturity, they become solid students of God's word and start to see life now and in the future through God's lenses, not their own. They realize there was a purpose and plan in their life for God's good work. They may not have attained much in physical value, but through their journey of life with the Lord by their side, they gained nuggets that will yield more value than anything tangible on this earth. And it will be evident in their children's coming generations!

During their selfless journey, they produced a fruit-bearing life of the Fruit of the Spirit that displayed their unmatched Christlike morals and values. They exhibited integrity and trustworthiness incomparable to others and were categorized as dependable and accountable. They were dedicated and loyal to their God-given gifts for the sake of others, portraying a life of Christlikeness second to none. The end result will lead to a life-changing story of today that will carry on tomorrow and for years to come for the benefit of others, but most importantly, for the glory of God.

Remember, leaving a godly legacy is not about earthly quantity but Christlike quality! It gives all of our loved ones a solid hope for what is to come that will help them endure and persevere through times of trouble in this world! This enduring legacy, rooted in hope, can shape people's lives in the future in powerful ways for God's glory. Can it make a difference in spiritual value for someone's permanent position in the future? I think the words from the Bible answer that question unequivocally.

Matt 7:24–27 says, "Anyone who listens to my teaching and follows it is wise, like a person who builds a house on solid rock. Though the rain comes in torrents and, the floodwaters rise, and the winds beat against that house, it won't collapse because it is built on bedrock. But anyone who hears my teaching and doesn't obey it is foolish, like a person who builds a house on sand. When the rains and floods come, and the winds beat against that house, it will collapse with a mighty crash."

2 Tim 4:6–8, "As for me, my life has already been poured out as an offering to God. The time of my death is near. I have fought the good fight, I have finished the race, and I have remained faithful. And now the prize awaits me—the crown of righteousness, which the Lord, the righteous Judge, will give me on the day of his return. *And the prize is not just for me but for all who eagerly look forward to His appearing.*" What a powerful passage of Hope to end this journey with at the end of Deuteronomy!

In Summary

"A Message of Hope!"

Moses, the great leader of the nation of Israel, was a man God chose to lead His people from bondage to a Promised Land full of God's enriched blessings. However, Moses felt he was not worthy to carry out the future plan God had in store for His children. He looked for every excuse and scapegoat in shunning his call from the Almighty One. He did not want this responsibility because Moses looked more at his failures in the flesh—versus what God's power could perform in all his weaknesses! That's how God can work in you and me today and in the future—when we surrender and submit to His will and plan (2 Cor 12:9)!

At first, Moses did not see himself as the one who could fulfill a duty and responsibility that God had drafted all the way back to His promise to Abraham. But you see, God would work out His promise through a man like Moses, who felt inferior and incapable of accomplishing this incredible feat. This storyline shows you and me just how the power of God can use one person who thinks they are a weak vessel for the glory of God that can impact generations of people!

In time, Moses would become God's humble and faithful servant, friend, great prophet, intercessor, leader, and lawgiver. More importantly, he would become the messenger of God's hope for His children of Israel, which still stands today! Once Moses gave it all to the Lord's guiding ways, the journey of hope began from the hands of the enemy towards the Promised Land of God.

In Deuteronomy chapter 8, we see a powerful undertone in how we should believe what God says in His word is true, which is our solid foundation of hope. God wants all His children to live by bread alone (His word), not the material things that will soon perish. As we've seen throughout this book, our priorities and choices must align with God's word 100% to help accomplish His long-term plan! Look at some of these profound comments from Charles Spurgeon below on the Truths of living on the word of God:

- "We don't live by God's word—because we *fight* with God's word: "The worst implement with which you can knock a man down is the Bible; it is intended for us to live upon—not to be the weapon of our controversies, but our daily food, upon which we rejoice to live."
- "We live by every word that proceeds from the mouth of God, not by every feeling we experience. You have never received a spiritual life based on your own feelings. It was when you believed God's Word that you lived, and you will never get an increase in spiritual life and grow in grace by your feelings or your own doings. It must still be by believing the promises and feeding on the Word." [1]

Before the Second Generation of Israelites started their quest for the Promised Land, they had to be well-equipped and prepared with God's guiding principles and the promise of His word engrained in their lives. They had to understand their absolute need for God's help and the purpose behind this pursuit, which was part of fulfilling God's plan. But they had to ensure that their core principles of obedience, faith, and hope were built on the foundation of God's word. Before they proceeded toward the land, there was a critical point: "If they ever got off course from God's will, they had to regroup, seek God, and cling to His promises. Once they did this, it would boost their confidence, help them progress, and achieve victory in the land."

The Second Generation of Israelites faced a critical question: Would their conquest of the land, guided and assisted by God, leave a lasting impression on their lives? Would it powerfully influence and inspire future generations? Would the future descendants be able to hear, see, and know about God's greatness and goodness every step of the way through the chosen Second Generation? Would their testimony of God's blessings become a godly legacy that would benefit future Israelites for years to come?

Unfortunately, God's nation failed to share its favorable results with succeeding generations in many ways. The facts of its successes and failures are recorded in the Bible for our use today as a guiding tool. Their tales should powerfully help every generation of concerned Christians in today's society. As we move forward in life as God's servants on this earth, will the older generations assist the younger generations for the well-being of their future success?

---

1. Enduring Word. "A Warning Against Pride."

"A Message of Hope!"

No matter our assessment of one generation to another, we need to be careful in pointing fingers at past, current, and future generations because God's word commands us in 1 Tim 5:1–2, "Never speak harshly to an older man, but appeal to him respectfully as you would to your own father. Talk to younger men as you would to your own brothers. Treat older women as you would your mother and treat younger women with all purity as you would your own sisters."

In the heart of this passage, Paul is telling Timothy that the basis of his ministry in a church will not only be how he teaches but also how he treats others. As spiritually mature Christians, we must treat all groups of people with Christlike respect. Why is this important? When we exemplify the Fruit of the Spirit with all ages, it strengthens the church body, creates an attitude more like Jesus Christ, and establishes solid unity. This should be our biblical guide on how the older and younger generations can work harmoniously in the power of God's word, which can be effectively passed down for years. It will positively affect not only the church but also the homes—and throughout the communities!

Never forget this: As a child of God, you and I are part of God's generational family because of His grace, mercy, and love—and through our faith in Jesus Christ. Yes, God chose the Jews to be His own people and, through the rest of the world, come to find salvation. And now, because of our faith in Christ, we are part of His family. 1 Peter 2:9 states, "We are a chosen generation that should be the same as his royal priesthood from generation to generation."

No, we are not part of the Jewish nation, religion, or family established from the beginning. But we were grafted into God's generational lineage because of Jesus Christ. Romans chapter 11 reminds us that we were an uncultivated, wild shoot, grafted in when we chose to believe in His Son, our Savior and Lord. You and I had no claim to the benefits of God's people from the beginning—but we now have a new status drawn up from the root of Israel that must be passed on.

We've been chosen as God's own to actively represent His Son to our family, friends, neighbors, and everyone within our proximity. The spiritual investment we put into our future descendants and others will exemplify our genuine relationship with God our Father, His Son Jesus Christ, and the Holy Spirit. What we allow Him to do in and through us for the benefit of others in expanding His Kingdom will demonstrate just how much worth we put in taking the time to impact and influence many lives for His glory, not in our own achievements.

As we move forward in the future, we will do one of two things: 1) We will either allow the change of man's culture by generation to affect and influence us in ungodly ways, or 2) we will comply with God's word, live by them, and teach them—so they can be passed down one generation at a time for God's good and mainly for His glory.

When we choose the latter, it keeps unity and all of God's teachings in one accord. And this is how we can all be part of God's generation—from beginning to end—United as One! The challenge is there for you and me "now" because once again, Jesus tells us, "The harvest is great, but the workers are few. So, pray to the Lord who is in charge of the harvest; ask him to send more workers into his fields." (Matt 9:37–38)

Don't we realize, as parents and the "supposed" wiser generation, that the first generation of Israelites (out of Exodus) were misguided by their ways of disobedience that led to their utter destruction? When God delivered them from bondage, He not only allowed them the opportunity to dwell in His presence, but He gave them a choice to enter His future of a new Promised Land that possessed a fulfilling life beyond their comprehension.

But here's the critical point: They could not possess the desires of the things of this world—and be in His presence at the same time (as we stated earlier). And we all know how that story ended for the first generation. It led them to a misguided hope apart from God's will and plan. When God's children place their hope in something or someone other than Almighty Yahweh, their seemingly temporary pleasures will lead them to a pit of despair.

Yes, it is evident that the first generation of Israelites failed the test because of their misguided ways! Even the second generation had to be reminded of their failures, false beliefs, and who God is. Though many of the second generation of God's children did not see the true hope of God lived out in their ancestors' lives (first generation), God gave them the undeniable opportunity to realize that there was hope for a blessed future.

Here's the key: "Adherence to the Heavenly Father's ways, like that of the Israelites of old, is a matter of choice—because this powerful word can determine our path." We should know by now that Almighty God desires His children to choose His divine ways, assuring all of us of His love and the presence of His promises, provision, and power in our next season of life, which is all we need. And like the Israelites, we, too, need this reminder of God's undeniable promise that will come one day.

It's that glorious day when we can step into the Promised Land that He's prepared for you and me—for the rest of our lives. That's the type of hope I want to place in my heart, soul, spirit, and mind—with all my strength each and every day that can be passed on to others! This will require my genuine love, respect, and obedience to my Heavenly Father and all His ways, and not the ways of the world. I genuinely want to aspire to be more of a Messenger of Hope that can lead others to something more encouraging and positive—versus one of hopelessness!

Moses, next to the last Book of the Pentateuch, the book of Numbers holds a significant lesson for us. It marks a turning point for the first generation of Israelites that led to their tragic demise and severed ties with God. Their downfall was their failure to trust and obey God's ways as they sought the wrong things in their lives. This should serve as a warning for every righteous soul, a lesson that should make us weep for these foolish people over time.

However, instead of pointing fingers, it would be wise that we examine our own hearts and make sure that the tragedy of Israel is not repeated in our own family lives. With that, is there a turning point in our children's lives that goes unnoticed, which could harm their lives, versus for the good of their spiritual well-being? Parents, once again, we must ask ourselves, have we firmly established our spiritual barometer of seeking the Lord first *in our own lives*? Why, you ask? So, our future descendants have the correct biblical and spiritual guiding compass in their life's journey!

We all talk about it today and realize that the first generation of Israelites suffered way too long and aimlessly wandered in the wilderness because they disobeyed God and did not seek Him wholeheartedly. However, in those 'fleeting' moments when they came to their spiritual sense, they called and wailed out to the God of Hope for help! What is so compelling is that they did not look to the false gods for help but sought the Only One Who could help them during their intense trials. Sadly, they were not consistently committed to clinging to God's promises and truths, which could have enabled them to endure and persevere through the next phase of their journey! If they had only been loyal to God, they would have eventually experienced victory instead of loss!

We must remember what God's word tells us in Isa 55:6, "Seek the LORD while you can find him. Call on him now while he is near." God's word also reminds us in Deut 4:29, "But from there you will search again for the LORD your God. And if you search for him with all your heart and soul, you will find him". Over and over throughout the Bible, God calls His people to repent, return to Him, and seek the Lord while He may be found before it's too late! Trust me, He wants us to experience all of His victorious ways in everyday life when we ultimately decide to follow Him and all His ways!

All believers, no matter how strong we think we are, will often get weary in our Christian life, just like the biblical heroes mentioned throughout the Bible. But God's power and strength will never diminish; it's the same yesterday, today, and forever. Does that give you comfort and Hope? Always remember this promise: "God is never too tired or busy to help us.

He will always listen to His faithful children and come to our aid—because His strength is our means of strength in everyday life."

Too often in our Christian journey, we lose focus on our 'Real Hope' and wander in the wilderness for way too long (like the Israelites). Why? Because we're not resting in the power of God's promises and truths. In those trying moments of our lives, many walk more by sight (the temporal) than our faith (the eternal)! It's when we go through intense trials and tribulations that get us off course in our Christian life, and we take our thoughts and hearts away from that close relationship with the Lord—which we desperately need every minute of every day. When we're out of sync with our Lord, we all need a spiritual awakening within our hearts, minds, and spirits to shake us up and reinvigorate, refresh, and renew our hope in the One Who can help us get back on track in our personal lives—but just as important for the sake of others.

Undoubtedly, the Christian life is not smooth sailing, and we all can get too complacent in our daily walk with the Lord. That's why we need Someone to prod us in our state of complacency—so we can get up and move when He moves. Throughout this book, we have seen this powerful underlying message: "If a generation of parents and family leaders are not wholeheartedly obedient to God, where genuine saving faith, love, and absolute reverence to our Lord are exhibited—there will be no hope of spiritual survival for our future heirs!" Always remember this—if we're not united and clinging wholly to the Lord, we will never be in sync with Him 100%. Once again, God's word reminds us in Amos 3:3, "Can two people walk together without agreeing on the direction?"

When we feel like life is crushing us, and we're about to have an implosion, and we cannot take another step forward, we can call upon the name of the Lord so He can renew our strength to get us through to that next phase in our life. The powerful takeaway from a very popular and memorable passage in Isaiah 40:31 is those who patiently wait on the Lord with the supernatural expectation (hope) that God will fulfill His promises and renew our strength. When we genuinely trust in Him and His word, patience will come like second nature, elevating our spiritual strength to rise above the difficulties in this life. And that internal and external action impacts our family, friends, and everyone we know!

Paul reminds us in Rom 8:24–25, "We were given this hope when we were saved. (If we already have something, we don't need to hope for it. But if we look forward to something we don't yet have, we must wait patiently and confidently)." As we wait patiently for God's will to unfold in our lives, we must convey and portray absolute confidence that in God's divine wisdom, it will all come together for the good—for those who love the Lord and are called according to His purpose and plan. But always remember this key point—in His perfect timing.

The Psalmist provides some powerful words of hope in Ps 33:18–22, "But the LORD watches over those who fear him, those who rely on his unfailing love. He rescues them from death and keeps them alive in times of famine. We put our hope in the LORD. He is our help and our shield. In him, our hearts rejoice, for we trust in his holy name. Let your unfailing love surround us, LORD, for our hope is in you alone."

Deut 31:6 also has a persuasive message of hope when Almighty God tells all His children, "So be strong and courageous! Do not be afraid, and do not panic before them. For the LORD, your God will personally go ahead of you. He will neither fail you nor abandon you." The promise and message of Hope in the Book of Deuteronomy are not just ancient words but a beacon of light in our modern world. Amid all the societal acts of unholiness and hopelessness, we must yearn for God's divine help and guidance like never before. Grounded in the Truths of His word, we understand the vital role of Hope in our everyday life, especially for the spiritual survival of our children and younger ones.

You see, the Israelites were taught the enduring foundations of God's word, which were continuously repeated to them so they would understand the difference between right and wrong—and good and evil. They were even commanded to tell their children the ways of Yahweh so future heirs would pass down the ways of God to their own descendants. Why? So they would trust, believe, and rely on the Source of Hope that never fades.

But you must love the final story of Moses' life's journey in his last book. Within sight of the Promised Land, Moses dies. God buries His friend and messenger on the barren slopes of Mount Pisgah. No worldly monument or epitaph marks his earthly grave as a remembrance of all the accomplishments he attained for His Lord. However, he chose something better than Egypt (his old servant) could ever offer.

The great prophet, servant, and messenger willingly traded earthly acclaim, accolades, and pleasure for a reward in an invisible spiritual realm. He cashed it all in—for a long-term and eternal relationship with the Almighty and Living God, a commitment that is the best trade anyone could have made. "What he lost, he couldn't have kept anyway—BUT what he gained, he could never lose." Powerfully, he dies in hope, listed among those who "placed their hope in the resurrection to a better life" (Heb. 11:35). And it seems he tasted the reality of the resurrection before any other (Jude 9; Matt. 17:3). We must recognize that we may not see hope fulfilled in our lifetime. However, that possibility doesn't diminish our hope, for the sleep of death is only a night while we wait for the resurrection of dawn.[2]

In his final address to the Israelites, Moses gives them a song of promise for the future (Deut. 32). Even in Revelation 15, we're reminded of the Song of Moses and the Lamb—a song of worship and victory. Undoubtedly, in today's time of turmoil and toil, genuine followers of the Living Hope long to sing this song, for that's when our hope is fulfilled forever. And it makes no difference whether we rest in the grave or remain alive at Jesus's return. Until then, we remain God's messengers of hope on a journey to the Promised Land. Today, we must build on that unshakable foundation of Hope, seek it, and always cling to it! It will steadfastly guide us until the end of this life, comforting us with God's presence in our struggles! And make no mistake—it will be worth the effort for God's glory—because it will surely impact so many lives around us, especially our close ones!

---

2. Manner. Bruce. "Moses: Hope Deferred."

"The Reason for Hope"

What would you say if someone asked you today about the driving force behind your genuine belief and trust in God? Do others, especially our loved ones, perceive a supernatural faith, love, and hope we inherently possess beyond explanation? Is it so outwardly profound that it cannot be denied when the storms of life assail you? How would you respond to this crucial question? God's word reminds us in 1 Peter chapter 3 of a fundamental question affirming our authentic position as a believer of Hope in the One who is and will always be there for you.

Once again, we're reminded of this passage in 1 Pet 3:14–16, "But even if you suffer for doing what is right, God will reward you for it. So don't worry or be afraid of their threats. Instead, you must worship Christ as the Lord of your life. And if someone asks about your hope as a believer, always be ready to explain it." You see, Jesus Christ is the reason for our Hope as genuine believers—it never wavers or waffles (it's rock solid).

Remember this critical statement as genuine followers of Christ: "If faith is our confident belief and 'yes' to all of God's promises, and our love is evident through our obedience to His word, then Hope is the confirmed "amen" in our lives to it all! It looks forward to seeing that God's plan will come to fruition—knowing it will happen beyond a shadow of a doubt! But we also know it's on His timetable of action, not ours. We simply trust in it! Does the world and our close ones see this type of godly assurance in our lives?

As stated earlier, many Christian Apologists often refer to this passage above in their defense of our undeniable hope in the One Who will sustain us through our most challenging days. It's a command to "always be ready to give an answer to everyone who asks you to give the reason for the hope that you have." But here's a thought-provoking question. If you never get asked this question when the times of struggle are so trying, is it because we're not exhibiting our Living Hope in the way God desires? Do we understand that our display of Hope in Christ is essential and paramount in today's world, invoking a sense of responsibility and purpose in our faith?

Visibly living out our genuine hope in Christ before others is crucial in today's time. How? It profoundly impacts the unbelieving world, the weaker in faith, and our young ones as they grow in their understanding of faith. When the world and our close ones witness this great hope in the face of persecution or suffering, they will naturally want to know why that Hope (Matt 5:16). This hope brings peace, joy, and contentment in our lives when the world cannot provide. Therefore, we must be prepared to share the gospel and our actual position of hope gently and respectfully—layered with empathy, humility, confidence, boldness, and passion.

This is so important. Why? Our children and the younger generation need to see the wiser generation as an example of relying upon the 'Source of Hope' tethered with all of these components above—especially when we are in our deepest despair. Our genuine faith, hope, and love need to be so spiritually contagious that they spread to our young ones for their well-being in the days and years to come. Trust me, they will need it sooner or later!

Many experts would tell you that one of the hardest things to say in life is—*I don't need help*! This baffles me when we have the Greatest Source of Power and Strength known to humans. With that, this is going to be a severe gut punch! Unfortunately, many parents don't seek God's guidance, wisdom, and knowledge because they've allowed their self-pride to get in the way of our Heavenly Father, Who is at our disposal—at every beckon cry. We don't come to Him for counseling because of all the substandard statistics regarding the parent-child relationship we saw at the outset of this book!

Parents, it is apparent that all of our hodgepodge ideas do not work as a godly guide for our children in this godless society & culture today. We must put our self-philosophies aside and focus on God's desires and what He commands in our lives as His mature ones. And what is that, you may ask? We all should know by now that one of the most incredible things we can achieve in life as parents and leaders in the homes and communities is this: "Teach hope, faith, and love in Christlike ways to the younger generations at the early stages of their lives by following these steps below":

- Be the daily role model and example of Christlikeness for our children and the younger generations (Prov 3:5-6, Matt 6:33, Col 3:17, Gal 5:22-23, Tit 2:11-14).
- Embody a vibrant prayer life where our younger ones see firsthand 'Who our real Source of Hope is' (Jer 33:3, 1 Tim 2:1-6).

- Implement daily times in the word of God where they see examples of hope in the scriptures and how it helped God's people overcome barriers in their lives—that's even life-applicable today. Read the stories of Noah in Genesis, chapters 6–10; Abraham starting in Genesis, chapter 12; Joseph in Genesis, chapters 37–50; Esther, Ruth and Naomi in the Book of Ruth, Daniel, Job, Paul, and the Disciples—to name a few.
- Teach them the importance of being surrounded by Christian friends who can provide them with positive support and unity (2 Cor 6:14, 1 Thess 5:11, 1 Cor 15:33).
- Demonstrate a consistent, obedient, and faithful life of committed service to the Lord. Why? Because a loyal servant to Christ exhibits genuine faith, love, and hope in Him alone (Mk 12:29–31, Josh 24:15, 1 John 3:16).
- Establish a diligent pattern of worship in the house of God so they will see the value it offers to a life of stability as Christians (united as one), especially during intense trials. (Ps 150:6, John 4:24, Heb 13:15).
- Encourage them to believe in the power of faith, love, and hope in the word of God so they can start reading and studying God's word independently (1 John 2:5, Psalm chapter 119, Jas 1:22).
- Teach them the importance of obeying God's word and heeding the guidance of the Holy Spirit (John 14:15, John 14:26, Luke 11:28, Acts 5:29, Rom 8:26, Gal 5:25).
- Ingrain this in our children's early stages: When we become followers of Christ, we will have friends and others to turn against us because they are of the world. But remember, our Lord is there to lift us up and let us know we're not in this world alone! (Ps 46:1–2, 1 Pet 2:11, 1 Chron 29:15, John 15:18–25, John 16:25–33, 2 Tim 4:16–18).
- Teach them about salvation in Christ—the Way, Truth, and Life. Reinforce that He's the only source and path to eternal life. Teach them about Jesus' life, death, and resurrection, which is the basis of our hope (John 3:16–17, John 14:6).

In 1 Corinthians chapter 13, Paul reminds us that only three things will last forever (faith, hope, and love), and it is clear that these are the things we should pursue and cling to throughout our life's journey. Why? Because they are the Perpetual Cycle of our Spiritual Life as His Citizens of Heaven on Earth! Think about it! When we look at these holy components—faith, hope, and love—they are all wonderful gifts from our Heavenly Father. These divine virtues are the most excellent qualities that humans can possess. Why? Because they come from our Creator, and by our application, they can lead blessings back to God. What an opportunity to send those sweet aromas back to the throne of our Heavenly Father and Lord when we live out His Hope in our daily lives!

These most precious elements intertwine and connect in all their beautiful and holy facets, producing a genuine follower of Christ. They are the biblical, spiritual, and foundational codes and characteristics of our godly beliefs! Hope is the gift that will encourage and motivate us to endure and persevere no matter the situation. But this is vitally important—you cannot possess Real Hope without a genuine life of faith and love built on Jesus Christ the Redeemer—our Lord, King, and the Rock of Salvation!

A powerful and profound passage that cements the worth and value of these moral principles is in Paul's writing in 1 Thessalonians 1:3: "We always thank God for all of you and pray for you constantly. As we pray to our God and Father about you, we think of your faithful work, your loving deeds, and the enduring hope you have because of our Lord Jesus Christ." Here, Paul complimented the Thessalonian believers for 1) Their work produced by faith—2) Their labor prompted by love—and 3) Their endurance inspired by hope. Just as love can be considered the motivating factor for faith and hope (1 Cor 13:13), so hope also encourages and builds up believers in the practice of love and faith (Col 1:3–5).

When these three transformative elements are at work in the Christian life, they shape the mindset, heart, and attitudes towards any activity, reflecting the work of the Lord. Their combined power, like the Trinity, should prompt us to ask: "Are these three components shaping my life for the betterment of our future descendants and others?" If they are, hope will rise to the surface, inspiring us to build up the future generation of believers in the practice of Christlike love and genuine saving faith!

Think about the power of each one of these glorious elements: *Faith* is the virtue of our solid belief in God—and without faith, we cannot please our Lord (Heb 11:6). *Love* is the virtue of seeking *what is best for the loved one*—and if we Love the Lord, we will obey His words (John 14:15). And always remember—love lasts forever. Finally, *Hope* is the virtue of being confident in our eternal life in Christ—it knows that we can rest in what He tells us in His word, which is faithful and accurate (2 Cor 5:1–10). After all, that is what His promises are designed to do: To inspire hope and give us the boldness and confidence to live and share it. Consider this statement: "When we lack Christlike hope, we're not trusting and resting on the promises of God's truths that others need to hear and witness in our lives."

Hope is the anchor that sustains our faith in the face of any situation, assuring us that regardless of the outcome, God will come through. This is the essence of hope. Consider the Israelites: "In all their weaknesses, as they cried out to God, many of His children still had hope while they were still in bondage—and even during their wandering years in the wilderness." Even today, when we are in our darkest times, we can hold onto our Hope in the One Who will carry us and sustain us through the trials. Hope is the link to our genuine faith in the Lord's strength—knowing He loves us and will never forsake us.

These profound words deeply move me from John MacArthur. "When we place our hope in God alone, that hope becomes the wellspring of our truest, purest, and highest joy (Neh 8:10). This is because God is our rock; He is unchangeable, faithful, and sovereign. His unfolding purpose cannot be thwarted, and this kind of hope leaves no room for fear. By faith, we know that God is for us, which means He will save and grant eternal life to those who trust Him. Most importantly, when remembered, this hope fortifies us against any doubts that may assail us, filling our hearts with a joy that is beyond measure."[1] How?

Hope is our shield against the assaults of Satan. No matter what trials we face in this world, we hold fast to the promise of a better life to come. Regardless of the troubles, trials, struggles, illnesses, diseases, disasters, or deaths that may befall us, we cling to the hope of a glorious future—and we eagerly anticipate its arrival. When Satan seeks to sow seeds of doubt in our hearts, we return to the revelation of our hope. As Paul urges us in 1 Thess 5:8–11, we stand firm in our hope, knowing that it is our greatest defense.

Let's return to a key chapter in the Bible regarding our genuine living faith and hope. The author in Heb 11:1–2, 6 reminds us: "Faith shows the reality of what we hope for; it is the evidence of things we cannot see. Through their faith, the people in the days of old earned a good reputation. By faith, we understand that the entire universe was formed at God's command, that what we now see did not come from anything that can be seen..." And it is impossible to please God without faith. Anyone who wants to come to him must believe that God exists and that he rewards those who sincerely seek him."

The assurance and conviction of genuine saving faith that pleases God begins with Him. Remember, *faith* is a gift of grace God gives us out of His love. Once we accept Jesus Christ as Lord and Savior by faith and live it out in our daily lives, it will bring to the surface our passion for the Lord—and genuine compassion for others' well-being in the future. The summation of this beautiful gift from God will reveal a powerful depiction of an undeniable Hope for something to come: our eternal resting place.

1. MacArthur. John. "Hope Under Attack."

This is a key takeaway for you and me: "From the true principles and foundation of faith and love, nothing is pleasing to God without the existence and our solid position of righteousness in Jesus Christ, God's only Son. And our hope in Him reveals that the Spirit is alive and well within us for the world to see. The way that faith and love connect with hope is through godly wisdom and that ongoing seeking of Him. Proverbs 24:14 says, *"In the same way, wisdom is sweet to your soul. If you find it, you will have a bright future, and your hopes will not be cut short."* What a sweet spot to be in life, not only for God's glory and for us individually—but for our loved ones and others to see visually.

That is why we must understand the magnitude of sharing the Gospel with others and leaving a legacy of genuine faith, hope, and love in our future paths for God's glory. Our undisputed lives of Christlikeness should portray this—"conveying and displaying the truth of God's active Word at work in us by the biblical and spiritual trail we lay forth that can benefit others today, tomorrow, and eternally." Yes, the Christlike qualities that we exhibit, as God's Citizens of Heaven on Earth (Phil 1: 27–30), can significantly make a difference in so many lives that we're in contact with (Read Colossians chapter 3 and Galatians chapter 5).

Don't we realize this fact by now, and it's this: You and I can metaphorically (resemblance) give so many people "a Taste of Heaven and God's goodness" through our actions and way of life by embodying and demonstrating godly attributes like humility, service, love, compassion, kindness, forgiveness, and peace, which reflects the characteristics often associated with a Heavenly realm on Earth. When we do this for the good of all within our proximity, we show others what a life guided by divine principles might look like.

Just think about the power and impact of our Christian lives on others when we live according to the truths of His Word—guided by the Holy Spirit. You and I have the undeniable opportunity to give a glimpse of what godly election, justification, redemption, and sanctification look like by the way we conduct our everyday lives as 'solid and genuine' Christians who have 'Real Hope' that will soon lead to a day of glorification. We all have a God-given choice and responsibility to make a difference in others' state of spirituality right now today!

Here's the power of genuine Hope in Christ and all His promises. It becomes a transforming reality in our daily lives, resulting in God being glorified through us, as Paul states in 1 Corinthians 10:31. God's word also reminds us in Tit 2:13 that our blessed hope from God brings us joy through the trials and tribulations we face in this world. This should cause us to stop and evaluate our thoughts, words, and actions so we can be a blessing to our

"The Reason for Hope"

Lord because of our Hope in Him! After all, He's given us this Hope for a reason! And that's to live, share, and ensure it's passed on to others.

Paul reminds us in Rom 15:13, "I pray that God, the source of hope, will fill you with joy and peace because you trust in him. Then, you will overflow with confident hope through the power of the Holy Spirit." Paul's description of God as the "God of hope" signifies that, even when the future seems uncertain and unpredictable, our steadfastness in God's love and faithfulness will keep our minds in perfect peace (Isa 26:3). If our lives are genuinely overflowing with confident hope in Jesus Christ our Rock—there are so many wonderful holy attributes we can spread to all our family, friends, relatives, and everyone within our reach!

Also, in this beautiful passage, Paul prays that the God of hope will fill us with "all joy and peace." Hope is connected to the qualities of joy and peace, which tells us that hope generates these two precious elements within us, even in adversity.[2] In these times of uncertainty, we all need these beautiful attributes to positively affect other people's lives—especially our children and the younger generation! As we've seen solidly throughout this journey, Hope is a powerful virtue that should be lived out in the Christian life.

With that, this should be our daily challenge for the good of God's creation: "To be imitators of Christ (Eph 5:1)." Then, watch the power of His Spirit change and affect lives for decades, if not centuries! But we must be committed to His cause today, tomorrow, and in the future—because that's His desire for you and me! Yes, parents can make "The Difference in Future Generations for the Glory of God!" Only if our priorities and choices are established on God's firm foundation and aligned with His long-term purpose and plan—will we be able to achieve our godly goals! Are you on board?

1 John 4:4, "But you belong to God, my dear children. You have already won a victory over those people, because the Spirit who lives in you is greater than the spirit who lives in the world."

---

2. Got Questions. "May the God of Hope Fill You?"

"Our Foundation in Hope!"

Let's recall the powerful message of the old hymn, 'Solid Rock': "My hope is built on nothing less than Jesus' blood and righteousness. I dare not trust the sweetest frame but wholly lean on Jesus' name. On Christ, the solid Rock, I stand: all other ground is sinking sand." This hymn echoes the Parable of the Wise and the Foolish Builders, a crucial lesson from Jesus about the necessity of building our Christian life on a firm foundation, which is the word of God. Let's not overlook this vital lesson and commit ourselves to this unyielding foundation of faith.

Jesus reminds us in His profound parable in Matt 7:24–27, "Anyone who listens to my teaching and follows it is wise, like a person who builds a house on solid rock. Though the rain comes in torrents, the floodwaters rise, and the winds beat against that house, it won't collapse because it is built on bedrock. But anyone who hears my teaching and doesn't obey it is foolish, like a person who builds a house on sand. When the rains and floods come, and the winds beat against that house, it will collapse with a mighty crash." This security and stability comes from building our lives on the solid foundation of Jesus Christ, our Living Hope.

Our Lord and Savior is reminding you and me that we can only build a solid foundation on Him by hearing and responding to His message—in other words, obeying every detail of His Holy Word. This is not a passive process but an intentional and active one. If we're not intentionally building our Christian life of faith, hope, and love on the foundation of Jesus Christ, we will not have a driven purpose in this life as obedient and loyal servants—and we will be headed down a path of deception.

The Apostle Paul even reminds us in 1 Cor 3:10–18, "Because of God's grace to me, I have laid the foundation like an expert builder. Now, others are building on it. But whoever is building on this foundation must be very careful. For no one can lay any foundation other than the one we already have—Jesus Christ. Anyone who builds on that foundation may use various

"Our Foundation in Hope!"

materials—gold, silver, jewels, wood, hay, or straw. But on judgment day, fire will reveal what kind of work each builder has done. The fire will show if a person's work has any value. If the work survives, that builder will receive a reward." This is the hope and inspiration that comes from a life built on the foundation of Jesus Christ.

"But if the work is burned up, the builder will suffer great loss. The builder will be saved, but like someone barely escaping through a wall of flames. Don't you realize that all of you together are the temple of God and that the Spirit of God lives in you? God will destroy anyone who destroys this temple. For God's temple is holy, and you are that temple. Stop deceiving yourselves. If you think you are wise by this world's standards, you need to become a fool to be truly wise."

Just like the church's foundation, our homes and individual lives are to be built on the foundation of our Lord, Redeemer, and Savior, and nothing else. This pertains to officials, preachers, teachers, parents, and all leaders. It is the responsibility of each of these highly appointed positions by God to ensure that the essence of all our groundwork and principles are built on the Cornerstone so they will sustain for years to come. It must comprise the right doctrine and righteous living to endure all the challenges confronting our holy structures. It must consist of spiritually mature, sound, sensitive, and discerning bodies that meet God's standards. Anything of lesser value will not meet the specifications of a Holy God.

This is crucial because if you look at Paul's passage in 1 Corinthians chapter 3, there is an underlying message *for those who 'are not' building a firm foundation on Jesus Christ*. It's this: If we use unspiritual material other than the principles of God's word as our daily source, we will be more identified with self, seeking the wrong things in life and compromising with the ways of the world. We will then find ourselves with no spiritual purpose, not moving with the Lord, which leads to a weakened spiritual life.

'Genuine Christians' who build their foundation on Christ will be responsible builders because they will form and structure it with the best their hearts, minds, souls, and strength can offer the Lord. Their lives are not just built on church services one day per week—but a daily life of fervent prayer, consistent Bible meditation, selfless and humble service, the actual application of God's word into their lives, diligent repentance, sincere obedience, unconditional submission, and sharing with their loved ones and others the importance of this firm foundation—so it will sustain the tests of time for years to come.

This is so vital because, as caring, compassionate, and wise Christians, we need to realize this fact: "There is a tactic and strategy by the work of the enemy that has been out to devour and divide one era at a time—since the beginning—until the Lord returns. Satan is subtly working in ways—creeping and maneuvering his deceptive ways into every tiny crack in the younger generation's lives. This has now become a distraction not only for the children but also for the parents. It becomes a rippling and crippling spiritual crutch that leads the family unit from a life of godly obedience and faith—to hopelessness in time. And when the enemy accomplishes those feats, he is on the path of complete and total destruction in our homes.

So, here's a key question for you and me: "Have we, as Christian parents and family leaders, built our firm foundation on *'Christ alone and His teachings'*—for the spiritual security of our children, their children, and all future heirs?" When they look at us as their role model in life, do we portray and convey (internally and externally) a life of righteous living that embodies genuine faith, hope, and love that will resonate with them for years to come?

As stated above, just like building a church on the guiding principles of God's Holy Word, which entails the *right doctrine and right living—that meets and adheres to God's standards*—so, too, we as individuals (as His church) should ensure that we're grounded in the sound preaching and teaching of the Bible. Why is this important? It will prevent our homes from having a cracked foundation in a world surrounded by so many falsehoods and deceptions—but also prohibit us from living a life by the status quo of hypocrisy. But just as important, we must pass on these Truths to our children and others for their well-being.

Just think—if all parents are aligned with God's ultimate guiding plan, this will be the outcome: 'Committed & Loyal Kingdom Builders' are not just building their lives on the unshakable foundation of Jesus' blood and His righteousness, but they are also spreading this foundation to everyone around them. How? These believers have developed both internal and external groundwork to withstand the trials of life. But their mission doesn't end there. They are also preparing future generations for their eternal home. The key to their success lies in their genuine heart that consistently seeks the Lord, yearning to fulfill His ways in their everyday life. Their work on this foundation is a testament to their unwavering dedication to God and their love for others!

Always remember the transformative power of reflecting on God's goodness, faithfulness, and promises in your everyday life. When we reflect on these throughout our life's journey, it transforms our response to the world. Instead of fear, we respond with hope. Resting in His provisions ignites our motivation and genuine compassion for others, compelling us to pass them down. When we discipline ourselves to remember His blessings and engrave them in our hearts and minds, they inspire us to act in the present for a future impact. Throughout the Bible, God's people are urged to trust Him and join Him in His work of restoration and redemption for the good of society. This happens when we continue to remind others of the significance of God's work today and His promises for the future!

So how can we, as Christian parents, raise godly generations on the firm foundation of Christ? Once again, let's return to the message Moses preached to Israel in Deuteronomy 6 as they prepared to enter the land of Canaan. They would face many temptations in the land as the pagans surrounded them with their wicked ways. So, they had to ensure they possessed a supernatural force enabling them to abide by God's ways and pass them on to future heirs.

His point is this: To raise up godly generations, we must love God fervently, talk about His goodness, love, mercy, and grace every day, and teach our children diligently the word of God and the importance of applying His ways in their lives. This next step is vital: "We must live in the world carefully by God's wisdom, knowledge, and guidance, not men." If our own relatives see the love of the Lord and His ways in us, it will make a difference in one way or another. And never forget this: Our Lord is worthy of our efforts in teaching others these Truths! [1]

Legitimate Followers of Christ—the wiser generation of today, are commanded by our Heavenly Father to teach the fundamentals of our faith, passed down to us—so they can be carried forward to our future descendants. It is our God-given responsibility to lead the newer generations to these foundational basics below for their spiritual and biblical well-being:

- The importance of God's word! It's the Truth! (Matt 7:24, 2 Tim 3:16–17, Heb 4:12–13, Psalm chapter 119, Isa 40:8, 1 Pet 1:25, Jas 1:22).
- Who is God? Creator, Holy, and Sovereign! (Genesis chapter 1, 2 Sam 7:22, John 4:24, 1 Tim 1:17, Matt 3:16–17, Mal 3:16, Ps 139:7–12, Ps 147:5, Isa 40:28, Ephesians 1; Revelation 19:6)[2].
- Who is Jesus Christ? Our Savior and Hope for the world! (John 1:1, John 3:16, 1 Tim 2:5, John 10:30, John 14:6, 1 Cor 8:6, Col 1:15–20, 2:9, Rev 1:8).
- Who is the Holy Spirit? Our Counselor and Comforter, Who leads into all Truths! (Matt 28:19, John 14:26, John 15:26, Galatians chapter 5, Acts 1:8, Acts 2:38, Eph 4:30, Rom 8:26, 1 Cor 2:7–11, 2 Cor 3:17).

---

1. Cole. Steven. "Raising Godly Generations."
2. Got Questions. "Who is God?"

- What is true Christianity? Our real identity in Christ—our Living Hope! (Gal 2:20, Galatians chapter five, Colossians chapter three, Eph 2:8–9, 1 & 2 Peter).
- When should I act on my Christian faith? Daily! (Psalm chapter 119, Rom 10:17, 1 John 5:4).
- Where should I exemplify my Christian beliefs? Everywhere! (Rom 1:16, 2 Tim 1:8–12, 1 Pet 1:13–16, 1 Pet 2:12, Col 4: 5–6).
- Why is my Christian faith important? It reveals our genuine hope and love! (Proverbs chapter three, Eph 2:8, Jas 2:17, Hebrews chapter eleven).
- How can I live out my faith? Genuine application of God's word through the power of the Holy Spirit! (Matt 6:24, Matt 16:24, Rom 8:11, 2 Cor 5:17, Col 3:17, 1 Thess 1:2–3)
- What is the importance of worshipping God? Draws us closer to Him! (John 4:24, Ps 95:6, Isa 25:1, Rom 12:1–2, Heb 13:15, Eph 4:11–12).

When we wholeheartedly embrace and apply these fundamental godly principles in our lives, we are not just living but also transforming. This transformation, fueled by the empowering presence of the Holy Spirit, has the potential to influence and change lives. It's not just a theoretical concept but a tangible reality, especially in a society and culture that is undoubtedly drifting from the Truths of God's word and His ways of righteous living.

We must take ownership of these teachings today, tomorrow, and for the rest of the years, God allows us on this earth. We have a crucial opportunity to shake the foundations of each individual in our homes, schools, workplaces, churches, communities, and every beating turn with the Power of God's word active in our daily lives! As disciples of Christ, we bear the weighty responsibility of planting and watering every seed of faith, hope, and love for the future of God's Kingdom.

This is imperative: We cannot live in a tunnel of oblivion, thinking it will happen without our involvement and engagement in a society and culture gradually falling away from the Word of God. Why is this urgent? Most current generations are becoming increasingly exposed to social media and artificial intelligence (as noted earlier). Their everyday function will become more and more "humanless" than ever before in history.

So, if current and future generations are not grounded in the foundation of God's principles, their way of communicating and interacting could structure their lives in ways conflicting with God's design. It is feared that the only truth they will come to know is falsehood, which is the opposite of

"Our Foundation in Hope!"

God's expectations in life. In time, they will engage with more ways of the world—than God's. Just go back to the disheartening statistics at the outset of the book.

But as passionate children of God who genuinely care for this country's spiritual future, we have the power to help alter our loved ones' ways biblically! [3] We fervently pray that accountable Christian parents and leaders can pass on their core principles of biblical living. This is not just a hope but a necessity so that future eras can preserve and sustain them, enhancing Christlikeness everywhere for the good of God—and not man! It is a call to action for you and me to put our godly heritage into motion by investing it into the lives of the younger generations today!

---

3. Skiena.Steven. "Why Generation Alpha Z are Non-Religious?'

"Hope in Action"

This is another critical phase of our lives as Christians and leaders within our household and abroad, and that's ensuring that the Living Hope we have in Christ is actively in motion. What does this mean? In God's word, we can clearly see that hope is an action word, which means once we put all our trust in God (internally), we physically make efforts to move it forward because we know that what He says in His word will happen. Look at it this way: Our genuine hope in our Lord is an internal movement to an outward display of our absolute belief in God's promises and our joint effort with the Lord in that journey. It involves taking steps towards what we hope for, even when it's complicated.

Another way to look at it is when our hope is in action, we depend upon the Lord for everything. The Bible shows us that we should put our hope in God and wait on him before acting on our own. The Psalmist reminds us in Psalm 27:14, "Wait patiently for the LORD. Be brave and courageous. Yes, wait patiently for the LORD". When we allow the Holy Spirit to work out Living Hope, it is an act of binding God's promises in our lives with all our hearts, souls, minds, and strength.

It's packing the power of His words and truth around our hearts and minds, and truth be known—in our everyday lives. This can involve choosing to surround our tragedies and personal wounds with what you and I know about God's love, redemption, protection, and provision instead of asking questions like, "Why did this happen?" Remember, it's ok to ask why, but we mustn't stay stuck in that rut of complacency! When troubles come, it's part of our growing process that should always lead to progress! It benefits us individually, our loved ones, everyone within our presence, and most importantly, God our Father. How? Because it establishes more Christlikeness in our lives for the benefit of all!

Always remember this PowerPoint: "Our actions of the Living Hope in our personal lives play a critical role in the Christian faith by offering comfort to those suffering and going through intense battles. Living out this undeniable confidence of good things to come can assist others in persevering through their own trials and tribulations." How? Through our active lives as Christians, living by every word of God, fueled by the Holy Spirit, others will see that genuine saving faith and hope can sustain and strengthen our spiritual lives. The effects of our active Hope can encourage and motivate all believers to live righteous lives—because they will come to believe that what's to come is real and will indeed happen, and that's our eternal home with Christ.

You see, our active Christian Hope can influence others in powerful spiritual ways. How? Because of our godly responses in motion, others and our close ones will come to believe and know that their actions of righteousness will one day be rewarded in heaven! It's not that they expect anything in return for their faithful works; this action is like a supernatural 'second nature' as part of our Christian Walk. Genuine saving faith, love, and enduring hope will yield God's working salvation in and through our lives!

We often think of hope as an emotion or sense of feeling. However, without action to back it up, hope won't help us endure, persevere, grow, and move forward in our Christlike lives in fruitful ways. Hope is actually more of a way of thinking or a state of being. As Christians, it's putting all those holy attributes of obedience, faith, love, and hope into practice. According to the Bible, putting God's word into practice is a spiritual habit or discipline that involves taking ideas and thoughts and turning them into actions and deeds. This is part of our growing and maturing phase as genuine followers of Christ. It impacts our daily walk with the Lord, but just as significantly, it positively influences our children and others around us! In our most challenging moments or seasons, we cannot rely on feelings alone. If so, it's dangerous.

Think about the power of putting God's word into practice and action daily! It demonstrates our genuine love for His word, our faith in all His ways, and Hope, knowing that it will all work together for the good, no matter what! This step in our Christian lives is so important because it illustrates that we have personally prepared, exercised, and repeated Christlike acts for ourselves, others, and, most importantly, our Heavenly Father.

God's word reminds us powerfully in Jas 1:22–25, "Do not deceive yourselves by just listening to his word; instead, put it into practice." The verse continues, "But don't just listen to God's word. You must do what it says. Otherwise, you are only fooling yourselves. For if you listen to the word and don't obey, it is like glancing at your face in a mirror. You see yourself, walk away, and forget what you look like. But if you look carefully into the perfect law that sets you free, and if you do what it says and don't forget what you heard, then God will bless you for doing it."

Even the great Apostle Paul tells us in Phil 4:9 to keep putting into practice all we have learned and received, and the peace of God will be with us! When we intentionally put our Christlike actions in motion, they will surely touch others! But we must engage with others so we can enforce this! Here's the power of putting our Christlike action of Hope at work. It shows we're students of God's word—because the Power of the Spirit is leading us, and we are more connected with the Fruit of the Spirit (Christlike love, joy, peace, patience, kindness, faithfulness, gentleness, goodness, and self-control)—than the ways of man and this world. This guidance from the Spirit reassures us that we are on the right path.

In Romans chapter 12, Paul profoundly reminds us of a sense of urgency for Christians in the body of Christ, but also for all family leaders and believers, and it's this: "To put sacrificial love into action," He tells us that our "Love must be sincere and we must hate what is evil. Paul points out that true believers love genuinely, without hypocrisy, and overcome evil with good." This is not just a suggestion but a command for us to follow. It's a call to show the depth of our faith and commitment, especially for parents and family leaders, for the sake of our children. Why, you ask?

You see, God's children are lovers of good, and they hate evil because it is the enemy of all that is good. Always remember, as God's creation, we're made in His image, and it's our calling to love what is good because God Himself is good—the source of all Goodness (Mark 10:18). Everything God created is "very good" in every aspect (Genesis 1:31). With that, our goodness as believers, our righteousness or moral excellence, is assured by being made right with God through faith in Jesus Christ (Ps 14:3; Rom 3:22; 10:4).

And no matter what, we cling to this source of goodness because it brings us joy and fulfillment in representing God for the benefit of our children and loved ones! By putting good deeds in motion and genuinely showing kindness and sacrificial love outwardly to others, we prove that we are the children of God. God's word reminds us in 3 John 1:11, "Dear friend, do not imitate what is evil but what is good. Anyone who does what is good is from God. Anyone who does what is evil has not seen God" (see James 3:13).

Let's return to the Israelites. God warned the people of Israel to turn away from their corrupt behavior and "do what is good" (Amos 5:14). If they would go against the prevailing corruption by hating evil behavior and clinging to what is good and righteous, and if they would defend justice instead of trampling on it (Amos 5:10–12), the Lord would stand by them as their defender rather than as their judge. Similarly, Paul asserted that to

"Hope in Action"

those who "keep on doing good, seeking after the glory and honor and immortality that God offers," the Lord will give eternal life. "But he will pour out his anger and wrath on those who live for themselves, who refuse to obey the truth and instead live lives of wickedness" (Rom 2:7–8).

Clinging to what is pleasing and good in God's sight is when we walk by the Spirit of God, and the Fruit of the Spirit is in motion in our daily lives. This is vital because it draws us closer to Christ, resulting in Christ-likeness of character that will indeed affect others around us. God calls us to do good, even if it means suffering, just as Christ suffered for you and me. He is our example, and we must follow in all His steps. We cling to what is good for the well-being of others by ensuring we're joined with the Lord, our source of Hope. Always remember that when Jesus Christ effectively works in and through us—by His Spirit—this is all the goodness we need to be wholly good (not perfect)—because this will surely display that our Living Hope is active and alive.[1] What a powerful and wonderful feeling!

Jesus reminds us in His Sermon on the Mount in Matthew chapter 5, "You are the light of the world—like a city on a hilltop that cannot be hidden. No one lights a lamp and then puts it under a basket. Instead, a lamp is placed on a stand, where it gives light to everyone in the house. In the same way, let your good deeds shine out for all to see so that everyone will praise your heavenly Father." This is the godly impact we can have on others and our loved ones when we cling to God's goodness—and convey and portray it in our daily lives! It can touch so many outwardly and internally!

In my last book, God's People Count, Connecting God's Dots, the main message was to discover common ground with others, so it enables us to connect with people more effectively. For you and me to impact current and future generations, we must find ways to relate with them—and there is no greater relevance than the foundation of mercy, grace, and love found in Jesus Christ. We need to clothe ourselves with tenderhearted mercy, kindness, humility, gentleness, and patience, and above all, clothe ourselves with love, which binds us all together in perfect harmony that will touch our young ones' lives. In doing this, parents will connect with their children and the younger generation in invaluable ways today that will make a difference. And this is vital. Why?

Make no mistake—as we've seen consistently throughout this journey, many of this new generation long for relationships and significance in ways that can glorify God. And this is key: As we relate to the younger generations, we will discover they are open to mentoring and coaching. Why? Because they want to interact with others and succeed in life. Don't

---

1. Got Questions. "What Does It Mean to Cling to What is Good?"

be fooled—millions seek hope that will lead them to a better outcome than ever before. I genuinely believe that if godly leaders lead them, they will become leaders who can make a difference in society for the good of God! With that, we need to instill in them (now) the importance of recognizing God's blessings and empowering grace when they live by the biblical teachings of His word.

Still, it will require the older generation, who should be wiser and more discerning, to relate differently to the younger generation with a similar godly approach as above. It should be the older generations' inspiration to take action and raise an era with a restored biblical worldview that will change how they relate to their culture, which can impact the world for God's glory in the future. But it will also require the next generation to be humble in their acceptance of these teachings in extending the Truths of the Bible to its farthest point in this life. However, for all generations to succeed in this progression of God's Kingdom, it starts with each one taking responsibility for planting the seed of God's word from their very lips of grace and love with each upcoming era (Col 4:6).

The wisest man in the Bible, Solomon, reminds us in Prov 10:11–13, "The words of the godly are a life-giving fountain; the words of the wicked conceal violent intentions. Hatred stirs up quarrels, but love makes up for all offenses. Wise words come from the lips of people with understanding, but those lacking sense will be beaten with a rod."

The influential power of this verse in Proverbs emphasizes the potential authority of our words and their impact on others around us. It suggests that a person's character is reflected in their speech and that the righteous and more mature Christians should strive to use their words to uplift and bring life to those around them, especially the next generation who can help carry the torch of God's work forward.

Our words and deeds possess an extraordinary power, serving as the very building blocks of others' lives. In the beginning, God 'spoke' the world into existence by the power of His words (Hebrews 11:3). As stated so often throughout this book, as God's creation, we are made in His image, and our words and deeds also carry a transformative power that can shape a generation—like a life-giving fountain that perpetually springs forth God's most divine characteristics.

This is important because many reports state that our young ones hear 18 negative statements for every positive one (so sad). Other reports even show that kids hear over 400 negative words a day. So, this makes me ask: How many positive words does it take to equalize this negative output? Here it is: Experts tell us it takes seven positive words to counteract one negative comment! This shows the incredible potential of positive words to counteract negativity, giving us a reason to be optimistic and motivated.[2]

To put this into a more biblical perspective, God expects parents to bring a child up in the instruction of the Lord, which means parents should treat their children the way God treats you and me. As our Heavenly Father, God is "slow to anger" (Num 14:18; Ps 145:8), patient, and forgiving—His discipline is designed to bring us to repentance and restoration (Heb 12:6–11), not brokenness.

The power of our words can weigh heavily on one's spirit, leading to discord and division and even inciting hatred and violence. However, when we yield to the Holy Spirit, our words and actions can also be so uplifting that they positively influence and spread to others with such spiritual impact that they can change a country of people to come to believe and follow the Lord (Read James chapter 3). But here's a gut punch: Is teaching the word of God to our future heirs and others even a priority within the foundation of family homes throughout this great land today?

Unfortunately, as we've seen with the earlier data, in America, our perspectives and views are twisted and distorted, just like the Israelites from the first generation. We define success and align our priorities around money, possessions, titles, positions, careers, or our family heritage, but God views success through a different set of lenses. He desires us to teach, raise, and ingrain His words of life in our family's lives so they can sustain in Building His Future Kingdom! Remember, when Moses leaned more upon God's ways versus his ways, unbelievable promises were fulfilled. You see, godly actions moved with unbelievable progress when this great leader, prophet, messenger, and friend of God allowed Yahweh to work through him!

Our #1 goal and prayer should be that our children will raise their future heirs on the core biblical truths of the Bible. In turn, continuing that cycle, that era will also raise their children to become devout believers in Christ as their Savior and Guide, which will continue to be passed on. It's the principle of 2 Tim 2:2, which says, "You have heard me teach things that many reliable witnesses have confirmed. Now teach these truths to other trustworthy people who can pass them on to others."

What Paul poured into Timothy was also to be poured into others; in other words, he was not to keep it to himself. The key takeaway in this passage is that they were also looking for trustworthy and faithful responders who would take responsibility and actively pass these truths on. Can we honestly say we are part of God's dedicated ones who will pass His Truths on to future eras?

---

2. Rhinehart. Deanna. "Kids Hear Over 400 Negative Words A Day."

In 1 Tim 4:10, Paul reminds us, "This is why we work hard and continue to struggle, for our hope is in the living God, who is the Savior of all people and particularly of all believers." Here, Paul is reminding you and me that our hope for this great salvation is only practical for those who genuinely believe in Christ as their Lord and hold on to all His promises, regardless of the trying times we will endure! We must cling to His promises during these trying times, for they are our beacon of hope and our strength to persevere.

However, the enemy does not want you and me to believe this truth, so he misguides us as often as possible! And when parents are misled and out of sync with God, our children and the younger generation will be off-kilter, too. We suddenly find ourselves not moving with God and all His plans and purpose in our lives. We cannot allow the enemy to do this in our personal and, equally important, family lives. We should all know by now that a key tactic of the enemy is to cease (stop) all our Christlike actions for the good of others. He will continue to do everything in his 'limited' power to prevent us from moving forward with acts of godliness. But remember, our Almighty God has infinitely more living power than the enemy will ever have, providing us with a sense of security and confidence in our faith and assuring us that we will prevail!

Once again, never forget what Paul tells us in this powerful set of verses in Colossians chapter 3, which is our new life in Christ—our Living Hope! Col 3:16-17, "Let the message about Christ, in all its richness, fill your lives. Teach and counsel each other with all the wisdom he gives. Sing psalms and hymns and spiritual songs to God with thankful hearts. And whatever you do or say, do it as a representative of the Lord Jesus, giving thanks through him to God the Father." As the Lord's representatives on this earth, we are charged and implored to teach and counsel others and all our loved ones about Christ, Our Hope. And this can only be done through the wisdom of God actively at work in you and me, empowering and guiding us in our faith journey!

So, you ask, why are actions of the Living Hope so important for our future heirs to seek and cling to? As our children and the younger generations grow, hope is one of the most important things they can learn in a world that is lost, blinded, and full of deep despair. Teaching our children biblical hope is vital because it is an invaluable lesson to help them endure and persevere through the trials and tests of times in this society and culture. It will give them a True Source to help them overcome those challenging life barriers.

The power of hope in Christ willingly and patiently endures suffering, no matter the intensity. How? Because it is convinced that this present suffering is nothing compared to our future glory with the Lord (Rom. 8:18). You see, by grace through faith, we are saved, and we can walk daily with our God and learn how to grow closer and closer to Him. And in love, we grow in our knowledge and relationship with God and others. And in hope, we endure hardship that helps us to keep our eyes fixed on God and our Lord and Savior.

In 2 Thess 2:16-17, Paul reminds us, "Now may our Lord Jesus Christ himself and God our Father, who loved us and by his grace gave us eternal comfort and a *wonderful hope*, comfort you and strengthen you in every good thing you do and say." You see, the power of our 'Living Hope' never gives up, and it does not stop praising our Lord—no matter what comes our way today, tomorrow, and the future."

Living Hope helps our younger generation press on toward their godly goals today and in the future without losing faith and their love for God's will and plan. It is one of life's most essential values and attributes that children need to develop. Why? Because children who understand the value of 'Real Hope' will be less likely to lose their faith or give up in life (as discussed earlier). And guess where it starts? It starts with the leaders in the homes, and that's you and me! So, you ask, how can I teach hope?

Cultivating is the beginning phase of preparing, developing, nurturing, and fostering something into growth. It is a process that requires diligence, discipline, and hard work with the expectation that something good will be produced. This same process applies to parents teaching hope to our children because it starts with you and me as the Christian leaders in our homes. You ask again, how? Through our active lives as genuine believers, we show them that the Lord is good, almighty, and trustworthy. In time, they will understand that they should set their hope in God alone because He's the Source of Hope. It will help them to keep His commandments as a guiding rule in their everyday lives.

With that, we must remember our Christian responsibility as parents is to educate our children and ensure they understand God's Word and the importance of His promises for the future. When parents do this, it assures them that there is a better chance of spiritual survival for their heirs if we plant this invaluable seed. And with hope and prayer, it will take root and manifest over time! When it manifests, it gives our children confidence and boldness and helps guard their minds and hearts against all the falsehoods and temptations in this life. How?

Because they know Who their source of Truth is—they will know what direction to take when they reach that crossroad in life. Because Living Hope encourages, builds up, motivates, and knows there is a more remarkable outcome, it never gives up—because real hope points them to

Christ, our Lord! It reassures them that He is their Way, Truth, and Life (John 14:6). This type of hope is sure and will never disappoint—it is the anchor to their soul (Heb 6:19).

Contemplate the wonder of this great treasure bestowed upon us by the power of the Holy Spirit. It's a precious gift demonstrating God's boundless love for you and me. When hope is lavished upon believers, this divine gift instills confidence, boldness, joy, peace, contentment, and power in us. With His unwavering presence, the Holy Spirit assures us that nothing can separate us from the love of God in Christ Jesus our Lord. Our unshakable trust in God's word and promises is the wellspring of our active Christian lives.

Let us always remember that this gift is not something we can achieve on our own; it is a gift of faith—given to us when we accept Christ as the Lord of our lives. For we now have the power of God's indwelling Spirit in us, Who can help us to put our hope into action! However, parents hold a significant role in this journey, leading their children and the younger generation to that Reliable Source of Hope through their way of life, teachings, and godly discipline. As we can see, our role as godly parents is of utmost importance in a world veering off course spiritually and biblically!

So, let us ask ourselves, are we truly living out our genuine Living Hope for the sake of our future descendants' well-being? What is our ultimate priority in life? If our genuine saving faith, hope, and love are in the Lord alone, and He is the Lordship of our lives, it should be evident and impactful for everyone within our sphere of influence! Is our Hope in action inwardly and outwardly in powerful ways? This is not just a gentle reminder but a stark warning for all of us, and I cannot stress this enough, and it's this:

If our hopes are focused more on earthly things than the ways of God, we will act foolishly, and we will always be mistakenly out of line with the Truth of God's teachings. Undoubtedly, the enemy's complicated and confusing traits of transgression, which are affecting the younger generations, are not going away; they will only heighten in the years to come—on this side of Heaven.

If our spiritual lives are not productively in motion, the enemy will exploit this vulnerability and continue his destructive ways, potentially leading us to despair. It's important to realize that this will not only affect us and the current generation but could also be a detriment to our future descendants. Therefore, we must progress and take *biblical steps in our own lives* for the betterment and benefit of our loved ones and others. When we do this in our active lives as concerned and caring Christian leaders, we illustrate absolute respect for our Heavenly Father, the kind of reverence and fear He wants us to possess in our lives.

"Hope in Action"

The Psalmist provides a profound passage that shows us the benefits of fearing the Lord with complete awe and respect, which leads us to work out our salvation for His glory. When we act out our genuine lives as followers of Christ, we sow things fruitfully in our family's lives, and in time, they will reap godly benefits for years to come. Psalm chapter 128 says, "How joyful are those who fear the LORD—all who follow his ways! You will enjoy the fruit of your labor. How joyful and prosperous you will be! Your wife will be like a fruitful grapevine, flourishing within your home. Your children will be like vigorous young olive trees as they sit around your table. That is the LORD's blessing for those who fear him. May the LORD continually bless you from Zion. May you see Jerusalem prosper as long as you live. May you live to enjoy your grandchildren. May Israel have peace!"

The key to enjoying these spiritual blessings through our family is recorded in Psalm 127:1: "Unless the Lord builds a house, the work of the builders is wasted. Unless the Lord protects a city, guarding it with sentries will do no good." Always remember, if our foundation of hope is not 'actively' built on the Truths and promises of Christ—our Lord and Savior—our efforts in helping to lead a future generation in godly ways will be futile.

Our role as parents and household leaders is a duty and a consequential responsibility. We must not allow the enemy to divert us from this crucial aspect of life—guiding the next generation through our godly actions in word and deed. This is not just important; it's vital for the next era of believers—because they are not just counting on us—but looking up to us. We must be vigilant and safeguard our family's best interests and future well-being for their spiritual survival. As the wiser generation of today, we should possess a discerning spirit that is so spiritually intuitive that it can detect even the slightest warning signs in our young ones' lives before it's too late!

Warning Signs

"Misguided Hope"

There is no greater danger in the American Family homes of today than this, and that's placing all our hopes, dreams, and wishes on the things of this world—versus the ways of God! When we put the value of our hearts, minds, and souls on the expectations of what man and the things of this world can temporarily offer us, we can easily take our focus off the value of our eternal perspective. Don't get me wrong; there is nothing wrong with wealth, education, maintaining a good family name, highly acclaimed positions, possessions, and even technology.

However, it's evident from the statistics at the outset of this book that the homes across this great land have succumbed to many of these temporal things that can easily misdirect and delude our Christian Walk. How? Because they are not grounded in the eternal matter—and do not place their faith, love, and hope in the Lord first! And that is a grave concern!

As parents and mature Christians today, we must accept this reality: "All of our misguided ways in the homes start with you and me as the wise ones." After all, who is the spiritual leader, nurturer, provider, and primary source of everything in our homes? It's the father, mother, and all guardians who rule the household! If the parents and leaders don't control spiritual imbalances at the early stages of these young ones' lives, there will be a wave of uncontrollable that we may never be able to rein in. I love this saying: "Control the controllable—before they get out of control and do more damage." The potential damage of not controlling these spiritual imbalances is immense, and it's our responsibility to prevent it.

In all our weaknesses, you would think that wise, discerning, and yearning parents would be crying out for God's guiding strength—especially with all the temptations confronting families in today's society and culture. This makes me ask: "Who would decline His empowering grace when it is so needed (2 Cor 12:9)?" Don't we realize that the Grace of God can help us overcome any developing barriers we face today? You see, God's grace transforms us from the inside out, affecting every aspect of our lives. It empowers us to live in freedom, joy, peace, and righteousness that can affect us individually and, most importantly, others. Remember that Almighty God wants us to stay united as one (under His divine power) because He has a beautiful purpose and plan for our family lives. His grace is our reassurance and our hope.

When we go through intense battles within our homes and need His strength more than ever, it is not a suggestion but a necessity to make God our first point of contact. He's not our second choice or backup plan. When we seek Him first, it is a powerful declaration that our spiritual choices and priorities are aligned with His will. When Christian parents seek the help of God's empowering grace—especially when they need it the most—it shows they are leaning and trusting upon Him more than anything else. This is not just important; it's critical for the sake of our children's state of spirituality—because, always remember, His strength works best in our weakness! Parents, we can be the source of spiritual and biblical strength and support for our children! We must be Rock Solid in our faith, love, and hope in Christ! Why is this so important?

When our Christian foundation of hope is cracked and misguided, the enemy will start hailing distress in our lives for various reasons. They are: 1) When believers are not consistently in the word of God, 2) Not applying and obeying His word in their daily lives, 3) Lacking a structured commitment of faithful service to the Lord, 4) Demonstrating a weak prayer life as individual(s) and a family, 5) Insufficient in their corporate worship, 6) Allowing too much of the world in their homes than the ways of the Lord, and 7) Not self-examining their genuine saving faith, hope, and love that should be grounded in Christ alone.

Christians, when we neglect the weakest areas in our lives, we inadvertently distance ourselves from God's word and the guidance of the Holy Spirit. This negligence can weaken our godly life in the family homes, making us vulnerable to the enemy's attacks. These hostile ambushes can damage us individually and, most importantly, our household—and even extend to our relatives and friends, creating a harmful domino effect spiraling out of control. It's vital to remember that maintaining a vigorous and sturdy spiritual life is not just a choice but a commitment we must uphold. The consequences of neglecting this commitment are severe, and we must act with urgency to prevent them.

Think about this key lesson! Suppose we don't address our areas of spiritual weakness, threats, and opportunities. In that case, this ill-fated condition can disconnect us from a genuine relationship with God, leading to a hardened heart, doubt, the wrong type of fear, worrying too much, and high levels of anxiety. We then get so out of sync with God that we start incorporating a cynical, critical, and judgmental spirit that leads to anger, frustration, discouragement, disheartenment, and even division. It's crucial to be aware that when the enemy has misled us down this path of vulnerability, he has us right where he wants us. We must remain vigilant and aware of his tactics to avoid falling into his traps.

The enemy knows how to bombard us in so many damaging ways that can lead to disastrous results. We then reach a point of damage control, trying to solve the problems we've allowed him to create in our lives—rather than resting in the promises of God's absolute truths from the beginning! I challenge you to return to the short four chapters Paul wrote to the Philippians! Observe, interpret, and apply these passages to counter these ill-fated vices! Scripture is a powerful tool that can empower us to counter the negative influences in our lives.

This is why Christian parents must teach their children and younger ones profound passages today, such as this one in Psalm chapter 1. "Oh, the joys of those who do not follow the advice of the wicked, or stand around with sinners, or join in with mockers. But they delight in the law of the LORD, meditating on it day and night. They are like trees planted along the riverbank, bearing fruit each season. Their leaves never wither, and they prosper in all they do. But not the wicked! They are like worthless chaff scattered by the wind. They will be condemned at the time of judgment. Sinners will have no place among the godly. For the LORD watches over the path of the godly, but the path of the wicked leads to destruction."

I cannot say this enough. When Satan sees a weak Christian structure in the homes—one that is so susceptible to His conniving ways, where our family focus is not grounded in obedience, faith, hope, and love in Christ, he will slide into our spiritually weak lives. We are now an open forum for his perpetual devious acts. You may ask, how does this happen? As discussed earlier, it occurs when the leaders in the homes (parents and guardians) allow inappropriate and unholy things to take root in their children's lives because of their unwise teachings, leading everyone to be misguided. Remember this: A misguided hope is when a person places their time, value, priority, choices, and needs in something *spiritually unfulfilling and has a flawed logic*.

This happens when someone has a weak spiritual foundation due to their carelessness—and doesn't have the discernment to choose the right things in life. It's because they are spiritually blind, foolish, and grounded in wrong information that leads them to a state of being delusional. The bottom line is that they have been duped with poor, unspiritual advice. In time, their thought process will become unrealistic or naïve in their expectations—because of the untruths in their lives. This will only lead to a path of no clear godly guidance!

Jesus reminds us in Matt 6:22-24, "Your eye is like a lamp that provides light for your body. When your eye is healthy, your whole body is filled with light. But when your eye is unhealthy, your whole body is filled with darkness. And if the light you think you have is actually darkness, how deep that darkness is! "No one can serve two masters. For you will hate one and love the other; you will be devoted to one and despise the other. You cannot serve God and be enslaved to money."

The Apostle Paul even tells us in Eph 5:5-11, "You can be sure that no immoral, impure, or greedy person will inherit the Kingdom of Christ and of God. For a greedy person is an idolater, worshiping the things of this world. Don't be fooled by those who try to excuse these sins, for the anger of God will fall on all who disobey him. Don't participate in the things these people do. For once, you were full of darkness, but now you have light from the Lord. So, live as people of light! For this light within you produces only what is good and right and true. Carefully determine what pleases the Lord. Take no part in the worthless deeds of evil and darkness; instead, expose them."

In these passages above, we can clearly see that we cannot be children of God who possess the Light and Hope of Christ—and dabble in the realms of darkness *at the same time*—because one has more control over our lives than the other (Galatians chapter 5). Always remember that our God is a jealous God (Exod 34:14). Why? Because He will not share His praise with other gods or idols that keep us from the presence of His holy and righteous ways of living. This is why our worship and honor should be dedicated and directed solely and wholly to Him, for this brings glory to His Most Precious and Holy name!

Warning—We need to bear this in mind each day of our lives on this side of Heaven: When anything or anyone takes over our Heavenly Father's position, which should always be #1, then we're off course to His guiding principles. When we get out of line with our Lord, we're now vulnerable to the enemy's attacks. That is why we must heed what the Apostle Paul teaches us in Romans 8:13 and Colossians 2:13-14, and that's: Put to death the deeds of our flesh and nail all our sinful passions to the Cross of Christ, once and for all!

Here's a gut punch that will strike an internal core with many parents. Seriously, think about this significant point. We cannot have biblical Hope in Christ—if our desires for worldly things and earthly expectations *are more of a focal point in our everyday lives than a yearning for God's purpose and plan*. If this happens, we've been misguided by the works of the enemy, the world, and our selfish desires (the flesh)! And when our lives as parents get to a state of selfishness—everyone else, including our children, doesn't matter anymore—because we're more focused on ourselves!

And when this happens, a void occurs, and we lose sight of our real hope in Christ and His saving grace. This will lead us to not hearing the actual voice of God and not heeding the guidance of the Holy Spirit! Hopefully, by now, parents should realize the importance of building our individual and family lives on Christ, the Solid Rock—because a cracked foundation and misguided ways from God's Truths will not produce a structured life with the Lord. Without that firm foundation in Christ, there will be no stability, growth, or signs of fruitful living. Once again, refer back to the Parable of the Four Soils in Matthew chapter 13.

Remember what Christ, our Savior, said about the Four Soils, which is so critical for our understanding today? Our Lord says, "To those who listen to my teaching, more understanding will be given, and they will have an abundance of knowledge. But for those who are not listening, even what little understanding they have will be taken away from them. That is why I use these parables, "For they look, but they don't really see. They hear, but they don't really listen or understand." Parents, if we're not genuinely adhering to the Truths of God's Word, applying and living them out, they will be taken away.

Why is this so vital? As stated so often throughout this journey, when we're not in line with God's plan, it affects us, our immediate family members, and other close ones within our homes and surrounding areas. And here's the root cause of the problem—that person lost their passion and desire for seeking the Lord first, which is a danger zone. Once again, seeking our Lord and His desires should be first and foremost because it can prevent us from being led astray—it helps us to secure our solid foundation in the power of His word (Matt 6:33, Prov 8:17, Deut 4:29, 1 Chr 16:11).

As we end this journey, we must acknowledge that the enemy is on the attack and will continue to intensify his efforts in these last days. He wants to snatch up the word of God from us, so we will lose our focus on all of God's ways and teachings. With that, this should be our daily banner in life as devoted Christian parents and stewards of the future generation: "We can only defend our cause of Christ by living on every word in the Bible and never losing that grasp!" It is the only foundation of hope that will get us through these trying times in today's world! If not, the enemy's vices, the world, and our flesh will continue to compound our worrisome spirits, hearts, and minds that could stretch for miles—with no end in sight. When this happens, we can come to a place of hopelessness and even helplessness; it will impact us negatively. How?

When a pessimistic heart, mind, and spirit consumes us internally, it can deter all our efforts and plans of planting seeds of hope for our descendants. This is imperative to understand because *pessimism is the antithesis of hope*. How can we model 'real hope' outwardly—when we internally possess a pessimistic heart, mind, and spirit? Think about that! This type of attitude can affect us in so many ways—because it can debilitate our total being. Don't be a phony by conveying a fake front (facade).

The earlier studies and research we conveyed at the book's outset show us discouraging trends because the view and teaching of God's word are diminishing one generation at a time. Parents, once again, this is how the enemy sneaks into our family lives and leads us away from the righteous ways of a Holy God. When we are not grounded in the depths, richness, and fullness of God's word and applying it to our lives (as a family unit), it leads to a spiritually weakened structure within our homes where people will stop going to church, cease from reading God's word, which will lead to a falling farther away from God—Our Source of Hope! By enforcing the Bible in our daily lives, we can only benefit from our walk with the Lord and help our future descendants' paths in godly ways. If we're not in God's word as an individual and family, how will we ever know who our Father, Son, and Spirit are?

Why is this imperative? Because woefully, the enemy is not stopping his onslaught of attacks and means of devastation—because he's not done with you and me. Why? Because parents are still allowing him to continue his defeating ways in the lives of millions of families through our poor leadership, lack of accountability, wrong choices, and spiritually lopsided priorities in life. And this is the spiritual gut punch! We fall into his traps of trickery—because we place our priorities, time, and value more on the things of this world—versus quality time with our Loving, Gracious, and Merciful God. In time, I only hope and pray that so many will come to understand all the wonderful things our Lord can provide for our future descendants—and us in glorious ways!

Always remember: "When the enemy sees an open door of weakness in our lives (like the nation of Israel) because of our lack of biblical structure, guidance, and discipline, he will seize his plans of disruption and corruption as he did thousands of years ago." Since Adam made that horrible choice that brought sin into our lives, we've been in an uphill battle for spiritual survival. And painfully, it will not get any better on this side of eternity. In today's unspiritual society and culture, and from the data reports we've seen earlier, it is evident—we have a lot of work to do in our family homes for our Heavenly Father!

Ever since the beginning of that fall, every person in each generation has faced the conscious choice of life they desire for themselves, but just as notably, their future descendants. And here's the takeaway: "It will either be a solid foundation and path of righteousness and holiness so everyone will know the importance of where their true Hope lies—or one that will lead down a road of lies, deception, and falsehood, which will eventually lead to the path of destruction." If anyone chooses the latter, many of God's children will continue to wail out for His mercy more and more in the years to come!

It's crucial to understand the pressing battle in many American homes today. The enemy, with his centuries-old strategy and cunning ways, is stealthily infiltrating the lives of parents, children, families, homes, churches, and schools across this great land and worldwide. His deceptive ways can dismantle our family lives if not vigilantly guarded against. Parents must awaken from their state of fleshly complacency and be the front-line defenders for our young ones' spiritual lives as soon as possible! The urgency of this cannot be overstated. Why is this important?

As long as that door is cracked open to his ways, the enemy's hunt will pursue, and he will persist his way into every generation, one person at a time, and create havoc and division and break down God's designed system of familyhood. And in time, we will lose all sight of Who our Hope in life is! If parents ignore God's guidance and put down their biblical guard for the spiritual sake of their children's future, they are not looking out for their best interests. But there's another PowerPoint, and it's this: They are also not looking out for the best interest of what God expects from them as Christlike parents! The consequences of this neglect could be dire and widespread.

Unfortunately, our children face so many issues today due to a simple fact! They are placing their most pressing matters, values, and blinded hopes on the things of this world—that will never lead to a productive life of godly obedience. As parents, it is our sacred duty and privilege to guide them toward godly obedience and to show them the path that leads to a life of fulfillment and purpose. Sorrowfully, our young ones seek more worldly stuff in everyday life than God's most divine ways! And if this continues, their spiritual future looks bleak! Parents, trust me, many of our children and the younger generation(s) are trying to fill a meaningful void in their lives—because millions of adolescents cry out from the depths of their hearts and souls for something better to cling to in life!

With that, this is going to be a severe gut punch! As parents and responsible followers of Christ, *we must STOP allowing our children to be misled by the ways of the world, the enemy, and their own sinful desires.* Unfortunately, there seems to be no parental guidance that could lead them to a life of "genuine" hope full of unimaginable promises that God has in store for His children. But just like the Israelites, *these promised blessings only apply to those who obey His word!*

Many Christian parents enforce "parental guidance" before watching a movie or doing anything that may bring harmful things into their children's lives. Then why don't we implement the same rules and guidelines as godly parents regarding the teachings of God's word? Proverbs 22:6 solidly affirms that parental guidance plays an essential role in the spiritual maturation of children. Why do we seek and cling to the world's advice more than the ways of God's guiding principles in the Bible?

As a mentor and teacher in the Prison Ministry and community, I witnessed too many cases of parents who were uninvolved, uncaring, dispassionate, and disinterested! They were too passive (unassertive), allowing their children and young ones to do almost anything in life. There were no biblical and spiritual guardrails. I've seen so many poor examples and evidence of the "lack of godly structure" in family lives! Unfortunately, I've seen the traumatic state of brokenness that it can bring to a family over time. Sadly, it also affects relatives, friends, and other close ones emotionally, mentally, and spiritually. It's a rippling crack that can cripple people's lives to hopelessness for years to come.

All parents and genuine followers of Christ need to heed these warning signs, come out from under that rock, and enforce a godly routine that can be passed on. Why? Because we can undoubtedly make a difference in the younger generations' lives *"if we genuinely desire and care about glorifying God's most precious Name!"* The takeaway for you and me is this: 'What is our true priority in life? What choices will we make as family leaders that will lead our children and the younger generations down a path of Faith, Hope, and Love in Christ?' It is so imperative today that the wiser ones never mislead our young ones in an ungodly fashion. If we do, we're treading on dangerous currents!

Our Lord Jesus Christ profoundly reminds us in Matthew 18:6, "But if you cause one of these little ones who trusts in me to fall into sin, it would be better for you to have a large millstone tied around your neck and be drowned in the depths of the sea." You see, children and our young ones are trusting by nature, and because they trust their parents and other adults, they can easily be led to faith in Christ—*if the elder ones live by that Christ-like example*. This scripture shows us that God holds parents and the wiser in faith accountable for how they influence God's little ones—mainly those who are young in their faith. Our Savior is clear in this profound passage: "Anyone who leads His children or the weaker in faith away from His path of righteousness will receive severe punishment."

This compelling passage in Matthew 18 refers to "little ones" as true disciples of Jesus, whether young or old, who are identified by their childlike trust in God. The key takeaway in this passage for the elderly generation is this: "As the mature and righteous ones, we are implored by our Heavenly Father to come to the aid of anyone weaker in faith—who looks to us as their example of Christlikeness and assist them in fruitful ways." With that, parents, please make no mistake about this: As our children are growing in spiritual maturity and they look to us as their role models, we are the ones who can either lead them to stagger and falter OR continue to walk in the straightness of God's guiding ways. It's up to you and me to lead them in righteousness!

These words from our Savior in Matthew should remind responsible Christians of this: "We need to be mindful of how our actions in word and deed impact others, especially those in God's family. Our responsibility is to be a positive, godly influence in their lives, helping them grow spiritually and avoid anything that could cause them to sin." That is why we need to start living and teaching them the holiness and righteousness of God in the early stages of their lives—built on the solid foundation of Jesus Christ—so it can be carried on for the future of God's glory!

Look at our history lessons in the Word of God! When the Israelites were crying out to God so often throughout the Old Testament, they realized that they had violated God's ways. Their disobedience brought them to a crossroads in their life's journey, which led to one of two choices: 1) Either repent and obey the ways of God—or 2) continue to follow the false gods and idolatrous ways of the world. The unfortunate choice of the latter would lead them down a path of destruction. Regardless, it was their choice to either choose life or death (read Deuteronomy chapter 30). But I firmly believe that those sincere cries from the children of God lay in this—"They genuinely believed there was Someone Who could save them from their pit of despair."

Undoubtedly, unbelief was at the root of the rebellion of the first generation of Israelites, mainly due to this fact—they walked more by sight than faith. In other words, they were more led by perception than Truth! Is that a danger zone? Please keep in mind that perception can lead to deception. What does that mean? When we perceive or misinterpret information

"Misguided Hope"

that is not for our good, it can create a thought pattern leading us down the enemy's path. And when we get off course, we can quickly lose hope in the One Who can help us in times of distress and confusion! But remember, faith is more powerful than sight and will guide us in the right direction.

We should all know by now that when we're grounded and guided by the Truth of God's word, we will establish the right perception of God and His accurate facts because we know it's faithful and true. If parents initiate and incorporate the foundation of God's word into their children's lives, it will develop and evolve over a lifetime for their spiritual good, but most importantly, for God's glory. How? Because God never changes, and His teachings are consistent with the same message of power daily. Each day brings a new revelation about Who He is and our understanding of Him in powerful, changing ways.

This is so vital because, in one foolish, blind, faithless choice, the first generation of Israel (from the Exodus) lost it all, which led to their tragedy. That first generation did not heed God's commands and believe in the God of Hope! As mentioned earlier, they were more guided by the sights of the flesh—than the Spirit of God! So, here's the key takeaway for you and me: "When people seek the Lord first and walk by faith, more so by sight—it's because they're grounded in the Truth of the Bible and guided more by the Spirit—than the flesh." Never forget this: "Our fleshly desires will always misguide us away from the presence of God!"

But always remember this comforting fact: "God never abandons His children who are crying out for His guidance and help! Like the days of old, He comes to the aid of His children today by putting up the necessary guardrails against the enemy's temptations that they will confront in this life. And here's the Goodness and Greatness of our Almighty God—He beautifully shows us the way out (1 Cor 10:13)."

The key is not opening our lives' portal to the works of the enemy but to the power of God's Holy Word and Spirit! Doing this will enable and empower us to develop new spiritual habits that will prevent so many unnecessary cries in the wilderness! It's a healthy, godly pattern for the old and young to seek and cling to daily! As you will see, this is a vital step to everyone's state of spirituality!

We cannot forget what Peter tells us in 1 Pet 5:8-9, "Stay alert! Watch out for your great enemy, the devil. He prowls around like a roaring lion, looking for someone to devour. Stand firm against him, and be strong in your faith. Remember that your family of believers all over the world is going through the same kind of suffering you are."

"Seek Hope"

Never forget this ensuring promise! "God will continue to look for people who are seeking Him with all their hearts, minds, and souls" of those He can strengthen in preparation for their spiritual battles on earth! In today's times of trials and temptations, God wants to show His strength to those whose hearts are genuinely committed to Him—as we saw so often throughout the Israelites' journey. Today, more than ever, we need that Source of Hope to seek and cling to, which will support, supply, protect, and defend those who are sincere and upright with good intentions to serve our Almighty God above all things. *Your commitment to God is recognized and appreciated, and He will strengthen you in your spiritual battles.*

Always remember this biblical fact: "Our Heavenly Father knows who seeks Him and who truly belongs to Him—because their foundation has been built on the Word of God. Their belief is grounded so firmly in Jesus Christ as their Lord and Savior, with the guidance of the Holy Spirit—they don't waver one inkling and never compromise with the ways of the world. No matter the tests, their hope rests in the promises of His word alone—because that is their stronghold and the anchor for their soul (Heb 6:19)!"

These compelling passages (below) in God's word confirm and remind us that He knows who belongs to Him, providing a comforting reassurance in His unwavering knowledge and care for His believers, a care that remains steadfast and unchanging, offering a sense of security and comfort in His constant presence.

2 Tim 2:19, "But God's truth stands firm like a foundation stone with this inscription: "The Lord knows those who are his," and "All who belong to the Lord must turn away from evil."

John 10:27-29, "My sheep listen to my voice; I know them, and they follow me. I give them eternal life, and they will never perish. No one can snatch them away from me, for my Father has given them to me, and he is

"Seek Hope"

more powerful than anyone else. No one can snatch them from the Father's hand."

Ps 139:1-2, "O LORD, you have examined my heart and know everything about me. You know when I sit down or stand. You know my thoughts even when I'm far away."

Jer 1:5, "I knew you before I formed you in your mother's womb. Before you were born, I set you apart and appointed you as my prophet to the nations."

Make no mistake: "God is searching high and low for hearts that will be loyal and committed to Him in these final days, those that listen to His voice! He is in strong pursuit of those who will seek Him and cling to Him with a desire and commitment to follow and obey Him to the very end of this life—and not give in and fall prey to the ways of this world." God's word reminds us in Ps 53:2, "God looks down from heaven on the entire human race; *he looks to see if anyone is truly wise if anyone seeks God.*"

This passage in Psalm chapter 53 challenges the wiser ones in today's world! In all the sin and evil around us, God is looking for one who understands His heart and plan and seeks Him for the sake of righteousness. From God's lofty position in Heaven, He is paying close attention to our hearts' truest intents and desires. He looks down on us to see if any human beings understand spiritual truth and genuinely seek Him first above all things, which should be the more mature generation (parents). This act of seeking God first is a testament to your value and importance in His eyes.

Regrettably, not one person is good in God's eyes, as His word confirms in Rom 3:10-18. However, there's something powerful for parents and wiser ones to think about and challenge themselves with each day: "How can the more developed generation of today turn this around for the good and betterment of our Heavenly Father—where they can impact and influence future generations for His glory?" This is not just a challenge but a responsibility that should motivate us to rely upon the power of God's word, with the guidance of the Holy Spirit—when dealing with all of life's unfortunate circumstances and difficulties.

Remember the distressing statistics from the book's outset where most parents do not seek, use, or rely upon the teachings of God's word? That is why parents must change their spiritual direction in today's American family homes and step up to the plate of godliness for our children's well-being. By now, family leaders should clearly understand that the word of God must be their first and primary source of teaching when searching for the correct answers in everyday life—for our young ones' state of spirituality. In other words, we must be godly parents each day for our children's spiritual good!

Never forget what the author in Heb 4:12–13 tells us, "For the word of God is alive and powerful. It is sharper than the sharpest two-edged sword, cutting between soul and spirit, between joint and marrow. It exposes our innermost thoughts and desires. Nothing in all creation is hidden from God. Everything is naked and exposed before his eyes, and he is the one to whom we are accountable." Parents, our primary choices are exposed through His written Word, the Bible. We learn in Scripture that the Word of God is *alive* and *active*—it lives and works.

This profound passage in Hebrews should lead all Christian leaders to ask this vital question: "Are our innermost thoughts and desires genuinely aligned with God's long-term purpose and plan, individually and most importantly, for the next generation of believers?" The Almighty One knows if the mature and wise generation is up for this most essential call—or if we even care! All things are visible in our Heavenly Father's eyes, and we will be held accountable for our actions!

Astoundingly, life-generating things can happen when God's Word goes forth for the good of society—for it can fully accomplish its purpose in our lives. Not only in our individual lives but when we lean and rely upon His guiding truths every day, they will undoubtedly impact everyone around us. Remember what Isaiah 55:11 tells us: "The rain and snow come down from the heavens and stay on the ground to water the earth. They cause the grain to grow, producing seed for the farmer and bread for the hungry. It is the same with my word. I send it out, and it always produces fruit. It will accomplish all I want it to, and it will prosper everywhere I send it".

The power of God's word should move all committed followers of Jesus Christ to conduct themselves with genuine lovingkindness and make efforts for the good of our loved ones and others; it doesn't just help them; it is mentally and spiritually healthy for us; too. We need to prioritize this in our daily lives for the current and future eras—because those little acts of caring and sharing can set off a tentacle of Christlike waves for years to come. It can impact the lives of our future descendants in powerful ways that will help them to seek and cling to the righteous things in this life!

So, I beg these questions: "Are parents and family leaders using God's wisdom to prepare the next generation with the spiritual foundation they need to help them through their most fierce wars?" "Are we doing our part as devout disciples of Christ in equipping our future heirs with the knowledge of how to be loyal and committed to the One Who will strengthen and help them overcome their most intense battles on this side of Heaven?" "Will they be ready?" "Most importantly, are they ready right now?"

Attention! Because those times are here, and they keep coming in relentless waves! The younger generation, our own children, desperately

"Seek Hope"

need the lesson of commitment and loyalty to God because their battles with society and culture have reached unprecedented levels. In this quest for guidance, which parent(s) will step up to teach the next generation the ways of unwavering commitment to our Lord, especially when the storms of life are so severe?

With that, here are some challenging and gut-provoking questions for you and me as the 'supposed' wiser generation: "Do we genuinely care about the future of humanity's 'spiritual state' through the ages?" "Are we blazing a path of godliness for our future heirs that can be passed on gloriously to others—so they will have a stronger sense and knowledge of Who their Real Hope in life is?" Hopefully, we are not so fixated on the Israelites' faults of years gone by that we're pointing our fingers back at them so often—we forget entirely about our own complaining, arguing, unrighteous, and discontented ways.

Parents, don't we realize that we cannot afford to suppress the lives of our loved ones in ungodly ways—because it will lead nowhere spiritually for God's glory? When we don't assume the godly responsibility for our Christian role as leaders in the household, it's because the eyes of our hearts, minds, and spirits are not focused on the things that matter to God most! "Shouldn't we respect all the things God respects, laid out in His word?" We will only establish the right type of reverence for our Heavenly Father in front of our younger ones when they see us seeking Him with all we have, and we cling to His promises no matter what comes! Living a life reflecting godliness is not just a choice; it's a commitment we must uphold for our spiritual growth.

Our loved ones and others should visibly see more traits of godly obedience and the 'Living Hope' in our daily lives as parents—versus the disobedient ways and signs of hopelessness—as in the case with that first generation of Israelites.' If we fall into the habits of that lost generation, and that's how our loved ones and the world label and remember us, we will find it challenging to teach our future heirs and others the ways of God!

Remember this: "If we consistently strive to live a life patterned with the ways of our Lord, guided by God's word and the Holy Spirit, we can enlighten future generations with the structure of God's holiness and the means of our Living Hope (1 Pet 1:3-9)." Our Lord expects us to seek Him above all things and live a divinely teachable life for our descendants. This is not a burden but a privilege and a source of hope for a brighter future (1 John 5:3). It's a journey filled with hope and inspiration, knowing we are shaping a brighter future through our spiritual values.

We must be mindful every day that the younger generations see parents and leaders as their example in many ways. As discussed frequently throughout this journey, the lifestyle we choose in everyday life can be highly influential in their personal lives because it can lead them to either godly obedience or fleshly disobedience. That's why Christian parents and guardians should aspire to be more of a spiritual blessing to the younger ones' lives for the well-being of their future state of survival.

It starts by seeking and holding on to the Truths of God's word in every area of their daily lives! We should not choose scriptures that fit our fleshly comfort zone because God wants us to seek and follow "all" of His Truths! If we pick and choose scriptures that suit our comfort level, we'll conform more to the ways of the world, allowing the enemy to lead us apart from God's purpose and plan that will affect everyone around us! Never forget this: Christ asks His followers to die to themselves, to take up their crosses, and to follow after Him first and foremost above all things (Matt 16:24).

Taking up a cross and dying to oneself are not "comfortable" actions. However, Christians should always be willing to step outside their comfort zone into any situation God may place them in, including parenting! Look at the followers of Christ in the New Testament. The apostles sacrificed everything in order to serve God (Matt 19:27), and they willingly went into dire situations regardless of the consequences. Their goal was spreading the Good News about Christ and discipling others so the Gospel would expand for the benefit of God's Future Kingdom. And in it all, they adhered to the Truth and did not deviate one bit!

Undoubtedly, the apostles put themselves well outside their regular routine and did things far beyond their comfort zones for God's glory. As Christian parents and leaders, we, too, should be willing to go into uncomfortable circumstances when our young ones are confronted with cultural ways that we may not feel comfortable with. We should consider how to best serve God through our gifts and talents and come to our children's aid—even if it seems daunting. Most importantly, we must seek and stand on the power of God's promises and truths for the sake of our future heirs. This steadfast adherence to His word during intense times will reassure our children and future generations of the Strength of our Faith.

This is a crucial truth we must never forget: Remembrance is at the heart of each generation. When the younger generation looks to us as their role model, what we seek in life and our choices can profoundly shape their personal and family lives in the years to come. They will remember the good, the bad, and the ugly. As they incorporate our lifestyle into their own lives, they can influence future societies and cultures in ways that can positively or negatively change a modern era.

Here's my point: Whatever shapes us physically, mentally, and *most importantly, spiritually* can trickle down to our heirs for decades and have lasting impressions on others for years to come. As wise and discerning Christians, we should all hope and pray that we will be the epitome of Christlikeness so our descendants will embody the mighty ways of godliness for the sake of God's glory in the future! The key to shaping our spiritual lives in Christlike ways is—"When we seek the Kingdom of God and His righteousness first (Matt 6:33)." When we do this with steadfastness, it forms us in godly ways that significantly affect our children and others!

Because here's the excellent news and impact of that commitment: 'We have a new story of Hope' to tell the world when we became a new creation as believers in Jesus Christ (2 Cor 5:17). It possesses genuine faith, repentance, obedience, love, and forgiveness while pressing on toward our eternal goal and storing treasures in Heaven and not on earth. This should become our top priority, passion, and motive to leave God's fingerprints on our lives for loved ones and others to witness and talk about for decades!

Today, more than ever, we need intentional, faithful, and loving parents who can be godly influencers in the lives of the younger generations for God's future plans. They must be breathing, living, sustaining, and teaching their children so it is passed down. Parents can only attain this status by having a daily experience with God through applying His word to their lives and heeding the guidance of the Holy Spirit. In today's culture, this is vital because God's word has much to say about the power of influence (Prov 13:20, Prov 22:24-25, Matt 5:16, 2 Cor 6:14,1 Tim 4:12).

Here's the power of that influence: "The deeper our love is for God, the more we will genuinely love what He loves, and that is Christ–His Son, family, children, people, the body of Christ, worship, our enemies, and our joyful obedience to His Word, with the guidance of His Spirit." When we do this, we find ourselves honoring and praising Him selflessly above all things in our everyday lives! This powerfully sets the precedence of one of the most critical stages as a parent and family leader, leaving a legacy for our young ones—as discussed so often throughout this journey. Do we get the message by now?

So, here are some critical questions for all Christian parents: "What motivates us in everyday life?" "Do we know what our purpose-driven life is—as God's servants on this side of Heaven?" "Does our assured hope that we possess in Christ yield so much internal strength that its power is displayed outwardly?" In other words, it is so radiant from the inside and out that people see a joy, peace, contentment, and comfort beyond all human understanding. "Most importantly, do our children and loved ones see this active in our daily lives, no matter life's difficulties?" Remember this key takeaway: Living a devoted, purpose-driven life as God's servant brings joy, peace, and fulfillment that surpasses all understanding.

Here's one thing for sure: If our driven hope in Jesus Christ is rock solid, then we are not pursuing the desires and expectations of this world and people. Instead, we're chasing after all the things of the Lord—because He's our Source of Hope that can get us from one day to the next. Paul is a perfect example of someone who invested his hope in Christ. After all, he's the only person in the Bible who said, "Follow me because I follow Christ" (1 Cor 11:1). This greatest apostle of all times exemplified the heart, mind, and spirit of obedience, loyalty, and reverence, which should be our model in everyday life. Why?

In many of Paul's letters, we see the powerful undertone of Hope in his message to believers. Paul could easily talk about this Hope because of his wholehearted commitment to the Lord. His faith, love, and hope in Christ led him to serve Him with passion, diligence, willingness, unwavering commitment, gratitude, joy, boldness, confidence, and enthusiasm—while enduring and persevering through the most intense trials imaginable. When he was down, he sought the power of His Lord, and he clung to it with all of his heart, soul, mind, and strength!

Regardless of Paul's tribulation, he gave us powerful words that should motivate us as Christians today, such as in Phil 1:6— "And I am certain that God, who began the good work within you, will continue his work until it is finally finished on the day when Christ Jesus returns." Also, once again, this profound passage in Rom 8:28 is one that many are familiar with and even memorize as their anchor in life: "And we know that God causes everything to work together for the good of those who love God and are called according to his purpose for them."

As God's children, we must never forget that God is not blind to the suffering and temptations we are experiencing today, and neither was the apostle Paul when he wrote this verse. The purpose of Romans 8:28 is to encourage Christians and allow the power of God to renew their minds and change their perspectives (Rom 12: 1–2). Our Almighty God is all-knowing, all-powerful, and all-present; He knows what we need—when we need it—and why we need it, BUT He knows that if we don't seek Him foremost, we will never know where and Who our Source is. Seeking Him first should always be our all-out attempt for all answers in everyday life—for the good of ourselves and our loved ones! It will never disappoint!

And trust me, I think all of you would agree with me on this— "We need a mindset that is more fixed on the realities of Heaven than the ways of this world more than ever" (Col 3:2 Phil 4:8). We need to seek this mindset because, in today's culture, we all get "down in the dumps and at times wallow in those pits of despair" because of all the unrighteous things swirling

"Seek Hope"

in our midst. When this happens, it is difficult to look beyond the immediate times of those trials and the future of our eternal hope.

But here's the excellent news and means of motivation for us as wise and mature Christians. Looking to the future is precisely what God wants us to do because He wants us to believe, trust, and rely on His strength and all His promises. He wants us to seek and cling to Him—despite our trials and tests of time. Remember what Paul tells us in Romans 5:3-4: "Tribulation produces perseverance; and perseverance, character; and character, hope." So, if you think about it, *hope* is the defining point in Romans 8:28.

Always remember that seeking our Lord daily is not just a choice but a weighty responsibility. It is the cry of God's heart—His appeal for people to repent and pursue His forgiveness while there is still hope of salvation. The message echoes in Isaiah's invitation recorded in Isa 55:6 reminds you and me: "Seek the LORD while he may be found; call on him while he is near." God wants us to return to Him with "pure and genuine" devotion (James 1:27), which is the foundation of our life and relationship with Him (our Hope). However, when we forsake the Lord, we must humble ourselves before Him, repent, obey His commands, and walk in His ways again. Only in this way can we receive forgiveness of sins and restoration (2 Chr 7:14).[1]

At the start of our new life in Christ, our Loving Father longs for us to pursue Him—seek Him with all our heart, soul, mind, and strength. We urgently need His strength to help His children endure and persevere through all our trying times. I want to think by now that we know beyond a shadow of a doubt we need His strength and that firm foundation today more than ever for the sake of the next generation of believers. Why?

Because Yahweh knows the enemy is creeping all over the earth, seeking to destroy and separate us from His loving arms. But God is not giving up on those who are willing to accept and heed all His ways and have based their steadfast hope and faith in His only Son! Always remember this: "God wants to include anyone in His Heavenly family—that chooses the path of the Way, Truth, and Life (John 14:6)." And no matter what, He will be with us—through it all—to the very end of our story on this Earth! His presence is our comfort, our security, and our strength. Undoubtedly, great things are to come! But we must strive for Him—and hold on to our Hope with all our might!

Lastly, let's return to the author of Hebrews, who reminds us in Heb 11:6 of this profound truth: "And it is impossible to please God without faith. Anyone who wants to come to him must believe that God exists and that he rewards those who sincerely seek him." Let us remember that God

---

1. Got Questions. "What Does God Mean, When He says Seek and Live?"

is not a passive observer but a loving Father who actively seeks out faithful people He can bless. His love for us is unwavering, and this is a true testament to the value and worth of our lives in the Eyes of Almighty God—our Creator—and Heavenly Father. Who would not want to pass this truth on to their loved ones—so they will have Someone supernaturally powerful to cling to—in all their life's battles that will surely come?

"Cling to Hope!"

Whether we like it or not, it's a guaranteed certainty that Christians will face storms in their lives for a reason and purpose. These disturbances, varying in intensity, are an inescapable part of our earthly journey. They will test our patience, emotions, and ability to show goodness, gentleness, love, and kindness toward others. They can elevate our worries, escalate our anxieties, lead us to doubt and a lack of faith, and even pits of distress, despair, and hopelessness. If we're not careful, they can debilitate us emotionally, physically, mentally, and, most importantly, spiritually.

However, how we handle these testing moments will determine if we will come out the other side—the same, weaker, or stronger. If we come out the same, it is apparent we did not learn from the storm of life. Unfortunately, if the storm weakens us, the storm gets the best of us, and we will not be able to progress in our Christian Walk. But always remember, our Almighty Creator puts us through the storms of life so we will come out the other side more powerful and more resilient—able to endure and persevere through more storms that will surely come into our lives.

It's crucial to remember that every storm is an opportunity to learn and grow. This strength of character allows us to be more Christlike and come out victorious, glorifying God in magnificent ways! This learning and growth in the face of storms empowers us, gives us hope for the future, and will influence others around us, showing the transformative power of faith in overcoming challenges.

God's word tells His people to cling to Him in several places, including Deuteronomy 10:20 and 13:4. Some say that sticking or clinging to God is one of the most critical stages of our sanctification process because it shows our absolute loyalty and undeniable commitment to our Father and Lord, Who has shown Himself to be faithful and true to all of His promises. When we cling to Him above all things, it demonstrates that we're showing Him our unswerving and relentless devotion because we know He's worthy of it and will never let us go!

But we can even go deeper—because clinging to God also illustrates that we're intentionally spending time with him through prayer, praise, and studying and applying His word into our lives. It also shows that we trust His ways, seek His favor, and care only about His approval. It also shows we're forsaking all other gods and holding on to His Goodness and Greatness that can be shared with others!

Always remember, God will allow or cause these storms in our life's journey because He does not want us to be complacent in this world today. As discussed earlier, He does not want us to conform to worldly comfort because this is not His plan for you and me—for this is not our final resting place. In all my years of teaching, mentoring, instructing, and even preaching, I've always conveyed this vital message to others, and it's this. When we're going through this life journey, think of the power of God's Spirit as the 5 C's of life:

1) He *convicts* us when we're off course to God's guiding principles, 2) He *counsels* us to get us back in line with His ways, 3) He *comforts* us so we will know He's with us, 4) He wants to *correct* our wrong ways back to His righteous ways and 5) He wants us to stay *connected* with Him to ensure we don't continue making the same mistakes. We do this by clinging to our Lord and holding tightly to all His ways, which is always for our good!

The author of Hebrews profoundly reminds us in chapter 12 that we're called to persevere and look to Christ as our example when the storms of life confront us. Why? Our Lord and Redeemer endured the shame of the cross to bring us into fellowship with God for a purpose and plan. Think about that for a moment. When parents and family leaders suffer through their trials and come out of the storm more Christlike as an example for our young ones, we can bring more fellowship and unity within our family unit. How? Because they witnessed the bad and horror of a tragic life situation transformed into something good—because of God and our hope in Him alone!

With that, we must always cling to Christ and keep our eyes on Him as we run the race of life. We must focus on more admirable, honorable, holy, pure, righteous, and good things that honor God our Father (Phil 4:8)! Never forget this: We have received His citizenship in an unshakable kingdom. Let us show gratitude and offer our lives in acceptable service by holding firmly to all His ways of righteousness that will impact others and carry over for years!

When we "cling to" our Lord, it means that we stick or hold together with Him through all the trials of life. No matter what, we resist separation because we want to be united and always embraced by His empowering grace. In other words, we're so attached to Him that nothing in the world could detach you and me from this committed holy good—because we're genuinely adjoined to our Father and Lord—by His Spirit!

When we're going through those difficult stages and storms of life, and we feel as if we are about to lose grip on His Almighty Power, we can always refer to the book of Psalms as a biblical and spiritual guidance that will help us to hold on to Him at all costs. A good example is Psalm 107: 28–30: "Lord, help!" they cried in their trouble, and he saved them from their distress. He calmed the storm to a whisper and stilled the waves. What a blessing was that stillness as he brought them safely into harbor!"

Please remember, those who never suffer or go through the trials of life may not appreciate God as much—versus those who have endured and matured through these hardships! Most importantly, when we set the example of godliness through these tests, they set the precedence of Who we rely upon, which will influence others around us. It will indeed move others and will exalt our Almighty God!

The author of Hebrews even reminds us in Heb 10: 23–24, "Let us hold tightly without wavering to the Hope we affirm, for God can be trusted to keep his promise. Let us think of ways to motivate one another to acts of love and good works." In this beautiful passage, we see a powerful point: "If we hold fast and stick firmly to the Hope we profoundly proclaim, we will find ways to help others to Christlike acts of love and His good works. This impacts not only the body of Christ but also our homes and communities. This steadfastness can carry on from generation to generation if that spiritual grip is held tightly within the body and the homes for the benefit of others! It can be a significant turning point and impact for future generations!"

This is a vital step for us individually as family leaders and most notably for our younger generation; it's this: "Clinging to God's promises with all our heart, soul, mind, and strength shows that we seek His will above all things (as discussed so often throughout the book)." It also illustrates that we care only for His approval—not the mere mortal man. It demonstrates that we desire to invest our time in His long-term service plan and will always keep His praise and honor on our lips no matter what storms come (Ps. 63:7–8). When we cling to the promises of God and our Source of Hope through all our trials and tribulations, we truly display our loyal commitment and love to His ways!

Once again, I cannot stress this enough: As Christian parents and the wiser generation, we must ensure that our lives are in biblical and spiritual order and that we cling to His ways *with all our hearts, souls, minds, and strength.* Why? Do we really think that our children and the younger generations, as they get older, are being taught a godly, disciplined life when we carry them to *"church periodically, pray together occasionally, read God's word sporadically, and serve the Lord randomly?"*

It's crucial to understand that a part-time approach to Christ in our children's lives will not foster a deep commitment to Him as they mature. Our Lord desires our wholehearted devotion, not just a partial one. He wants every part of us to embrace His divine teachings. This is urgent because it's our responsibility as Christian parents and disciples of Christ to establish a structured life of godliness in our children from their earliest years.

When we hold tightly to our Source of Hope, He works His righteousness in us. This is a crucial step because when we cling to what is good, pure, and holy, it demonstrates our love for God and brings us a sense of security and peace. You see, when we're dedicated to obeying His word, it shows that we trust His wisdom and guidance. When this comes to life in us, we can firmly believe He is transforming us from within, teaching us His good and perfect will, which will undoubtedly impact others. And in His perfect timing He is working everything in our lives for His good.

Some of Paul's final instructions to his great servant Timothy are recorded in 2 Timothy chapter 2, entitled "A Good Soldier of Christ Jesus." And the only way you and I can be a good soldier for Christ, for the benefit of our loved ones, is by holding fast to God's divine Word so we can avoid all the dangerous errors of falsehood in the world today. This is so important because if we get caught up in foolish talks, behaviors, and attitudes, it can lead to strife and division within our family and even the body of Christ. The only way we can explain and teach the Bible correctly and effectively is by studying the Word of God personally to understand what it means, which can help us interpret it correctly to our children and others!

In 2 Tim 2:11–19, Paul reminds us profoundly, "This is a trustworthy saying: If we die with him, we will also live with him. If we endure hardship, we will reign with him. If we deny him, he will deny us. If we are unfaithful, he remains faithful, for he cannot deny who he is. Remind everyone about these things, and command them in God's presence to stop fighting over words. Such arguments are useless, and they can ruin those who hear them."

"Work hard so you can present yourself to God and receive his approval. Be a good worker, one who does not need to be ashamed and who correctly explains the word of truth. Avoid worthless, foolish talk that only leads to more godless behavior. This kind of talk spreads like cancer, as in the case of Hymenaeus and Philetus. They have left the path of truth, claiming that the resurrection of the dead has already occurred; in this way, they have turned some people away from the faith. But God's truth stands firm like a foundation stone with this inscription: "The LORD knows those who are his," and "All who belong to the LORD must turn away from evil."

Always remember, living in obedience to our Lord, where we're sharing the Good News of the Kingdom with others—He will take care of our business as He promised—and if that's the spiritual arrangement we have in our daily lives as His family leaders, where is worrying? In other words, Jesus is teaching you and me that our focus should be shifted away from this world—with all its deception and lying allurements. It should be fixated and placed upon the things of God's Kingdom. Then, people will see our investment in Hope, especially all our loved ones!

Remember that Real Living Hope is the expectation and desire to receive something—knowing it will happen. As we've seen, our genuine Christian hope is a virtue that our children and the younger generation need today more than ever. Trust me, as times of evil intensify in our last days, many of the younger ones throughout the communities and around the globe are longing and crying out to receive something that will get them through their most intense trials. As stated earlier, so many of them have a void that needs to be filled in their lives, and they want something more positive and supernaturally powerful and good to cling to.

And it starts with you and me as godly leaders living as obedient, faithful, and loving followers of Christ—who display that solid foundation of Hope for their good! And to put this application into a more robust perspective— "Our Lord expects you and me to build that foundation for their future!" He awaits devoted Christian parents and leaders to be the example of His faith, hope, and love to everyone around us-by holding on to all His Truths and never compromising, no matter what comes in life.

This is all so critical because, in his last letter, 2 Timothy, chapter 3, Paul reminds us that in the last days, people will love only themselves and the things of this world. They will be disobedient, ungrateful, unforgiving, and scoffers at God with no means of self-control. They will act religiously but resist the One who could make them godly. A master key to this passage is this: "If we're not hanging on to the Truths of the Bible, we can easily find ourselves engulfed in a world overflowing with pervasive evil." With that clarity, the urgency of our task as godly parents and leaders becomes clear. This is not just a matter of personal concern but a crucial responsibility we bear for the younger generations' state of spiritual survival! It's a call to action that we cannot ignore.

But also nestled throughout this epistle, we see Paul giving biblical instructions to Timothy that the key to his teachings to others is this: "Hold on to the pattern of wholesome teachings you learned and keep fanning in that flame of God's empowering Spirit to help you. *Don't be ashamed of telling the truth you were taught, and carefully guard the precious truth entrusted to you!"* This is not just a suggestion but a command to hold onto the biblical truths, which serve as the unshakable foundation of our faith and the unwavering guiding light in a world filled with darkness.

In this powerful chapter, Paul reminds you and me of the immense responsibility we bear. If we're not carefully guarding the precious truth of God's word for the benefit of others, we're not only neglecting our God-given responsibilities but also letting our Heavenly Father down because we're disobeying His commands. He's entrusted you and me as accountable followers of Christ to teach, equip, and prepare others for years to come until our Hope in Christ returns. This is vital because if we don't train our children and the younger generation on the importance of God's teachings, they could easily drift further away—which is clearly evident today, as we've seen so far.

So, what are we genuinely teaching our children and the younger generation to seek and cling to more in life today? Once again, Jesus Christ, our Lord, tells us in Matt 6:19-21, "Don't store up treasures here on earth, where moths eat them and rust destroys them, and where thieves break in and steal. Store your treasures in heaven, where moths and rust cannot destroy, and thieves do not break in and steal. Wherever your treasure is, there the desires of your heart will also be."

In this compelling passage, our intentions should be driven by our true inner devotion to God alone, no one or nothing else! Jesus' point is not that Christians cannot have wealth or own anything (as discussed earlier), but His ways should be our primary choice in everyday life. When the parent's choices align their lives with God's purpose and plan, it will not only enrich their spiritual journey but also bring hope and contribute to the well-being of their future heirs. This alignment with God's purpose is not just a duty but a source of inspiration and motivation, as it leads us to hold this profound treasure in our hearts and aspire for our loved ones to join the Lord in building His coming Kingdom!

Here's the impact! When we store treasures in Heaven, we assist in Building God's Kingdom, not just through our tithes, offerings, God-given gifts, and talents—BUT also through our descendants. This is so important for all believers to understand because storing treasures in Heaven is an act of obedience and wholehearted commitment to God. It clearly demonstrates that we're holding more closely in our hearts, minds, and spirits the realities of Heaven and not the things of this earth (Col 3:2). In other words, we're fulfilling God's word in our daily lives, not just for ourselves but for the sake of God's next generation. It exemplifies that all we say and do as

"Cling to Hope!"

His servants, ambassadors, messengers, and representatives on Earth are aligned with His will and plans for the future.

Parents, don't we realize by now that we cannot afford to let our children and future generations cling to the unspiritual things of this culture today? If they do, they can easily conform to the acceptance of worldliness, which can lead to a tolerance of sinful ways in their daily lives. Today, it starts with you and me. We, as parents, have the power and responsibility to set spiritual boundaries and establish a deep-rooted plan of godly structure in our respective families' lives! Let's face it: There needs to be some accountabilities outlined and enforced in Christian homes today! If your household is in a downward spiral out of control from God's guiding ways, turn it around. Why?

The Blessed Hope is a powerful force that we need in our lives today. It is the Light that guides us through our most troublesome times. It serves as a constant reminder that Christ, in His selfless act of sacrifice, redeemed even the lowliest of us from wickedness, purifying us for His glory. Hope is a defining characteristic of the followers of Jesus, for God is the very foundation of our hope. When we accept Christ as our Lord, God gifts us His Spirit, a divine light that should illuminate our daily lives. This genuine Hope is our beacon of light in the darkness and one of the most extraordinary distinguishing characteristics between believers and those who do not know Christ. Let's remember this hope is not just for us but for our loved ones, too. Do they see this Living Hope, this unwavering assurance, active in us today? Let this Hope uplift and encourage us in our daily lives for the well-being of others.

In Psalm 37:23-24, David reminds us that God not only wants us to be in spiritual order but also guides us step by step to put us in a position to be used by Him. This divine guidance is not just a random occurrence but a strategic plan to align us with His purpose and put us in a position to help others for His ultimate glory. Did you know that Almighty God strategically places His gifted servants in key positions to Build His Future Kingdom? And this can only be accomplished by attaching our lives wholeheartedly to the Power of God and all His ways! This assurance of God's guidance should fill us with confidence in our journey of faith for the benefit of others in our path.

Another profound takeaway from this passage in Psalm 37 is that God knows those who are fully committed to Him so He can guide their steps to be aligned with His purpose and plan for the future. And the power of this verse lies in this assuring promise—He's holding our hands each step of the way. But here's the underlying message for you and me, as stated earlier: "Are we genuinely seeking and clinging to Him with all we have, no matter what the world throws our way?" "Do our loved ones see us connected, fastened, and anchored in all of God's ways, where they know beyond a shadow of a doubt that we're walking in His presence every day?" Do the younger generations visually witness the older and wiser generations' motivation by the new mercies of God in their daily walk? How transformative and impactful this could be in the lives of so many for years to come—if we would only do it!

"Walk in Hope"

Without question, the greatest quest in everyday life is our all-out search for God, where we're walking in all His ways of righteous and holy living, which are conveyed in His Holy Word. Individuals, families, communities, and even nations have sought God differently for various reasons throughout their journey in life. But here's the key: God is already searching for people to come along beside Him who possess a willing and loyal heart and are committed to His purpose. What about us?

This leads me to ponder a question: Are we, as His chosen ones, searching in the right areas and walking in the right direction that is aligned with His will and long-term plan? In other words, is our eager pursuit genuinely focused on the Source of Hope in these uncontrollable times of restlessness today? Are we doing everything with our heart, soul, mind, and strength to be in His presence every day of our lives?

Do you ever wake up in the mornings and feel as if you're not seeking the right things in life, which leads you to go the opposite direction of God (like Jonah)? Could we be holding on to the wrong things in this life that will not help us endure and persevere through the tests of time? But also for the benefit of our young ones, who desperately need His guidance daily! Trust me, our younger generation needs to be walking in the presence of the Lord today more than ever with all the tempting times they are confronting! And the parents and leaders can set the precedence of those daily steps of righteousness and newness for the younger generation!

The great prophet Jeremiah reminds us in Lam 3:22–23 that God's mercies are new every morning of every day! We should rejoice in being renewed, refreshed, and regenerated in our daily lives to new spiritual heights. The power of Jeremiah's cry in Lamentations chapter 3 vividly depicts suffering and despair under God's wrath. However, his tone shifts later, transforming his lament into a testament of hope in God's mercy, faithfulness, and ultimate redemption.

Think about it: God's mercies are new every morning, which means He shows us His compassion daily, which knows no bounds; it's immeasurable. With each rising and setting of the sun, He supplies a fresh measure of His grace upon us as His devout children. He has good and spiritually refreshing things to give you and me today that weren't available yesterday. However, we can only obtain this experience of God's mercy by being in His presence daily.

This should reassure and reaffirm our expectations for what's to come through our Living Hope (Jesus Christ). It should cast a flaring beam in such a positive light that it influences and impacts our loved ones and others in powerful ways—that will carry over for generations. Just think—that one ray of undeniable Hope can nourish and empower hearts, minds, souls, and spirits so they can overcome their most tragic times on this side of Heaven. But that ray of Hope cannot be visible if we're not in step with our Heavenly Father!

I don't know about you, but I need that blessed assurance in my daily life to get me through those times of distress and despair. But to feel absolutely confident in that guarantee, I know that I must be 100% committed and loyal to my Lord every day—where I am walking in His presence—so I can receive His empowering strength through His word and Spirit. I am sure many of you feel the same as me, and it's this:

"With all the unspiritual behavior we're experiencing in this world, we can all get to the point of being mentally, emotionally, and spiritually weary and tired of fighting some of these battles in our own strength! Don't forget what Jesus tells us in Matt 11:28-30. In that constant fight, do we find ourselves, on a daily basis, not as committed to the Almighty One as much as He would desire?" What prevents and keeps us from that daily closeness to our Heavenly Father? Have you self-examined your spiritual walk? Never forget one of the key tactics of the enemy is to deceive and lead us astray and entirely away from the path of our holy Lord!

Each morning of a new day, we must ask ourselves, "Are we walking in all of God's ways?" For me, I know I must seek the One who is more powerful than me, the One who can help me overcome my most intense trials. When I feel disconnected from His power source, I know I am going in the wrong direction in life. That void is mainly there because I am not seeking and walking in the righteousness and holiness of my Lord. But when I do, I am filled with His strength and reassurance, knowing He is always there to guide me, directing my steps and decisions (Psalm 37:23-24).

This makes me ponder even more: "Could it be that many of us are not walking in that blessed hope because we're not wholeheartedly loyal and committed to God and seeking Him as we should in our daily lives?" Maybe

"Walk in Hope"

it's because we're continuously fighting one worldly battle after another in everyday life—beating and wearing our hearts, minds, and spirits to the point of defeat (as stated earlier).

But let's not forget that we're fighting a battle that has already been won (1 John 4:4). When we try and take on these fights in our own strength, we can lose all sight of hope, which is where the enemy wants us. But once we completely submit and surrender it all to Him, He's got it! Do we genuinely believe in the promise of what Jesus tells us in John 16:33? "I have told you all this so you may have peace in me. Here on earth, you will have many trials and sorrows. But take heart because I have overcome the world," a victory that should fill us with hope and encouragement.

Paul also reminds us in Rom 8:35, "Can anything ever separate us from Christ's love? Does it mean he no longer loves us if we have trouble or calamity, or are persecuted, or hungry, or destitute, or in danger, or threatened with death?" The answer is this, "No, despite all these horrific things we will experience on this earth, overwhelming victory is ours through Christ, who loved us" (Rom 8:37). But we cannot take rest and peace in that promise from the Living Hope—if we're not in unison with our Lord every day—for the good of our ourselves and others!

Walking in Hope is not just a phrase but a powerful concept that can transform our lives. In my first book, 'God Values Our Daily Steps,' I emphasized the importance of being in step with God in our daily lives for a reason and purpose. Since we are created in the image of an Almighty and Holy God, we share many of His divine characteristics. And we cannot display those critical attributes for the benefit of others if we're not in unity with our Heavenly Father in everyday life. Remember the power of this passage in Amos 3:3, "Can two people walk together without agreeing on the direction?" This unity with God's will is our reassurance and our guide.

Our daily steps with God can be categorized in one of two areas—intentional or unintentional, and this distinction is a wake-up call! In simpler terms, and this is a heart-pounding diagnosis—believers are either actively and intentionally walking with the Lord, or they're inactive and unintentional, essentially going nowhere! Here it is in a nutshell: "They are either impacting other people's lives for the glory of God—or leading others in a meaningless manner that is not of our Heavenly Father." So, which category do you choose to be in?

Here are the facts: Our intentional or unintentional actions hinge on this—the condition of our heart. Because the heart is the driving force behind our motives and desires. Remember what Jesus tells us in Matt 6:21, wherever your treasure is, there the desires of your heart will also be. Once again, Jesus reminds us in Matthew chapter 13 in the Parable of the Sower that the seed is the word of God, and when it was scattered amongst four soils, how it is produced is based on the condition of that person's heart. In other words, it comes down to the state of that person's attitude and behavior: It is either one of the flesh or Spirit. It will not be productive if it is one of the fleshly and worldly desires. However, if it is one of the Spirit, it will produce abundantly for the well-being of others and our Heavenly Father! If you think about this, it comes down to our wholehearted intentions of daily priorities and choices.

Here's the key takeaway: When we take intentional steps with God, we experience His closeness, guiding direction, and timely help in those moments of need. Just think, when we walk with the Lord, we are in unity with His Spirit, and we are enveloped in His comforting presence, His peace, and His understanding of what is right and wrong in our lives, which can benefit everyone within our sphere of influence (2 Tim 3:16–17). When we walk in the Spirit, we find that the sinful appetites of the flesh have no more dominion over us. And what a powerful Christlike display that can profit our children and the next generation!

A "Walk" in the Bible could be viewed this way: It is a way of practical and biblical living in our daily Christian life because our everyday journey should lead to spiritual growth. God calls us to Walk it so others will see our consistent progress toward our eternal prize (Phil 3:12–21). When we conduct this type of spiritual activity in our daily lives, it shows we yearn for more of God in our lives, where we yield to His control, follow His lead, and allow Him to utilize His influence over us, which strongly impacts other people around us. And here's an essential PowerPoint: To Walk in the Spirit is the opposite of resisting or grieving Him (Eph 4:30), like most people do today.

We must understand and feel the profound impact of our spiritual walk with our Lord each day because it should reflect our 'Christlike' behavior and what truly matters to God. If we commit to this daily, we can reap the rewards of these intentional steps because they showcase our 'true' worth in the eyes of the One who lovingly created us! You see, God cherishes our efforts and time with Him because they bring glory to His name that touches others. The only way to have a genuine relationship with our Lord is by being in His presence daily through the power of His word and Spirit.

The power of walking in unison with our Lord demonstrates that we aim more to be imitators of God than the ways of the world (Eph 5:1). It will exhibit that we will respond more out of Christlikeness than react like the ways of the worldly man. When we're in that proper heart set of His daily presence, we rely more and more on His promises, which lead us to be all in for our Lord and King. It gives us a different perspective, one more of holiness than worldliness. This closeness gives us more of His insight, which helps us go to Him for counseling and comfort, leading to that inward change He desires for you, me, and others (Read Proverbs chapter 3).

Walking in Hope means we're more in tune with our genuine saving faith, where the attitude of our heart and mind is fixed on the eternal versus the sight of humankind and all its temporal state. This harmonious and glorious stance is needed by leaders in homes and communities today because it can help so many who are weaker in faith and need someone to show them the path of righteousness. This is imperative because, without hope, our walk by faith will falter in this life's journey.

You see, walking in our Living Hope is not just a journey; it's a source of joy and strength. Without this master component (Hope), we will wander away from walking with God and, in time, come to the point of despair. Hope is essential to live in the joy of the Lord fully. Neh 8:10 reminds us, "The joy of the Lord is my strength." And God, in His love and faithfulness, has given us all that we need to have hope in every step we take to our eternal home. Always remember that this hope gives us Christlike joy because we have an unbelievable promise of glory to come (John 11:25, Col 3:14).

Think about it this way: Walking in the Living Hope means we are in Christ, and He is in us. Never forget the very words from the lips of our Lord, Jesus Christ, in John chapter 15, "Abide in Me, and I will abide in you." As we've seen throughout this book, if we don't have a solid relationship with our Lord and Savior, we will be like strangers, not knowing which way to go. Once again, remember what Amos 3:3 tells us: "Can two people walk together without agreeing on the direction?"

When we walk in the Hope of our Lord, Jesus Christ, we become more spiritually adept at diligently enduring and persevering through the troubled waters of life. It's hope that helps us to be more patient and wait for His guidance and teaching. Doing this enriches our learning while enabling us to become more of a Christlike role model for our children and others. In this daily walk with our Lord, we grow and mature and utilize our God-given gifts to enhance God's Kingdom.

In this state of maturity, we now seize those opportunities to fervently prepare our loved ones for this bound life to come—because we are more fixed on the Spirit versus the flesh (Read Romans chapter 6). This is because we believe beyond a shadow of a doubt that genuine godly faith trumps all fear. We desire to be in this togetherness with our Father because He's appointed us for a position in a time that needs to point others to His goodness rather than evil!

Once again, let's return to a very popular and memorable scripture in Jer 29:11–13: God reminds us, "For I know the plans I have for you," says the LORD. "They are plans for good and not for disaster, to give you a future and *a hope*. In those days when you pray, I will listen. If you look for me wholeheartedly, you will find me." This passage shows us that our minds and hearts must be fixed on the Lord 100%, so our hope in His plans aligns with His will for our lives, now and in the future. This promise of God's plans for us is a source of hope and reassurance in our journey with Him.

When our hearts, minds, and spirits are focused on the Lord, foremost, it establishes a lifestyle of persistent hope because we're encountering a personal relationship with our Heavenly Father—and that type of daily experience renews our faith and confidence in His word perpetually (it never ends). Why is this so important? As parents and leaders, our walk with the Lord' first' greatly impacts the spiritual growth and development of our children. This walk, closeness, bond, growth, and pressing on will never perish and won't disappoint our hopes for a joyful and blessed life—starting here on earth that will reach its fullness in eternity (Col 3:1–4).

That is why we must cultivate, plant, nurture, water, and feed every word of God into our young ones today—because the tests are continually intensifying on this side of Heaven. If we're not built on a solid foundation and anchored in the hope of Christ and all His ways, the enemy will misdirect us daily, as the staggering data earlier showed. We must be steadfast in all of God's ways to fight off the enemy's tactics.

This is so important in our lives individually and as parents and leaders of the future generation, now more than ever! Why? When we're not seeking and walking with our source of Living Hope first, we will find ourselves off-course in this life of confusion and get easily led astray. When that happens, we will enter a bewildering stage where we can end up in that lonely place known as the wandering wilderness (just like the Israelites).

As Christian parents, we must acknowledge that we will inevitably face spiritual challenges, especially when it comes to our children and loved ones. However, it's important to remember that these challenges are not just trials but opportunities for joy. Therefore, we must establish our spiritual barometers as family leaders. This preparation will give us a better chance of survival when we find ourselves in these unfortunate situations. Remember what Jesus' half-brother (James) tells us in the first chapter of his epistle. "When" trouble comes (not if), consider it an opportunity for joy. This mindset allows us to grow and become more like Christ, which is spiritually healthy for parents and the entire household!

When Christian parents find themselves in the unfortunate stage of their wandering lives, they must step up as Christlike role models. By doing so, they can show their children and the younger generation the Perfect Escape Route—our Hope in Christ and all His promises conveyed to us in

God's word. This will lead us out of the place of despair by the power of His Spirit. The beauty of this is that we are paving a solid path of godliness for our future heirs to witness firsthand as a visible guide!

Regrettably, when we stray from God's guidance and structure in our daily lives, we will feel that emptiness and disconnect. It's like living in a house built on shifting sand, constantly swaying and on the verge of collapse. We may try to fill this void by acting religiously, reading verses randomly, and occasionally listening to Christian music and sermons on social media. However, none of these actions can replace the constant presence of the Spirit of Christ in our hearts, which is what we truly need every minute of every day.

However, if you ever feel that you're in a rut of complacency and not in step with our Lord, always remember the compelling stories of Joseph, Elijah, Job, Moses, David, Ruth, Jeremiah, Peter, and even the great Apostle Paul (to mention a few). As God's faithful and loving servants, they went through significant bouts of despair and discouragement at various points in their lives. Still, their hope and faith were so grounded in the Truth of God's promises that they would eventually prevail through their personal storms, get in step with their Lord, and persevere for God's glory.

Even the twelve disciples of Jesus, while walking with the Lord on this earth, were not wholly dedicated to genuine faithfulness and hope in the Messiah. What rattled their Christian lives was when their friend, Lord, and Savior would die and then resurrect back to life, fulfilling what He told them would happen. In time, they would come to an unbelievable height of renewed hope and faith in the One Who was faithful and true to His very words that He conveyed to them. Their journey from doubt to unwavering faith should inspire us all. It took time, but they did not lose what they inherently possessed 'internally' from the beginning in their hearts, minds, and spirits. Do you have that same internal feeling?

The resurrection of Christ, which took place approximately two thousand years ago, is the cornerstone of our faith and the hope that brought our lives to new levels. When Jesus arose from that grave and cracked the foundation of the earth, He conquered death and sin for all times. He has now given us the incredible opportunity to accept this atoning sacrifice by faith and believe in all He did, said, and will do for you and me in the future. If we don't get engulfed in the truths of God's word, engage and embrace it with every fiber of our being, we will have difficulty finding daily encouragement. Yes, His words are that powerful!

With that, this is a fundamental truth we all must understand. "Spiritual death is our greatest enemy, and we cannot defeat it on our own." Our Lord and Redeemer came to this earth to address the problem of sin and eternal death that created all our issues, which separated us from a Holy God. His life, death, burial, and resurrection have assured genuine believers a victory over all our problems once and for all. He has given us the privilege of going from the old to the new, from the darkness to the Light. The only way to prevent that separation from His presence is to commit to a daily Walk with our Lord and all His Ways. This daily walk is not a burden but a cherished privilege that guides and supports us in our faith journey!

We need to remind ourselves daily that when we are out of step with God, we're not in line with a purpose and plan that will be for our good, but most importantly, our loved ones! So, when something or someone redirects our steps, our internal red flags should be significant if we're connected to the power of God's Spirit! Why? Because that's when the Holy Spirit convicts and counsels us, trying to lead us back to the right course in our lives for our well-being. Once again, read Galatians chapter 5 and Eph 5:18–20.

If your heart, soul, and mind need renewal, refreshment, restoration, and reinvigoration, God's word is your source. The benefits will be rewarding for you, your family, and your future descendants. The power of God's Word is transformative, as it always produces fruit, accomplishes all He wants it to, and prospers everywhere it is sent (Isa 55:11).

Each day, we are entrusted with the responsibility to self-examine our spiritual lives and ask ourselves: "Are we in step with God's plan in our appointed role to fulfill His will?" This self-examination is not a burden but a sacred duty that Yahweh has given us as His accountable children and leaders. If we're not living up to this calling, the missing tie could be that we're not placing all our love, hope, and faith in His empowering grace!

Then we must ask ourselves and put ourselves to the true test: "Are we putting all our aspirations, eagerness, enthusiasm, expectations, and ambitions into the will of our Lord? Are we aligning our spiritual yearnings, hunger, thirst, and cravings with our Heavenly Father's daily desires?" In other words, are our spiritual desires of the right choices and priorities aligned with God's long-term plan? This is so imperative because our choices and priorities in our daily lives can have a profound impact on all our loved ones. If we're not living up to our sacred responsibility as godly parents and leaders, our lives have an apparent spiritual shortfall, and our loved ones may be affected.

Could it be that we're living more of a life of hopelessness, which is a lack of optimism and genuine passion for the Lord's ways in our lives, rather than Living Hope? You see, the power of Hope in our lives can affect others in so many positive spiritual ways. However, finding ourselves in a shortfall clearly indicates that we may be holding onto the wrong things in our daily lives because we're not walking with our Lord daily where we should be the spiritual and biblical influence in our children's and younger ones' lives. But it's never too late to shift from a path that is not leading anywhere—to the righteous pathway of our Lord. We can realign our life's purpose with His divine plan, where we can surely experience a transformative power of faith that can guide us and others to a fulfilling path of Hope!

When you feel like you're on the wrong path and not making progress in your daily walk with the Lord and need His empowering strength, always take comfort in the power of God's word in Isa 40:31. "But those who trust in the LORD will find new strength. They will soar high on wings like eagles. They will run and not grow weary. They will walk and not faint."

What a powerful promise! Our Heavenly Father will renew our strength and bring his people through the storms and obstacles they face in their daily lives. There's also a reminder for us of what's to come gloriously. But the key is that we must absolutely Trust in Him and all His ways. And the only way we can rest in that promise is to be in His presence daily. Who would not want this wonderful experience every morning and throughout each passing day on this side of Heaven?

Don't we realize we have an undeniable privilege to be in His presence each and every day, where we can have great heights of Hope and Joy for what's to come? And just as important, we can be the vessels and channels of His empowering hope that can lead upcoming generations in powerful ways for our Lord to that final resting place! You and I have the unbelievable freedom and opportunity today to walk in all His ways from this day forward—to our eternal home! Once again, always remember what Paul tells us In Galatians 5:25 and Romans chapter 6: "If we live by the Spirit, we will be in step with the Spirit of God."

3 John 1:4, " I could have no greater joy than to hear that my children are following the truth."

"Freedom in Hope"

Please consider the power of this statement: "There is not one person alive today who may be suffering from anxiety, addiction, affliction, abandonment, adversity, abrasiveness, agony, aggressiveness, arrogance, ashamed, atrocious acts, anger, abnormality, adulterousness, attacks, alienation, and any awful things in their lives that can keep them from an All Loving, Gracious and Merciful God! How? When we come to that point in our life where we accept salvation in Jesus Christ by faith, it is indeed a comforting feeling of all the relief we can experience in this life because of what He has done, is doing, and can do! You see, in our new lives as Christians, he has made us right and complete because we're saved from the penalty of our sins, eternal death, and all the horrors in our lives. We have now been redeemed, reconciled (made right), justified, forgiven, and adopted into God's blessed and eternal family.

Think about the power of these two words: Freedom and Hope. Our freedom in Christ removes all our darkest stains and most profound feelings of shame from our gloomiest days to the purity and perfection of His righteousness. When Christ arose from the dead, all our blemishes, sins, and impurities were cleansed. And when we're in Christ as His faithful followers, that exact depiction applies to you and me. And He's not done.

Now, He's given us another power source, Hope! When we accept Him as our Lord and Savior, His Spirit gives us hope that can transform our thoughts and actions on all our dealings with the horrors of this life to the realities of Heaven, where everything is perfect. Yes, we must rest on that Freedom and Hope to help us endure and persevere in our most challenging times on this side of Heaven. You see, freedom and hope in Christ will lead us to a new place where there are no more pains, sufferings, anguish, and personal defeats—because we now have eternal victory in Him!

Walking in the freedom of Hope and Faith in Christ alone involves living under God's extraordinary grace: Paul reminds us in Rom 6:14, "For sin shall no longer be your master, because you are not under the law, *but under grace."* We must understand that freedom in Christ doesn't mean we can do whatever we want—it's all about being free from the power of sin so we can be a slave to righteousness and bring glory and honor to His name by exemplifying genuine Hope (Rom 6:17–18)! When we incorporate this into our personal lives, it will impact our loved ones!

The Christlike freedom we boldly exhibit is not just a personal journey but a beacon of hope for others. It shows that we've been rescued, redeemed, restored, refreshed, and renewed for extraordinary things. And this will lead us down a path of righteousness in unbelievable ways that will impact and influence other lives. It clearly demonstrates Romans 12:1–2 in our lives because we're no longer conformed to the things of this world but yielding to the power of God's Spirit, which enables Him to re-establish our new life in Christ for the well-being of any and everyone throughout our life's journey. This transformation is not just for us but for everyone within our reach, offering a glimmer of hope and a promise of a better future.

So, today, if you had the formula for spiritual freedom, would you apply it to your life and seize the opportunity to release yourself from an area of spiritual bondage preventing you and your close ones from growing closer to Christ? First, we need to understand spiritual freedom. It's not just a concept but a personal journey where our lives align with the power of God's Spirit, revealing our choice in the only One who can deliver and free us from any circumstance. It's about identifying who is Lord over our life, and *we've submitted and surrendered it all to Him.* When we're at that point of submission—*willing and ready* to receive His support—we will know who holds the key to our freedom because there will be no doubts! And it is then that our Living Hope will be illuminated for everyone to see! This is so imperative for parents in homes today—for the sake of their children!

Please pay close attention, parents and family leaders, to this call of urgency! Because of the freedom we now have in Christ, we have the God-given opportunity to impact others by investing our godly heritage into the lives of our loved ones today. We must take the roots of God's word and embed that foundation into the next generation's lives. If we are not putting these things into biblical practice, how can the future of God's Kingdom be successful? That is why today's older and wiser generations must be the example of a Christlike legacy for the younger generation. It is so crucial for parents and all family leaders to embody our true Freedom in Christ, our Hope, rather than the bondage of the enemy's tactics in this world!

Parents, always bear in mind this truth. If we are not adorning ourselves with the righteousness of Christ, living by the Fruit of the Spirit, forgetting our past, and aiding others in their journey towards our eternal rewards, we are not living up to the Living Hope that Peter reminds us of in 1 Peter 1:3–4. In today's chaotic society and culture, we must set an example of being more aligned with our Lord than with the ways of the world. Home leaders must embody a Christian life filled with worship, service, and biblical and spiritual Truths. We cannot allow the enemy to steer us from these Christlike ways. If we give in to the enemy's ways, even in the slightest, we will not influence our loved ones and God's future Kingdom! In other words, we are not putting the freedom of hope and salvation we possess in Christ to work for His purpose and plan!

In His sovereignty, God can accomplish His Kingdom without us. However, as His chosen ones, He expects us, as His true leaders of the Christian faith, to build His future city through our succeeding eras. He expects all of His mature ones to use their God-given freedom and hope for great things! Yes, God is Holy, Eternal, Almighty, and totally Self-Sufficient, and He does not need any created being, but here's the key—we do need Him.

No, God does not need us—but, amazingly, He loves us passionately, and in His goodness, He wants us to live with Him forever. After all, he freed and redeemed us for a reason! So, He commands us to pass on His goodness to future heirs because He wants as many people as possible to experience His freedom by accepting His Son by faith—and live out this 'Living Hope' that He provides (1 Tim 2:3–6).

You may ask, how does our Freedom in our Living Hope (Jesus Christ) affect my role as a parent or leader in the home? The answer lies in the transformative power of Christ's death on the cross. Once we accept Christ as our Lord, the indwelling Spirit begins a work in us, enabling us to fulfill a destiny and function as one in terms of God's ultimate goal. Christ's death on the cross freed you and me to become the people our Heavenly Creator designed us to be. God intends us to be His vessels of love, joy, peace, patience, gentleness, goodness, faithfulness, kindness, and self-control to benefit God's plan. If we initiate these components in our daily lives, we can indeed be the Christlike channel that will flow these elements to our loved one's future—to benefit God's Kingdom (Galatians 5:22–23).

Unfortunately, based on the patterns we've witnessed so far with the parent-child relationship, it is apparent that the spiritual foundation within today's family units is insufficient to sustain the younger generations' faith and hope once they leave their homes. It seems there is more of the enemy's bondage in the homes today than Christlike freedom. Why is this important? Parents can set the precedence for their children and the younger generations of faith and hope as they age—if they consistently ground their lives in the roots of God's teachings and the freedom we genuinely possess!

"Freedom in Hope"

This is so crucial because the future of the younger generations hangs in the balance, and it is up to parents, guardians, and family leaders to step up and provide the biblical and spiritual guidance they need. We must recognize the urgency of this task, as one day, Almighty God will hold us accountable for our role as His faithful servants. Parents, we must choose to influence our children and the younger ones with a Life of Hope in the One Who will always be there during their darkest days. Why? Because Hope is that holy virtue that helps us all to endure and overcome this life of perpetual worldly challenges!

Just consider this fact: "If our children continue to descend into this evil abyss that we're seeing in today's society and culture, are we close enough to their hearts, minds, and spirits to hear their silent cries for help?" More importantly, do they know Who to turn to and seek—when their temptations and times of bondage become overwhelming? With that, are we, as parents, the living example of Hope throughout our children's lives, as 1 Pet 1:3 suggests? These questions are not just rhetorical. They are crucial. Why, you ask?

It's critical to recognize the urgency of the situation: "When you compound all the significant struggles and misleading's in adolescents' lives today—with the decreased teaching of God's word (as noted earlier)—the divide will become greater and more significant over time." The wedge that the enemy is driving into our personal lives, homes, and communities today will only separate us from God's plan—and drive us farther away from God's loving arms of grace and spiritual freedom!

Here's another way to put our Freedom in Hope in perspective—from a biblical and spiritual point of view. We experience true freedom in Christ by knowing Him, walking in all His ways, and engaging with the changes He makes in and through us as we focus on service to Him and others. This Christlike liberty and New Hope now transcends the 'human freedom'—that once preferred and longed for the things of this world—to a new spiritual longing in our Christian life. It now provides joy, peace, comfort, and contentment in the life He desires in us, but also for the benefit of others. It alters our hearts, minds, and spirits from the things of this world to the hope and freedom we now possess with Christ forevermore.

With that, as obedient followers and leaders of Christ, we cannot afford to sit idle, be complacent, and watch younger and future generations make the same mistakes that we're seeing today in the current society. As accountable family leaders, we cannot ignore what's happening in our children's lives. Our young ones must understand this: More of our liberty in everyday life should be dedicated to Christ and His word than worldly things! And parents can set that example!

Parents, the choices we make today are not just about us; they are about the spiritual survival of our future generations! As household leaders, it's our duty to prioritize our family lives by seeking God daily and taking ownership of building a godly path and legacy for the current and future eras. Why? So our children can know where and to Whom to turn when their trials are unbearable. They must learn how to rely upon the One Who can help them—especially when they are struggling in those times of anguish and suffering (1 Pet 1:3, Rom 15:13, 1 Cor 15:19–20).

Let us not underestimate the potential consequences: "If we're not utilizing our 'Liberty in Christ' to its fullest, and raising our children on the importance of being genuine seekers as Bible-believing, God-honoring, Christ-following, Spirit-filled, Worship-Praising, and Obedient and Faithful Bondservants—that's in line with God's teachings—we are not in sync with our Heavenly Father's purpose and plan." If this happens, our younger generation will not know Who to turn to when times are intense. The only way to be in unity with God's faith, hope, and love so our children know where to go is by applying God's word to our daily lives, and we're repetitiously teaching these basics to our children—with the reassuring support and guidance of the Holy Spirit. It is then, we can be confident in our parenting journey.

Parent, don't we realize that we have been crucified with Christ (Gal 2:20) and that we have been reborn as entirely new creatures (2 Cor 5:17). The Christian life is one of death to self and rising to "walk in the newness of life" (Rom 6:4), and that new life is characterized by daily thoughts about the One Who saved us, not thoughts about the dead flesh that has been crucified with Christ. Remember, parents, when our flesh consumes us more than the Power of the Spirit around our children and the younger generations, we're not impacting them in the spiritual freedom God desires!

When we are continually thinking about ourselves and indulging the flesh in sinful ways that we have already been freed from, we are essentially carrying around a corpse full of rottenness and death. This is not the Freedom of Living Hope! But remember, the Spirit is our source of strength, the only way to bury the old life entirely. We strengthen the new nature by continually feeding on the Word of God, and through prayer, we obtain the power we need to escape the desire to return to the old life of sin. Let's draw strength from the Spirit and feel empowered in our new life, a life of freedom and hope in Christ!

Once we embrace the transformative power of becoming a new creation in Christ, we are guided by the Holy Spirit from an old path to an entirely new path. This new road is a testament to our beautiful liberty in our Lord and Savior, empowering us to overcome all the barriers in our

"Freedom in Hope"

everyday lives. We can now surrender our heavy burdens and the weight of the world's anxiety, stress, and worries to Someone Who counsels and comforts us on this new journey in life. We are no longer sojourners wandering around in life with no apparent purpose and meaning; now, we are filled with the freedom and understanding that comes with living in Christ. Let's revel in this liberating freedom!

You see, the critical solution comes down to this! 1) How badly do we want a close relationship with God? 2) Are we willing to relinquish control of our weakest areas and submit them to Him? And here's the gut punch! 3) Do we want to *seek Him more than our selfish desires? So, here's the answer—it starts with you and me*! While I may disagree with some of Martin Luther King Jr.'s doctrinal beliefs, I do like this quote where he said — "If you can't fly, then run; if you can't run, then walk; if you can't walk, then crawl, *but whatever you do — you must keep moving forward.*"

Moving forward means pressing on from the past to the future with determination and never giving up. However, it requires one critical component—choosing a faithful and obedient life in Christ, one that consists of spiritual freedom and Hope! This choice will impact our loved ones and others within our presence! Yes, it can have a high-powered impact! Is that the path of freedom we've chosen for ourselves, but most importantly, all our loved ones?

However, unfortunately, many Christians are living in the middle of the road. What does this mean? We are so centered on pleasing friends, neighbors, and family members (within their worldly comfort zone) that we lose focus on making a spiritual impact for our Lord and Savior in other people's lives—especially our own children. If we have goals to seek meaning and purpose as followers of Jesus Christ, our #1 objective should be to live a God-honoring life that has labeled us in all His righteousness that will affect current and future generations.

Memorize these powerful passages below, which can genuinely affect us and our loved ones as we progress in the freedom and hope we have in Christ when we seek and serve Him wholeheartedly!

Psalm 118:5: "Out of my distress I called on the Lord; the Lord answered me and set me free."

Psalm 119:45: "I will walk in freedom, for I have devoted myself to your commandments. "

Romans 6:5–8, "Since we have been united with him in his death, we will also be raised to life as he was. We know that our old sinful selves were crucified with Christ so that sin might lose its power in our lives. We are no longer slaves to sin. For when we died with Christ, we were set free from the power of sin. And since we died with Christ, we know we will also live with him.

Galatians 5:1: "So Christ has truly set us free. Now make sure that you stay free and don't get tied up again in slavery to the law."

Galatians 5:13-15: For you have been called to live in freedom, my brothers and sisters. But don't use your freedom to satisfy your sinful nature. Instead, use your freedom to serve one another in love. For the whole law can be summed up in this one command: "Love your neighbor as yourself." But if you are always biting and devouring one another, watch out! Beware of destroying one another.

Luke 4:18-19: "The Spirit of the LORD is upon me, for he has anointed me to bring Good News to the poor. He has sent me to proclaim that captives will be released, that the blind will see, that the oppressed will be set free, and that the time of the LORD's favor has come."

John 8:36: "So if the Son sets you free, you are truly free."

Please never forget this powerful reminder! Once we genuinely surrender and submit our lives to Christ and believe in Jesus for our salvation, we can start living out our spiritual freedom! We can do this because of the power that comes from the Spirit of our Lord and Savior residing in us as His committed believers and followers. You see, we've now been freed and redeemed, and God justifies us and frees our conscience from condemnation (Rom 8:1). We are now free to believe, accept the gift of salvation, and live our days as devoted followers of Christ, made holy and acceptable in the sight of God that can undoubtedly impact everyone in our life's journey! The power of this rested assurance gives us hope beyond comprehension and will surely help others in their journey, too!

Always remember what the great Apostle Paul tells us in 2 Cor 3:17-18, "For the Lord is the Spirit, and wherever the Spirit of the Lord is, there is freedom. So, all of us who have had that veil removed can see and reflect the glory of the Lord. And the Lord—who is the Spirit—makes us more and more like him as we are changed into his glorious image." What a powerful source of hope and promise for our children—if the wise ones would reflect the glory of the Lord in their lives—for the young ones today!

"Whatever, Never Lose Hope"!

This segment is so crucial for all of us! When we find ourselves amid our most intense and fierce battles on this side of Heaven—when our losses in this life seem to outweigh all our victories—when the weights of the world have worn us down to mental, emotional, and spiritual defeat, and we see no signs of hope and help on the way, there is one verse that most believers turn to in their deepest woes. It's Psalm 23:4, where David's words serve as a beacon of reassurance and strength, "Even when I walk through the darkest valley, I will not be afraid, for you are close beside me. Your rod and your staff protect and comfort me, filling my heart with courage and my spirit with peace."

Most account this as a Psalm of David's maturity, but with vivid remembrance of his youth as a shepherd. Charles Spurgeon wrote, "I like to recall the fact that this Psalm was written by David, probably when he was a king. He had been a shepherd and was not ashamed of his former occupation. This Psalm has charmed more griefs to rest than all the world's philosophies. It has shut up the most felon thoughts, black doubts, thieving sorrows—than there are sands on the sea-shore."

"It has comforted the most noble host of the poor. It has sung courage to the army of the disappointed. It has poured balm and consolation into the hearts of the sick, of captives in dungeons, of widows in their pinching griefs, and orphans in their state of loneliness. It has elevated the hearts of the spirit of humans from the depths of the deepest sea to new grounds of hope and restoration!"

"Dying soldiers have died easier as it was read to them; ghastly hospitals have been illuminated; it has visited the prisoner, broken his chains, and, like Peter's angel, led him forth in imagination and sung him back to his home again. It has made the dying enslaved Christian spiritually unchained from his earthly master and powerfully consoled those who are dying in their final moments on this side of Heaven. Millions of people have memorized this Psalm, even those who have learned few other Scriptures. Ministers have used it to comfort people suffering from severe personal trials, illness, or dying. For some, the words of this Psalm have been the last they have ever uttered in life." [1]

The power of this Psalm in 23:4 can be paraphrased as follows: "Either you can struggle against life's difficulties, or you can turn them over to the Lord and ask Him to give you the wisdom and strength you need to handle each one." That is the point of absolute surrender and submission from self—to Him! Joshua 1:9 reminds us profoundly, "This is my command—be strong and courageous! Do not be afraid or discouraged. For the LORD your God is with you wherever you go." In other words, as followers of Christ and with the indwelling Holy Spirit active in us, we should possess such internal strength and courage that we have undeniable hope and faith in the One Who will always be with us, no matter the intensity and grave realities of the trial. But He does require us to seek Him in all things—so He knows we're relying on His empowering grace."

Paul reminds us in Tim in 2 1:7, "For God has not given us a spirit of fear and timidity, but of power, love, and self-discipline." In addition to living bold and courageous lives as Christians, never losing hope, we are called to live without fear." Jesus even taught us in Matt 10:28, "Don't be afraid of those who want to kill your body; they cannot touch your soul. Fear only God, who can destroy both soul and body in hell."

When Paul was imprisoned, he wrote these profound words in Phil 1:14 for our benefit: "And because of my imprisonment, most of the believers here have gained confidence and boldly speak God's message without fear." While there is a sense in which we are called to fear God, which is to live in respect and reverence of Him, Scripture is clear that we are to live with confidence in God's promises and power. If we lack confidence and absolute trust in His Sovereign Power, then something is missing in us! Think about this passage we quoted above in Joshua 1:9.

What God commanded Joshua is also seen in the Great Commission: "Surely I am with you always, to the very end of the age" (Matt 28:20). Also, we have the promise of Hebrews 13:5: "God has said, 'Never will I leave you; never will I forsake you.'" Do we truly believe in that message? God calls us to live courageously, without fear, with complete confidence, knowing that God is always with us. If we feel a void and disconnect from our Lord, we must self-examine our spiritual lives and decipher and filter out the things that prevent us from our Living Hope. Then yield to His Word and Spirit,

---

1. Enduring Word. "The Lord is my Shephard and Host."

"Whatever, Never Lose Hope"!

draw closer to Him, and allow our Heavenly Father to lead us in all His ways!

As we've witnessed throughout this long journey, the enemy is working in powerful ways, cunningly luring parents and our younger generations away from the very foundation of God's guiding principles. He is aggressively pursuing us from the outside, affecting us all on the inside. We must acknowledge this fact: "He's out to break down our internal structure of godliness—so we will lose all focus on the holiness and righteousness of our Holy God?" The enemy is out to sever and separate parents, guardians, and our young ones from the holy foundation of the godly home that our Heavenly Father desires in His family today! You see, the enemy wants all of God's children to live in a world of hopelessness; he does not want us to possess the Living Hope in our everyday lives, which can help us to overcome so many barriers in life!

But no matter your life's difficulties, never forget this astounding fact! Regardless of the magnitude of the enemy's work around us and all the trials and tests we will confront, there's a beautiful promise from our God of Hope—when His children cry out and seek Him for help. It's this: "Nowhere in all the whole wide earth is there one child that is so lonely, one mind so darkened, one heart so broken, one spirit so heavily burdened and crushed, and one soul that feels so confused and lost beyond hope and help—that would escape the eyes of a Loving and Caring God" (Ps 46:1, Ps 34:18, Ps 147:3, Prov 3:1-8, Luke 15:6, 24, 1 Cor 4:5, Rom 8:26-29). If you and your family seem so lost and confused with all the turmoil in everyday life—always remember this—' we all need to seek the One Who can carry us through the storms of life. He's simply waiting for our response to His call!'

We must always keep this in our hearts, minds, and spirits: "God always considers the end result—the big picture, which is going to be the best plan for you and me—and nothing else matters." The character we develop through our sufferings will prepare us for the Kingdom of God, which is the ultimate fulfillment of Romans 8:28. But it also helps and will impact our children when they witness firsthand the end and lasting result in our lives, as parents and leaders, which is to be more Christlike.

The wisest man in the Bible (Solomon) even reminds us in Prov 8:17, "I love all who love me. Those who search will surely find me. Seek me while you can find me before it's too late." In other words, seek and build your lives upon the One Who will carry you and me through the battles and temptations of this ill-fated, severely lost world. Why is this so crucial? If we don't grasp the Hope of Life, we will find it difficult to sustain a biblically sound life in all His teachings.

We must always hold on to the One Who will carry us through our most horrific times—so we can leave a legacy for our loved ones that will carry over for years. And we do this because it brings our Heavenly Father glory, honor, and praise! The Psalmist reminds us in Ps 27:4, "The one thing I ask of the Lord— the thing I seek most—is to live in the house of the Lord all the days of my life, delighting in the Lord's perfections and meditating in his Temple."

Always remember, no matter how misguided we may get in this journey of life, once our lives are rested in the assurance of our faith, love, and hope in Jesus Christ, Paul reminds you and me, once again, in Rom 8: 1–2, "So now there is no condemnation for those who belong to Christ Jesus. And because you belong to him, the power of the life-giving Spirit has freed you from the power of sin that leads to death." What a beautiful and encouraging promise!

When we seek and place our hope in the One that can motivate and entice all believers to start building their lives on Christ alone, it will enable you and me to leave a legacy of hope for our future descendants in lasting ways. This legacy will give them something real and tangible to hold on to during all their life battles, and its impact will carry over for years, underscoring the significance of our actions.

Seeking and Clinging to God and Walking in all His ways will give us Real Hope when we are in that seemingly bottomless pit. Paul expounds, "He will give eternal life to those who keep on doing good, seeking after the glory, honor, and immortality that God offers. But he will pour out his anger and wrath on those who live for themselves, refuse to obey the truth, and live lives of wickedness" (Rom 2:7–8).

When the ways and works of the enemy snare us into a state and rut of despair, he is not only stealing our joy and hope, but he's depriving you and me of leaving something precious for the sake of our loved ones and others—and that's a Christlike legacy. And that's what our younger generation needs from us today—because this selfless and sacrificial act and godly heritage can bring a glowing glimpse of hope into their life for today, tomorrow, and years to come.

"All parents must ensure that their foundation is genuinely built on the Living Hope in life—Jesus Christ from the beginning." Don't we realize that He is the Only One Who can help each of us during the most confusing and difficult times of our lives, as times of evil intensify in ways that defy Almighty God? As genuine followers of Christ, our discerning spirits should pick up any danger signs when we're off God's path of righteousness, empowering us to stay true to our faith and responsible in all our actions!

"Whatever, Never Lose Hope"!

Yahweh reminds us profoundly in Psalm chapter 34 of some powerful words of comfort, peace, and hope. Read these passages and always realize that God is there no matter the troubles in our lives. Always remember, there is hope when the sinner cries to the Lord for help because—He helps the helpless, provides hope for the hopeless, frees us from all our fears, gives us joy in our darkest times, saves us from all our troubles, empowers us in our weakest moments, hears our cries, is close to the brokenhearted, rescues those whose spirits are crushed, redeems those who serve Him, protects the bones of the righteous (not one of them is broken), and all those who take refuge in Him will not be condemned.

What an enduring and ensuring promise from our God of Hope. This reminds me of an idiom that I love, and it's this: "When we're going through troubled waters and stormy seas, our Hope in Christ alone can carry us over the waves of difficulties in life." No matter who you are or what you've done in life—He's there for those who call on Him (Rom 10:13, Acts 2:21)! This even reminds me of the most memorable passage in the Bible, which is recorded in John 3:16–17. "For this is how God loved the world: He gave his one and only Son so that everyone who believes in him will not perish but have eternal life. God sent his Son into the world not to judge the world, but to save the world through him." This passage's operative words are: "Those who truly believe!"

Once again, let's return to this beautiful promise from the Lord in Rom 8:38–39, "And I am convinced that nothing can ever separate us from God's love. Neither death nor life, neither angels nor demons, neither our fears for today nor our worries about tomorrow—not even the powers of hell can separate us from God's love. No power in the sky above or in the earth below—indeed, nothing in all creation will ever be able to separate us from the love of God that is revealed in Christ Jesus our Lord."

In this powerful passage that millions are so familiar with and have memorized, the great Apostle Paul provides us with a list of the most dreadful things we will encounter in this life, including fear of death, unseen forces, demons, powerful rulers, unknown future events, and even the fear of heights and drowning. Paul is convinced that none of these dreaded things can isolate us from the love of God in Jesus Christ.

These compelling verses express a full assurance that nothing could ever separate those from God's love—who genuinely believe in Christ Jesus as the Lord of their lives, for He's their Source of Hope and Empowering Strength. But the key is those who have genuine saving faith and truly believe in Him and all His ways (as stated earlier)! And when we're grounded in the sound truths of His scriptures, just like this one, they will renew and strengthen our hope in the One Who will see us through all the trials, temptations, and tests of time.

We all need to be cautious when going through major warfare, where everything seems lost, and it's this: We cannot allow ourselves to get into a state of self-pity. Why? This is not spiritually and mentally healthy for you and others, and it does not honor and please God. Look at it this way: When we focus more on ourselves during our intense times on earth—versus what the Lord wants us to gain from our tribulations—it's almost like we assess ourselves and our circumstances more through our own perspective than trusting in God. After all, isn't He our gracious, merciful, ever-present, all-powerful, all-knowing, and loving Father Who has our best interest at heart? The danger is that when we take God out of the picture, we rely more on ourselves to fill in those life gaps! When self comes to the surface more than Christ, it will never lead us to an exemplary of our Living Hope and becoming more Christlike!

You see, a living hope in our Lord and Savior is part of our makeup as Christians because it exhibits something supernatural that the unbelieving world cannot understand. It's an absolute knowing and belief that all the things God says and stands on will happen! This blessed assurance keeps us grounded as sound and solid believers for today, tomorrow, and the years to come! Plus, it will help us prepare others for eternity! How? Because it displays our genuine life of faithfulness, obedience, and love, where real hope is illustrated for our future descendants' well-being, it can significantly impact their future walk with the Lord.

Our genuine need for hope and the purpose of this beautiful attribute should be apparent in our lives today. Remember this: A genuine internal and external sign of a Christian has built their foundation of Hope in Christ alone and all His promises! This makes them more than just believers—they are living messengers of hope, ready to make a difference in the world for others' well-being. If we don't, we risk getting misguided in our life's journey as parents and family leaders, which will not benefit our future descendants.

However, if we finally surrender and submit as Moses did, we will grow closer to God—guided by the Holy Spirit. In His wisdom and guidance, we will discern when we're off course and when something is wrong. This discerning spirit will lead us to seek Him and cling to all His promises of grace. These building blocks will help us realize the urgency of leaving a life of Christlikeness for our future eras. It will impact so many in lasting ways—to the very end of our time on this side of Heaven!

When we know beyond a shadow of a doubt that we have not lost our Hope no matter what, it means that we trust and believe in God's word and all His promises. How? Because of our life and hope in Christ, we now have salvation, freedom from sin, and eternal healing that gives us the peace, love, joy, and strength to overcome it all! Never forget this: "Great things are to come for those who cling to the Living Hope to the very end!"

Nah 1:7, "The Lord is good, a strong refuge when trouble comes. He is close to those who trust in him."

The End!

"Hope is on the Way!"

In the Gospel of John, Jesus provides us with some compelling words in chapter 16, v.16, that should give us a lasting hope to overcome the troubles of this world. And in this spiritual triumph, we inherently possess joy, peace, and comfort that will get us through to the end of our life's journey. The verse reminds you and me, "In a little while, you won't see me anymore. But a little while after that, you will see me again." While this verse probably refers to His death and His resurrection, many of us cling to this verse, knowing that our time on this earth is coming to a close and, in just a little while, our Savior, Redeemer, Light, and Hope of the world is coming back to take us home—to our eternal resting place, a promise we can hold onto in these uncertain times.

With all our focus on the problems in the world today, where we easily get distracted from His presence, do we fully grasp that our Lord is always nearby? Our Heavenly Father reminds us in Psalm 34:18 that He is close to the brokenhearted and the crushed in spirit. Do we genuinely believe He holds us in His Almighty Hands and has pledged never to abandon us? He is with us, behind and ahead of us—shielding, nurturing, and providing for us.

Most importantly, He has given us His Counselor and Comforter to guide us through our most daunting challenges. He reminds us that He has conquered the world, so losing hope is unnecessary. Christ also assures us that He is our Way, Truth, and Life, and no one can reach the Heavenly Father except through Him, our Living Hope! By now, we should know that nothing can separate us from a Loving and Caring God—if our hearts and actions align with His purpose and plan!

On the last night before His betrayal and death, Jesus was preparing His disciples for the days ahead. These chosen men had followed Christ and learned from His teaching and example for over three years. They had placed their hopes in Him as the Messiah, the Promised Deliverer, yet they still didn't understand how He was going to accomplish that deliverance. Christ profoundly tells His devout followers in John chapter 16 that He is going away to the One Who sent Him.

Astoundingly, the disciples did not even question where their Lord was going. Instead, they were grieving that He was leaving. He tells them that He should leave so the Advocate can come and lead them into all Truths and convict the world of its sin. The followers of Christ would get it in time because once the Holy Spirit came into them (as we read in the book of Acts), great things would happen, and their sadness would be turned into Joy! This undeniable joy lies in the hope that Christ will save us and take us to our eternal home. The key to that reassurance comes from the Holy Spirit. Do you know it? Can you feel it? Have you shared it with so many? Are you and others ready?

Jesus Himself offers comfort around this topic in John 14:2-3 where He promises that there are many rooms in His Father's house, and He goes to prepare a place for you and me. The implication is that we'll join Him (and our loved ones if they are ready) when our time on earth ends. Can you even imagine Christ, our Lord, and King, wiping away every tear from our eyes—because death shall be no more, neither shall there be mourning, nor crying, nor pain anymore, for the former things have passed away!

I cannot even fathom this great day, for an hour is coming when all in the tombs will hear his voice and be called up to glory. Evidently, those who are called up were ready for this day of glorification. This leads me to ponder: Have we truly prepared our loved ones and others on this biblical fact; "they have been delivered from this evil world because of their genuine saving faith and Hope in Christ?" Do we know for a fact that by their fruitful living, they are ready? Our Lord's teachings and examples are there for us today to pass on to others. The most important question today is this; have we prepared others, as our Lord has commanded? If so, then we've shared it with others—before it's too late.

You see, only our Heavenly Father knows when He will grant our Lord permission to sound that glorious horn. But I often find myself questioning: In our earthly timeline, will there emerge a generation of Evangelism Explosion followers? A generation that will passionately teach the Truth, spread the Gospel, lead others to Christ, and help to save souls, no matter the cost? Could there be one final celebration on this side of Heaven before His return and our entry into the Promised Land? And if so, have we prepared our future heirs to carry the banner of Christlikeness to its farthest reaches?

All of this is so pressing because there's no greater purpose in our Christian lives on earth for those who long to hear these words from our Lord Jesus Christ in Matt 25:23 when the Master said, "Well done, my good and faithful servant. You have been faithful in handling this small amount, so now I will give you many more responsibilities. Let's celebrate together!" What a wonderful reunion and time of rejoicing with all our loved ones when we come before the presence of our Lord—every generation that chose to follow the ways of Christ. The investment of our godly heritage into others for their well-being in the future can assuredly reap a return of eternal rewards.

Always remember, God created you and me to magnify and exalt Him and make His Name great to everyone within our reach—every day God has endowed and allowed us on this earth—until Christ comes back (Matt 12:36-37). God has indeed designed each of us in unique ways that can influence the world and our close ones in a godly fashion, enfolded in His Faith, Love, and Hope that will last for years while we're here on Earth (1 Corinthians chapter 12, Rom 12:6-8 and Eph 4:12). God reminds us in Isa 43:7, "Bring all who claim me as their God, for I have made them for my glory. It was I who created them."

This powerful passage in Isaiah should remind us how God wired you and me; it is to bring glory, honor, and praise to Him. He 'spiritually' wired you and me to inject shock waves of His holiness, righteousness, and Hope into everyone standing near us. We need to convey and portray a life of joy, happiness, and assurance for the spiritual well-being of our future descendants—versus a life of regret, sadness, and disappointment! That opportunity for you and me is today—because tomorrow may never come!

Don't we realize that our life on this earth is short—it's like a vapor (Jas 4:14), which means we may not have tomorrow? However, eternity awaits us, and we should think about living in light of this eternity as His Citizens of Heaven on Earth right now. Why? Because it should motivate and entice us to leave a legacy of Christlikeness that will radiate for years to come in our loved ones' lives. This biblical mindset will keep us focused on the things that matter, which will always have eternal significance. When we live with eternity in view, we are more interested in storing treasures in heaven, as discussed often throughout this journey (Luke 12:33). Most importantly, it's for the good of others' future state of spirituality!

Even Jesus felt the urgency of being about God's work while the opportunity remained for Him on earth. In John 9:4-5, He said, "We must quickly carry out the tasks assigned to us by the one who sent us. The night is coming, and then no one can work. But while I am here in the world, I am the light of the world." These are compelling words from our Lord, Savior, and Hope of the world that should deploy us to imitate Him in this same model. So, I beg the question: "Are we being that Light of Hope in someone's life today in lasting ways? Are we imitators of Christ daily in front of our loved ones?"

We must recognize that our brief lifetime on this planet is imperative. Why? So we don't squander the time our Merciful God has given you and me in times of sharing, serving, and spreading His Good News. Psalm 90:12 says, "Teach us to number our days, that we may gain a heart of wisdom." God wants us to live with purpose, recognizing that our clock is counting down to the moment when we step through death's portal and enter our eternal state. At that moment, the books are closed. But, in the meantime, hopefully, the life we've sowed as faithful servants to Christ, will begin to reap the righteous and fruitful paths that we laid for others for years to come. Not a lack thereof (like that first generation of Israelites)!

If we are genuine followers of God's word and we know that life is nothing but a vapor, it should cause us to be uncomfortable with a restless heart "if" we're wasting time. It should lead us to invest our Christlike heritage into God's work for the benefit of our future eras. The fruitful results will ground them more in their faith—while loving God's commands and leaning on the One Who will see them through their most challenging battles.

We all must remember a time will come when all of God's children will come together to recognize and worship Him as one complete family! And because God is full of love, mercy, and grace, He extends the invitation to every generation to come to know and accept His Son, Jesus Christ, as Lord of their lives so they will possess a "Real Hope" in their trying times on this side of Heaven. Why is this so important? As we've discussed so often throughout this walk in Deuteronomy, without Hope in Christ that is enfolded in genuine faith and love, our future descendants' state of spiritual survival is in jeopardy!

As we transition into new eras, the current and future society must see clear evidence of parents' and the wiser generations' transformed lives of Christlikeness for all the young ones' spiritual good. It should depict a life of obedience to all of God's ways in His word, demonstrating our genuine faith, love, and hope in the Lord. Always remember this: "When our children and the younger generations see more godly responses from us through all life's circumstances, this gives them a stronger sense of that Real Hope in what we truly believe and live by."

Today, we have the power to transform our world by prioritizing our Christian responsibilities. By incorporating the biblical teachings into our own lives, we can initiate and implement them in training and teaching future generations. This transformative power will help mold a younger era for the good of God and society. We all have this God-given ability because Peter reminds us in his second epistle, in chapter 1, that as God's chosen ones, "We have all the resources we need to live a godly life." This spiritual prescription will change us individually and impact others for decades—if not centuries! The choice hinges upon you and me today!

By now, we should all know that Almighty God commands you and me to ensure our children and others take on His High calling. It should be an honor and privilege to tell and teach our descendants about God's goodness and scriptural ways of living, which should be practiced daily for His glory. He desires that you and I, as faithful and obedient followers of the Lord, pass on His divine ways to future generations for their state of spiritual survival—now more than ever.

Always remember that God has promised a glorious eternal home for all those who love Him and have trusted in Christ Jesus for salvation—our Hope for today, tomorrow, and the future. This promise is not just a distant hope but a reality we can look forward to. God's eternal Promised Land is the inheritance of all who come to Him through His Son (John 14:6). And never forget this: "The path of our invested godly heritage can be the legacy that leads our young ones to this blessed land." Let this promise fill us with hope and reassurance as we move toward our Heavenly home. Have we prepared our loved ones and others for their "right" ultimate destiny? This cannot be stressed enough as our final days on earth wind down—and gradually draw to a close!

As discussed earlier in this last chapter, in one of the most potent chapters in God's word, we see Christ telling us in Matthew chapter 25 probably some of the most profound words recorded in the Bible. It's these two statements: 1) "Well done, my good and faithful servant," and 2) 'Away with you, you cursed ones, into the eternal fire prepared for the devil and his demons.' The storyline and takeaway in this passage refer to those who used their investments for the growth of God's Kingdom. Jesus reminds us, "Those who use well what they are given, even more, will be given, and they will have an abundance. But from those who do nothing, even what little they have will be taken away." This powerful verse applies to us today and for the future to come! Once again, please refer to the Parable of the Four Soils in Matthew chapter 13 for its compelling lesson, which will help us all determine if we're in the business of God's fruitful way of living—or not!

Our primary focus should be on seeking the things of God, prioritizing them over the things of the world. When we do this, we are actively taking care of God's business, which is the most pressing matter in our lives for the well-being of others. This aligns with Paul's exhortation in Philippians

2:12, which reminds us to 'Work hard to show the results of your salvation, obeying God with deep reverence and fear. For God is working in you, giving you the desire and the power to do what pleases him.'

Parents, our new life in Christ should be reflected in our actions of righteousness and holiness. This involves obeying the Lord's calling, serving Him without griping or complaining, and relying wholly on God's grace. You see, God's empowering Grace (through His Spirit's work) helps us respond to God's Most High call. It enables us to overcome the restricting power of sin because it sustains us in every moment of our lives. This powerful Grace leads us to feel the favor and blessings of an Almighty God—when we know that we don't deserve it. It brings effective change in our hearts and minds, renewing our thinking and transforming our lives, undoubtedly impacting and influencing everyone within our realm. It helps us all realize and know that the reach of eternal life is within our grasp and real!

But another essential PowerPoint: When we take care of our Lord's business today, for the future, it also means that we are yielding to His Word with the guidance of the Spirit. As we repeat this in our everyday lives for the well-being of others, it will create a repeated yearning and desire to do God's will in lasting ways. The beautiful thing is that His grace is sufficient to supply us with the internal strength to carry on (2 Cor 12:9). You see, working out our salvation is a way of offering ourselves to God in selfless service that impacts others to build His Kingdom, which glorifies Him!

Up to this point, you and I should be fully aware of this fact by now—how we conduct our daily lives as a Christian leader is doing one of two things: 1) Honoring our Heavenly Father—2) or not (there's no middle ground)! Our life story and biblical teachings that we've attained throughout our lives, as the wise ones, should strongly emphasize godly obedience, respect, faith, and love in ways that label us as His true representatives to all generations. When this is spiritually intact in our lives as followers of Christ, others, especially our future heirs, will see our Real Hope in the One Whom we trust and believe in for what's to come—it's our power source in everyday life! And when it's at work in us internally (through the power of the Spirit), its outer impact can carry on for years!

With that, here's a high-powered question for you and me as disciples of Christ: "Should our blessed hope of Christ's return—at any given moment—be so powerfully alive in us that it portrays a genuine Christian life that others want?" It is so full of peace, joy, boldness, enthusiasm, confidence, and contentment that it is infectious. Others want to gravitate to it because they want this supernatural inner working in their own lives. But equally important is this: "Teaching and living that pattern of life for our loved ones' future state of spirituality." John reminds us in 1 John 3:3, "And all who have this eager expectation will keep themselves pure, just as he is pure." What does this mean? It means we are responsible for living a life that others want to emulate.

The genuine believer, eagerly anticipating Christ's blessed return, is transformed by the power of the indwelling Holy Spirit. This life of purity is not just for our own benefit, but it will surely influence our children's lives and future descendants. Remember, "We will all stand before the Lord one day and give an account of how we lived for Him on this earth as His faithful servants" (2 Cor 5:10). Did our lives have a godly impact and influence on others that will carry over for years? Our anticipation of Christ's return should be so compelling that the world wants a piece of it!

Memorize these motivating passages that Paul gave us as reminders—because, as a new creation, we possess the ability to do far more for the glory of God. He reminds us in Eph 2:10, "For we are God's masterpiece. He has created us anew in Christ Jesus, so we can do the good things he planned for us long ago", and once again, 2 Cor 5:17 tells us, "This means that anyone who belongs to Christ has become a new person. The old life is gone; a new life has begun!" And when we possess that new life in Christ, His Spirit will give us a hope that can affect so many lives!

However, if you ever come to that crossroad in life, take comfort in this passage from the Apostle Paul in Phil 4:6–9, "Don't worry about anything; instead, pray about everything. Tell God what you need and thank him for all he has done. Then, you will experience God's peace, which exceeds anything we can understand. His peace will guard your hearts and minds as you live in Christ Jesus. And now, dear brothers and sisters, one final thing. Fix your thoughts on what is true, and honorable, and right, and pure, and lovely, and admirable. Think about things that are excellent and worthy of praise. Keep putting into practice all you learned and received from me—everything you heard from me and saw me doing. Then the God of peace will be with you."

Every believer must realize that seeking God first and clinging to His Hope in these final days is essential because it can bring a sense of spiritual strength, joy, comfort, contentment, and an unbelievable peace that surpasses all our understanding—especially when times are so intense. And when we are the inspiration of godly faith, love, and hope, this stage of our sanctified life aligns our daily priorities with our Heavenly Father that will surely affect others. Trust me; this godly lifestyle will motivate us to seek the Lord through a lifelong relationship with Him—no matter what's good, bad, or ugly.

And here's an amazing and beautiful promise. As we set out to seek Him relentlessly and wholeheartedly, our Heavenly Father responds with his presence, blessing, and power. This deepened relationship with God helps us better understand His will for our lives and elevates our Christlike character with enhanced faith, love, and hope. It gives us a greater sense of purpose as His children each day.

Plus, it helps us resist the temptations the enemy throws our way. This leads us to better understand His wisdom, which will help us attain a discerning spirit. Trust me, when these wonderful holy attributes (faith, love, and hope) are exhibited in our lives, they impact and influence our children and the younger generations, making us feel responsible and committed to passing these beautiful assets on to future heirs.

Once again, as responsible Christian parents, in these final days of intense spiritual battles, do our children genuinely know where to turn when times seem hopeless— and they feel helpless? Have we embedded the depths and fullness of God's word so profoundly in their hearts, minds, and souls that their spirits long and lean toward His presence and guidance in each passing moment (Col 3:16)? When we teach them about Hope in time, they will firmly believe that what God says is true and will come to fruition. And regardless of their deepest valley, loudest cries, and lowest of times, they know Who will be there no matter what!

When our children and the younger generation see parents and wiser ones clothed with the new empowering life in Jesus, and they know where our true hope and faith lies, over time in their growing stage of life in Christ, they will learn these guiding principles: 'Who to seek (Christ)'—'What to seek (His empowering grace)'—' When to seek (when times are harsh)'—' Where to seek (His Word)'—' Why to seek it (to overcome and be more Christlike)'—and 'How to seek it (connecting with Him in prayer and yielding to His Spirit)!' Teaching these fundamental facts throughout their lives will aid them in those difficult times! When we seek the God of Hope for all things in life, we set the guiding essence for the younger generation's future.

Once again, Paul reminds us powerfully in Col 3:1–5, "Since you have been raised to new life with Christ, set your sights on the realities of heaven, where Christ sits in the place of honor at God's right hand. Think about the things of heaven, not the things of earth. For you died to this life, and your real life is hidden with Christ in God. And when Christ, who is your life, is revealed to the whole world, you will share in all his glory." What a profound promise that should give us an undeniable Hope to pass on to our future heirs! By now, we should unequivocally know Who our Living Hope is—and the rewards that will spring forth through our efforts for our Father.

One of the most significant questions ever posed by our Lord during His time on this earth was these very words, "Who do you say that I am?" (Luke 9:18–20). This severe question has consequences not only in this lifetime but also for eternity because it's a question that, sooner or later, all of us will have to answer for ourselves, and here's the key takeaway: "If Christian parents and leaders do not take the spiritual inheritance that they possess in Christ, and invest that life-changing story into today's younger generation's lives, they will be ill-equipped for what will come!" Most importantly, they will never be able to answer Jesus' question, "Who do you say that I am?"

The answer to this question for our loved ones' benefit hinges upon the parents' and older generations' setting the precedence through their genuine identity in Christ. So, parents, "Who do you say that Christ is?" When that question is posed to you, your immediate response should be, "He is Our Living Hope, Light, Savior, and Redeemer." This should reflect a lifestyle that points others back to our Lord, Jesus Christ, God's only Son.

Trust me, when parents and family leaders confidently, boldly, and passionately set the preface of who they are in Christ and their relationship with Him, this will impact our family and others forever. If we're not investing our *real inheritance* into our children's lives, we're not only disregarding our godly heritage, but we're not passing on a Christlike legacy for our loved ones' state of spirituality. As stated so many times, we could be their only source of the Gospel.

Parents, throughout this long journey, we should clearly be aware of this critical point, and it's this: If we get too complacent and reliant on the things of this world, God will allow unpleasantries into our lives—think about that first-generation of Israelites. When we get too far away from our Holy Father, He will remind us that this world is not our home (Phil 1:27; 3:20). One day, we're here, and the next, we are gone. However, all those born into the family of God will, at death, gather in their eternal home and enjoy the rewards of serving the Lord forever (1 Cor 3:12–13). As mentioned earlier, don't we long for our family members and others on this earth to hear those words from our Lord, "Well done, my good and faithful servant?"

In time, when we live by the Truth of the Word where we're applying it, it will help all of us to identify with our Source of Hope, Jesus Christ, genuinely. And here's the crucial point! When our identity rests in Christ alone, we will believe and live by His words with all our heart, mind, soul, and strength! This will help guide and strengthen our children during the difficult days ahead—because, make no mistake about it—those times will come! Remember, as noted earlier, being a devoted godly parent is not a part-time position!

You see, our Creator is fully aware that the enemy is distracting us from His purpose and plan by misguiding the believers' hope—and sending them into a rut of despair in these final days on earth. Because undoubtedly, there's a lot of darkness prevailing in our homes and all around us—we cannot escape it! Satan is intensifying his acts of devious ways where millions are doubting their salvation, and their hope is misguided. When this happens, the enemy steals our joy, disturbs our peace, hinders our prayer life, and keeps us from the Truth of God's word. When we start falling further away from a Holy God, it can dangerously lead to spiritual blindness and even a departure of our faith. That is precisely why godly parents must be fully committed to their appointed positions as God's leader in the household. Why?

Because when the enemy leads us down a path of spiritual impairment, he deprives us of God's mercy, which prevents us from godly obedience and misleads our Christlike direction in everyday life (Acts 5:39). Unfortunately, the enemy continues his relentless efforts because he wants us to ignore God's promises, disregard His genuine love for us, and deceive ourselves of God's grace. He wants to sever us from every biblical fact of God's Loving Word and promises in his last days! The enemy will use any tactics and strategies possible to get the familyhood of God going in the wrong direction in life.

In today's disturbances amongst our younger generation, I often hope and pray that in these final days, a generation of faithful Christian parents will aim to raise a godly generation that will leave an indelible mark of Christlikeness that can last for decades and centuries. With that, as mentioned earlier, could there be one last ditched effort to spread the Good News to a lost generation? "Could there 'possibly' exist one last great development on this earth—as its final bullet point in life—for the sake of humankind in saving others—for God's glory?"

Finally, shouldn't we pursue the best interest of our children's state of spirituality like God pursues us? God has designed parents to be the first and most important people to model His loving relationship with our children. Our Heavenly Father is searching for parents who have a willing and committed heart to start training their descendants in the ways God desires. As noted earlier, we must tell and teach our children the profound message of this passage in Prov 8:17, "I love all who love me. Those who search will surely find me." We must do this now before it's too late! Our time to pass on the Good News of Hope to our future descendants is now, for tomorrow may never come!

Always remember, there is a danger when we choose to turn to the world for provisions in times of difficulty or ease; it means *we have turned away from God and our Lord as our Guiding Source.* As we've seen repeatedly throughout God's word, it is better to trust in the Lord Jesus Christ and place all our hope in Him—than to put our confidence in man and the ways of this world. We must be the living example of Christ today!

In Titus 2:12-14, God's word reminds us to reject this world's passions and ungodliness and live in a godly fashion with controlled lives in this present age. It also teaches His children to seek our blessed hope in Jesus Christ. This is so vital because, in God's search, He desires and even commands us to point others to His Son, Jesus Christ—our Light and Hope of the world. We do this by exemplifying the 'Living Hope' in our own lives that impacts and influences others, especially our loved ones, for the rest of our days on this side of Heaven (1 Pet 1:4-5). It's our God-given choice and call today!

Once again, only time will tell if we left our mark on people's lives for the spiritual good of others—and mainly for the benefit of God's Kingdom! It all comes down to our decision to make a difference in the younger generations' lives for a change in the future that will honor God in magnificent ways. It's our individual choice as His children today to honor Him—or not! What will be the testament of our genuine legacy for the ages? Will these ending passages exemplify our Christian legacy for future generations' spiritual well-being? We cannot disappoint them, but most importantly, we cannot let our Heavenly King down! He's counting on you and me today, which can carry over for years until we enter our glorious resting place!

Heb 12:14-15, "Work at living in peace with everyone, and work at living a holy life, for those who are not holy will not see the Lord. Look after each other so that none of you fails to receive the grace of God. Watch out that no poisonous root of bitterness grows up to trouble you, corrupting many."

Acts 20:24, "But my life is worth nothing to me unless I use it for finishing the work assigned me by the Lord Jesus—the work of telling others the Good News about the wonderful grace of God."

Gal 1:15-16, "But even before I was born, God chose me and called me by his marvelous grace. Then it pleased him to reveal his Son to me so that I would proclaim the Good News about Jesus to the Gentiles."

Gal 2:20, "My old self has been crucified with Christ.[e] It is no longer I who live, but Christ lives in me. So I live in this earthly body by trusting in the Son of God, who loved me and gave himself for me."

Ps 57:2, "I cry out to God Most High, to God who will fulfill his purpose for me."

2 Cor 6:10, "Our hearts ache, but we always have joy. We are poor, but we give spiritual riches to others. We own nothing, and yet we have everything."

"Hope is on the Way!"

Rom 1:16–17, "For I am not ashamed of this Good News about Christ. It is the power of God at work, saving everyone who believes—the Jew first and also the Gentile. This Good News tells us how God makes us right in his sight. This is accomplished from start to finish by faith. As the Scriptures say, "It is through faith that a righteous person has life." It is a life that looks forward to their eternal home but also ensures that others can possess this same life, too!

Ps 130:5, "I am counting on the Lord; yes, I am counting on him. I have put my hope in his word." Are we genuinely putting our hope in the One Who will see us through to the end of this age? Are we teaching and sharing with everyone on our path the goodness of our Lord from the beginning to the very end of our lives? Time will tell! Hopefully and prayerfully, we are preparing as many as possible for that day of eternity!

Bibliography

Ang. Carmen. Visual Capitalist Site. "Ranking U.S. Generations on Their Power and Influence Over Society." May 6, 2021. https://www.visualcapitalist.com/ranking-u-s-generations-on-their-power-and-influence-over-society/

Barna Group Site. "Research Shows That Spiritual Maturity Process Should Start at a Young Age." November 17, 2023. https://www.barna.com/research/research-shows-that-spiritual-maturity-process-should-start-at-a-young-age/

Barna Group Site. "How Concerned Are Christian Parents About Their Children's Faith Formation?" March 30, 2022. https://www.barna.com/research/christian-parents-concerns/

Barna Group Site. "Signs of Decline & Hope Among Key Metrics of Faith." March 4, 2020.https://www.barna.com/research/changing-state-of-the-church/

Centers for Disease Control and Prevention Site. "U.S. Teen Girls Experiencing Increased Sadness and Violence." February 13, 2023. https://www.cdc.gov/nchhstp/newsroom/2023/increased-sadness-and-violence-press-release.html

Christian Quotes. Fifty John MacArthur Quotes. https://www.christianquotes.info/quotes-by-author/john-macarthur-quotes/

Christianity.Com. Thirty-Six Powerful Christian Love Quotes: Scriptures and Sayings About Love. June 15, 2020.

https://www.christianity.com/wiki/christian-life/inspirational-christian-quotes-about-love.html#:~:text=It%20has%20the%20feet%20to%20hasten%20to%20the.That%20is%20what%20love%20looks%20like."%20-%20Augustine

Cole. Steven J. "Raising Godly Generations. Deuteronomy 6:1–25." Bible.Org Blog. December 3, 2017. https://bible.org/seriespage/10-raising-godly-generations-deuteronomy-61-25

Cushman. Ward. To Every Nation Site. "Five Facts About Our Acceptance by God. Our Position in Christ Assures us of Acceptance." https://toeverynation.com/5-facts-acceptance-by-god/

DeAngelis. Tory. American Psychological Association. "Teens are spending nearly 5 hours daily on social media. Here are the mental health outcomes." April 1, 2024. https://www.apa.org/monitor/2024/04/teen-social-use-mental-health

Earls. Aaron. Lifeway Research. "Americans most want to avoid fear and anxiety, gain freedom and safety." August 5, 2021. https://news.lifeway.com/2021/08/05/americans-most-want-to-avoid-fear-and-anxiety-gain-freedom-and-safety/

BIBLIOGRAPHY

Eisenberg. Richard. Forbes Article. "Leaving a Legacy No Matter How Much Money You Have." February 8, 2019. https://www.forbes.com/sites/nextavenue/2019/02/08/leaving-a-legacy-no-matter-how-much-money-you-have/?sh=3defd20941e

Ekstrand. Dr. D.W. The Transformed Soul Site. "The Influence Parents Have on Their Children." http://www.thetransformedsoul.com/additional-studies/spiritual-lifestudies/the influence.

Enduring Word. "Deuteronomy 8, A Warning Against Pride." https://enduringword.com/bible-commentary/deuteronomy-8/

Enduring Word. "Psalm 102, Afflicted, But Full of Trust." https://enduringword.com/bible-commentary/psalm-102/

Enduring Word. "Isaiah 1. Indictment and Invitation." https://enduringword.com/bible-commentary/isaiah-1/

Enduring Word. "Joshua 4. Memorial Stones." https://enduringword.com/bible-commentary/joshua-4/

Enduring Word. "Deuteronomy 34. The Death of Moses." https://enduringword.com/bible-commentary/deuteronomy-34/

Enduring Word. "Deuteronomy 31. Final Instructions to Moses." https://enduringword.com/bible-commentary/deuteronomy-31/

Enduring Word. "Psalm 23, The Lord is My Shepherd and Host." https://enduringword.com/bible-commentary/psalm-23/

Enduring Word. "Deuteronomy 29. Renewal of the Covenant." https://enduringword.com/bible-commentary/deuteronomy-29/

Enduring Word. "Deuteronomy 28. Blessing and Cursing." https://enduringword.com/bible-commentary/deuteronomy-28/

Enduring Word." 1 Corinthians 15. The Resurrection of Jesus and Our Resurrection." https://enduringword.com/bible-commentary/1-corinthians-15/

Enduring Word. "Deuteronomy 22. Various Laws." https://enduringword.com/bible-commentary/deuteronomy-22/

Enduring Word. "Deuteronomy 1. Moses Remembers the Journey of Israel from Mount Sinaia to Kadesh Barnea. https://enduringword.com/bible-commentary/deuteronomy-1/

Enduring Word. "Deuteronomy 12. The Worship God Commands." https://enduringword.com/bible-commentary/deuteronomy-12

Enduring Word. Gruzik. David. "Deuteronomy 10. Recovering After a Fall." https://enduringword.com/bible-commentary/deuteronomy-10

Enduring Word. Gruzik. David. Deuteronomy 4. "A Call to Obedience." https://enduringword.com/bible-commentary/deuteronomy-4

Foley. Ryan. The Christian Post Site. "Americans Who Read the Bible Have Far More Hope Than Those Who Don't." April 16, 2023. https://www.christianpost.com/news/americans-who-read-the-bible-have-more-hope-in-times-of-stress.html

Francis. Alannah. Christian Today Site. "What is the biblical concept of commitment? And what does it mean for our faith lives?" September 14, 2016 https://www.christiantoday.com/article/what-is-the-biblical-concept-of-commitment-and-what-does-it-mean-for-our-faith-lives/86202.htm

Front Gate Media Site: "Victorious Family Special: Exclusive from the Washington Times." November 15, 2023. https://www.frontgatemedia.com/victorious-family-special-exclusive-from-the-washington-times/

Bibliography

Germano. Maggie. Forbes Article. "Despite Their Priorities. Nearly Half of Americans Over 55 Still Don't Have a Will". February 15, 2019. https://www.forbes.com/sites/maggiegermano/2019/02/15/despite-their-priorities-nearly-half-of-americans-over-55-still-dont-have-a-will/?sh=79f1609a5238

Got Questions Ministry. "What Does the Bible Say About Being Wholehearted?" https://www.gotquestions.org/Bible-wholehearted.html

Got Questions Ministry. "What Does it Mean to Cling to What is Good?" Romans 12:9. https://www.gotquestions.org/cling-to-what-is-good.html

Got Questions Ministry. "What Does the Bible Say About Sharing?" https://www.gotquestions.org/Bible-sharing.html

Got Questions Ministry. "Why Did God Choose Israel to Be His Chosen People?" https://www.gotquestions.org/why-God-choose-Israel.html

Got Questions Ministry. "What Does the Bible Say About Family?" https://www.gotquestions.org/Bible-family.html

Got Questions Ministry. "What Does It Mean to Cling to What is Good?" https://www.gotquestions.org/cling-to-what-is-good.html

Got Questions Ministry. What is the Meaning "May the God of Hope Fill You?" https://www.gotquestions.org/may-the-God-of-hope-fill-you.html

Got Questions Ministry. "How Can We Be Rejoicing in Hope?" (Romans 12:12). https://www.gotquestions.org/rejoicing-in-hope.html

Got Questions Ministry. "How God Is Our Refuge?" https://www.gotquestions.org/God-our-refuge.html

Got Questions Ministry. "How Can I Become a More Cheerful Giver." https://www.gotquestions.org/cheerful-giver.html

Got Questions Ministry. "What Does It Mean to Be Pure in Heart." https://www.gotquestions.org/pure-in-heart.html

Got Questions Ministry. "What Does the Bible Say About Acceptance"? https://www.gotquestions.org/Bible-acceptance.html

Got Questions Ministry. "What is Christian Spirituality?" https://www.gotquestions.org/spirituality-Christian.html

Got Questions Ministry. "What Does the Bible Say About Sensuality." https://www.gotquestions.org/Bible-sensuality.html

Got Questions Ministry. "What Does God Mean When He Says Seek Me and Live?" https://www.gotquestions.org/seek-me-and-live.html

Goodreads Site. William Shakespeare Quotes. https://www.goodreads.com/quotes/604765-life-is-too-short-so-live-your-life-to-the

Got Questions Ministry. "What is the Significance of the Valley of Achor in the Bible?" https://www.gotquestions.org/Valley-of-Achor.html

Got Questions Ministry. "Who is God?" https://www.gotquestions.org/who-is-God.html

Got Questions Ministry. "What Does It Mean to Take the Lord's Name in Vain?" https://www.gotquestions.org/Lords-name-vain.html

Got Questions Ministry. "What Does the Bible Say About Acceptance?" https://www.gotquestions.org/Bible-acceptance.html

Got Questions Ministry. "What is the True Meaning of the Second Commandment." https://www.gotquestions.org/second-commandment.html

Got Questions Ministry. "What is the Meaning of Christian Worship." https://www.gotquestions.org/Christian-worship.html

BIBLIOGRAPHY

Got Questions Ministry. "What Does It Mean that Without Faith. it is Impossible to Please God." https://www.gotquestions.org/without-faith-impossible-please-God.html

Grace Quotes Site. 2023 https://gracequotes.org/quote/the-christian-is-a-person-who-makes-it-easy-for others-to-believe-in-god/

Greatest Things and Others. "The Analysis." https://ccel.org/ccel/drummond/greatest/greatest.ii.ii.html#:~:text=Have%20you%20ever%20noticed%20how%20much%20of%20Christ's.people%20happy%2C%20in%20doing%20good%20turns%20to%20people.

Gryboski. Michael. The Christian Post Site. "Only 9% of Gen Z Youth are Bible-Centered Survey. August 11, 2021. https://www.christianpost.com/news/only-9-of-gen-z-youth-are-bible-centered-survey.html

Hillman. Os. "In Order to Impact the Next Generation. We Must Relate to Them. Christian Post Article. December 10, 2013.https://www.christianpost.com/news/in-order-to-impact-the next-generation-we-must-relate-to-them

Jones. Jeffrey. Gallup Poll. "U.S. Church Membership Fall Below Majority for First Time." March 29, 2021. https://news.gallup.com/poll/341963/church-membership-falls-below-majority-first-time.aspx

Kummer. Tony. Ministry-To-Children Site. Children's Ministry Statistics. "How Do Kids Come to Christ?" February 17, 2022. htttps://ministry-to-children.com/childrens-ministry-statistics/#What%20Happens%20When%20Kids%20Miss%20This%20window?

Laurie. Greg. Crosswalk. "How to Conquer a Giant in Your Life." September 27, 2017. https://www.crosswalk.com/faith/spiritual-life/how-to-conquer-a-giant-in-your-life.html

Lydon. Michael. Vocabulary.com Blog. "The Power of If." March 26, 2012. https://www.vocabulary.com/articles/wc/the-power-of-if/

MacArthur. John. "Hope Under Attack." Master's University Blog. https://www.masters.edu/thinking_blog/hope-under-attack/

Manners. Bruce. Adventists Review. "Moses: Hope Deferred." September 27, 2006. https://adventistreview.org/2006-1527/2006-1527-6/

Mathis. David. Desiring God Site. "Are We Living in the Last Days?" June 8, 2017. https://www.desiringgod.org/articles/are-we-living-in-the-last-days

Merriam Webster. Finders Keepers (Losers Weepers) https://www.meriam-webster.com/dictionary/finders%20keepers%20(losers%20weepers)

Miller. Sarah. Jefferson Health Site. "The Addictiveness of Social Media; How Teens Get Hooked!" June 2, 2022. https://www.jeffersonhealth.org/your-health/living-well/the-addictiveness-of-social-media-how-teens-get-hooked.

Morrow. Jonathan. Impact 360 Institute. "Only 4 Percent of Gen Z Have a Biblical Worldview." New 2018 Barna and Impact 360 Institute Research Shows. https://www.impact360institute.org/articles/4-percent-gen-z-biblical-worldview/

Muacevic. Alexander. Adler. John R. "The National Library of Medicine Site. "The Effect of Parenting and the Parent-Child Relationship on a Child's Cognitive Development: A Literature Review." October 14, 2022. https://www.ncbi.nlm.nih.gov/pmc/articles/PMC9678477/#:~:text=Positive%20parenting%20helps%20the%20child,and%20social%20and%20cultural%20problems

No Sweat Shakespeare Site. Eat. Drink. and Be Merry https://nosweatshakespeare.com/quotes/famous/eat-drink-and-be-merry/

BIBLIOGRAPHY

Nunnery, David. Diligently Site. "What is Going on With Families in America Today?" https://teachthemdiligently.net/what-is-going-on-with-families-in-america/

Pierce. Jerry. Decision: The Evangelical Voice for Today Site: Barna: "Only 2% of Parents of American Preteens Have Biblical Worldview." March 10, 2022. https://decisionmagazine.com/barna-only-2-of-parents-of-american-preteens-have-biblical-worldview/

Renner. Ben. Study Finds Site. "American families spend just 37 minutes of quality time together per day, survey finds." March 21, 2018. https://studyfinds.org/american-families-spend-37-minutes-quality-time/#:~:text=After%20polling%202%2C000%20parents%20of%20school-aged%20children%2C%20researchers,polled%20described%20their%20average%2C%20daily%20lives%20as%20"hectic."

Rhinehart. Deanna. Championeers Site. https://www.championeers.com/single-post/kids-hear-over-400-negative-words-a-day-how-many-positive-words-does-it-take-to-make-up-for-them

Rothwell. Jonathan. Gallup Poll Site. "Teens Spend Average of 4.8 Hours on Social Media Per Day." October 13, 2023. https://news.gallup.com/poll/512576/teens-spend-average-hours-social-media-per-day.aspx

Rouis. Rex. The Mechanics of Faith; Hope, Faith, and Prayer Site. "If—The Biggest Word in the Bible". https//www.hopefaithprayer.com/biggest-word-bible/

Santora. Frank. Bible Study Tools Site. "Are you Leaving a Godly Legacy?" June 23, 2022 https://www.biblestudytools.com/bible-study/topical-studies/are-you-leaving-behind-a-godly-legacy.html

Segal. Marshall. Desiring God Site. "Honor the Parents God Gave You." https://www.desiringgod.org/articles/honor-the-parents-god-gave-you. April 22, 2021

Skiena. Steven. Ward. Charles B. "Who's Biggest?" The 100 Most Significant Figures in History. *Time Magazine Article.* December 10. 2013. https://ideas.time.com/2013/12/10/whos-biggest-the-100-most-significant-figures-in-history/

Source Site. Why Generation Alpha and Z is non-religious? https://thetruthsource.org/why-generation-alpha-and-z-is-non-religious?

The Bible Says Site. "Deuteronomy 30:15–20 Meaning." https://thebiblesays.com/commentary/deut/deut-30/deuteronomy-3015-20/The Truth

United States Census Bureau Site. "Census Bureau Releases New Estimates on America's Families and Living Arrangements." November 17, 2022. https://www.census.gov/newsroom/press-releases/2022/americas-families-and-living-arrangements.html